Saul Bellow: vision and revision

to Cara, Margot, Sabrina

Saul Bellow: vision and revision

Daniel Fuchs

6568

Duke University Press   Durham, N.C.   1984

Library of Congress Cataloging in Publication Data

Fuchs, Daniel, 1934–
  Saul Bellow, vision and revision.

  Includes bibliographical references and index.
  1. Bellow, Saul—Criticism and interpretation.
2. Bellow, Saul—Technique.   I. Title.
PS3503.E4488Z665   1984   813'.52   83-9061
ISBN 0-8223-0503-8

Contents

Prefatory note   vii

Acknowledgments   ix

Abbreviations   xi

Part I. Bellow's literary milieu

1. Saul Bellow and the modern tradition   3

2. Saul Bellow and the example of Dostoevsky   28

Part II. The works: craft and composition

Introduction   53

3. *The Adventures of Augie March*   57

4. *Seize the Day*   78

5. *Henderson the Rain King*   98

6. *Herzog*   121

7. *Herzog*, the intellectual milieu   155

8. *The Last Analysis*   179

9. *Mr. Sammler's Planet*   208

10. *Humboldt's Gift*   233

11. Bellow's short stories   280

Epilogue. *The Dean's December*   305

Notes   311

Index   339

Prefatory note

As the title of this study suggests, I have approached Bellow's work in two ways. First, in chapters one and two, I attempt to define the writer's literary and cultural milieus. These chapters of cultural criticism are the "vision" part of the title. Chapter one deals with Bellow's reaction to the dominant modernist strain (Flaubert) and is an attack on aspects of its aesthetic ideology. It concludes with a contrast of contemporaries. Chapter two deals with the opposing moral, even religious strain (Dostoevsky) of that tradition, one to which Bellow feels an affinity. Chapters three through eleven are a critical reading of the work from the point of view of how it was composed; scholarly as well as critical, the "revision" part of the title, they are essays which incorporate textual criticism. These chapters begin with *The Adventures of Augie March*, the first novel for which there is significant manuscript material. There is an epilogue on Bellow's recent novel.

This study is directed to the serious reader of Bellow, the serious reader of twentieth-century literature; many such will be found in the universities, many outside of them. Consequently, I have tried in the studies of particular works to be as plain as possible in the description of compositional points, using, for example, words like "early," "middle," and "late" to describe manuscripts.

It is a pleasure to express thanks to Robert Rosenthal and the staff of Special Collections at the University of Chicago Library, where almost all of the Bellow manuscript material is held, and to the Humanities Research Center at the University of Texas. Any study benefits from the body of informed critical opinion in the field and I wish to thank the tillers of the field. My greatest debt is to Saul Bellow for allowing me sole access to all of his manuscripts with permission to quote. Needless to say, many a novelist would be understandably reluctant to be scrutinized in this way.

My thanks to Curtis Harnack and Yaddo for fellowships in 1975 and 1977 which enabled me to pursue my work in idyllic surroundings. And to the Research Foundation of the City University of New York for grants when I was getting started and when I was finishing up.

My most pervasive debt is to my wife Cara.

Acknowledgments

Chapter 1, "Saul Bellow and the Modern Tradition," is an expanded version of an essay which appeared in *Contemporary Literature*, Winter 1974. A version of the final section of this essay was delivered as a lecture at faculty seminars of the University of Bergen and the University of Trondheim, Norway, under the auspices of the United States Cultural Foundation in Norway, April 1976. A recent version of the present essay was given as a lecture before a Humboldt University audience in East Berlin under the auspices of the League for Friendship Among People, January 1981. Chapter 2, "Saul Bellow and the Example of Dostoevsky," appeared in a somewhat different version in *The Stoic Strain in American Literature*, edited by Duane MacMillan, University of Toronto Press, 1979. It was delivered as a lecture at the second annual meeting of the Austrian American Studies Association, Schloss Leopoldskron, Salzburg, October 1975. An earlier version of Chapter 3 appeared as *"The Adventures of Augie March:* The Making of a Novel," in *Americana-Austriaca*, Wilhelm Braumüller, Vienna, 1979. Chapter 6, in a version abridged by the editor, appeared as *"Herzog:* The Making of a Novel," in *Critical Essays on Saul Bellow*, edited by Stanley Trachtenberg, G. K. Hall, Boston, 1979.

I would like to thank Richard G. Stern and Jascha Kessler, from whose correspondence with Bellow I have quoted.

I recall with pleasure the avidity of graduate seminars in Bellow I taught at the former Richmond College of the City University of New York (now the College of Staten Island), the Dolmetsch Institute of the University of Vienna, and the John F. Kennedy Institute of the Free University of Berlin (West Berlin).

Abbreviations

AD   *An American Dream*, Norman Mailer (New York: Dell, 1970)

AdM   *Advertisements for Myself*, Norman Mailer (New York: Berkley Medallion, 1966)

AM   *The Adventures of Augie March*, Saul Bellow (New York: Viking, 1953)

AN   *Armies of the Night*, Norman Mailer (New York: Signet, 1968)

BK   *The Brothers Karamazov*, Fyodor Dostoevsky, trans. Constance Garnett (New York: Modern Library, 1950)

D   *The Double*, Fyodor Dostoevsky, in *The Short Novels of Dostoevsky*, trans. Constance Garnett (New York: Dial Press, 1951)

DD   *The Dean's December* (New York: Harper & Row, 1982)

DM   *The Dangling Man*, Saul Bellow (New York: Meridian, 1960)

EH   *The Eternal Husband*, Fyodor Dostoevsky, in *The Short Novels of Dostoevsky*, trans. Constance Garnett (New York: Dial Press, 1951)

H   *Herzog*, Saul Bellow (New York: Viking, 1964)

HG   *Humboldt's Gift*, Saul Bellow (New York: Viking, 1975)

HRK   *Henderson the Rain King*, Saul Bellow (New York: Viking, 1959)

MSP   *Mr. Sammler's Planet*, Saul Bellow (New York: Viking, 1970)

ND   *The Naked and the Dead*, Norman Mailer (New York: Signet, 1948)

SD   *Seize the Day*, Saul Bellow (New York: Viking, 1956)

V   *The Victim*, Saul Bellow (New York: Signet, 1965)

VPN   *Viking Portable Nietzsche*, Friedrich Nietzsche, trans. Walter Kaufman (New York: Viking, 1964)

WV   *Why Are We in Vietnam?* Norman Mailer (New York: Berkley Medallion, 1968)

Part I

Bellow's literary milieu

Chapter 1

Saul Bellow and the modern tradition

i

Novelists are often our best critics and nowhere more so than in the novel itself. Art may best be a criticism of life by being a criticism of art. No American writer since the war has given us as level-headed, vibrant, and true a description of contemporary life as Saul Bellow, and no one has delineated so clearly and so deeply the relationship of the way we live now to what we read now, of character to ideas, of personality to books. The Bellow protagonist often bears his most intense feelings through an arena of the most palpable cultural props. Survival depends equally on how he feels and what he thinks, which are inseparable. In carrying this weight of seriousness, Bellow runs counter to the popular (and populist) image of the novelist whose mistrust of ideas and even words qualifies him as still another rugged saint of adventure. In American literature physical acts are eloquent (Hemingway, Faulkner) but the reflective consciousness is often muted or blaring. But if Bellow is a novelist of intellect, he is not an intellectual novelist. He eschews the thesis novel, one which proceeds because of an idea; this he considers "French" (Gide, Sartre, Robbe-Grillet). Bellow sees his characters in their personal realities, sees them as selves, or better, souls, whose thoughts move with the inevitability of emotion. This is, in his view, the "Russian" way with ideas (Tolstoy, Dostoevsky). If there is something unfamiliar to the American common reader in this mind and body involvement—as opposed to one or the other—there is something perhaps even more unfamiliar to the uncommon reader in the grounds of the argument. For no one has so persistently and successfully gone against the grain of modernism, which is still a kind of orthodoxy in the universities and even the quarterlies. In this respect Bellow is the postmodernist par excellence:

his very inspiration often comes from a resistance to the celebrated aesthetic ideology of modernism, with its tendency toward monumentality and its perhaps inevitably concomitant tendency toward coldness.

Any description of this ideology had best begin with illustrations taken from its origins in late nineteenth-century French literature. A radical subjectivity, an idealism of the word marks the aesthetic realism of Flaubert and symbolism of Mallarmé. "The story, the plot of a novel is of no interest to me," Flaubert says. "When I write a novel I aim at rendering a color, a shade. . . . In *Madame Bovary*, all I wanted to do was to render a grey color, the mouldy color of a wood louse's existence."[1] As Bellow has remarked, where Phaedra embodied the passion of Racine, the new aesthetic aristocrat manifested his passion in virtuosity. *Madame Bovary* is a great book partly because Flaubert's attitude toward Emma reflects an element of charity that transcends the strictures of his letters. This element is not present in *The Sentimental Education*, whose protagonist, Frederic Moreau, is the first of the nauseous heroes. Contemplating the flood of Parisian Sunday perambulators, Frederic feels "the knowledge that he was worth more than these men mitigated the fatigue of looking at them."[2] Frederic's king's-eye view, his "atrophy of heart," his self-destructive reduction of illusion (Flaubert seems to be engaged in homeopathic self-cure) appear again and again. Modern life appears as a wasteland. "As for the living, we will let the servants do that," concludes the aesthete artist in *Axel's Castle*. And Eliot's "young man carbuncular," which Allen Tate has called the high-water mark of modern poetry, shows that the servants may not even do that.

Like most saints, Flaubert was fortunate in his choice of disciples. Martyrdom was converted into religion—the religion of art. In *Dubliners*, Joyce's style of "scrupulous meanness" was a nod to the master, as were the variations on Flaubertian themes: the death of illusion in "Araby," the irony of "Grace," the aesthetic virtuosity of a story about still another unlived life in "The Dead." *A Portrait of the Artist as a Young Man* may be viewed as a resolution of the Flaubertian problem. For subjectivity to assert any kind of real freedom under modern conditions, it must be extraordinary. The tragedy of Emma Bovary is that she is ordinary. In *Portrait*, heroism resides in the character as well as in the work of art. In its extremity, the heroism develops into a self-deification, clearly echoing the theory of impersonality in Flaubert's letters.

To the extent that they make style the subject of their books, subordinating personality to form, character to artifact, event to irony, action to words, making experience the reflection of some higher truth, these writers reduce the historical to the point where it is merely a reflection of a perfection that can never be known. This is the imaginative utopianism of the modern. To the degree that the actual is debased, the ideal is exalted.

Flaubert and Dedalus are like "a god"—god over what? Stephen thinks of himself as a "priest of eternal imagination." But eternal and imagination are logically contradictory. When, in his review of *Ulysses*, Eliot says that Joyce's method works "towards making the modern world possible for art," we see where the cart stands in relation to the horse. The modernist aesthetic invented the New Criticism, in which judgments of form preceded judgments of meaning.

This movement on the part of an aesthetic aristocracy was an emasculation of rational, experience-oriented, liberal man. Subsequently, in place of history we found myth; in place of Freud, Jung. Commenting adversely on this, Bellow says that the Jungian primordial experience brings illumination through drill, orthodoxy, and imitation, so that the golden moment will return. Weeping by the waters of Babylon, we sadly live.[3] Eliot and Jung are cast in the same mold. Jung's comments on art subordinate the merely personal to the higher impersonality. The artist is not a self but a medium. In its most extreme form this appears in Rimbaud: "It is a mistake to say: I think. One ought to say: I am thought. . . . *I* is someone else."[4] It is no accident that Rimbaud also says, "Man is finished! Man has played all the roles." Rimbaud, the arch-hipster, in "Bateau Ivre" took the archetypal bad trip in search, no doubt, of the prelapsarian. What modernism often unfolds, what Flaubert, Joyce, and Eliot offer us, is the secular equivalent of Original Sin (in Eliot, of course, we later get the religious "equivalent"). Joyce is the greatest of these writers in that he often transfigures his characters in the face of this condition. Like Eliot, in "Ash Wednesday," though in a totally different ambience, they achieve an inconclusive purgatorial nobility.

Volumes have been written in support of the greatness of *Ulysses* by exegetes of the sacred text, yet the book, great as it is, illustrates the weakness of modernism. In one sense, *Ulysses* represents a move back to *Madame Bovary* in that the youthful energy of Stephen, sublimated and idealized as it is, comes to nothing. Though Joyce is left with only the ordinary voices of Dublin, the greatness of *Ulysses* is that the ordinary is seen to be heroic. This is made possible by Joyce's rejection of Stephen's king's-eye view, since the ordinary, Joyce would have us believe, transfigures even him. Nonetheless the famous reconciliation at the end of *Ulysses* between the "father" and the "son" exists as a brilliant rhetorical pattern rather than an authenic "reconciling" experience, for two men urinating together in the street is hardly the moral equivalent of an artistry which exhibits the most dazzling aesthetic virtuosity of any novel ever written, and Molly's recollection of Bloom, moving though it is, will scarcely change the status quo between them. Despite the sort of honor Joyce displays towards his characters, everyone exists in a moonlike relation to emotion, and all remain almost as isolated as the characters in *Madame Bovary*.

In *Ulysses* Joyce is a student past master, but the gap between words and deeds is, if anything, even more glaring with such a weight cast on such an inconclusive frame. Stephen, the character who might have been noblest, falls hardest, while Bloom, our Ulysses, has a mind remarkable for its activity, but even more for its passivity. And the shape of this quester's life—the sense of significant event—is amorphous. As Bellow once remarked to me, for Bloom, going to a funeral resembles taking a bath. In *Finnegans Wake* we get the logical extreme of Joyce's aesthetic—not a day in the life of everyman, but all days in the lives of all men. In trying to express all of history, Joyce becomes ahistorical, as myth obscures individuality in an ambience of imposed fatality. In this astonishing reading of the collective unconscious, language itself must be a merely historical description; so Joyce invents a new one. *Finnegans Wake* shows us that it is not Stephen Dedalus but Joyce himself who is a priest of eternal imagination. If only there were one.

"The last sick sufferer from the complaint of Flaubert." So D. H. Lawrence describes Thomas Mann in a review of *Death in Venice*: Flaubert "stood away from life as from a leprosy. And Thomas Mann, like Flaubert, feels vaguely that he has in him something finer than ever physical life revealed. . . . And so, with real suicidal intention, like Flaubert's, he sits, a last too-sick disciple, reducing himself grain by grain to the statement of his own disgust, patiently, self-destructively, so that his statement may be perfect in a world of corruption."[5] If the relatively balanced *Death in Venice* elicits this blast against aestheticism, what would Lawrence have said of *Doctor Faustus?* In Aschenbach, perversity, disintegration, and disease, the revenge of the Dionysian, is attended by a nobler sense of life's possibility, in which a generous illumination, an enlargement of soul, accompanies the destruction of the body. This cannot be said of Mann's last artist-hero, Adrian Leverkühn.

The remarkable thing about the encounter of the modern Faustus with the devil is the condition of the pact. Faustus will sell his soul, not for knowledge, not for worldly power, not for Satanic freedom, not for experience, not for pleasure, not for love—but for art. But what is art without these qualities? When this Faustus makes his pact, he is losing not only his salvation, he is losing his humanity. The Promethean is reduced to the aesthetic as art is reduced to a merely intellectual version of the demonic. The crucial clause in the contract is one with which the modern artist-hero is all too familiar, involving as it does alienation from ordinary life. Hell profits him, says the devil in archaic "Lutheran" German: "if you renay all living creature, all the Heavenly Host and all men . . . thou maist not love. . . . Thy life shall be cold."[6] Later in life, Leverkühn, in a fit of mellowness, does wish to marry, but in terms which do not violate the pact: "Not only for the sake of comfort, to be better bedded down; but most of all because [I hope] to get from it good and fine things for [my] future work."[7] Like Eliot, he wishes to make life possible for art; for life is cold, but art is warm. The devil purveys "towering flights and illuminations . . . colossal admiration for the made thing . . . the thrills of self-veneration" which, as we have seen, are indistinguishable from self-hatred: "yes, of exquisite horror of himself, in which he appears to himself like an inspired mouthpiece, as a godlike monster," who sinks into "unfruitful melancholy but also into pains and sickness."[8] In his assault on "the bourgeois order" and "bourgeois raffinement . . . a culture fallen away from cult," the devil opts for a new mythic barbarism: "excess, paradox and mystic passion, the utterly unbourgeois ordeal."[9] Serenus Zeitblom, the devoted humanist, shrewdly sees a connection between aestheticism and barbarism, and understands when one of Leverkühn's masterworks is reproached for both "blood boltered barbarism" and "bloodless intellectuality." (Appropriately, it is called *Apocalypse* and signals the end of the world; the aesthetic is predictable: "in it dissonance stands for the expression of everything lofty, solemn, pious, everything of the spirit; while consonance and firm tonality are the world of hell, in this context a world of banality and commonplace.")[10] *Doctor Faustus* carries to one logical extreme the reactionary ideology implicit and sometimes explicit in the modern tradition. These tendencies mirrored an even more sinister combination of "blood boltered barbarism" and "bloodless intellectuality"—political fascism.

There was a time when the poet could be compared to the lunatic and lover. In *Doctor Faustus* the devil says that "the artist is the brother of the criminal and madman,"[11] a significant shift. The artist-hero, as we have seen, may be beyond the pale of ordinary life, beyond good and evil as it is defined in "conventional" morality, a morality which is found wanting, if it is found at all. The artist appears as the creator of a higher morality, a superman, an immoralist. But what if the exceptional man is not an artist? What of the undignified aspect of immoralism? Where then do his explosive insights flare? Where does this energy, often plebeian, go? In the character of Julien Sorel, the first of the plebeian, immoralist criminals, *The Red and the Black* provides an original answer. The central assumption of the book—a Romantic one—is that however devious a brilliant *ambiteux* Julien is, his deviousness is justified given the social circumstances. Julien is an immoralist insofar as he conquers the world he despises, but the "murder" and sequel to it show that he is not an immoralist at heart; the real reason for his death is his intransigent rejection of the value of class distinction. As usual, there is a sort of premodernist balance in Stendhal: energy and morality are not yet totally disjunctive.

They appear to be in Raskolnikov, in whom the crime, though premeditated, is impersonal, symbolic if you will. Like Sorel, this penniless, powerless, incipient intellectual lives in the shadow of Napoleon. His breakthrough into "heroism," a grim caricature of power, stems from his contempt for ordinary life. The fatal catalyst is his obsession to find out whether "he was a louse like everybody else or a man," whether he could be a Napoleonic superman beyond good and evil. The didactic point of *Crime and Punishment* is that crime must be punished, that the superman, however sorrowfully approximated, must fail. Dostoevsky's account of "bourgeois" morality (e.g., Luzhin) is, however, Nietzschean. And the dramatic force of Raskolnikov's contempt for ordinary life (including his own) has, not surprisingly, often been taken as the vital energy of the book. His immoralism has found imitators.

Gide's Lafcadio is one of these. What is passional in Dostoevsky becomes theoretical in Gide, as the desperate longing for freedom becomes a meditation on the gratuitous act. The murder of Amedeé has no dramatic motive other than Lafcadio's desire to prove his freedom, but the psychological motive is clear and familiar—he is still another protagonist with a king's-eye view of ordinary life. Genevieve, his Sonia, is attracted to him because he is "hedged in by all the ludicrous conventions of their world,"[12] and, in this *sotie*, Gide presents us with nothing but ludicrous conventions (family, church, literature, science). Although we would never know it from the book itself, Gide did not intend this to be an affirmation of nihilism; it has, however, often been taken as such. Lafcadio's attitude, in a minor key, is part of recent popular culture. When Phoebe Zeitgeist, as she is being murdered, asks, "Why? What have I ever done to you?" she is told: "Poor child! Be not so naive as to believe that cruelty and violence must necessarily be motivated! The malicious act, set apart from the commonplace, lackluster treadmill of goal-oriented drives, attains a certain purity of its own being."[13] What Lafcadio shows us is crime as aestheticism. Who would have thought he would become a folk hero?

Though Camus's Meursault has a venerable lineage, his fate reveals a certain purity of nihilistic design which is new: "One might fire, or not fire—and it would come to absolutely the same thing."[14] Meursault's crime is not an isolated event, but part of a general soullessness: he is totally devoid of piety or feeling at his mother's funeral; he is willing to marry his girl if she is keen on it, but answers "no" when she asks him if he thinks marriage is serious. Since we have in Meursault a rigidity, a mean excess, a human being acting like a machine, why isn't this book a comedy? Why aren't our sides splitting? Because the author's assumption—and the assumption of the age?—is that nobility attaches to belief in nothing; honesty transcends the stupid, normative judgments made upon it. In a typical modernist reversal, the center of judgment, common sense, is seen as ludicrous. While this is true enough in many instances of our lives, the intensely sympathetic portrayal of murderous nihilism breaks new ground. "It's common knowledge that life isn't worth living anyhow,"[15] says our hero. Isn't that what Flaubert said? What is most disturbing about Camus's novel is that the immoralist position *in extremis* has become the property of everyman, for the starkness of the novel proceeds from the sense that there is no aesthetic release, no superman alternative. Camus is in the modern tradition in that in *The Stranger* he has written a book beyond which one cannot go. In its modernist extremity it is still another novel in which a tradition comes to an end.

ii

The central thrust of Bellow's fiction is to deny nihilism, immoralism, and the aesthetic view.[16] He wishes to make art possible for life. Where the artist-hero sought isolation, the Bellow protagonist longs for community, and ironic distance gives way to the nearness of confession as we are on a personal standard. The *noli me tangere* of modernism gives way to "I want, I want," the cold exquisiteness of modernist art to a superjournalistic accessibility. This is the formal meaning of the breakthrough of *Augie March*, where stasis gives way to speed, radiance to ordinary daylight, spatial form to temporal form; narrative is back and the formal meaning reflects a moral one. Augie's excited belief in the "axial lines of life," though somewhat undercut by the subsequent narrative, is typical of the reassessment of common possibility which is the burden of Bellow's mature work. If the artist-hero proper is nowhere present in Bellow, what may be called the citizen hero is often there: the dangling man and Augie have hopes for a colony and a school; Herzog wants "politics in the Aristotelian sense"; Artur Sammler had desired an international fellowship. The aesthetic gives over to the ethical, the artist to the thinker—one may even say, the beautiful (in the French sense of *le beau*) to the good. Indifferent to myth, Bellow brings us into the wildness of current history, the citizen's arena. For authenticity of vision we are given not the collective unconscious but the "glittering eye" of full historical consciousness, since the emphasis is not on the artist but on the event, not on "divine impulse . . . surface polish . . . the law of numbers"[17] but on issues, description, and emotion recollected in some semblance of tranquility. Bellow is the heir of the first modernists, the Romantics, rather than the archmodernists. Like Keats, he is certain of nothing but "the holiness of the heart's affections"; he has not lost belief in the self or even the soul. In Bellow we may have trouble locating good and evil, but we are never beyond it. Immoralist activity, the ultimate nihilistic act, may be a temptation, but it is a temptation which must be overcome. Perversity is not a metaphor of release from civilized inhibition, as it is in *Death in Venice* and its bedfellows, but a form of *mishigas*, tolerable comic madness. Bellow, like others in the postmodern period, illustrates what one wit has called the power of positive sex. What is perhaps the quintessential symbolist poem, "L'Après-midi d'un faune," in its rendering of a fugitive animal sensuality, is about coitus interruptus. The effective missionary style of Herzog reminds us that morality pays.

The general characteristics of modernism—alienation, fragmentation, break with tradition, isolation and magnification of subjectivity, threat of the void, weight of vast numbers and monolithic impersonal institutions, hatred of civilization itself—are obviously authentic in one way or another. Any definition of postmodernism assumes them, as does any postmodern writer. What Bellow does is resist total absorption by them and repudiate the ortho-doxy of "experimentation" which derives from these characteristics of the modernist aesthetic. Above all, he tries to dramatize states of emotion and consciousness that prove there is more to life than this aesthetic assumes. His prose—of course it varies from book to book—reflects the tension in-volved in this resistance, balanced as it is between affirmation and skepti-cism, the manic and the depressive, action and revery, common sense and mystical feeling, the ordinary and the abstruse, the colloquial and the learned, Yiddish inflection and Latinate elongation. From *Augie March* on there is always an energetic temperament, a personal voice speaking through the contraries, making them one. There is neither the sort of irony that implies a split between public and private, nor is there coterie appeal. A writer for whom the mundane does not eclipse subjectivity but intensifies it, Bellow, in this sense, transcends Stephen Spender's distinction between the modernist novel of sensibility and the antimodernist novel of sociology, the novel of poetry and the novel of prose. While Pound was trying to purge the language of poetry of abstraction and to make poetry as well-written as prose, Joyce and Virginia Woolf, in reaction to Bennett, Galsworthy, and Wells, showed that prose could be as well-written as poetry. Bellow shows that prose can be as well-written as prose. His creative repudiation of the modernists makes him a virtuoso in spite of himself.

But one must choose between Spender's categories, and Bellow is in the camp of the prose contemporaries, not the poetic moderns; the realists, not the visionaries. He has always been critical of what he calls the "dismal revolutionary style" derived from modernist visionaries and their belief that man is finished. In the followers of two major classical visionaries, Rimbaud and Lawrence, he notes these characteristics: "trance, dream-utterance, androgynous, homosexual, antinomian, squalor, mesmerism, charlatan-ism."[19] Shamanism is part of the current dislocation. But self-appointed grace is always suspect because it implies too easily, as we have seen, legions of the damned. Bellow sees Lawrence's views of sex as analogous to antino-mian salvation through art: "There are the saved and the damned, the elect and the lost, the orgastic and the impotent."[20]

Characteristically, Bellow prefers Lawrence's art to his doctrine, admires *The Lost Girl* and dislikes *The Plumed Serpent*.[21] The relationship between Alvina and Ciccio is a margin of hard-won authenticity, and Alvina is so well-realized partly because her past is so well-documented. The portrait of Mr. Houghton and his Manchester House is one of the best things in Lawrence. In *The Lost Girl* Bellow is won over by the triumph of an instinctively ascertained fulfillment, but the ideology of sex, the absurd "political" dimension, shows us the hubris of the visionary. Where the doubt of Alvina becomes the pervasive disgust of Kate, Lawrence needs a system to convince himself; so, the world failing her, Kate flees into myth. Don Ramon is the "Natural Aristocrat" who will be "Savior" to the peons: "One must disentangle oneself from persons and personalities," he says, "to turn beyond them to the greater life."[22] This is protofascism. It is well and good to say that Lawrence was not "interested" in politics—but politics, to paraphrase Trotsky, is interested in Lawrence. Bellow has always insisted that the deepest truth is to be found in the personal. In this sense, his rejection of *The Plumed Serpent* parallels his rejection of *Doctor Faustus*, of which he has said: "We cannot continue to build in every novel such total systems in order that we may know what, for example, a woman feels when her husband deserts her, what a man feels on his deathbed. We must take our chances on a belief in the psychic unity of mankind."[23] The monumentality and coldness of modernism, then, is to be countered by the primacy of merely personal emotion. The Bellow novel generally brings a reduction in scale and a corresponding increase in human warmth.

Bellow's first paragraph as a publishing novelist is an attack on modernism. In an obvious allusion to Hemingway, the protagonist of *Dangling Man* complains that emotion, inner life, is suppressed in "an era of hard boiled-dom."[24] Hemingway (in his irony, restraint, mistrust of emotion, disillusioned style, deflation of public rhetoric—all related to his tough-guy manner) is still another disciple of Flaubert.[25] When Bellow's Joseph says, "most serious things are closed to the hard-boiled," he is valuing emotion in a way which makes sense when describing Bellow's career as a whole. But, considering Joseph's inner life, one may well choose the tough-guy alternative. Full of the modern disgust and self-pity, he is cast as a victim in a landscape that might be out of Flaubert or *Dubliners*. Yet he has the energy to write in the confessional style, and the principal virtue of the psychological age in which he is living—honesty. Here is established, albeit in a minor key, Bellow's first link to the Romantic "I" of Rousseau, Goethe, Wordsworth, Stendhal, "who felt no shame at making a record of their inward transactions" (*DM*, p. 9).

Things were not always bad for Joseph. The alter ego, the healthy man he was last year, had an essentialist view rather like Bellow's own. "In all principal ways, the human spirit must have been the same," (*DM*, p. 25) he says. Related to this, he expresses the *amor fati:* "In a sense everything is good because it exists. Or, good or not good, it exists, it is ineffable, and for that reason, marvelous" (*DM*, p. 29). He asks himself, "How should a good man live?" and plans "a colony of the spirit."

A bad party, however, shatters the idea of a colony and separates the old enlightenment Joseph from the new modern one. He quotes Hobbes. What particularly bothers him about the party is the victimization of a girl through hypnotism: "it had been so savage because its object could not resist" (*DM*, p. 57). Passivity, victimization, nonentity—modern qualities too real to let his subconscious rest—drive him invariably into a rage; indeed, this is the main line of action though he is scarcely conscious of it. He insists on being recognized by a functionary of the Communist Party to which he once belonged because he fears nonentity. In his spite, in his self-hatred, in his mixture of intellection and powerlessness, in his flair for the embarrassing, violent flare-up, he is like Dostoevsky's underground man (from the book of that title to which *Dangling Man* has obvious technical affinities as well). In a moment of rare serenity, Joseph is moved by Piatigorsky playing Haydn but is displaced by his niece's Cugat records. She says, "What you call me or think doesn't matter" (*DM*, p. 70), which hits him where he can least afford to be hit. When she becomes more explicit, "Dirty no-account" (*DM*, p. 71), he spanks her. Later, his smug, profession-oriented friend Abt makes him reflect on the declining idea of greatness, a legacy of Romantic (secular) salvation with its images of heroic immoralism and benign criminality. From the "great sadness" of Werther and Don Juan to "the great ruling images of Napoleon" to "those murderers who had the right over victims because they were greater than the victims; to men who felt privileged to approach others with a whip" (*DM*, p. 89) and so on until we get to Hollywood mass culture, we "have been taught there is no limit to what a man can be" (*DM*, p. 88).

The rest of the fragmentary story shows us, however, that there is only limit. The self-pity becomes so oppressive that when Joseph tells the Spirit of Alternatives, "I'm a chopped and shredded man," we want to get him that opening in the cereal factory. Joseph proves too weak to be free and welcomes the regimentation of army life. At one point, thinking of a painter friend, he says: "Those acts of imagination save him. . . . My talent, if I have any at all, is for being a citizen, or what is today called, most apologetically, a good man" (*DM*, p. 91). But regimentation remains the height of his goodness.

Similarly, in *The Victim*, the central character overcomes apathy in a tawdry urban landscape. Despite considerable temptation to the contrary, he will not accept the notions that man is nothing and that we are not responsible for one another. Here regimentation is not the answer because dignity—the way between superman indifference and underground man envy—is.

Yet the real break from modernist apathy occurs in *Augie March*, for Augie does not have to choose dignity; it is a quality of the world he inhabits. The city, the neighborhood, the family, the affair—all have reality. In writing a picaresque novel, Bellow commits himself to a world whose surfaces are worth beholding, whose activities are worth recording. The one is involved with the many, as the marginal man goes through a panoply of social types. Ambition, passion, soul, fate—these are living concerns. The claustral quality of his first novels gives way to a wide open world, depression to larkiness, obsession to ease. In proclaiming his unity with the large, expansive quality of the older novel, Bellow is trying to bypass the modernist syndrome. In Augie, Bellow attempts to portray the most estranged of modern qualities—charm.

If Augie is a rogue, he is a thinking, compassionate rogue. His civilized voice tells us that his education has gone well beyond the college of hard knocks into the school of soft abrasions. The tone of the novel, therefore, is one of qualified buoyancy: "I am an American, Chicago born—Chicago, that somber city" (*AM*, p. 3). If, as he asserts in the face of the oppressive doctrine of determinism, "a man's character is his fate" (*AM*, p. 3), he is well-aware that "his fate, or what he settles for, is also his character" (*AM*, p. 154). With his keen eye for corruption, he sees that Simon's closed, moneyed milieu and its resultant mere "success" is a perversion of the heroic will. Despite the break, the brothers cannot help feeling for each other. Though Augie recognizes the "worldwide Babylonishness" (*AM*, p. 70), he will not believe that "we are at the dwarf end of all times" (*AM*, p. 60), will not accept the modern cult of the past. If he were capable of being a disciple, he would compare Einhorn to Caesar, Machiavelli, or Ulysses. History is alive in even the minor, passing character, like Mr. Kreindl, the Klabyasch player, who is seen in his Napoleonic aspect. Similarly, Bellow suspends the ironic attitude. When Grandma Lausch puts on her corset "to take the eye of a septuagenarian Vronsky or Des Grieux" (*AM*, p. 15), she is seen not with contempt but with affection. Even when she may deserve contempt, as in her paranoid farewell, Augie would rather think of her noble admonition to be a somebody. The desire to be a somebody—this is at least half of Einhorn's greatness: the refusal to be a victim although fate seems almost to have made him one.

Just as he rejects the past as a golden age, utopianism of any sort is suspect in Augie's view. Thea's belief that "there must be something better than what people call reality" (*AM*, p. 316) is an ominous indication of her self-enclosed version of reality. Augie tags along uxoriously and must sooner or later be victimized. Basteshaw, the utopian who has "created life" (*AM*, p. 509) and the solution to all the ills the flesh is heir to, is a brute in his personal life and subjugates Augie to his will. As he falls asleep in the crazy lifeboat, Augie has the chance to kill him but nurses him instead, feeling pity

for him. If Augie keeps his bearings through all the conflicting realities that
people seem to like to impose on him, it is because he is in touch with "the
axial lines of life" (AM, pp. 454f.), an intuitive knowledge expressed in
unabashed traditional abstractions—"Truth, love, bounty, usefulness, harmony." Since life itself perpetuates human value, man doesn't have to die to
be reborn, like Osiris, a wasteland mainstay. In a related idea, Augie later
thinks: "I don't know who this saint was who woke up, lifted his face, opened
his mouth, and reported on his secret dream that blessedness covers the
whole Creation but covers it thicker in some places than in others. Whoever
he was, it's my great weakness to respond to such dreams. This is the *amor
fati*, that's what it is, or mysterious adoration of what occurs" (AM, pp.
526f.). Considering the difficulties he has been experiencing with his wife,
Stella, one detects a note of unearned optimism, but like the old Jacqueline
dreaming of Mexico, it is the hallmark of this *ingénu* to "refuse to live a
disappointed life" (AM, p. 536).

Seize the Day may be considered a reaction to the somewhat excessive
exhuberance of *Augie March*. If *Augie March* was his clearest rejection of
modernism to date, *Seize the Day* seems to be in a phase of agreement with
its negative power. It is his most piercing study of alienation, of the depravity of bourgeois society—the radical's Bellow. But if *Seize the Day* is about
the alienation of a good man, the goodness is there and not ironically given,
for Tommy's vision of love in the subway is a strumming of the axial lines.
Similarly, when his wife drives at him in her impersonal, mercenary way,
Tommy says, "Thou shalt not kill! Don't you remember that" (SD, p. 112).
Above all, the image of the dead man—a surrogate for humanity, for his
father (whom he has just seen in that position in the steam room), and for
himself as well—brings an upwelling of sympathy and pain before the fact of
mortality. "The consummation of his heart's ultimate need" are the tears that
betoken the burning need for human connection. Norman Podhoretz has
suggested that the story would have been better if Tommy had murdered his
father, but Podhoretz was not aware of the symbolic meaning of this act for
Bellow. A work of great force, *Seize the Day* is possibly Bellow's most
perfectly realized work; consequently, some think it his very best. But I
believe that the breakthrough into a larger, wilder, aggrandizing subjectivity
that we get in *Henderson the Rain King* and *Herzog* makes the next phase of
his work his most original and most valuable.

Bellow has commented that Henderson, "the absurd seeker of high qualities," is the character most like him.[26] Although the scene is Africa, *Henderson the Rain King* is a personal idyll. Myth serves the cause of personal
transcendence; the primitive, the voice of civilization; the heart of darkness,
the heart of light. As some of the critics have noticed, it is a parody of
Conrad, Lawrence, and Hemingway rather than another note on the decline

of the west. Dahfu encourages Henderson in the belief "that chaos doesn't run the whole show. That this is not a sick and hasty ride, helpless, through a dream into oblivion" (*HRK*, p. 175). The Covent Garden school of anthropology, comically employed, yields not a wasteland but some measure of fruition; instead of the Fisher King, the Rain King. In his movement from innocence to experience, from the Arnewi to the Wariri, the voice of wisdom is partly the voice of Blake. Henderson's cure, such as it is, owes much to a Romantic, vitalistic naturalism. Henderson can think of Dahfu as "a true artist" and a superman in his benign aspect, as when he tells the threatening tribesmen: "Sometimes these great men go beyond themselves. Like Caesar or Napoleon or Chaka the Zulu. You ought to be glad that he's not a Chaka and won't knock you off" (*HRK*, p. 251). Here Henderson defends the voice of civilization, and the tablets he wishes to break embody what seems to him a harsh, ritualistic primitivism. Henderson is transformed by Dahfu to the extent that he becomes a "Be-er" rather than a "Becomer." This accounts for his giving up the violin, an event symbolic of his transformation: "*I wanted to raise myself into another world. My life and deeds were a prison*" (*HRK*, p. 284). In escaping to Africa Henderson exorcises the escapist in himself.

In *Henderson the Rain King* and *Herzog* Bellow is offering us the new comedy, one which he sees beginning with Svevo's *Confessions of Zeno*. Introspection, self-knowledge, hypochondria, so solemnly treated in the modern tradition, are here the subject of humor. The novelist enjoys laughing at himself, as he does at others: "The inner life, the 'unhappy consciousness,' the management of personal life, 'alienation'—all sad questions for which the late romantic writer reserved a special tone of disappointment, of bitterness, are turned inside-out by the modern comedian. Deeply subjective self-concern is ridiculed. *My* feelings, *my* early traumas, *my* moral seriousness, *my* progress, *my* sensitivity, *my* fidelity, *my* guilt—the modern [read contemporary] reader is easily made to laugh at all of these." (Bellow gives the population explosion, the political and scientific revolutions, wars, failures of religion as reasons for the change.) Bellow sees, for example, *Lolita* as a reworking of *Death in Venice*, with Nabokov mocking the Nietzschean, Freudian theme: "Humbert is not impressed by sickness, nor does he associate it with genius; perversity is a concept from the whiskered past with its notions of normalcy"—perversity as a sign of a special fate, normalcy being associated with dumb health. The new comedy is "our only relief from the long-prevalent mood of pessimism, discouragement, and low seriousness (the degenerate effect of the ambition for high seriousness) . . . the comic spirit is also the spirit of reason opposing the popular orgy of wretchedness in modern literature."[27] In saying this, in appealing to a norm of rationality, Bellow is reversing the dark, outsider strain of comedy which, in many variants and tones, from desperation to gaiety, constitutes the dominant strain of the modern tradition. Bellow is appealing to a community that apparently exists. *Herzog* and *Lolita*, two of the best American novels since the war, are also two of the most seriously read and widely popular, though *Herzog* seems the better book in that the comic intention is nowhere mitigated by a diminished seriousness in the conceptions of the central self and climactic action.

The "plot" of *Herzog* is given in the first paragraph. What is important is the dramatization of consciousness, the movement toward recovery, the clairvoyance of a comic tone. *Herzog* begins in gloom and ends in light. The physical action of the book runs parallel to, and is at one point identical to the shift in consciousness. The flexible third person–I narrator, taken over from Donleavy's *The Ginger Man*, another postmodern comedy of consciousness, gives us maximum illumination. We view Herzog and view Herzog viewing Herzog. Yet the most brilliant innovation is the renovation of the epistolary technique, allowing as it does a blending of discursiveness and intimacy, the argumentative and the personal, *kulturkampf* and the *cri de coeur*. Ideas are never free of the passional element and learning wears a common grace. In his Kant and Hegel, he wants his lox and bagel. No system is substituted for human response, nor do the ideas direct the psychological states. Eventually, the private content of the letters attains the positive outlook of the rather consistently elaborated ideas (though, tonally, the idea-letters move from tension to tranquility). The pathos of the letters is heightened by the fact that they are never sent.

As private man and as scholar Herzog battles the wasteland outlook. He, too, senses the axial lines of life: "His study was supposed to have ended with a new angle on the modern condition, showing how life could be lived by renewing universal connections; overturning the last of the Romantic errors about the uniqueness of the Self; revising the old Western, Faustian ideology; investigating the social meaning of Nothingness" (*H*, p. 39). Here Herzog attacks nihilism, the aesthetic aristocracy, immoralism, and existentialist dehumanization, indicating that the revision of the Faustian ideology would be in the direction of Goethe (including, of course, the rejection of Mann); accordingly, he later refers to his new energy as "a Faustian spirit of discontent and universal reform."

Herzog's rejection of Heidegger's "fall into the quotidian" is another variant of his resistance to Nothingness, his refusal to give up on ordinary life. In this vein, he chastises his friend Shapiro for "a merely aesthetic critique of modern history" (*H*, p. 75), derived doubtless from Burckhardt and Nietzsche, with their contempt for mass democracy. Nietzsche has Herzog's qualified admiration; it is that he has become debased, the master of those whose view is "aesthetic"—Lafcadio, Dr. Faustus, Hulme, Pound, Eliot—which Herzog finds distracting. To have assumed that "the deterioration of language and its debasement was tantamount to dehumanization led straight to cultural fascism" (*H*, p. 76). Though Herzog can give a certain assent to Hulme's rejection of Romantic "dampness," he recognizes that, for all his degeneracy, Rousseau had an openness, an honesty, a sense of himself, that made him large, larger than his detractors: "I do not see what we can answer when he says 'Je sens mon coeur et je connais les hommes' " (*H*, p. 129).

Corollary to the wasteland aesthetic is "the new utopian history, an idyll, comparing the present to an imaginary past, because we hate the world as it is" (*H*, p. 163). Our self-awareness has indeed been purchased at a great cost to instinct. But when we then fabricate a golden past, the only outlet for inspiration in the absence of this past becomes a "negative transcendence" or kind of immoralism: "This is pursued in philosophy and literature as well as in sexual experience, or with the aid of narcotics, or in 'philosophical,' 'gratuitous' crime and similar paths of horror" (*H*, p. 164). The immoralist "tradition" from Sade to Mailer, from Raskolnikov to Lafcadio to Meursault is included herein. Herzog refuses to give credence to Proudhon's belief that "God is *the* evil," and thereby rejects the immoralist view that everything is possible.

How do these complex but familiar ideas relate to the central physical action? *Herzog* can be described as the story of a murder that does not take place. We have been speaking of the ideational content of *Herzog* in a way that is necessarily restrictive of the novel as a whole, for the murder scene—like the portraits of Gersbach, Mady, and Herzog—is comic. Herzog with his antique gun zeroes in on the villainous Gersbach—who has just given his daughter a bath! "Herzog saw faint wisps of powder that floated over Gersbach's stooping head. His red hair worked up and down. He was scouring the tub. Moses might have killed him now" (*H*, p. 257). But, of course, no! "The tenderness of such a buffoon to a little child" and the thought that Gersbach and Mady, too, can bring up a little child mitigates his contempt. The triumph of Herzog is that he refuses to see them as wasteland characters; the taking of a life has meaning, since life has meaning. In his actions, as in his thoughts, then, Herzog rejects the nihilist view. This scene is given by a master of the new comedy in which, as Bellow says, deeply subjective self-concern is ridiculed. The release Herzog feels after his decision is psychological as well as moral, for he is not trapped in his ego.

Is Ramona the answer? Not, in the last analysis, any more than her Marcuse or Brown; sexual utopianism is simply the loveliest modernist falsification. Herzog is left with an intellectual and emotional balance that can only be called affirmation. His prayer to God is another version of the *amor fati*, which is itself an instinctive rejection of the modernist negative apocalypse.

The comedy and intellectuality of *Herzog* is rounded out by a tone of personal elegy vis-à-vis Herzog's familial past. His father, like Simon Dedalus, is an elaborate failure, but this does not at all dispel the strong feeling of son for father, or deny father Herzog's depiction as a man whose "I" had dignity. Similarly, like an anti-Meursault, he feels his mother's death as no one else can. "Whom did I ever love as I loved them?" (*H*, p. 147) says Herzog; yet the weakness of excessive dwelling on this deep filial emotion is known to the depressive Herzog. Here, as elsewhere, however, Bellow is affirming universal connections at the risk of being square.

On the face of it *Mr. Sammler's Planet* looks as if it might be a work similar to *Herzog* in as much as its central intelligence is an introspective man whose professional life, to say nothing of his personal life, is something of a shambles. Sammler is another man who affirms deeply felt traditional and intuitive conceptions in the face of the dual assault of aestheticism and utopianism. Again Bellow makes no compromises with his reader, rendering in detail the contemporary metropolitan climate—one of violently conflicting ideas which are inseparable from emotions. But there are great changes. Bellow has left behind the subjective, lyrical quality of *Herzog* and *Henderson the Rain King*, the "special comedy" of these central characters, and written a book whose times are darker and whose protagonist is more witness than agent. When the focus of madness is in the age rather than the hero, we do not need the embodiment of a powerful, crazy style but the preserver of a quiet sanity that will hold. There is, in other words, an increasing objectivity in the new work, a movement away from the dramatization of obsessions; accordingly, the third person narrative illustrates the greater difference between author and protagonist. What dramatizes it even more is the fact that this is Bellow's first postsexual character, a desired distancing effect achieved by the creation of a seventy-two-year-old man. This characteristic can be viewed not only as a quality in the nature of things but as a witness to a life whose scars and tensions have not left much room for the ease of sex. Think of old Einhorn, the Commissioner, "still an old galliard, with Buffalo Bill vandyke . . . he swanked around, still healthy of flesh, in white suits, looking things over with big sex-amused eyes" (*AM*, p. 61).

Sammler is the witness to a universal dissonance. In its rendering of a broad, social panorama this is Bellow's harshest book. New York has always been enervating to the Bellow protagonist. Chicago has been relatively normal, but in New York the malevolence is palpable. The pollution, the guarded aproaches, the ripped-out, urine-smelling phone booths, the universal dog dung—this is only the landscape of a deeper rot. Most important, it is clear that the rot is a result of the oblique triumph of modernism, a triumph of sorts, for the aesthetic aristocracy is now the aesthetic mob: Mallarmé is spinning in his grave; Raskolnikov has a fellowship; nihilism is alive in the murderous behavior of the revolutionary. Reason seems to retreat in the face of "the century's great crime," the holocaust, seeking explanations in the bureaucratic, dehumanized[28] quality of modern life, denying the possibility of simple moral judgment. Hannah Arendt (never named) is, in Sammler's view, the victim of modernist, mass-man, Weimar assumptions. Indeed, reason is in danger of becoming another lost illusion—even in the view of Sammler himself.

Sammler's Anglophilia, his admiration of H. G. Wells, is an expression of civilized possibility, rationality, sanity. Wells, who is political "in the Aristotelian sense," views literature as a means to the greater end of social harmony, international community. Sammler opposes this to Weimar intellectualism (whose popular American embodiment is the stalinoid Herbert Marcuse), which is an expression of the modernism we have been defining. Yet Wells, too, came to be depressed by the century of war. What, thinks Sammler, has come of the *Cosmopolis* project for a World State, or his articles in *News for Progress* and *The World Citizen*. Lecturing at Columbia on this ideal of "a service society based on a rational scientific attitude toward life," Sammler feels "what a kind-hearted, ingenuous, stupid scheme it had been" (*MSP*, p. 41). His feeling seems justified as the new brutality is made flesh when Sammler is violently attacked for pointing out that Orwell said British radicals were protected by the Royal Navy. One would not ordinarily think of Orwell as a defender of the Establishment. Beyond that, of course, why attack Sammler for reporting what Orwell said? Orwell is, as the phrase goes, "counter-revolutionary." And Sammler? An "effete old shit," whose "balls are dry." The Freudian-Marxism of Reich is in the wings here. Revolution cannot be merely political or economical, since authority—all authority—should and can be destroyed only by a crusade of unrepressed children. Sammler is attacked by still another mad utopian.

The other stunning event of the brilliant opening of *Mr. Sammler's Planet*, the menacing self-exposure of the black pickpocket, is equally indicative of a world gone topsy-turvy. (Significantly, the doorman is not there—one of several failures of the guardian function; nobody coming to the besieged Feffer's aid is another.) Authority resides in the size of a man's member. It speaks for itself: "It was a symbol of superlegitimacy or sovereignty. It was a mystery. It was unanswerable, the whole explanation" (*MSP*, p. 55). Speak about transcendence downward! The situation is grim as immoralism appears in the most astonishing guises. Sammler's implicit allusion to Edmund's famous speech in *King Lear* is taken without a break in narrative stride: "Make Nature your God, elevate creatureliness, and you can count on gross results." Sammler muses pessimistically, "Maybe you can count on gross results under any circumstances" (*MSP*, p. 55).

The bleakness of *Mr. Sammler's Planet* derives from the fact that the suffering of the central character is no longer inseparable from pleasure.

Comedy is reserved almost exclusively for the secondary and minor characters—though there is much of this—because normalcy is *in extremis:*
where the comedy of *Henderson the Rain King* and *Herzog* depended on the
resiliency of good will, the last-ditch confidence of reason, the ability to
establish a normative perspective, Sammler has all but lost this ability. The
major character in later Bellow who is closest to being alienated, he is the
most precarious of Bellow's yea-sayers. If this is partly due to his age, it is
also due to his experience—Herzog thought of himself as a kind of survivor,
but Sammler literally is one. Moreover, Sammler is the only character in
Bellow to take a life. Considering the symbolic meaning this act has for
Bellow, it strikes us with shattering force, for it is an acknowledgment, as in
King Lear, that the world can present an animal pattern. Sammler has his
bizarre Cordelia, but Gruner has none. Sammler's real Cordelia is his consciousness, which is not entirely isolated. Sammler tells Wallace of the
section in *War and Peace* in which the captive Pierre's life is spared because
he has exchanged "a human look" with the cruel General Davout: "Tolstoy
says you don't kill another human being with whom you have exchanged
such a look. . . . I sympathize with the desire for such a belief . . . men of
genius . . . are almost forced to believe in this form of psychic unity. I wish
it were so" (*MSP*, pp. 188f.). This is the most tenuous statement of the axial
lines or universal connections or moral-self theory in Bellow.

But when recalled to the battleground of ideas by Lal's physics and metaphysics of the moon, the irreducible moralist in Sammler is revived. In his
own way, Lal is still another embodiment of the modernist negative apocalypse. His utopianism is pragmatic: "the species is eating itself up. And now
Kingdom Come is directly over us and waiting to receive the fragments of a
final explosion. Much better the moon" (*MSP*, p. 219). Lal, who has read the
symbolists, embodies one of the ironies of history. It is not the symbolists
but the mechanists they despised who may make the incredible voyage: "the
invitation to the voyage, the Baudelaire desire to get out—get out of human
circumstances—or the longing to be a drunken boat, or a soul whose craving
is to crack open a closed universe is still real, only the impulse does not have
to be assigned to tiresomeness and vanity of life, and it does not necessarily
have to be a death-voyage. The trouble is that only trained specialists will be
able to take the trip" (*MSP*, p. 219). Lal defends the plausibility of his utopia
since he sees around himself a widespread death wish, at which point
Sammler affirms the moral being of man, the "pain of duty which makes the
creature upright" and the "instinct against leaping into kingdom come"
(*MSP*, p. 220). The overleaping of ordinary life is again proscribed. Sammler
has the good Gruner as an example of present decency and living proof that
there is "a bond." He also has his saintly Meister Eckhart.

When, walking down Broadway, Sammler sees what seems to him a host of "Hollywood extras. Acting mythic. Casting themselves into chaos, hoping to adhere to higher consciousness" (*MSP*, p. 149), he feels the value of the ancient imitation of good. In the debasement of modernism, life has become art. "The standard is aesthetic" (*MSP*, p. 147) in the same sense that Shapiro's critique of modern history is aesthetic. There is an attempt "to rise above the limitations of the ordinary forms of common life" (*MSP*, p. 147), a middle-class bohemianism that is a caricature of the avant-garde. In playing sexual fantasist, guerrilla, or desperado, one can fantasize a life beyond the ethical. Never mind that Sade's blasphemy is reduced to hygiene; never mind the consequences of symbolic crime. For Sammler, this is an area where even Kierkegaard was a fool to tread. Indeed, the vogue of Kierkegaard's *Fear and Trembling* is of a piece with the eccentricity of the age. Sammler would understand that the point of the biblical story is that though Abraham is superhuman in his obedience, God does not exact an immoralist tribute. But as he looks around him Sammler sees once again an equation of the aesthetic and immoralist positions: "He thought often what a tremendous appeal crime had made to the children of bourgeois civilization. Whether as revolutionists, as supermen, as saints, Knights of faith, even the best teased and tested themselves with thoughts of knife or gun. Lawless. Raskolnikovs" (*MSP*, p. 63). The meaning of Sammler's life is that the ethical can never be suspended. Civilization depends upon it. Nowhere is Bellow more Jewish than in his constant insistence on this point. *Mr. Sammler's Planet* has its own special "poetry" of decadence and pathology. The device of the septuagenarian alien allows Bellow to present the strangeness of contemporary reality with unexampled distance. But if Bellow is playing Dostoevsky to the young's possessed, he has not achieved the pathos of the master.

Though Bellow went all out in the composition of *Humboldt's Gift*, it received a mixed critical reception. The critical displeasure expressed on the occasion of its publication is in good part attributable to Bellow's violation of modernist shibboleths. The novel is his first to deal centrally with the most sacred of modern archetypes, the artist-hero, a figure notably absent from the work of a writer so aware of the modern tradition. For Bellow has resisted identification with the type just as he has resisted the aesthetic ideology which makes so much of it. The reviewers' response to the novel was to a significant degree a resistance to this resistance. No one likes to see his god abused, and Bellow will not bow to the religion of art. Moreover, Von Humboldt Fleisher is portrayed as a failure because he is all too typical of the ideology. He is the victim as modernist. To tell the story of someone trapped by his own consciousness in not new in Bellow, but to tell the story of a genius trapped by his own consciousness is. Humboldt is not only a student of, but also an embodiment of Rimbaud, Eliot, et al., the great naysayers, the desperate idealists trapped in the modern prison. The question is, why can't Humboldt develop his extraordinary poetic gifts? The answer is that his view is self-confining, his sense of entrapment a self-fulfilling prophecy. He turns every insight into a form of damnation, every situation into a conspiracy. Yet his failure is often taken as a form of success. As *poète maudit*, he is evidence for the reality of the wasteland view.

If Humboldt is indeed a paranoid who has enemies, he is also a man who has friends. Charlie Citrine counts himself as one of them, despite the fact that it was impossible to have a relationship with him without being an enemy at one time or another. Citrine is the necessary complement to the *poète maudit*. Himself something of an artist—he has a successful play—he is primarily an historian and biographer, a scholar whose stated professional interests are more political than aesthetic. Once again the Bellow surrogate is cast as citizen. Once again the state totters. The theme of civility has worn thin. Partly because of Citrine's age, partly because of the increasingly implacable incongruities of American life, the religious theme replaces the political, Steiner replaces Aristotle, mysticism replaces enlightened skepticism. That Bellow is as convincing a dramatist of mystical connection as he is of moral obligation is doubtful. Not that the religious element has been absent: Wilhelm, Herzog, and Sammler address God; and Henderson thought of himself as mediumistic and attuned. Their *other*worldliness, such as it was, only served to establish the primacy of this one. But Citrine's yearning for transcendence, an explicit preference for a higher world, is sustained. Corresponding changes occur; where the Bellow protagonist used to be hard on Jung, he now treats him with great respect. There is a switch in *Humboldt's Gift*, a realignment of allegiances. How seriously can it be taken? Even Citrine considers himself an amateur, albeit a sincere one, in the Steinerian scientific mysteries.

More than this, it is hard not to see the Steiner dimension as part of the overall comedy of the book, Bellow's claims for its seriousness notwithstanding. While there is often a creative tension in his work between the soul and the world, never before has the string been so taut. The novel virtually divides the world into Platonic *doxa* (appearances) and *episteme* (real knowledge), and with the addition of Steiner, the spiritual becomes the occult. Can one really be a scientist of the invisible? His particularly otherworldly appropriation of Steiner also induces an uncharacteristic quietism. Willy-nilly—and he often enough wills it, capitalizes on the joke—Citrine's spiritual assumptions work partly as comedy, a sort of Hyde Park quixotry in an environment every bit as unpromising as La Mancha.

But Citrine's distance from ordinary Chicago is never so great as to amount to a surrender to alienation. The wisdom of the novel is its wry jelling of disparate elements. Where Humboldt is spirit ultimately debased by vulgarity, Cantabile is ultimate vulgarity seeking to capitalize on spirit;

where Citrine is soul attracted to body, even unto its literary possibilities, Renata is body attracted to soul, and the substantial amount soul has managed to accumulate in the bank; where Steiner sees a world beyond the chaos of mere appearance, the divorce courts show us *that* chaos with perfect clarity. In its wrenching polarities, the plot itself is thus a a conception of wit. *Humboldt's Gift* is nothing if not masterly comedy. Citrine is the Bellovian presence straddling the contraries. Once again, the sympathy, the suppleness, the humor of a Bellow "I" assures us of the reality of the human comedy.

iii

Many periods hinge on contradiction and the post-modern period in American fiction is one of them. If there is one salient characteristic of the era, it is polarity. Coherence, a dominant center—no; antithesis, adversary alignments—yes. One can not be certain what it is that the age demands. It is doubtful that historical proximity alone creates this uncertainty. From time to time literary history presents an ideal polarity which goes a long way toward defining the complexity of an age. One thinks of Richardson and Fielding, Tolstoy and Dostoevsky, or, closer to home, Fitzgerald and Hemingway, T. S. Eliot and Wallace Stevens. It is not surprising that our own post-war period, prodigal in its incoherence, adds luster to the lists of *kulturkampf*. This is not an instance of literary bloodlust or gladiatorial nostalgia. When the two major literary reputations of the post-war generation form a thesis and antithesis with no synthesis in sight, the matter compels attention. For their opposition is based on antithetical attitudes toward the modern tradition.

Mailer and Bellow are well aware of each other as living alternatives in the arena of culture. Mailer may be seen as Bellow's cultural anti-self. The central distinction is political, for Bellow represents the conservative liberalism Mailer affects to despise. For Bellow there generally is a politics of civility, a possibility of more than fragmentary consensus, a middle grasped from the periphery in an often exasperating but finally decent society which represents a civilization worth preserving. If *Mr. Sammler's Planet* and *Humboldt's Gift* call this into question—and they do to some extent—they do so in favor of a deeper conservatism. Yet Bellow's recent essays show that he has not abandoned this political stance. In a recent piece, we find Bellow chastising Sartre for saying, in his introduction to Fanon's *The Damned*, that the oppressed must redeem themselves by violence.[29] Mailer, on the other hand, has spent a good part of his career making violence respectable. His justification for this, a familiar one, is that "individual acts of violence are always to be preferred to the collective violence of the State."[30] As if this were the only quality of the state, as if America were embroiled in an eternal Vietnam. "The route to control could best masquerade under a conservative liberalism" (*ND*, p. 556), says Mailer's proto-fascist General Cummings. For a long time Mailer thought that if you had anything good to say about America, you were an unwitting tool of fascism.

Much of the positive emotion in Mailer is generated by the act of murder, fantasized and often enough achieved in his writing. But the wife he stabbed was harder than the knife. George Schrader asks, "How . . . are we to understand the behavior of a man who is conscious and sane and yet performs a motiveless destructive act? I haven't the slightest doubt that Mailer not only knew what he was doing but performed the action only because he was aware of it—all too much aware of it perhaps."[31] We are to understand it as the gratuitous act. Yes, there is an aura of self-conscious confession, the gratuitous act as examplary! Mailer's comment in the newspapers to the effect that the writer acts out what the ordinary man only fantasizes indicates that being a superman of sorts was the motive. But how can you kill your wife with a penknife? It suggests that Mailer may be a liberal after all.

"There is no crime of which I do not deem myself capable," said Goethe, but he didn't commit any. Mailer "commits" them mostly in imagination, reaching for some return of the instinctual, the natural, as if rape and murder were primitive. Psychology and anthropology have taught us that this is not the case, that instincts are conservative, that the id can be as tyrannical as any superego, the superego as repressed as any id. The white Negro is as much conditioned by pathology as he is liberated by spontaneity. Yet Mailer's creative characters are violent and must be; indeed, for Mailer creativity is a form of violence. His successful lovers are sadistic, even murderous. It is not for nothing that Sergius, in the masterly "The Time of Her Time," calls his penis "the avenger." It could be no other way in a society he judges to be monolithically repressive, a judgment contingent on his own insufferable narcissism. In *Why Are We in Vietnam?*, the rational, liberal part of Mailer can not help condemning the killing in Vietnam, but the dark, subconscious Mailer, willy-nilly, goes along with its psychological necessity. D.J. is both creative and murderous, Croft imperious and violent, Faye romantic and sadistic. Killing Deborah gives Rojack "a view of . . . Heaven"; it is like coming "in a woman against her cry" (*AD*, p. 35f.). Here we have negative transcendence in all its black purity. Orgasm has often been associated with death, as a transcendence of time, but rarely with murder, as a destruction of the other. This is the wisdom of our Sade.

Mailer's fascination with murder and the gratuitous act remains perhaps his deepest vein as we see in his sympathetic portrayal of Gary Gilmore, a man more interesting to Mailer than the rest of us because he is a murderer.

What is most troublesome about this portrait is Mailer's occasional lapse into sentimentality, as in the following romantic equation: "If you put a profile of what an artist at thirty-five might look like, Gilmore would fit that physical profile."[32] Mailer compares his lovers to Romeo and Juliet, but Shakespeare's Romeo does not ask Juliet to die—in a one-way suicide pact! Though the love theme is not sentimentally drawn, it has its sentimental aspect; it is the sort of relationship that exists primarily in ideal separation, the kind a life-term provides. The more recent Jack Abbott episode shows how the very questionable veers off into the disastrous. Despite its modernist fundamentalism, Abbott's book is a remarkable document. But to claim, as Mailer does in his introduction to the prisoner's book, that we may have a writer of the greatest stature among us is to be victimized by the notion of the artist-criminal. "You didn't have to kill me," were Richard Adan's dying words as Abbott testified at his trial—the dying words, as it happens, of an artist. Abbott killed him because he could not use the employee's bathroom, because he mistook Adan's gestures of aid for gestures of menace. A tragedy of toilet training? Like Rojack, who wanted crime without punishment, Abbott seems to believe that anyone with a philosophical mind never comprehends the concept of guilt. At least the mellow, elderly Mailer does not have the courage of his earlier convictions. He expressed contrition, admitted some kind of guilt.

Mailer and Bellow are nearly direct opposites. Mailer is far more sympathetic to modernist assumptions. Mailer's missing middle is Bellow's tenuous center. The characteristic Bellow movement is of a marginality moving toward the center. This is true in different ways of Augie March, Tommy Wilhelm, Henderson, Herzog, Sammler, and Citrine. In place of negative transcendence we see a reaching for transcendence normally understood. Bellow could hardly be more spiritual, but he is more ethical in a traditional sense. He is recognizably Jewish. He resists the knee-jerk Nietzscheanism, the immoralist trans-valuation of values, that Mailer gives us. While his characters, from Augie to Sammler, from Joseph to Citrine, are not unfamiliar with the appeal of crime, none (including Sammler, who kills but does not murder) is familiar with murder.

Where Mailer is drawn by magic, Bellow is attracted by morality defined in Judeo-Christian terms. Mailer finds stasis in battle, Bellow in peace. States of triumph in one correspond to states of harmony in the other. Mailer wants greatness, Bellow goodness. For all his intellectuality, Mailer is sympathetic to the redskin; for all his sensuality, Bellow to the paleface. While both write about Narcissus in the Big City, Mailer, romantically, is drawn to the heroic attitude; Bellow, skeptically, to the unheroic. The one errs on the side of swagger to the point of megalomania, the other on the side of quietism to the point of depression. A gaudy adventurousness is

countered by a wise passiveness. Dionysian, Mailer is radical by temperament; Apollonian, Bellow is liberal. Bellow admires the sociology of Edward Shils, Mailer deplores the sociology of David Riesman. Mailer is
attracted to ideology where Bellow is wary, and to melodrama where Bellow is to psychological realism. One is moved by the politics of ecstasy, the
other by the politics of civility. Mailer is propelled by diabolical event,
Bellow by redemptive character.

Mailer typically writes a romance, Bellow a realistic novel. Almost all of
Bellow's novels take place in a recognizable city; virtually none of Mailer's
do (*Barbary Shore* is almost accidentally in the city: *An American Dream*
dissipates city with dream). While neither slights subjectivity, Bellow is not
in danger of dismissing the actual world. Neither considers fiction to be
autonomous; both consider it to be a moral comment on that world even to
the extent that both tend toward the abstract and tendentious, writing
novels that often end with beginnings which are moral resolutions, ironic
or true. Both are mimetic, though Mailer's recent fiction approaches sheer
verbality. Mailer swims in the extreme, somewhat Byronic; Bellow in the
middle, Wordsworthian perhaps. A moderate Romantic, Bellow wants to
explore everything; an extreme Romantic or Modern, Mailer wants to per-
mit anything.

A figure of the fifties who was amenable to the sixties, Mailer prophesies,
contemptuous of the past. A figure of the fifties who was contemptuous of the
sixties, Bellow is anchored in history, skeptical of the future. Where Mailer
gravitates to the Manichean, Bellow is pulled toward the Stoical in the sense
of anti-millenarian. Bellow sees "evil" as privative, a falling away from essence, Mailer as positive, a weakness in the Creator. Existentialism finds
Mailer a friend, Bellow an adversary. Both dislike psychoanalysis: Mailer
finds it totalitarian, a devourer of instinct;[33] Bellow finds it meanly utopian, a
destroyer of pure motive. Yet Mailer was influenced by Reich; Bellow by
Freud, Reich, and others. Mailer remains intransigent, while Bellow criti-
cizes psychoanalysis from within, his sense of character owing much to it.
Mailer eschews tradition, Bellow tries to salvage it from the wreck.

Mailer has no normal family life or childhood in his work; Bellow has or
would like to have. Publicly exhibitionistic,[34] Mailer avoids the personal in
his work; fiercely private, Bellow is often confessional. Neither, it has been
said, can live with or without women. Jewish Don Juans, they keep getting
married. Bellow often views the new woman sympathetically but not perhaps seriously enough (could the central character in a Bellow novel ever be
a woman?); Mailer views her antagonistically. Bellow guards his independence, Mailer his *macho*. For Bellow woman may be squaresville, lotusland,
or Waterloo, but never the apocalypse. Both resist victimization, but where
Mailer's antidote is in the rebellion of the hipster or a hip version of the

superman, Bellow's is in the humanist's search for the dignity of the ordinary. Mailer's nostalgia for the revolutionary is matched by Bellow's for common sense. Mailer has been to Cairo, Bellow to Jerusalem—and back—and that as much as anything else tells us about the way they go.[35]

Though both of them will be read and considered for some time, no one can like these writers equally and in the same way. Considering the mutually exclusive views of reality they give us, it seems likely that the literary reputation of one will decline if that of the other ascends. Or they will both preside for a time over a polarized literary community, if they preside at all. For the polarization of late has become more complex with the coming of the new metafiction usually called postmodern. While Mailer's virtuoso work and deliberate confusion of genres make bows in that direction, both Mailer and Bellow seem, in comparison, positively Victorian in their relative moral strenuousness. With its emphasis on the central and the true, Bellow's quest in particular—like Jewish-American writing in general—seems out of synch with this verbal phenomenon expressive of formlessness, characterlessness, meaninglessness, entropy. Where fragmentation was once lamented, it is now made an aesthetic. It is a literature of synechdoche, a literature of fancy. So much is icon, so little is reference. Language is everywhere; feeling is where personality is—and where is that? Ironies echo in a hall of mirrors. We are in a labyrinth. There is a detotalization of mind, a demystification of heart. Since everything is aesthetic, the past is a neutral plural. How do we distinguish between pasts? How do we discriminate between the true and the false? Where is value? What are the consequences of such nihilism? In axing the axiological they are effing up the ineffable. Whatever happens, one must be grateful for two writers who have, over decades now, responded so vividly, though antithetically, to the assumptions of the modern tradition.

Chapter 2

Saul Bellow and the example of Dostoevsky

i

It is no longer possible to say that all modern American literature comes from *Huckleberry Finn*. In a literal sense it was never possible, whatever *éclat* Hemingway's famous hyperbole has had. In view of recent developments in the novel, it sounds with the resonance of another era. True, Salinger is oblique witness to the life of a tradition that includes Anderson, Hemingway, Lardner, and Faulkner, but the figure of the innocent initiate cannot be the only iconographic center of a literature which is focused on the adult genital ego in culture, and on its corresponding mental sweat. It was once possible to think of a pure adolescent heart as symbolic of hidden virtue still resident in the young country, a natural, redeeming reality deeper than all worldly appearances. But the difference between Huck and Holden Caulfield is instructive: solitude has become isolation, traumatic experience fullblown neuroticism, lighting out for the territory retiring to the mental institution. Adolescence is no longer an example but a case. Salinger is on Mark Twain's side, on his far side—civilized life is scarcely worth living—but we no longer have the freedom of the asexual idyll; we have urban, claustral impotence. Holden's grey hair symbolizes the end of an American myth, a time when America comes of middle age.

There are, however, advantages to growing all the way up, fallen though that state may be: what is lost in innocence is gained in knowledge. Though this moral has often been full of possibility in American literature, the force of it is no longer widely considered to be dramatic in itself. America has moved closer to Europe, and much, not "all," contemporary American literature comes from Flaubert or the Russians if it "comes from" anywhere. We have seen what the Flaubert tradition affords.

Bellow, on the other hand, seems to be the leading contemporary exponent of the "Russian" way. The idea of a writer as teacher rather than martyr, citizen rather than artist, journalist rather than aesthetician; the idea of literature that is flexible enough to be tendentious and broad enough to be inspiring; a literature that refuses to adopt the pose of objectivity, detachment, and disenchantment with life in quest of the compensatory salvation of form and avoids comparing the artist with God—all this bears witness to the Russian influence. The Russians would never think of art as religion, yet moral feeling in their work is charged with an energy, a yearning, a hope, that may finally be described as religious. Their art respects, indeed thrives, on mental effort and expresses, as Irving Howe has remarked, "that 'mania for totality' which is to become characteristic of our time."[1]

The postmodern Jewish writers have brought to American literature a dramatics of the mind which, generally speaking, recalls the Russians. V. S. Pritchett has suggested that there is an affinity between the American writers of Yiddish background and the Slavs. They know what the western writers have long ago forgotten, says Pritchett, "the sense of looseness, timelessness and space."[2] Pritchett's impressionistic remark acknowledges the essentialist affirmation, desperate though it may be, of irreducible moral truths that define a sort of rhythm of the ethical sphere. The artist-god comparison implies the need for a total subjective originality that denies the reality of this timelessness. These generalizations may be illustrated by a comparison between Bellow and the Russian master whose example is most instructive to him, Dostoevsky.

The central impetus in both writers, in periods marked by ideological confusion and in novels full of explainers, is the quest for what is morally real. Ivan Karamazov's "if there is no God everything is permitted" is the sort of immoralist proposition that they must refute. When Dostoevsky says of the "enthusiast," Belinsky, "He knew that the moral principle is at the root of everything,"[3] we have a statement in tune with Bellow's idea of "axial lines." To begin with a conventional illustration, both writers use the image of the child as the embodiment of innocence—sometimes offering it with an unabashed naiveté. We recall, for example, Augie's *après vu* of his fatherhood, or Myshkin's story of the peasant woman with a baby who says, "God has just such gladness every time he sees from heaven that a sinner is praying to Him with all his heart, as a mother has when she sees the first smile on her baby's face."[4] While such an image may embarrass the properly jaded reader, we know that a character like Myshkin could not exist without such sentiment. The contemporary reader has, perhaps, less difficulty with Ivan's conception of the child as victim, as symbol of unspeakable injustice, as is seen in incidents of child beating so vividly represented that even Alyosha agrees that the sadistic perpetrator should be shot. Similarly, a courtroom re-enactment of child beating is a blow sufficient to turn the civilized Herzog to murderous thoughts. Of course, child abuse has a seductive force in Dostoevsky, who is sometimes called the Russian Sade; but its thematic effect inverts Sade in order to expose nihilism, not to promote it. The poetry of crime—fully orchestrated and directly dramatized in Dostoevsky, muted and usually the subject of a lyric polemic in Bellow—comes to serve as a last-ditch proof of the existence of God or, at least, of the existence of moral imperatives since, in modern literature, God typically enters through the back door. The creator of Raskolnikov might almost have written (though it was actually Bellow) that "there are friendships, affinities, natural feelings, rooted norms. People do on the whole agree, for instance, that it is wrong to murder. And even if they are unable to offer rational arguments for this, they are not necessarily driven to commit gratuitous acts of violence."[5]

To be sure, the words of the Grand Inquisitor to Christ—"Dost Thou know that the ages will pass, and humanity will proclaim by the lips of their sages that there is no crime, and therefore no sin; there is only hunger?"[6]—carry great force in an age of behavioral environmentalism. We are familiar with Brecht's paraphrase of "Feed men, and then ask of them virtue." And it develops into the argument of Mailer's "The White Negro" where he excuses the murder of a storekeeper by young killers. *Anomie* issuing in desperate boredom does link characters like Stavrogin and Mailer's Marion Faye. Stavrogin wishes to "put powder under the four corners of the earth and blow it all up"[7]—as does Marion in similar words. The difference is that Dostoevsky, like Bellow, ultimately has a contempt for the immoralist Stavrogin, whereas Mailer's essential sympathy lies with the immoralist (now hipster) Faye.

Even greater is Dostoevsky's contempt for the radical Pytor Verkovensky, whose vision of the revolution come to pass is one of crime as the norm. Speaking to Stavrogin, he counts his troops: "The lawyer who defends an educated murderer because he is more cultured than his victims and could not help murdering them to get money is one of us. The schoolboys who murder a peasant for the sake of sensation are ours. The juries who acquit every criminal are ours. The prosecutor who trembles at a trial for fear he should seem advanced enough is ours, ours." Pytor concludes that "crime is no longer insanity, but simply common sense, almost a duty; a gallant protest."[8] True, in Czarist Russia any protest was credible, but what we get in Pytor is a prefiguring of Stalinist manipulators. On his part, Bellow has always been mistrustful of the clairvoyance of radical solutions, but it is not until *Mr. Sammler's Planet* that he dramatizes a comparable political hysteria.

Dostoevsky's attack on nihilism, then, is political as well as ethical. Not confined to hysteria, the assault often expresses itself as comedy at the expense of ideology, which is seen to be utilitarian, socialist, individualist, western. The underground man is, perhaps, the most conspicuous illustration of the assault on the radicalism of the 1860s (as opposed to the more humanitarian radicalism of the 1840s with which he has some ambivalent sympathy, as did Dostoevsky himself), which is imaged as the wall, the piano key (determinism), the ant hill, the chicken coop (the urban mass and that utilitarian haven, the apartment house), and the Crystal Palace (the new cathedral of utilitarian perfection). As Ralph Matlaw says, Dostoevsky is attacking the utopia of Chernyshevsky, Fourier, and Saint-Simon, which tried to reconcile Hegel and Rousseau, the world historic process and the man of feeling, historical determinism and individual will.[9]

In *Notes from Underground* and elsewhere Dostoevsky makes no distinction between ideology and utopia, which he uses in its pejorative sense. The uncensored version had intimations of Christian belief; however, the censor seems to have done well in deleting them if his aim was the dramatic coherence of the work. Despite the underground man's brilliance and authenticity, he is trapped in the atom of his ego, unable to love, unable to be more than a caricature of the "freedom" he claims to represent. But with *Notes from Underground* the genre of ideological comedy is established. The ruthless, loud honesty, the intellectual acuity, the comic dramatization of mental suffering—all these appear earlier in Diderot's *Rameau's Nephew*, but the full head of self-consciousness, historical awareness, and philosophical depth is Dostoevsky's addition. The underground man knows more than the nephew and enjoys less; he is isolated and, generally, impotent.

Ideological comedy—which is to have an impact on Bellow—is not confined to *Notes from Underground*. In *Crime and Punishment*, for example, there is the marvellous Lebeziatnikov, a rarely noticed character. After describing the "anaemic, scrofulous little man," the usually neutral narrator tells us that he was "really rather stupid; he attached himself to the cause of progress and 'our younger generation' from enthusiasm. He was one of the numerous and varied legion of dullards, of half-animate abortions, conceited half-educated coxcombs, who attach themselves to the idea most in fashion only to vulgarize it and who caricature every cause they serve, however sincerely." Lebeziatnikov is a theoretician and, in a wildly comic scene, expounds Fourier and Darwin to the smug bourgeois Luzhin who despises him as a man of no connections. Luzhin, ready for any praise, accepts Lebeziatnikov's commendations for being ready to contribute to the establishment of a new "commune," for abstaining from christening future children, for acquiescing "if Dounia were to take a lover a month after marriage, and so on." Luzhin, who is the most tyrannical, self-absorbed, money-mad character in the book!

When Luzhin asks to make certain that Sonia is a prostitute (later the

sinister depth of this request is revealed), Lebeziatnikov says, in the tone
of airy emancipation that Dostoevsky scorns, "What of it? I think, that is, it
is my own personal conviction that this is the normal condition of women.
Why not? I mean, *distinguons*. In our present society, it is not altogether
normal, because it is compulsory, but in the future society it will be perfectly normal, because it will be voluntary. . . . I regard her actions as a
vigorous protest against the organization of society." From Dostoevsky's
point of view—and from her own—Sonia's life of prostitution is a martyrdom. This point of view is conservative, sympathetic to monogamy,
privacy, Christianity, chastity. It is characteristic of Dostoevsky to scorn
"advanced" ideas, to characterize them as utopian schemes masking the
self-interest of the idea-monger. (Lebeziatnikov does "wait in hopes" of
Sonia.) Dostoevsky, profoundly mistrusting meliorist realism, often sees
the cause itself as the caricature. Lebeziatnikov says, "I should be the first
to be ready to clean out any cesspool you like . . . it's simply work . . .
much better than the work of a Raphael and a Pushkin, because it is more
useful,"[10] and thus gives us the first statement of a theme which becomes
major in *The Possessed*. Here, as elsewhere, Dostoevsky treats the ideologue as the buffoon. When, in his concern about the distraught Katerina,
Lebeziatnikov tells Raskolnikov that "in Paris they have been conducting
serious experiments as to the possibility of curing the insane, simply by
logical argument,"[11] we have a delicious reduction of the excessive faith in
rationalism which Dostoevsky condemns as western.

Dostoevsky's rare allusions to America suggest that he believes that the
new land is about as western as you can get. In *The Possessed* it is for the fop
Lebyadkin to sing its praises. He speaks glowingly of an American millionaire who "left all his vast fortune to factories and to the exact sciences, and
his skeleton to the students of the academy there, and his skin to be made
into a drum, so that the American national hymn might be beaten upon it
day and night."[12] The experience of Shatov and Kirillov in America gives this
rationalist optimism the lie. America, with its capitalism, its science, its
utilitarianism, is, in Dostoevsky's mind, a desperate place. He must sometimes have thought that Russian culture by comparison was concerned with
the smiling aspects of life.

In Bellow and Dostoevsky the world that we know is in good measure a
world of ideas, positions, solutions. The letters of Herzog are only the most
celebrated instance of the endless interplay of explanation which strikes
Bellow as the most salient characteristic of an anxious age. Some of the ideas
are worthy of Lebeziatnikov—like the theory of the Bulgarian aesthetician
Banowich, who believes that telling someone a joke means that you want to
eat him, or, more seriously, the various Sadean theories of negative tran-

scendence which espouse creative criminality. Basteshaw, Dahfu, Bummidge, Lal are among those heavy theoreticians in Bellow in whom ideology is open to the charge of utopianism. Dostoevsky's attack is centered on the utilitarian and the revolutionary; while not excluding these, Bellow's is directed at more recent utopian attitudinizing, including the psychoanalytic, the technocratic, the modernist visionary. The mold is the same but the material has changed somewhat, partly because Bellow has a common-sense sympathy for a number of the liberal utilitarian propositions which Dostoevsky burlesques. For Dostoevsky suffering is the mother of human consciousness; Bellow is willing to grant this, provided one holds, as he does, that pleasure is its father. Still, both writers reduce the Babel to a comic dimension from the point of view of a more traditional truth to be told. Both take confidence from older, "obsolete" truths, residues of a religious tradition.

ii

Bellow's outlook is analogous to that of social theorists such as Raymond Aron and Edward Shils. A *précis* of their key arguments sheds a clearer light on his aims, and on those of writers like him.

Raymond Aron's *The Opium of the Intellectuals* implies in its title the reduced attraction of the Marxist ideology and revolutionism that had once greatly appealed to a number of the post-war liberal revisionist writers in America. Aron maintains that revolutionism had benefited from the prestige of aesthetic modernism, that the artist who denounced the philistines and the Marxist who denounced the bourgeoisie could consider themselves united in a battle against a single enemy. Aron notes, however, that none of the big literary movements was allied with the political left. Exceptions seem tangential and only prove the rule: "Sartre's itinerary toward quasi-Communism appears to be dialectical. Man being a 'vain passion,' one is inclined in the last analysis to judge the various 'projects' as all equally sterile. The radiant vision of the classless society follows on the description of the squalid society of today."[13]

Bellow shares his view not only of high culture, but also of the mythicized proletariat, of whom Aron writes: "Servant of the machine, soldier of the Revolution, the proletariat as such is never either the symbol or the beneficiary or the leader of any régime whatsoever. . . . The common source of these errors is a kind of visionary optimism combined with a pessimistic view of reality."[14] As for the justification of such pessimism, Aron points out that by comparing the division of wealth and the standards of government of a century ago with those of today, we can see that "the growth of collective resources makes societies more egalitarian and less tyrannical. They remain, nonetheless, subject to the old, blind necessities of work and of power and, *ipso facto*, in the eyes of the optimists, unacceptable."[15]

This "doctrine of sustained tensions" with its emphasis on "the courage . . . to endure," as R. W. B. Lewis describes it, in a review of Lionel Trilling's *The Liberal Imagination*,[16] gives us what Lewis calls "the new stoicism," which is analogous to the Burkean view of history. Though the word has little of its original meaning, there is a similarity between the "old" Stoic rejection of Platonism in favor of sense perception and the late forties' stoic rejection of Marxism in favor of a pragmatic sense of possibility. Both posit a dignified self-sufficiency in a world of failed illusion. In Aron's dichotomy the essentialists and the utopians are at odds. We have seen Professor Herzog lecturing in a similar vein on the modernist "*new utopian history, an idyll, comparing the present to an imaginary past, because we hate the world as it is.*"[17]

Along with Aron, perhaps the clearest exponent of the stoical view is Edward Shils, a student of Karl Mannheim, sociologist and Bellow's colleague at the University of Chicago. Bellow would seem to admire the tone that these men assume—totally unapologetic—in their critique of modernist utopianism. Like Aron, Shils must place the Marxist view in what he feels is its proper perspective. He points out that Trotsky thought "the average human type will rise to the heights of an Aristotle, a Goethe or a Marx. And above this ridge, new peaks will rise." But Shils feels that the working class, even where it is Communist, is uninterested in revolution, in the moral transformation of itself and the rest of the human race. Shils believes that all ideologues (e.g., Marxists, French monarchists, Southern agrarians) are hostile to human beings as they are. A revulsion against their own age makes intellectuals think of the elevated cultural life and dignified peasantry of a non-existent past (e.g., Tönnies, Simmel, Sombart, Marcuse). He denies the validity of the *Gemeinschaft/Gesellschaft* distinction, since it assumes a small-scale, perfectly consensual, theological society that never existed.

Shils does not believe that bourgeois individualism, urban society, and industrialism are an impoverishment of life. For him, as for Bellow since *Dangling Man*, the "fundamental problems of humanity are the same as in antiquity." He wants a pluralistic society rather than a completely integrated one, with a bow to British utilitarianism and Burke's critique of ideological politics, and with another to the British liberals, like Milton and Locke, who saw that society could be effective even if it had no uniformity of belief, no unifying ideology, and to Mill who, taking the next step, held that diversity of viewpoint was a necessity for a healthy society. Moreover, Shils believes that in mass society there is actually "more of a sense of attachment to the society as a whole, more sense of affinity with one's own fellows, more openness to understanding, and more reaching out of understanding among men than in any earlier society of our western history or in any of the great oriental societies of the past"; that is, "it is the most consensual."

Indeed, the "uniqueness" of mass society is its "incorporation of the mass into the moral order of its society." Since the mass means more to the elite than in other societies, we see an enhancement of the dignity of ordinary life. Again, with a bow to Weber, "the unique feature of the mass society is . . . the dispersion of charismatic quality more widely throughout the society" (e.g., working class, women, youth, ethnic groups previously disadvantaged). Shils does attribute some truth to the view which he is compelled to deny, saying that while there is alienation, there is another side to the conventional Marxist critique of mass society. The other side of alienation is disenchantment with authority; of egotism and hedonism, the growth of sensibility; of the decline of local autonomy, a more integrated society. Beyond all this dynamism the primordial attachments—kinship, locality, sexuality—will change but persist.[18]

Shils attacks "ideology," a term that he defines with strict constructionist precision. Ideology is a highly systematized pattern of belief integrated around a few pre-eminent values—salvation, equality, ethnic purity. Political coherence overrides every other consideration, with supreme significance going to one group or class—the nation, the ethnic folk, the proletariat, the party leaders. It has a Manichean cast, positing uncompromisable distinctions between good and evil, sacred and profane, left and right, we and they; the source of evil is a foreign power, an ethnic group, or a class (e.g., bourgeois). There is a distrust of traditional institutions—family, church, economic organizations, schools, conventional political alignments. Shils distinguishes ideology from outlooks (e.g., Protestantism), which are pluralistic, containing creeds which shade off into ideology but do not take a sharply bounded and corporate form, and have much less orthodoxy. He also contrasts ideology with systems and movements of thought, which, like ideologies and unlike outlooks, are elaborate and internally integrated, but do not insist on total observance in behaviour, complete consensus among its adherents, or on closure vis-à-vis other intellectual constructions. Ideology, too, is distinct from programs, which involve specification of a particular limited objective, often in the form of a passionate rejection of one aspect of society.

Opposed to ideology is civility or civil politics; civility is the virtue of the citizen who shares responsibility in his own self-government. It is compatible with other attachments to class, to religion, to profession, but it regulates them out of a respect for tradition and out of an awareness of the complexity of virtue, an awareness that every virtue costs, that virtue is intertwined with vice. With characteristic benignity Shils, writing in 1958, says that "There is now in all strata, on the average, a higher civil sense than earlier phases of Western society have ever manifested." In the manner of civility Shils does not believe that ideology should be "completely dismissed"—the desire for greater equality, the distrust of authority, the need for heroism, all have "some validity." It is not the substance but the rigidity of ideological politics that does damage. Ideologies fail in their notions of global conquest because "normal" values assert themselves, compromises are made, and the world changes. As for the phrase "end of ideology," it applied only to a very specific time and in a very specific way; it did not mean that ideology could never exist. It was wrongly taken to mean that ideals, ethical standards, and general or comprehensive social views and policies were no longer either relevant or possible. Both sides failed, at times, to distinguish between ideology and outlook and between ideology and program. No society can exist without a cognitive, moral, and expressive culture; there can never be an end to outlooks and creeds, movements of thought and programs.[19]

It is worth briefly noting objections to these views which, like the views themselves, bear on a comprehension of Bellow and Dostoevsky. Needless to say, historical events of the late sixties represented an anger, a sense of injustice, that does violence to the tonality of these remarks and to a number of the propositions themselves. This is not the place for a weighing of arguments. To an amateur observer, however, it appears that Americans now and in the past have often been passionate about what Shils defines as programs, and that ideology is a concept resonant with the struggles of *Mitteleuropa* from which a number of liberal and radical intellectuals derive perhaps too much of their vocabulary. Ideology, as Shils defines it, is as bad as he says it is. But it is difficult to gainsay Dennis Wrong's questioning of the total view: "If 'ideology' is by now, and perhaps with good reason, an irretrievably fallen word, is it necessary that 'utopia' suffer the same fate? . . . [Utopia] is the vision of a *possible* society, a vision that must deeply penetrate human consciousness before the question of how it might be fulfilled is seriously considered—and by that time we will already have advanced a long way towards its fulfillment."[20]

The impatience or dislike shown by radical readers (adherents, say, of C. Wright Mills) for a book like *Mr. Sammler's Planet*, in which "ideology" is presented as brutality, or a book like *Herzog*, whose hero feels that the "occupation of a man is in duty, in use, in civility, in politics in the Aristotelian sense," not in ideology or politics in the Marxist sense, is another way of drawing the lines. One recalls Lenin's view of *The Possessed: "great but repulsive."* Bellow has his own personalist, novelist's point of view, but his explicit utterances about ideology, by which he means what Shils means, are in the manner of Aron and Shils: "Ideology is crippling to attention. It has no finite interests but makes a wholesale distribution of innumerable human facts. Its historical or biological schemes dispose of human beings by classification." In support of a deeper, contrary wisdom, he then quotes Dostoevsky, who writes in an accent Bellow comes to adopt: "We cannot exhaust a phenomenon, never can we trace its end or its beginning. We are familiar merely with the everyday, aparent and current, and this only insofar as it appears to us, whereas the ends and the beginnings still constitute to man a realm of the fantastic." The moral is then drawn by Bellow: "Ideology commands an end, imposes a law, speaks the first and last words and abolishes confusion. But it has no interest in the miracle of being which artists endlessly contemplate."[21] This "mystery of mankind," as Bellow is later to call it, this inexhaustibility, is indicative of the personalist, anti-ideological view.

Even more so are Dostoevsky's critical remarks on *Anna Karenina*. Addressing himself to the question of Anna's guilt, Dostoevsky repudiates the "physician-socialists," saying that, for the Russian author, "no ant-hill, no triumph of the 'fourth estate,' no elimination of poverty, no organization of labour will save mankind from abnormality, and therefore—from guilt and criminality . . . that in no organization of society can evil be eliminated, that the human soul will remain identical; that abnormality and sin emanate from the soul itself, and finally, that the laws of the human spirit are so unknown to science, so obscure, so indeterminate and mysterious, that, as yet, there can neither be physicians nor *final* judges, but there is only He who saith: 'Vengeance belongeth unto me; I will recompense' " (the epigraph to the novel). This is deeper than environmentalism, which says, "inasmuch as society is abnormally organized, it is impossible to make the human entity responsible for its consequences. Therefore, the criminal is irresponsible and at present crime does not exist." But, Dostoevsky continues, Tolstoy, knowing in this case the consequences of adultery and equal "crimes," expresses his older wisdom in an "analysis of the human soul."[22] Though Bellow is far more sympathetic than Dostoevsky to the environmentalists, he gives us in Alexander Corde of *The Dean's December* a man who does not want to see crime go unpunished. And Corde is sorry that in the murder of a white woman by a black psychopath, "Nobody actually said, 'An evil has been done' " (*DD*, p. 202).

One of the truisms of Dostoevsky criticism is that the writer who excoriated the ideology of political radicalism himself embraced the ideology of pan-Slavism with its belief in the messianic mission of the God-bearing Russian people, the truth of Russian orthodoxy and the falsehood of western Roman Catholicism, the sanctity of the Russian soil, and the even more sacred quality of the Russian peasant; here we have the we–they, sacred–profane dichotomy, which Shils says characterized the ideologist. But Dostoevsky scarcely knew the peasants he idealized. And, as Philip Rahv has said, the manner in which he embraced orthodoxy was so apocalyptic as to undermine orthodoxy, subvert dogma, shatter the notion of institutionalized religion itself.[23] If, in *The Possessed*, he saw the failure of revolutionary ideology, he was too honest not to portray the nihilistic vacuum which revolution must fill. Perhaps anyone viewing political reality in Czarist Russia with a clear eye would see a chaos beyond the politics of civility to set right. Dostoevsky dreaded the Antichrist whose arrival he intuited, which accounts for the gloom behind the comic balance of the book. As for his belief, does he ever really convince us of anything more than Shatov's "I—I will believe in God"? And for all his sweet clairvoyance, the final point about Myshkin is that he fails.

iii

·Above all, the dramatic force of Dostoevsky's art often works against his didactic intention with a brilliance that illustrates the subtle uniqueness of literature—the exposition, in action, of ambivalence, the complex of feelings in the face of which any idea must be a simplification. The underground man, Raskolnikov, Ivan—all characters whom Dostoevsky fundamentally rejects—are creations of a child of light who saw best in darkness. But the metaphor should not confuse. Dostoevsky was nothing if not a personalist. In saying of him that "nobody was less preoccupied with the empirical world. . . . His art is completely immersed in the profound realities of the spiritual universe,"[24] Nicholas Berdyaev gives us what is, at best, a half-truth. How can one be a non-empirical psychological genius? More to the point is the description by Strakhov, who knew Dostoevsky intimately: "All his attention was upon people, and all his efforts were directed towards understanding their nature and character. People, their temperament, way of living, feelings, thoughts, these were his sole preoccupation."[25]

This personalism is consonant with the intellectual depth of his work; for he is, as Arnold Hauser puts it, "a romantic in the world of thought" in that "the movement of thought has the same motive power and the same emotional, not to say pathological, impetus in him as the flood and stress of the feelings had in the romantics."[26] In this lyricism of ideas combined with a centrist conception of character Bellow finds Dostoevsky the acknowledged master. Typically, in a Bellow novel, an essentially urban man—usually "cracked," often intellectual, portrayed in his solitude or isolation, usually unemployed in one way or another, whose business turns out to be personal relationships—is thrust forward at the moment of intense subjective crisis. Everyday apprehension is shattered by a welling up of the demonic. What George Steiner says of Dostoevsky also applies to Bellow: his "characters—even the neediest among them—always have leisure for chaos or an unpre-

meditated total involvement."[27] Virtuosi in mental suffering, these characters embody the heady balance of disequilibruim. When Dostoevsky, in
his famous letter to Strakhov, wrote, "I have my own view of art, and that
which the majority call fantastic and exceptional is for me the very essence of
reality," he was a pioneer, not aware that he was writing a motto for much of
the literature of the future. It is this merging of realism and fantasy in a
context of pained, obsessive, often funny subjectivity—this art, as Philip
Rahv has it, of psychic distortion, moral agitation, and resentment,[28] the way
of Gogol rather than the "objective" way of Pushkin—that Dostoevsky and
Bellow take as their aesthetic norm. Herbert Gold called the author of
Henderson the Rain King the "funniest sufferer since Gogol,"[29] to which one
can only add, with the possible exception of the creator of *The Double*, *Notes
from Underground*, and *The Eternal Husband*.

"All Dostoevsky's heroes are really himself,"[30] says Berdyaev, offering a
version of the distinction between Dostoevsky, a writer of subjectivity and
obsession, and Tolstoy, one of objectivity and proportion. This is a distinction of convenience, but it is a contrast that can tell us something about
Bellow as well. Both present a theater of self-realization where the heart is
laid bare in the act of defining what is real. In this personal quest sociological
categories are secondary to the spiritual. If this implies a distance between
object and subject, society and self, action and temperament, it is a distance
which both writers feel must be bridged. In both, brotherhood is a refrain
whose melody they are trying—and often failing—to recapture. Both attempt to break out of what Edward Wasiolek has called *"the circle of
hurt-and-be-hurt,"*[31] the network of sado-masochism, which appears to be a
governing principle in Sammler's era. But, in both, meekness or mildness is
largely its own reward. *Caritas* is typically confounded by *Eros* in a scenario
where man-woman relationships testify to the potency of moral tenuousness
or disintegration. In Dostoevsky, as Berdyaev says, "The mystery of marriage is not consummated," and in Bellow the marriage is consummated, but
the mystery is not dispelled. For both, in Berdyaev's phrase, "love serves
only as an index of . . . inner division."[32]

Yet the delineation of similarities points significantly to differences, for
Dostoevsky presents us with a drama of extremes, a moral *chiaroscuro*, an
acting out in fact of what in Bellow often remains fantasy or suggestion.
Raskolnikov commits the murder; Herzog does not. Herzog thinks of and, in
some ways, embodies the strength of mildness; Myshkin is its apotheosis; hit
by a block of wood and his senses clarified, Henderson says that truth comes
in blows, but when Dmitri Karamazov says, "I understand now that such
men as I need a blow," he has been condemned for a parricide he wished for.
The self-willed in Dostoevsky are pathological, the meek incredibly self-
effacing. And sometimes both extremes inhabit the same soul. Corde skeptically, reluctantly admits that he cannot accept such paradoxes: "It was for-

eign, bookish—it was Dostoevsky stuff that the vices of Sodom coexisted with the adoration of Holy Sophia" (*DD*, p. 130). When a "murderer-saviour" type appears in *The Dean's December* in the person of Toby Winthrop, Bellow does not do much more than include him as part of the grim local color. Respecting his male-nurse qualities, he nonetheless considers him a "case," part of abstract modern consciousness rather than Christian miracle. Still, in his articles, Corde finds it necessary to mention the Antichrist.

Czarist Russia had a way of rendering fantasy literal, making for a dramatic, even operatic, quality which in a kindred comtemporary spirit more usually comes out as *opéra bouffe*. Dostoevsky's ideological preferences lent substance to an often Manichean opposition of forces. The outcome in Dostoevsky is typically tragic in overtone, a Dionysian coming to grips with the demonic, leaving one with a sense of waste nobler than the hidden cause. In Bellow even the Dionysian inspiration—e.g., Henderson, Herzog—is ultimately comic in that the painful, headlong quest is inseparable from knowledge that constitutes the self—the western, Dostoevsky-doubted ego, the last court of appeals; the self that, in its constant exposure, cannot be taken as seriously as it once was, yet is most of what we have to take seriously. Where Dostoevsky dramatically records the disintegration of the self, Bellow tentatively assumes it, and the tragic is converted into the comic. In Bellow, accordingly, more often than in Dostoevsky, the soul is finally restored to a firm outline.

The one point at which the two writers would seem to differ most is the apprehension of the self in its full sensual regalia. Here Bellow appears to be positively Tolstoyan. A character like Stiva Oblonsky, in *Anna Karenina*, lives in the literary love of an author whose judgment is otherwise morally proscriptive of him. Many of Bellow's characters exist in this way. Ramona, for example, illustrates the delights of inner division. The observation of sensuousness implies the "normal" world, but the dramatic situation implies the Dostoevskian "extreme." It is precisely this integration of opposites which describes a good part of the course of the current literary *zeitgeist*, for what we see in Bellow, and in other recent writers, is the normalization of the extreme—making it comfortable, cozy, charming. "If I'm out of my mind, it's all right with me," says Herzog and any reader of the book would understand him.

iv

Bellow's work offers some extended illustrations of the Dostoevskian influence—unconscious or otherwise. It has not been noticed, for example, that the dialogue between Joseph and the Spirit of Alternatives in *Dangling Man* is a low-keyed recasting of the apparition of the devil to the hallucinated consciousness of Ivan Karamazov. Ivan recognizes that the devil is his double: "You are the incarnation of myself, but only one side of me . . . of my thoughts and feelings, but only the nastiest and stupidest of them" (*BK*, p. 775). The devil appears as a shabby genteel Russian, whom Dostoevsky sees as a type. They "have a distinct aversion for any duties that may be forced upon them, are usually solitary creatures, either bachelors or widowers. Sometimes they have children . . . brought up at a distance, at some aunt's. . . . They gradually lose sight of their children altogether" (*BK*, p. 773). That is, the devil is worldly self-absorption divorced from the essential ties. Child abandonment, while not quite the equivalent of child abuse, is closely related.[33] Yet this prince of darkness is a gentleman, "accommodating, and ready to assume any amiable expression," possessing, in Dostoevsky's view, the complete western veneer and the basic western wisdom. He does not know if there is a god; he knows only *je pense, donc je suis* and, Descartes's "proof" of the existence of God to the contrary notwithstanding, its attendant solipsism (a sort of fantasy extension, in Dostoevsky's view, of the rationalistic, ego-oriented west): "Does all that exist of itself, or is it only an emanation of myself, a logical development of my ego which alone has existed for ever" (*BK*, p. 781).

Goethe was enough of a traditional humanist to create a Mephistopheles who desired evil but did only good; Dostoevsky's Mephistopheles, however, operating in a universe much more attuned to the modern saturation of alienated consciousness, sees that he desires good but does only evil—which perfectly describes Ivan's predicament (culminating in his harrowing scenes with Smerdyakov, whose suicide he hears of immediately after the apparition vanishes). Ivan realizes at the outset that the devil embodies his "stupidest" thoughts, yet so attractive are they that they threaten to destroy his "intelligent" ones. "God is dead," "the man-god," "will," "science," "all things are lawful," "the old slave man," parade so tantalizingly before his hallucinated view that Ivan can dispel them only in the way Luther with his inkstand set the devil to rout—he throws his glass at him. If this is a breakthrough for Ivan, the devil himself remains *déclassé*. Konstantin Mochulsky notes that "in his *Legend* Ivan represented the devil in the majestic image of the terrible and wise spirit, and here he has proved to be a vulgar hanger-on. . . . The spirit of non-being is an imposter: this is not Lucifer with singed wings, but . . . the incarnation of world boredom and world vulgarity."[34]

Precisely. And it is this note of boredom and vulgarity that Bellow strikes in his ostensibly reasonable, genteel representative of non-being, the Spirit of Alternatives. There is no nightmare, no sickness here—at least in the first meeting. Consistent with the meandering movement of the work itself, the encounter is "relaxed." So reasonable is the Spirit, so plausible to the dangling man are his alternatives, that he is also called "On the Other Hand" and "*Tu As Raison Aussi*." Yet it is clear that in his equivocal manner, his indeterminacy, his inevitable drift to the negative, the alienative, his flirtation with ideology, his attitudinizing in a vacuum of conviction, and above all, in his compulsion to the center of indifference, to death, he is the dangling man's devil-double in the same sense that the apparition is Ivan's— a representation of his own worst, his own "stupidest" ideas and tendencies. (Joseph, we recall, is already separated from the older, benevolent, rational, Enlightenment Joseph.) This apparition is even quieter than Joseph; his point must be elicited, but when it is seen to be "alienation," Joseph retorts that "it's a fool's plea." Not that there is no alienation, but "that we should not make a doctrine" of it.

Trying another route, the Spirit suggests "changing existence" through politics, but Joseph rejects the revolutionary and even politics per se. He does, however, admit the value of "a plan, a program, perhaps an obsession." When the Spirit converts this typically American ad hoc impulse into "an ideal construction," Joseph notes the "German phrase," and wonders about the ideological exemplar or type. He concedes that an "obsessive device" may be "the only possible way to meet chaos" and sees the apparent "need to give ourselves some exclusive focus, passionate and engulfing," but the essentialist in him asserts itself: "what of the gap between the ideal construction and the real world, the truth? . . . Then, there's this: the obsession exhausts the man. It can become his enemy. If often does." When the Spirit has no answer to this, apparently having no real convictions to defend, Joseph drives him out, flinging "a handful of orange peel" at him (*DM*, pp. 137f.).

Like Ivan, Joseph seeks that which "unlocks the imprisoning self," and in order to escape being "self-fastened" he himself is willing to entertain the "highest 'ideal construction,' " though, more or less, as a passing fancy. Still, he feels that *Tu As Raison Aussi* stands refuted; Joseph has confidence that the "final end" of everyone is "the desire for pure freedom," which he defines in Dostoevskian fashion, not simply as free will but as will defining itself as spirit, "to know what we are and what we are for, to know our purpose, to seek grace" (*DM*, p. 154). This is as far as Joseph will go towards religion. But the resolution is offhand and represents only a moment of equilibrium.

Joseph's depression worsens, and in the next encounter the Spirit appears as an almost old-style Mephistopheles, the Spirit that Denies, tempting Joseph to "give up," to succumb to indifference, to die, to "worship the anti-life." Joseph recognizes his "inability to be free," and this is the cause of his "weariness of life." Unmistakably, and despite his noble wish to share the pain of his generation, Joseph joins the army in the same way one joins the Grand Inquisitor's church: "We soon want to give up our freedom . . . we choose a master, roll over on our backs and ask for the leash" (*DM* pp. 167f.). When Joseph utters the hollow cry, "Long live regimentation!" he is aware that he is "relieved of self-determination, freedom cancelled" (*DM*, p. 191). This conclusion has little of the ambiguity sometimes attributed to it. In the end Bellow's devil-double emerges as one who ascertains one's doubt of selfhood, uniqueness, "separate destiny." Joseph is rendered almost as pale, sickly, chilled, and enervated at the end of his encounter with the double as Ivan is with his.

The dramatization of guilt leading to confrontation with the double becomes conspicuous in comparing Bellow's *The Victim* with Dostoevsky's *The Eternal Husband*. This comparison has not gone unnoticed, but the context of extended comparison here affords us a wider view of its meaning. Actually, Dostoevsky's *The Double* is the precursor of both. A solitary spirit in a dreary urban landscape is the necessary beginning to each crisis of subjectivity. In *The Double* "the damp autumn day, muggy and dirty, peeped into the room through the dingy window pane with such a hostile, sour grimace that Mr. Golyadkin could not possibly doubt that he was not in the land of Nod, but in the city of Petersburg, in his own flat on the fourth story of a huge block of buildings in Shestilavotchny Street" (*D*, p. 477). If his living is compartmentalized, so is his job, for Golyadkin is a result of the dehumanizing Russian bureaucracy. The crisis in his life breaks out when the moral qualities that the system exacts of its lesser lights—bootlicking, toadying, a fidgety, manipulative quality, a nastiness masking as playfulness, a choreographed self-interest—appears in the shape of Golyadkin Junior who, like Ivan's devil-double, is the embodiment of Senior's worst self.

As the story begins, we see Golyadkin "satisfied" with the "insignificant" face and bald head he views in the morning mirror. He feels so good that he counts his money. Beware!—a sure sign of anal-retentive meanness in Dostoevsky is viewed here as a sign of life in the bureaucracy. A volatile mixture of self-esteem and self-abasement (before his superiors, or any other male authority figure), this isolated, hostile, sado-masochistic urban bachelor is Dostoevsky's first underground man. "Sick," he goes to see a physician, palpitating before the meeting but greeting him with a schizoid "figuratively crushing" glare. He is suffering from "the perfumed compliment," the "masquerade" (*D*. p. 485), and a sense of his own unimportance; this feeling of insignificance is intensified when a rival in love, with better bureaucratic connections, wins out. In one of those scenes of comic humiliation of which Dostoevsky is in a class by himself, Golyadkin is rebuffed at the entrance to an important party only to stand in an obscure corner near the garbage—for three hours! Attempting to crash the party and dance with his beloved Klara, he is thrown out. Shaken, even his "secure" office life seems to be disintegrating. At this point the doppelgänger appears, full of Schilleresque sentiment. Raggedly clothed, he tells a three-hour story which makes Golyadkin sob, "even though his visitor's story was the paltriest story" (*D*, p. 530). Senior, on his part, confesses his personal torment, saying, "It's from love for you that I speak, from brotherly love" (*D*, p. 532). But the very next day Junior is formal, official, self-important, a hypocritical mask-wearer who usurps Senior's place and wipes his hand from Senior's handshake; later he condescendingly pinches Senior's cheek and finally has him committed. His attempt at *Bruderschaft* and all the worthy emotions a failure, it is no wonder that Senior goes crazy.

The Eternal Husband presents us with another comedy of self-exposure, another crisis in the life of an ostensibly well-ordered existence, another confrontation with the double. Where Golyadkin represented the harassed little bureaucrat out of Gogol, Velchaninov is the smug bourgeois; in Wasiolek's terms, where Golyadkin was the "mouse," the underground man, the sexual loser, Velchaninov is the "bull," the sort who abuses him, the sexual winner. He is confident, muscle- and ego-bound, apparently immune to suffering or guilt. Mysteriously, he is smitten by an attack of "higher ideas." For a long time he had felt a vague malaise, a nervousness, a hypochondria; for an equal time solitude has replaced his social life. The "higher ideas" are the kind "he could not laugh at in his heart," but are forgotten the next day.

Aware that his night thoughts are radically different from his day thoughts, Velchaninov consults a doctor friend about his sleeplessness and is informed that being "too conscious of the double nature of [his] feelings" is a symptom of approaching illness. Why is it that he forgets the recent past but remembers things that happened fifteen years ago? "Why did some things he remembered strike him now as positive crimes?" (*EH*, p. 348). His vulnerability to conscience, among other things, distinguishes him from unfeeling characters like Luzhin or Totsky. Like Ivan, like Golyadkin, he is pursued by the embodiment of his worst thoughts. This embodiment takes the elusive form of Pavel Pavlovitch Trusotsky, whom Velchaninov finally confronts, recognizing in this changed man the cuckold of nine years ago. Attempting to redeem his idle life, Velchaninov is genuinely moved to do what he can for his natural daughter.

Pavel is the buffoon, the mouse, the sado-masochist, who had been cruel to the child—though his cruelty once took the oddly reflexive form of hanging himself before her—out of resentment. *Ressentiment* is the key to his character, explaining his alternate wallowing in bland *Bruderschaft* and intimations of revenge. As with Golyadkin and the underground man, he is seized by a compulsion to humiliate the humiliator. But between the guilty and the shamed there is some question about who the real predator is. Pavel tells the story of Livtsov, the best man at Golubenko's wedding, who was insulted by Golubenko and who lost out in love to him; he stabs Golubenko (but does not kill him) at the wedding, saying, "Ach! What have I done!" When Pavel says, "he got his own back," Velchaninov roars "Go to Hell!" (*EH*, pp. 405–6), and their understanding is clear.

Pavel invites Velchaninov to meet what he hopes will be his fifteen-year-old bride-to-be, and the situation threatens to be a repeat of their original one. Velchaninov pulls back: "We are both vicious, underground loathesome people" (*EH*, p. 443), he tells Pavel, recognizing a grim mutual dependency. Pavel later appreciates Velchaninov's not telling him about the girl's true feelings for him and nurses him with tea and compresses when he, exhausted and suffering from chest pains, seem to have a constitutional breakdown. "You are better than I am! I understand it all, all" (*EH*, p. 455), says Velchaninov shortly before embarking on a sleep from which he nearly never awakens. Pavel attempts to murder Velchaninov with a razor in a not precisely premeditated act: he "wanted to kill him, but didn't know he wanted to kill him." Velchaninov sees that "it was from hatred that he loved me; that's the strongest of all loves" (*EH*, pp. 460–1).

Though Bellow's *The Victim* is strikingly similar in certain respects, the emphasis is almost as much metaphysical as it is psychological. Whereas, for example, the child-victim of *The Eternal Husband* dies as a result of humiliation derived from the guilt of both men, the child-victim in *The Victim* dies from a fated physical disease. Accordingly, the double here is not so much a projection of a particular guilt as it is a conception of suffering. In *The Eternal Husband* Velchaninov is clearly at fault; his subconscious wells up for release. With Bellow's Leventhal it is much more a question of obligation or responsibility, in that disillusioned, late-forties sense. An illustration of the end-of-innocence stoicism of liberal ex-radicals—like Trilling's *The Middle of the Journey* and Mary McCarthy's *The Groves of Academe*—*The Victim* gives us a picture of the victim as victimizer, the tyranny of the disadvantaged and outcast. To complicate the tough-mindedness, *The Victim* also subverts the image of the benevolent Jew of popular fiction dealing with anti-Semitism.

The general scene of *The Victim* can fairly be called Dostoevskian: the hallucinatory, nocturnal, numinous quality; the unpromising urban backdrop; the steps, the room, the heat; the hide-and-seek beginning; the protagonist wishing to be decent but caught up in a petty bureaucracy which is a temptation to the contrary; the urban "bachelor" (Leventhal is married, but his good wife is necessarily out of town). But there are differences: where Velchaninov was directly guilty, Leventhal's real guilt is in unfeeling. His eyes are indifferent, not "sullen but rather unaccommodating, impassive"

(V. p. 20). Physically large, he has none of the *amour-propre* of the Dostoevskian bull for, unlike him, he has not had a privileged life. On the contrary, it is not the softness but the "harshness of his life [which] had disfigured him" (V, p. 22). Meeting with the modest success of a respectable job and marriage, he tells his wife, "I was lucky. I got away with it," having avoided "the part that did not get away with it—the lost, the outcast, the overcome, the effaced, the ruined" (V, p. 26).

Allbee represents precisely this reality, as Leventhal comes to realize, but in a way that makes it very difficult for one to accept responsibility, even if direct in an attenuated way. Allbee is a victim of his own inadequacies and circumstances rather than any malicious action on Leventhal's part. Since Allbee is a determinist, his claim on Leventhal is more a gesture of revenge on conditions than it is an argument for individual agency: "The day of succeeding by your own efforts is past. Now it's all blind movement, vast movement, and the individual is shuttled back and forth. . . . Groups, organizations succeed or fail, but not individuals any longer . . . people have a destiny forced upon them" (V, pp. 68–9). Determinism is the cuckoldry of thought, but we are far from the direct guilt of *The Eternal Husband*. (And even there one can argue that Pavel needs Velchaninov and feels a sexual attraction to the man who brings him such masochistic undoing.) For his part, Leventhal will accept responsibility. (Allbee was fired as an indirect result of a scene between Leventhal and his boss.) But Allbee plays so heavily on the sentiment of guilt that it comes out as self-righteousness, despite the fact that he is not so much Leventhal's psychological double as he is, so the speak, a metaphysical one; for, as the story develops, he comes to represent, in Leventhal's mind, a necessary allegiance to those who are not lucky, the ruined. This is the meaning of the two epigraphs to the novel. Responsible or not, we are responsible. There are, after all, these faces in a sea of suffering.

Allbee claims an ideal relationship with his ex-wife, but the more we know about it, the more sentimental it seems to be. He cries when he sees the picture of Leventhal's wife because she reminds him of his own. It seems that their relationship was so good that she left him, because, he claims, he could not get a job. True love? Did Leventhal then break up his marriage as well? It turns out that Allbee had been fired at a number of places before and that his drinking really is something like the problem that the excessively restrained Leventhal thinks it is. His alleged depth of feeling for his wife is refuted by his not attending her funeral. (Pavel did not attend the funeral of his "daughter.") They were separated; it was hot; he would have had to see her family. Surely this is one of those instances, common in Bellow and Dostoevsky, where fine sentiment is travestied by contrary action. For both writers it is a *spécialité de la maison*. In *The Eternal Husband* Pavel attempts to kill Velchaninov after effusiveness, tea, and hot compresses: "it's just with a Schiller like that, in the outer form of a Quasimodo, that such a thing could happen," says Velchaninov. "The most monstrous monster is the monster with noble feelings" (*EH*, pp. 46–7). Velchaninov might just as well be speaking of Allbee.

Part of Allbee's "nobility" is hereditary. The depth of his *ressentiment* stems from his being the dispossessed Wasp, a *ressentiment* from above, deeper socially than Pavel's is from below. It explains his gloomy determinism, his excessive drinking, his difficulty in performing well at a job. When Allbee accuses Leventhal of ruining him "out of pure hate" (*V*, p. 74), we see an instance of pathology. Even more pathological is Allbee's virulent anti-Semitism; in New York "the children of Caliban" run everything, whereas "one of my ancestors was Governor Winthrop" (*V*, p. 131). He asserts that his "honor" tells him not to ask Leventhal for damages—though this is what he is doing, and then some—because he does not want to act like a "New York type." If things were not bad enough, books on Emerson and Thoreau are written by people with names like Lipschitz (*V*, p. 131). Later Leventhal finds Allbee in his own bed with another woman, and the degradation of the sentimental widower proceeds apace. Ousted, the resentful Allbee sets the gas jet in Leventhal's apartment. He "tried a kind of suicide pact without getting my permission first," thinks Leventhal; and in a rare judgmental remark, never quoted by those critics making a case for Allbee, the narrator says, "He might have added, fairly, 'without intending to die himself' " (*V*, p. 249).

Leventhal does err on the side of suspicion—though Allbee shows that this is sometimes impossible to do. Leventhal has none of the charm and little of the energetic temperament of later Bellow central characters. *The Victim* is the only longer work of Bellow with no comic element to speak of. There is a scrupulous meanness in the description of the milieu—between father and son, brother and brother—which goes with the Flaubertian-Joycean texture of the whole. Leventhal notices that the lights over the Manhattan building are "akin to the yellow revealed in the slit of the eye of a wild animal, say a lion, something inhuman that didn't care about anything human and yet was implanted in every human being too, one speck of it" (*V*, pp. 52–3). If this is the aura of sinister New York, it is also an intimation that the sympathetic heart is in danger of being lost.

Allbee is the double of Leventhal's impassivity—both are finally overcome, exorcised by Leventhal. When Leventhal finds out that—because of the office dispute (his boss "made [him] out to be a nothing," something he could ill afford to hear)—he was indirectly responsible for Allbee's losing his job, he wonders if he unconsciously wanted to get back at Allbee for some of his anti-Semitic jibes. Leventhal dreams of missing a train and of trying to catch the second section of it, from which men divert his path. His face is covered with tears. On awakening, "he experienced a rare, pure feeling of happiness. He was convinced that he knew the truth . . . [that] everything without exception took place as if within a single soul or person." Yet "he knew that tomorrow this would be untenable." Still, he recalls the recognition in Allbee's eyes, which "he could not doubt was the double of something in his own" (*V*, p. 151), a natural sympathy. Bellow, like Dostoevsky, does not end with a tearful wallowing in *Bruderschaft*. Despite the occasional closeness, even physical intimacy of a sort, the gain for Leventhal is in consciousness, not in a new relationship.

Like *The Eternal Husband*, *The Victim* ends with a coda which affirms the dubious character of the double. In a scene which takes place a few years after the main action Allbee, like M. Trusotsky, seems to be reincarnated— fancy clothes, wealthy woman, and all. Cantankerous, accusing, Jew-baiting by habit, pushing his lady around but speaking of her in ideal terms, denying any guilt in the murder attempt—he is changed only in circumstance, and Leventhal notices an underlying decay. Unlike Leventhal, Velchaninov does not seem to have changed: money, good food, and other creature comforts once again define his life. Pavel remains the eternal husband, subservient, harassed by infidelity, resentful of Velchaninov.

In a well-known speech in *The Victim*, which has no counterpart in *The Eternal Husband* but does in Dostoevsky's general outlook, wise old Schlossberg say, "It's bad to be less than human and it's bad to be more than human. . . . I say choose dignity. Nobody knows enough to turn it down" (*V*, pp. 127f.). These are sentiments to which the creator of Raskolnikov, the underground man, and Dmitri Karamazov would say "Amen." "More than human" is like that "sense of Personal Destiny" leading to "ideal constructions" for wisdom, bravery, cruelty, and art, which the dangling man thinks about. The man Leventhal meets in the men's room during a Karloff movie comprehends the type: "He really understands what a mastermind is, a law unto himself" (*V*, p. 96). Similarly, Caesar is Schlossberg's illustration of "more than human" in his idealized bravery (self-overcoming, casting out any human weakness) and his aspiration "to be like a god" (*V*, p. 121).

There is an attraction-repulsion in both writers to the "ideal construction," the "obsession [which] exhausts the man," superman transcendence, as there is to underground-man envy, self-laceration, and unfeeling (e.g., Golyadkin and Pavel, Joseph and Allbee). Leventhal, Bellow writes, "disagreed about 'less than human.' Since it was done by so many, what was it but human?" He adds: "he liked to think 'human' meant accountable in spite of many weaknesses—at the last moment, tough enough to hold" (*V*, p. 139). A nice touch this, recognizing as it does the common denominator of secular selfhood and its attendant anxiety, it establishes more-than-human/less-than-human as a continuum of gain and loss, up and down, in the struggle for subjective freedom. This is something of what Nietzsche meant when, in a remark attributed to him, he claimed that Dostoevsky's underman and his overman were the same. But this famous admirer of Dostoevsky's psychology misconstrued the Russian's relation to his character, for his transvaluation of morals, unlike that of Dostoevsky or of Bellow, was not related to Judeo-Christian roots. Did Nietzsche understand the anguished cry of the underground man—"They won't let me—I can't be good"?

Part II

The works: craft and composition

Introduction

Bellow has spoken freely about the question of revision in a number of interviews. With characteristically anti-Flaubertian animus, he has said that "the main reason for rewriting is not to achieve a smooth surface, but to discover the inner truth of your characters."[1] This is his single most important statement on the subject. For, to vary an old distinction, if there is one thing that the manuscripts underscore, it is that Bellow is a novelist of character rather than plot or surface. From conversation, letters, interviews, and articles it is known that Bellow usually begins a work with a particular "real" character or two in mind. The character then undergoes a varying number of transformations, from few, as in Humboldt, to many, as in Henderson. Bellow typically starts a novel in a state of excitement. Like a circus performer hopping onto a moving horse, he likes the flying start. Yet beginnings are generally difficult for him, involving much trial and error. Speaking of *Humboldt's Gift*, for example, he told Keith Botsford, "I wrote it in my usual way: lots of beginnings, three years on the middle and then the last third in six weeks flat out."[2]

It is clear, then, that one cannot speak precisely of how many times Bellow "wrote" any particular novel. Some sections may be very reworked, others slightly reworked. He writes his way directly into a book, rarely making notes. Some things came easily—the Chicago chapters of *Augie March*, for example—but much did not, and like many novelists he does not so much write as rewrite. Parts of *Herzog*, for example, were written twenty times, sometimes with minor changes, sometimes with major ones. Mastering the right tone of voice, establishing the appropriate distance—these were the essence of revision. All of the central characters are transformed into Bellow surrogates, yet in saying this, one is saying that none of them is Bellow himself. His central characters beginning with Augie March are all Bellovian, but may be as different as Augie and Mr. Sammler. "In every case," Bellow has said, "I'm as distant as I can possibly be, and if I'm not distant enough, I throw the thing away and start over again." Bellow's "possibly" refers to characters who are sometimes quite close. So after alluding to the problem of distance in *Herzog*, he goes on to say, "I thought in *Herzog* I was having a certain amount of fun at my expense, or if not at my own expense, I was making fun of my own type."[3] Character is at once the point of germination and the pinnacle of achievement. Bellow has said, "It seems to me that I've been dealing with a new sort of person and that's been the excitement of the books."[4] He here describes accurately the centrality of his spiritual seekers daunted in their quest.[5]

It is possible to believe as much as Bellow does in sympathetic character yet have a different sense of revision. Henry James is a case in point. His famous reworking of the canon was done not so much for substance as for surface. "The essence of the matter is wholly unaltered," said James of his revisions, "save for seeming in places, I think, a little better brought out."[5] While Bellow's revisions are not without the urge to verbal perfection, the essence of the matter is frequently altered, sometimes radically so, even in character and scene. But Bellow would not, as James did, impose a late style on early material. There is no going back to a book for him—except in pleasure or regret—once it is published. Yet, to go to the other compositional extreme, there is no falling into a novel almost by accident as there is, say, in Dostoevsky's *The Possessed*; that started as a totally different novel and was interrupted for a political pamphlet which itself became the novel. But like Stavrogin of that novel, some Bellow characters are transformed in the writing. Dostoevsky, too, revised with not the surface, but the truth of his characters in mind.

The logical contrast should be with Flaubert and Joyce, and this is the case. Bellow writes and rewrites profusely, prodigally, turning out five to ten pages a day when things are going smoothly. Flaubert might work weeks on a single page, though his usual rate was a page every four days. Francis Steegmuller writes, "Every sentence, every paragraph, it seemed would have to be forged painfully, read aloud, and worked over again and again like lines of verse."[6] Joyce's method of composition, too, was in the words of his friend Frank Budgen "that of a poet rather than a prose writer."[7] Joyce called the corrected galleys of *Ulysses* "mosaic"; like the mosaic worker he collected and sorted material—notes, quotations, references, ideas, essays in various styles—to fit the design, an elaborate, painstaking process of drafts and revisions. Budgen recalls that Joyce had been working hard all day on two sentences. When he asked Joyce whether he had been seeking *le mot juste*, Joyce answered, "No. I have the words already. What I am seeking is the perfect order of words in the sentence. You can see for yourself how many different ways they might be arranged."[8]

This is a perfect expression of the aesthetic ideology of modernism, and Bellow could not be further from it. As Walton Litz maintains, the accretion of intricate motives and complex patterns in the later revisions of *Ulysses* implies a world in which "it is the artist who creates the significance through language."[9] For Joyce, as for Mallarmé, "Tout existe pour aboutir à un livre." Joyce's obsession with form is countered by Bellow's obsession with character and event. For him, new experience rather than new technique is the wellspring of vitality. Where Joyce worked to a predetermined pattern, where as Budgen put it, the "words were far advanced in his mind before they found shape on paper,"[10] Bellow's method is more spontaneous, if more conventional. "How do I know what I think until I see what I say," is one of his ready aphorisms (from E. M. Forster). Far from mosaics, there are scarcely any notes in Bellow's voluminous manuscript material. Bellow is a classic illustration of a writer who writes himself into a work with no clear design. "I don't really know what I'm going to say," he told an interviewer. "In the end it's a process of discovery, rather than of putting something in that I know beforehand."[11]

Though all novels are contingent on both, Bellow's are the result of discovery rather than invention. This implies a subordination of imagination to the real world, a reversal of the modernist order. Where Joyce for a long time wrote *Ulysses* from both ends meeting in the middle, Bellow always begins at the beginning (or somewhere near what the final beginning is) with an energy that takes him a fair way into the book. In Bellow, too, though, the process of composition does not always correspond with the final order of the episodes, and he, too, did not always work on a novel sequentially. Some parts required extensive replanting. Tonal shifts frequently take place, with some of the richest comic bits in particular being written somewhere in the middle of composition. Many of his most memorable formulations come late, though often he hits expressions off early and will stick with them through many revisions. Like the pre-*Ulysses* Joyce, like most novelists, he revises centripetally, reworking key dramatic situations. And he comes back again and again to authenticity of voice. But unlike the early Joyce, his method is expansive rather than selective, inclusive rather than exclusive. Nowhere is there the mature Joycean centrifugal expansion and inclusiveness. Bellow gives us, generally, a subjective appropriation of traditional novelistic properties. Nowhere is the ordinary world under notice of dismissal, dissipated by symbolist subjectivity. But there is nothing in Bellow—or anybody else— that corresponds to the revolution in invention within a few years that marked most of the distance from *Dubliners* to *Finnegans Wake*. If Joyce's problem is over-organization, Bellow's may seem to be questionable focus. "My ambition is to start with an outline," he told an interviewer, "but my feelings are generally too chaotic and formless. I get full of excitement which prevents foresight and planning." His own best critic, he sees the difficulty in this: "I regret it when I get into trouble: a book two-thirds done and I don't know how it is going to come out."[12]

When things are going well enough, which means usually, Bellow writes every day. "I generally write for three or four hours at a sitting; mornings as a rule. No sabbath," he has said.[13] Though he claims "no ascertainable working method,"[14] he has no discipline problem. Bellow recalls that "someone once called me a bureaucrat (among writers) because my self-discipline seemed excessive."[15] With good humor he often likens himself to the tenor in the joke who must sing until he gets it right; he must "thresh and sift and winnow until I have a clear notion of what I am doing."[16] It is with no exaggeration that he calls himself a "very dogged . . . very persistent fellow."[17] So it is not uncommon to find extensive verbal revisions going on even into the galleys. When such qualities are matched to the greatest novelistic gift of any American writer in the last thirty-five years, the results are worth examining.

Chapter 3

The Adventures of Augie March

In an otherwise laudatory review of *Augie March*, Robert Penn Warren was perhaps the first to comment on what is now commonly regarded as the central problem of the novel—Augie's character. "It is hard to give substance to a character who has no commitments,"[1] said Warren, implying that it was particularly at big moments that Augie seemed somewhat insubstantial. Augie is, for Warren, a "static" character, redeemed, though, by a style which is itself a powerful device for characterization. Some critics, less generous, have thought that too much of the burden was placed on the style, finding it hysterical in its optimism. Others, who have found the style a triumph and Augie charming, found nonetheless something willed in its lyrical speechifying and intellectual farce, found the final third of the book something of a letdown. These criticisms had basically to do with some uncertainty in the conception of the central character. The manuscripts show how Bellow coped with this uncertainty.

Study of the manuscripts breaks conveniently into three parts. I have taken them in reverse chronological order, according to the amount of difficulty they gave Bellow in the writing. The final section of the novel, which posed some relatively difficult compositional problems, shows whole episodes deleted because of some doubt as to Augie's stature and direction. Corresponding tonal and verbal shifts work toward Augie's refashioned simplicity and buoyancy. In the crystallization of the upbeat, a minor character is transformed, a famous lyrical speech materializes, some of Augie's negative thoughts are cast away. The middle, Mexico, section exhibits similar but less frequent and far less thoroughgoing transformation. But in the reworking of the love affair Bellow risks a momentary high seriousness for his protagonist. The first, or Chicago, section, where Augie's character generally rests easily in youthful innocence, shows relatively few changes. One episode is recast to show the reality of this

innocence to best advantage, but one important minor character is transformed, raised from triviality to seriousness, because he expresses, even
in this brightest section, the case against happy innocence. He reappears
in the revised final section where experience reigns, and his views carry
that much more force. The manuscripts show that the dramatization of
even a relatively moderate innocence met a formidable resistance in the
world of experience.

The manuscripts of *Augie March*, unlike those of most of his other works,
do not show a great metamorphosis. To be sure, there are substantial
changes in character and scene, but the first two-thirds of the novel came
with the compositional equivalent of ease. The words "early" and "late" in
this essay do not therefore have the same force as they do in the more
elaborately revised works. The manuscripts show extensive holograph material, some of which is remarkably close to the final version. The holograph
material is contained in twenty-two notebooks (about 1100 pages, B.1.15 to
B.2.14). The typewritten fragments (about 280 pages, B.3.1 to B.3.13) are
relatively sparse, composed at various stages, many of them earlier than
some of the holograph material. Then there is the final draft (over 900 pages,
B.3.14 to B.4.4) with minor corrections, very close to the published novel.
There are no galleys. In addition to the changes already mentioned, there
are numerous verbal changes. In this novel of inclusiveness, Bellow did take
some care to exclude; historical comparisons, lists of nouns, catalogues,
endless apposition—much of this was excluded! The final version, in addition to limiting excessive allusion and deleting obvious psychologizing,
shows minor changes of a different sort: excessive colloquialism is toned
down, relative pronouns are checked, obscurities are clarified, verbs are
made more concrete.

There are few notes, but there is an occasional nugget in them. On the
inside of the back cover of a notebook (B.1.18) Bellow writes, "My resistance—and Augie's—to what I was 'born to be'; a son of my family like my
brothers. When I appear to be doing nothing I am doing that, resisting."
Since Bellow tells people from time to time that Augie was modeled on a
character he knew in Chicago, it is good to have this confirmation, not that
any was needed, that there is a good part of Bellow in the character. It is
worth noting that Bellow thought of Augie in terms of strength, independence. But that is not all, for the sentence goes on: "and 'doing nothing' is
not understanding what I have already done, and even what I am doing,
'doing nothing.' " This speaks to the opposite of strength, to innocence as
ignorance. Bellow's task was to define Augie March within this contradiction. In this he was largely, but not entirely, successful.

i

What is discarded or enlarged in the manuscripts, taken together with the novel itself, gives us the clearest perception of Bellow's intention in this novel of mixed intentions. The novel's dual nature has been often remarked. In the picaresque, with its world of episodes, accidents, surfaces, notation, a world in which respectability is close to crime, the hero cannot be too deep for a constant *disponabilité*. If there is a moral heroism it is unexpected, unlikely and in the process of receding. The *Bildungsroman* or, if you like, *Entwicklungsroman*[2] element implies more emphatic development, greater moral strenuousness and conclusive self-discovery.

But in the novel these two elements are not discrete. Augie's resistance to the social role, the "function," is consonant with the picaresque,[3] but this evasiveness is also a kind of wisdom. For the protean Augie there seems to be no social role worth having, and he is not the first American to give us a life of "evasion according to plan."[4] Whitman was. Perhaps it is not accidental that the singer of the more recent song of myself receives illumination lying supine, à la Whitman, intuiting the axial truth when all striving ceases. Wise passiveness transcends mindless activity. And yet, and yet—the will to moral certitude may well imply function, and Augie clearly longs for community, wants to be of use. But love is the only activity he unequivocally embraces. Does Augie succeed in this? Or does he succeed in any of the other affairs of development, challenges of *bildung?* The manuscripts show that Bellow had such functional plans for Augie, plans he was forced to withdraw. They show ways in which Bellow was forced to temper the *Bildungsroman* and let the picaresque have its way. Beginning with an *ingenu*, Bellow had to end with him.

The final, post-Mexico, section of the novel is the most elaborately revised and the most relevant to this problem. Having failed to make love his function, Augie, in the manuscripts, begins to think of function in more conventional terms. Love takes a back seat to use. As in the novel, there is no chance for a rapprochement with Thea, though Augie usually yearns for one. Bellow almost invariably keeps the possibility of Thea remote. That she "had died in New Guinea of a fever" (B.2.10) suggests too convenient a resolution; more typically, she promises to come back, but he never hears from her, or she sends him a letter from San Francisco telling him that she has married an Air Force captain, or he sees a picture of her in a horse-show on Long Island and knows that she has made up her quarrel with her family (B.2.10). Augie's response is either post-Thea depression or, in the final version, a combination of this and relief at being freed of the burden of an adventuress who would never change. But then the novel has Stella; Bellow, late in the game, develops her into a sustained love interest, indeed, a wife. Stella is a minor character in the earlier drafts, where love is secondary to a political theme. A love interest who later develops into Stella, Donna Byers—a scriptgirl with whom he travels to Vézélay and Chartres—does not want to marry. None of this has dramatic wings.

What *is* interesting is the development of the political Augie, one who sounds a bit like an Ur-Herzog. Contemplating an aimless drift to his life, Augie thinks: "I didn't know what to do, but yearned till I quaked for a summary, and to be bound into one. And not for myself, but to have a use, serve an end, give my powers satisfaction" (B.2.10). Shades of the five-cent synthesis and of "civility, use, politics in the Aristotelian sense." Augie's outlet is a postwar group called The Committee for a Reconstituted Europe (CRE).[5] His organizational superiors are Frazer and Robey, both of whom function differently than in the novel. We remember Frazer as the superior, somewhat callous intellectual who is surprised to find a guy like Augie in a place like Paris. That comic deflation is immediately expunged when we see Frazer, recently returned from China as a presidential advisor to Chang, now in Spain sending a written apology to Augie for his former attitude towards him and praising Augie's work in Robey's *The Needle's Eye*. Robey's book is not the intellectual travesty we see in the novel but a serious work. Influenced by Frazer's theory of gigantism—great states become tyrannous—Augie reads political theory: the Greeks, Rousseau, Burke's *Reflections*, J. S. Mill, and *The Brothers Karamazov*. Inspired by the "legend of the Grand Inquisitor," Augie reflects on "the universal ant heap or world state," a segment that appears in the novel, not as organically related, as his speech prior to departure for the war. The CRE can combat the threat politically. The idea is to preserve the individuality of ancient communities—Basque, Catalan, Piedmontese, Bohemian, Welsh—so that the old states can be met with an effective passive resistance and a new federation formed. There would be land distribution and socialism in industry. While Augie is skeptical at first, he is soon, in his manner, enthusiastic. The enterprise is backed financially by Robey, who is not presented here as a parody of an idealist but as a serious, learned philanthropist. His letters contain classical sociological terms—*Gemeinschaft, Gesellschaft*, secular folk civilization—which seem to be sly indication that the program will not be a force in reality. Robey's marriage and consequent welching on his financial obligation to the group is a serious version of his farcically contradictory character as it appears in the novel. Predictably, the first CRE Congress in Bruges "attracts ideologists and that's where the astonishment begins" (B.2.10), says Augie; very few of them had any notion of what the organization was about.

Augie is their man in Spain and, the reader soon learns, the prototype for the character of Clarence Feiler in "The Gonzaga Manuscripts," into which the most dramatic part of the Spanish episode is transformed. Briefly, Augie is disillusioned by his meeting with two Spaniards who are supposed to be sympathetic to the CRE. Alvarez-Palvo (or Guzman del Nido), a Falangist who is nevertheless sympathetic to the organization, enrages Augie with vaguely Spenglerian cant about the decline of the ideology-lacking west. Luis Estriner, neither an intellectual nor an ideologist, is very much interested in the American, not for the sake of the plan but as a customer for his hereditary stock in a Moroccan pitchblende mine; all Americans, for him, are adequately represented by the atomic bomb. An American, Augie is presumed to be a financier, a bit of typology which is easy for Augie to resist. But the effect has been depressing: "As usual, stormy with inside blackness, I lit out for the station"—an emotion that is not typical of the character as he is finally conceived. The temptation here and in the entire political episode was to take Augie too seriously, the *Bildungsroman* (here the term is perfectly legitimate) threatening to totally disintegrate the picaresque.

Augie is on the verge of becoming the citizen hero of the later works, a role that is reduced to minimally comic traces in the final version. Here, on the other hand, upon his return to Paris, when Frazer attacks J. S. Mill liberals for their want of hardness and says that hateful as the concentration camps were, they were proof of serious intention, Augie explodes, exclaiming that "the Germans were destroying the subject itself of politics" (B.2.12). This is a good argument, but it sounds more like Artur Sammler on Hannah Arendt than it does Augie March of the final version. Nazism, like Hiroshima and Nagasaki, though figuring in the manuscript, is virtually of a different world from the one Bellow is conjuring up in *Augie March*. You cannot put Tom Jones into a tragedy. In manuscript Augie confronts Frazer as an intellectual equal, which he does not at all do in the novel. There, like Huck Finn in the concluding section of Twain's novel, he falls back into anonymity, remaining in stylized awe of Frazer (even at his own wedding), as Huck does of Tom. On his return to Paris, it is Augie in manuscript (B.3.12), but Frazer in the novel, who expatiates on Paris as "the capital of the hope that Man could be free without the help of gods, clear of mind, civilized, wise, pleasant" (*AM*, p. 521). This seems to have been too lofty a sentiment for the comic *ingenu* Augie finally remains. For better or worse, Bellow's narrative strategy is to have Augie necessarily fall short of the self-knowledge that the *Bildungsroman* hero has—he is left with the limited perception of the picaro.

Consistent with the politically unproblematic conclusion of the novel is its attempt at a generally restored buoyancy. Through whatever shades of dusk, Augie remains the laughing creature. The general description of Paris itself is emblematic of the change. In an early version, permissive Paris is seen almost as a prototype of Sammler's New York. Augie describes it as a city that did not oppose you: "Thus there were thousands of forms of 'true life' and its 'independence' was the hidden joke of each. Nothing stopped you from putting on a toga or a zoot suit or a stovepipe hat or cowboy boots. Each was right because none mattered in the place—one set of words was no worse than another. Back of it all was an irony that concealed a horselaugh that diverted tears and rages" (B.2.12). Though Bellow is consciously satirizing what he has called "an anarchy of views upon normalcy"[6] in the novel generally, he wishes to subdue these somber implications. Despite considerable equivocation, the novel retains a larkiness to the end. A slightly later description gives us Paris as a merry-go-round, as in the novel, with its bridges, Greek statues, maypole obelisk, all-color ice-cream, adding what the novel excludes, "the whole outside darling play, the remainder grimness and suspicion" (B.2.13; *AM*, p. 521). While the goings on of Stella and others in the novel support this caveat, its exclusion represents a desire not to indict civilization itself.

Indeed, the stock buffoonery of Augie's cuckoldry is much lighter than the grim wrangling between Arthur and Mimi that occupies a considerable portion of Augie's Paris life in manuscript. The disintegration of their affair is scarcely alluded to in the novel. They have a child whom they leave to Einhorn's "wives" to bring up. The parents "never came to see nor sent to ask about her" (B.2.10), an unforgivable offense to the familial Bellow. Augie discovers this at Einhorn's funeral (again, the sort of solemn occasion that is likely to be excluded from the last part of the novel and is), where he cries profusely. Arthur, who speaks of Spinoza's *conatus*, striving, while living on money from his mother, is in the tradition of the alienated artist-hero. A devoted reader of Rimbaud, we see him in the novel "in the middle of an essay on the poet and death" (*AM*, p. 322), suggestive of some *maudit* transcendence. It is characteristic of him to say, "Whenever I write a dramatic poem I can't understand why the characters should ever want to be anything but poets themselves" (*AM*, p. 438).

In manuscript he has a long-winded discussion with Augie about identity and superfluousness, concluding with the rhetorical "Suppose you are superfluous?" (B.3.7). Yet Arthur is inclined to take Augie's fate seriously, telling him, "Sometimes I think you're preparing for a great undertaking, but you don't know what it is yet." Augie answers, "It'll come" (B.2.8.). Bellow erases this last bit of dialogue, since it implies too dedicated a self-consciousness for the final Augie. As for Arthur, the other side of superfluity is perhaps most clearly seen in his intellectual favorite, Kierkegaard, who writes that "the regenerated *oprakte* wanted the sinners to mock them so that they could enjoy the wickedness of the world" (B.3.13, 833f.). It is not so much Kierkegaard's soulfulness as his iconography of heroic alienation that captures Arthur. Arthur's projected book on contemporary French thought seems to imply further long-range involvement with alienation. Where Augie is trying to live a lifelong love, Arthur maintains that "Love dies in marriage" (B.2.13), which Mimi once said to Augie. These two liberated spirits clash. Mimi sports a bloody face and puffed eye in the Paris streets as Arthur stands "terrified" and the French say, "Voilà, qu'est que c'est que l'Amérique." This is the last scene in the early manuscript. Clearly the novel was going off in a grimly violent and psychologically difficult direction that the author wanted reversed. Arthur and Mimi figure minimally in the last section of the novel. Bellow is out to conclude differently about America.

"Love is adultery," says Mintouchian in an early fragmentary version of the chapter in which he appears (B.2.14). As it stands in the novel, the Mintouchian chapter reverses this bit of cynicism. Most manuscript descriptions of Mintouchian are quite brief, nowhere near a character sketch. "The dirty-picture runner across state borders" (B.2.14) or, alternatively, the man who "did some special service in the rackets like disguising wanted hoodlums" (B.2.9) becomes "a crack lawyer [with] global interests" (*AM*, p. 478) in the novel, though he is still somewhat shady. His elevation in vocation comes with an elevation in humanity. Mintouchian assures Augie of the reality of love when he needs some assurance. The first of Bellow's marvelous divorce lawyers, Mintouchian has the wisdom of a loony Tiresias. Augie is enraged when he suggests that Stella's, in fact, everyone's deeper consciousness is outlaw and that in this sense he would just as soon marry another. Ironically, the narrative seems to bear him out. So does his own life. Granted full immunity by virtue of an invalid wife (with whom he dines every night), Mintouchian is himself an adulterer truly in love with his mistress. But Mintouchian is not a cynic, and it is interesting to note that in the entire gallery of Bellovian doubletalkers, up to Von Humboldt Fleisher, this adulterer is the only one to receive praise. In the novel it is a parasitic lecher whom he repudiates who maintains that "love is adultery." Mintouchian's life illustrates that the converse may be true. He recognizes that Augie's love, rare as it is, "obeys the laws of life" (*AM*, p. 483), as does his own. Yet considering that Augie's love may well be illusory and that, in any case, the much worked-over Stella sequence can be taken seriously mainly as bedroom farce, the Mintouchian chapter comes off as a fog of affirmation. Augie says, "I have always tried to be what I am," which prompts some critics to talk about identity and the *Bildungsroman*. But what is Augie here but an *ingenu* cuckold? To his credit, Bellow himself consciously deflates this flirtation with rosy optimism through a comedy that reduces but does not destroy. And Augie is too grateful to Mintouchian for telling him that "you will not invent better than God or nature," since he himself had already said essentially the same thing to Kayo (*AM*, p. 450). The effect of the chapter is one of stylized optimism, and the narrative undercutting indicates that the author is himself uneasy with it. It is a forced attempt to keep the upbeat rhythm of the final section.

Augie's conversations with Clem in this section risk high seriousness. Clem, as others before him, lectures Augie on the value of having a function, saying, "the whole mystery of life is in specific data" (*AM*, p. 434). No realistic novelist could dispute this. Augie's slogan (taken from Padilla), "Easy or not at all" may be a motto for a picaro, but not for a novelist—unless you exclude the Chicago scenes of *Augie March*. The two important talks with Clem (*AM*, pp. 431–36, 454–56) did not come easily however; at least they do not exist in early versions of the manuscript (B.3.7, 744f.; B.3.9, 772f.). Clem, who presumes to speak for Freud, is armed with psychological jargon and appears to have the answers to Augie's worries about specialization leaving him behind. For Clem, Augie "can't adjust to the reality situation" (*AM*, p. 434); man needs function. Augie is too concerned with "trying to cheer up the dirty scene" (*AM*, p. 436). When Clem sets up as a vocational-guidance counselor—in the typical *buffo* reality of the last part of the book, Clem has never done a day's work in his life—to tell people where their aptitudes lie, this elicits, in resistance, Augie's axial lines declamation. The manuscript shows us that this aria—perhaps the most quoted speech in the book—is a very late inclusion (not even appearing in the late B.1.19). Essentially Augie is affirming his notion of personal fate precisely in the face of the pressure of function, and not quite out of the post-Thea depression at that.

As Lionel Trilling has pointed out, Bellow is "in the tradition of American Personalism which insists that a person has a fate rather than a function, and powers of enjoyment and love rather than achievement."[7] This tradition includes figures as diverse as Emerson, Whitman, Thoreau, Twain, Cummings, Saroyan, Henry Miller and Wallace Stevens. Trilling, like a number of characters in the book, believes that without a function it is very difficult to be a person and have a fate, and the manuscript indicates that Bellow has an inclination to believe the same. Indeed, the fact that Augie considers "usefulness" as well as "love" to be "axial" indicates clearly that Augie himself recognizes the value of function beyond love. Yet this recognition is an occasion for immediate comic diminution. Citizen Augie's planned colony–school—with Stella as professor of what?—will not materialize. The famous affirmation of the diminished Augie remains lyrical, but memorable. Yet Clem's skepticism is, in this important instance, justified.

Conditionality undercuts high seriousness when the war comes as well. There is a kind of determinism even larkiness cannot penetrate, though Augie in the final verson almost manages to succeed in doing so. In earlier versions, however, Augie is somber and not at all altruistic. We find Augie thinking about the impersonality of war and the valuelessness of man; we find him thinking nostalgically of Philip of Valois and Edward III. Augie is not the eager recruit, but when faced with no way out of military service reluctantly joins the Merchant Marine, which offers greater independence and easier discharge (B.2.8). In one early version Augie spends most of his liberty in the 42nd Street Library. His ship is torpedoed, but this time off the New Jersey shore when, despite great danger from submarines, the rummy captain wants to get his ship back to Philadelphia so he can get ice for his martinis. Augie is saved, but there is no mention of the Basteshaw episode (B.2.10), a late inclusion. Instead we have Augie spending a long time in a Brooklyn hospital, with a random description of the clientele and Augie's depression at leaving his thirties. All this seriousness, even lugubriousness, goes nowhere and is cast aside in favor of the intellectual farce and comic gusto we get in the Basteshaw episode, one of the latest and best things in the final third of the book.

The chapter is as close as we come to an adventure story in the novel, and, since it is Bellow, it is not surprisingly an adventure in ideas. As we have said, Basteshaw is the mad utopian, ideology gone haywire. Suffering from an hypertrophy of the rational, he is a beast in his private life. Brutal to the memory of his (tyrannical) father, sadistic to his fiancée, he belongs more to the realm of pathology than that of salvation. With his visions of power and his actual powerlessness, he is a parody of the ideologist. He recounts the story of his catatonic Aunt Etta, who slept for fifteen years and woke up one day to go about her business. "While she slept she ruled," says Basteshaw, and he might as well be speaking about his entire life. He also tells the story of the German goldsmith who sees his masterpieces melted to bullion—a powerlessness raised only by a belief in God. But what if one does not have such belief? A parodic superman, Basteshaw's collegiate ambition was to be a Renaissance cardinal, with his mother in a nunnery, his father in a gunnysack. In the face of the threat of anonymity he imagines himself to be Hymie Basteshaw, *Stupor mundi:* The astonishment of the world—here is power. Nothing less than words used to describe Christ will do for this new messiah. Augie maintains his skepticism about this version of Utopia. Although he has "created life," Basteshaw admits that "I am not God" (*AM*, p. 500f.). He is not quite man either. Willing to let Augie drown at the beginning of the episode, he subjugates him to his will at the end of it. "I will be Moses and you Joshua," he tells Augie in a parody of Augie's desire for the axial. Augie seems to be confronted with "a murderer," but he proves to be merely a tyrant. Bound hand and foot for the scientific good of humanity, Augie slips his bonds and can murder the sleeping oppressor. But in a typically Bello-vian casting aside of the killer's role, revenge is transformed into pity, the murderer into the male nurse—Henry Ware and Timmendiquas, Augie says, in an apt historical parallel. In his crazy way, Basteshaw wants the good. Isn't Augie, in the axial lines speech, on the verge of a similar leonine assertion? But heroic certitude, even Augie's, is undercut by the logic of the picaresque.

During the hazardous journey with Basteshaw, Augie had dreamed of an ugly, old panhandler whom he gives money. In turn, she wants to treat him to a beer. Augie touches her hair and is thrilled to find that she has "the hair of an angel." This unanticipated grace of the common is the opposite of Basteshaw's burlesque heroism. In its extravagant comedy, the episode illus-trates Augie's mistrust of heroic impulse and trust in ordinary, unheroic reality, a preference established in youth. It was Simon, with his "English schoolboy notions of honor" (derived from *Tom Brown's School Days*) that "we were not in a position to afford," who does not hustle at the dispensary; Simon, with his "Old South honor and his *codo-duello* dangerous easiness" (*AM*. 19), who bore grudges; Simon who developed that look of "unforgiving cosmological captaincy" (*AM*, p. 110). What outlet is there for the heroic energy of this "Francis back from the hunt" (*AM*, p. 424), this figure too large for the law. He leaves his heraldic Cadillac triple-parked in front of his apartment! More seriously, he has a liaison—which proves to be a disaster. Greatness is opposed by goodness, in the unheroic view, power by decency, achievement by enjoyment, destiny by happenstance. Augie is accordingly disenchanted with Einhorn for grumbling over Augie's tenderness toward the brother who cheated him. One cannot consider brotherly relationships as power politics. But Einhorn judges on the basis of "the same principle for persons as for peoples, parties, states" (*AM*, p. 183). Augie renounces all heroism, even the Romantic sort that comes close to home: "I was no wizard, for sure, nor gazetted as anything illustrious, nor billed to stand up to Apollyon with his horrible scales and bear's feet, nor slated to find the answer to all my shames like Jean-Jacques on the way to Vincennes sinking down with emotion of the conception that evil society is to blame for all that happened to warm, impulsive, loving me" (*AM*, p. 424).[8]

Augie wants an independent fate, but is wary of the egotism which often attends this quest. He does not want it for its own sake, and the (unheroic) heroism of self-conscious exposure often betrays a peculiarly modern moral weakness. So much more vulnerable is the conventional heroism. As Trilling has pointed out, the defeat of Thea's eagle—the conventional emblem of heroism—is really a triumph for Augie. *Il faut avoir un aigle,* says Gide, in what might serve as a motto for modernism, but for Augie it is *un aigle manqué.* Caligula—the name, in addition to sounding like "eagle" in Spanish, is mischievously symbolic of berserk power—does Augie's heart good when he retreats before the lizard. But isn't Augie moved by the struggle, beginning with Danton and Napoleon, of "this universal eligibility to be noble" (*AM,* p. 29)? And don't the "axial lines" imply a moral heroism? Yes, but a marginal nobility and a muted heroism is what our innocent hero must settle for, which is why the final part of the book relaxes into burlesque.

In an interesting early version of the scene between Clem and Augie (one that predates the speech), Clem, referring to the subject of moral heroism, says, "Your brother Simon read all those Walter Scott and Fenimore Cooper and Henty novels and they took on you, not him. . . . You've got lofty ideas. Did Einhorn do you harm by calling you Alcibiades!" Augie answers, "You've stuck me with Alcibiades. My preference is for Pericles, Moses" (B.3.9, 779f.). The reversal is significantly toward law, which in its deepest meanings is the one heroism Augie will admit to. Resisting Clem's jibes from the side of personal *Realpolitik,* Augie, in what is the germ of the axial lines speech, says:

> Think of Garibaldi in his red shirt riding in front of the fortress and saying to the driver of the carriage, "Slower, slower." The soldiers are on the walls but he knows nobody's going to shoot. And he's not shot. That's the start of something that Pio Nono and the Holy Alliance have to reckon with. Life is not in its last long night. Not finished. Mutual understanding of a high order is back; enthusiasm is back; natural agreement is back; glances with the truth in them, unarguable facts, apprehended in a second by the eye and brain. That's the great and deep mystery, that highest desires are the desires of other men, too, and not erratic.

Clem retorts that "five minutes . . . [is] how much Risorgimento you can expect" (B.2.8). Like Tolstoy's Pierre and General Davout, like Trotsky's workers eyeing the friendly Cossacks, this incident affirms, quickly as lightning, a moral truth. Augie's enthusiasm for moral heroism is nevertheless undercut by the war, and in manuscript, by a subsequent disintegration of the CRE. Deflatingly enough, it is Augie who utters the sentiment about Risorgimento lasting five minutes—in the context of final breakup with Sophie Geratis from a later version of the manuscript (B.2.8). If not Moses, then Columbus. The lawgiver remains a somewhat remote eminence, the explorer signifies the search for more accessible human shores. Yet it is typical of Bellow to recall that Columbus was carried back in chains. There is no heroism that soars beyond life's intractability. It is also typical of him to add that this "didn't prove there was no America" (*AM*, p. 536), that hope has its intractability as well. Bellow gives Augie a fragmentary nobility of assertion but not of activity, a heroism of sentiment but not of event, an unheroic heroism. The function of the final section of the novel is to show that even this is comically qualified. As is often the case in comic picaresque, the protagonist is valued more for what he experiences than what he concludes. Bellow himself, it seems, could not take what in a *Bildungsroman* would be the solemn conclusive section—the last (post-Thea) part of the book—too seriously.

ii

In the central, second, Mexico section of the book, idea is subordinated to event and, above all, to personality. This is the strategy most congenial to Bellow, and it marks the superiority of the first two parts of the book (generally, Chicago and Mexico) to the third. To speak of personality in the Mexico sequence is to speak of Thea Fenchel. In the earliest versions her name is Sophie, and the switch from "wisdom" to "goddess" may tell us something. Sane judgment on her part would be not quite to the point, whereas an heroic, unreachable quality would be. Is Augie a Julien Sorel to her Mathilde de la Mole? Differences in style, class, money, and direction attract him to this independent, original, and extreme woman. But Julien never really loves Mathilde; he uses her to achieve advancement in the world. On her part, Mathilde is at least romantically in love with the idea of Julien, who stands as a mysterious, dark rebuttal to the life of privileged boredom which surrounds her. Thea's attraction to Augie, although it stems partly from a sense of isolation, does not bring into question the idea of society itself; indeed, she clearly remains wedded to a bourgeois version of hereditary privilege rather than Augie. Our hero is the opposite of Julien in his willingness—one almost says his eagerness—to conceive of love as surrender. In the absence of function, love becomes the sole object of headlong committment. Augie has always had the capacity—or perhaps the talent—to leave the world well lost, which is precisely what Julien can never do with Mathilde and can only do in a gesture of romantic renunciation with the image of an idealized Mme. de Rênal in mind. Augie is a lover, and his relationship to Thea is easily the most interesting part of the manuscript in this section.

The final version shows us a Thea extreme in gesture rather than expression. She hires a detective to find Augie; she extracts snake venom. These are consistent with such neurotic quirks as keeping money in the refrigerator, using towels to wipe the kitten's messes and never being "anywhere without an animal" (*AM*, p. 313)—this last is particularly ominous for Augie in retrospect. On the other hand, what she says, her termagant manner, is toned down: "What I see is mere humanity and detest it. There's no genuine life" (B.2.5). How could Augie have fallen for someone who so explicitly refutes his central sense of things? Or someone quite so domineering: "I thought, if I had been, instead of so interested and willing to go along, more definite, I wouldn't have lost her. At the same time I couldn't imagine how I or anyone else could keep her. . . . She gave orders" (B.2.9). True, something like this is in the novel: Augie says, "I had to accept her version of everything, this being the obstinacy of assertion I spoke of. Also it was evident that she was used to having what she wanted, including me" (*AM*, p. 316).

The precision of the impersonal at so early a stage in their relationship might have signified more to Augie than it did, as might have her refusal of Augie's marriage proposal when her divorce comes through and Augie's recollections of her fear of pregnancy and her equal fear "of explaining to her family that I was the father" (*AM*, p. 372). A late inclusion meliorates her intransigence somewhat when Augie says, "as she couldn't count on me she wouldn't cut herself off from her family for my sake." But one feels that even if Augie had kissed her snakes they would not have, finally, made it. Thea says as much in a late manuscript: "even if Millicent (Stella) had never been in the picture . . . we'd have fallen out" (B.2.5).

There is much fine comedy—the lover's test—in the affair (e.g., the eagle, the snakes); though Bellow did not intend this, the episode is marvelous as picaresque victimization, unconvincing as drama of the self. In this sense, the Stella relationship is an echo of the main event. There Bellow is surely putting Augie through the comic wringer. Weak chest, bitch eyes, soft ass, hard delivery, Thea is the first of a feminine kind in Bellow, whose latent inaccessibility is the prime condition for an affair. (Mady, too, keeps her money in the icebox; *vide*, Freud). A spoiled, if original, upper-middle-class princess, Thea will not tolerate Augie's deviation with Stella, though Augie becomes aware that Thea "went hunting without me" (*AM*, p. 472). Interestingly, even in a late manuscript version (B.2.5) of the Stella adventure, Augie and Stella are perfectly chaste that night; it is like a Joseph Andrews replay of the Mimi abortion incident, with Augie helping Stella (Millicent) gratuitously and Thea not believing. "I was blamed for an offense I did not commit," says Augie. "I'm tired of being told the truth that knocks me down" (B.2.5). But any parallel between Joseph Andrews and Augie March—Bellow told me that he had been reading the Fielding book off and on during the composition of his novel—in point of rosy innocence might well stop at the threshold of the bedroom. And Bellow did not want Thea to come off as a sort of female, disbelieving Simon. This is consistent with his softening of Thea's rough edges in the final version; consequently, the falling out can be more traumatic, with Augie doing the jilted-lover-tearing-his-hair-out bit.

Much of this sequence of elaborate, self-lacerating psychologizing (*AM*, pp. 400–02) is not in the late manuscript, or, one should say, not there in its present form. For much of the substance of these pages is delivered excoriatingly by Thea, not by Augie. Enraged at Augie's ingratiating manner, she accuses him of self-deception in thinking that others are better than he is and in developing a seductive manner so that others will be kind to him. Thea sees no one who "leads a genuine life . . . who has the strength to live his nature. . . . They make up a life. If you see a million men you see a million different inventions. And everyone tries to recruit others to hold up his make believe. That's what power is—that you get other people to call your invention real." Augie can only reply, "I listened with an astonished, bitter emotion to this and saw indeed a general significance of my life described" (B.2.5). What has Thea been doing but exerting this power over Augie?

In the novel the confrontation is not as explicit, the recrimination has more to do with clashes in personal style: "It was too extreme a way of making out," says Augie, "that couldn't be satisfied by ordinary pursuits" (*AM*, p. 370). Thea's offended *amour-propre*—at Augie's suggestion that he went along with her eccentricities out of love—cuts the relationship off without a further thought from her. It is appropriate, therefore, that *les souffrances* be left for Augie, who was the one possessed by at least the illusion of love. Thea's speech becomes transformed in Augie's words from headlong denunciation to a painful, dialectical self-assessment: "I didn't want to be what they made of me but wanted to please them. Kindly explain! An independent fate and love, too—what confusion! . . . It wasn't right to think that everyone else had more power of being." The closest Augie comes to Thea's detestation of humanity is his recognition that the masquerade of selfhood distorts—"that's disfigured, degenerate, dark mankind—mere humanity" (*AM*, p. 401). Nor does Augie include himself in this negative picture. To Thea's insight about invention distorting nature, Augie adds that "the invented things never became real for me." Finally, in a late manuscript Bellow undercuts even this modified *Weltschmerz* by comedy, and we have somewhere near a dramatic node of the novel, a mock-murder scene. Augie goes to Chilpanzingo to revenge himself on Thea's Talavera—with a penknife. But he is gone, and the only real murder is in Thea's heart. In sum, the affair gives us an ostensibly deeper Augie, but one who remains confused, a stranger to conclusions.

The Thea-Augie-Stella triangle is the most worked over aspect of the Mexico section, unless we consider it to be the relatively brief Trotsky episode. So minor in the novel, it has a number of variations in manuscript. In the novel it appears largely as buffoonery; all of a sudden, condescending

Frazer has a place for Augie—travelling companion of the man being intensely hunted by the Russian police, headed by Chief Mink. Augie had glimpsed the great man briefly during fiesta time, his youthful heart "wild with enthusiasm" (*AM*, p. 374). The thought of being so close to history causes Augie to consider Frazier's offer, but his anxiety is relieved when Trotsky, whom he has seen only once, vetoes the idea.

The manuscript versions come much closer to history. In an early version, Augie appears before Trotsky who says, "fous moi le camp" ("Get the hell out") (B.3.6). A related version has Augie called upon to guard Paslavitch—not the teary, Francophile, player of Chopin of the novel, but now the rival of Trotsky and author of "A Dialectical Interpretation of Balkan History," which Augie thinks makes more sense than Trotsky's "law of combined development" (B.2.7). In another version he visits cold-ridden Trotsky who, looking into the Indo-China situation, has a traditionally imperialist vision of power—the world is a glass ball held by a talon. In a later version, Augie, describing himself as a sympathizer rather than a comrade, replaces a sick guard. A cast of minor characters who do not appear in the book is described. Depressed by Stalin and the Moscow trials (such specificity is deleted in the novel), Augie regards Trotsky as "so clearly in the line of great personality" (B.2.60)—a vision, as it were, of a non-ideological Trotsky. Another version has Augie contemplating the politics of assassination and the grimmest meanings of whatever is is right (B.3.6, 727). In still another version Augie can "remember seeing his murder at the gate" (B.2.10). In other words, the novel gives us Trotsky at the greatest possible distance, panorama rather than scene, subduing Realpolitik and drama to a line describing Augie's diminished, picaresque self. It would have been hard to do anything more with Trotsky without involving serious political considerations.

Minor as the Trotsky incident appears to be, it is mentioned in a rare early scenario which tells us something about the metamorphosis of the themes of love and politics. Augie is "picked up by the girl from St. Joe and runs away to Mexico with her. Spends a year in Taxco reading books—till they betray one another" (B.1.20). Bellow describes a "big political plan," corresponding roughly to the CRE, with Augie, under Frazer's direction, in charge of the Latin countries (Spain, France, Italy). He is introduced to a silent millionaire backer called Dowling (later Robey). In Mexico he meets Frazer who makes him one of Trotsky's guards. He is "tired of dissolute life with Fenchel and hoods in Taxco. . . . Fenchel follows him to Europe" (B.1.19).

What is clear, then, is that at first Bellow thought of *Augie March* as something of a political novel, with Augie possessed of a more serious mind; here, as in the early version of the Army episode, he is a hero who reads a great deal. It is as if, with such seriousness, he were invulnerable to victimization, comic or otherwise, by woman. Now Thea follows him. Think of

Herzog, desiring politics in the Aristotelian sense, putting sexual politics in its proper perspective, leaving the lover-victim bit to George Hoberly, "that sobbing prick." In the final version, on the other hand, the political theme is virtually non-existent. The closest we get to it is his brief fling as a proletarian hero, which only ends in Augie's realization that "I couldn't feel the importance of the cause much, or that it would benefit anyone for me to fight on in it. . . . No, I just didn't have the calling to be a union man or in politics" (*AM*, p. 310). This clarity of disillusioned perception occurs on the way to Thea's apartment. Heroism seems remote compared to the adventure of personality, politics abstract compared to the adventure of love. It turns out that even in love Augie's quest for noble identity must remain inconclusive though charged. This is all the *Bildungsroman* freight Augie can carry, the Thea episode being a fusion of *Bildungsroman* and picaresque. (With Stella it is straight picaresque.) As the novel evolves, Bellow must have Augie remain vulnerable, not become masterful. Humor is Augie's major defense, but he does not know enough to always see the joke. The larger questions of identity and proportion are not for him.

iii

Still, the more nearly pure picaresque of the first (Chicago) section of the book is generally considered the best. Constituting more than half the novel, this longest part came easiest. Long swaths of prose come down on the blank page virtually untouched; characters spring full-blown as if from the head of Zeus. Bellow's comment on the composition, however, recalls another miraculous birth: "It was like giving birth to Gargantua."[9] Much of the energy comes with the release from modernist inhibition already described. As Bellow's remark implies, however, no birth is that easy and a flood of articulation creates its own kind of weight. The very prodigality of inspiration in a realistic novel whose principle is inclusion can be a kind of difficulty. The novel is the sort of literary celebration that evolves fairly directly from experience—surface becomes substance as much of the writing spends itself on an enlargement of the nominal. The cake of language is not, however, the Flaubertian *gateau* but a homemade penny-pastry eaten in the kitchen or gobbled on the run. Surface is substance but self-referential, not symbolic. Present participles hyphenated by adjectives or nouns ("loud-breathing" Winnie, "West-moving" parents); hyphenated verbal adjectives ("sex-amused" old Einhorn, "garbage-nourished" Augie, "catarrh-hampered" genius, "Aeneas-stirred" Mediterranean); proper nouns as generic nouns (a "dark Westminster of a time," "a tremendous Canada of light," "a coal-sucking Vesuvius of chaos"); nouns in their own engaging facticity as in the marvelous catalogues of the Einhorn chapter, and even names for their own colorful sake ("Hrapek, Drodz, Matuczynski these dealers were called"); and verbal nouns ("child-ruiners," "human barbecuers")—these locutions are representative of an original, if occasionally breathless, prose in which ordinary activity is named and naming is an ordinary activity. It is not a question of *le mot juste*, but a case where anything named will do; not an aesthetic mysticism, but a fascination with the mystery in all men; a prose with a centripetal rather than centrifugal force. If the sentences sometimes risk nominative anarchy,[10] rarely has the thumbnail sketch been raised to so high an art. The small is named in conjunction with the large, the present linked with the past. So Mr. Kreindl is seen in a line of military panache. Napoleon, Frederick the Great, Kreindl—three names to conjure with. And if Kreindl was a foot under the required height, so was Napoleon.

Even the briefest linguistic analysis of *Augie March* points to activity, event, history, the social nexus, the traditional focus of the novel. The language works to enhance temporality, not to oppose it. Indeed, *Augie March* is best understood as a writer's expression of a particular historical moment, the revisionist liberal early fifties. Occasionally advertised as beginning in the roaring twenties, going through the grim thirties and so on, this Chicago novel belies our conventional expectations of these periods. There is no break in narrative stride or tone between the twenties and the thirties (and on into the forties) in that the twenties experience as we get it typically in literature (money, expatriation, aesthetic primitivism, historical doom) does not touch Augie. As for the thirties, this is when Augie turns down the plushness of the Renlings, remaining in an ideal condition of orphanage. Individuality transcends the merely economically determined. These twenties don't roar and these thirties don't bark. A consistent, buoyant, ingenuous, energetic marginality—a marginality working toward the center—is maintained; and even reinforced, since sharp-wittedness in helter-skelter conditions is at a premium in picaresque, as the twenties break into the thirties. The prose, mandarin picaresque, is designed to record, in addition to those elements already mentioned, bumpy shifts, personal discontinuities, reversals and encrustations of circumstance. In the immigrant milieu, the twenties is the time before the thirties. Nor do the thirties reflect any particular heroism to Augie. Looking in flophouses for stiffs to swell the union rolls reminds Augie of the time he recruited coal-hikers for Simon: "No use assuming that I had reversed all and was now entering those flophouse doors from the side of light, formerly from that of darkness" (*AM*, p. 292). The opposite of a Marxist, he does not view the proletariat as the wave of the future. No, what he sees as he appears before the beseeching workers is not at all revolutionary expectation: "what struck me in them was a feeling of antiquity and deep crust. But I expect happiness and gladness have always been the same, so how much variation should there be in their opposite?" (*AM*, p. 289). Viewing the world as ideological struggle conceals the essentialist reality for Augie. A sensuous will to life, a self-assertion, even in materialist circumstances, strikes his eye. The labor leader Dawson is like the businessman Karas: moneywise, well-dressed, leisurely. The recollection of Simon in a proletarian cell is amusing, but then he went for the big girls in black jackets and berets. And Augie himself has more to fear from union hooligans than from the other side. A number of characters who in one way or another "proposed a different kind of humanity altogether" (*AM*, p. 379)—Thea, Robey, Basteshaw—serve to make a similar point about ideology.

One cannot, of course, espouse such bracing skepticism and be considered "larky." Indeed, Bellow's Chicago stands up because it is seen in its contradictory perspective. The celebratory notes of the novel's beginning, "I am an American, Chicago born" are immediately qualified by "Chicago, that somber city," an indication of a habitual cast of mind. There is no one way of seeing Chicago. The approach to the city, via Gary, is lyrically evoked, compared to the "like greatness of place" (*AM*, p. 90) of winter London and Alpine Torino. Despite all the teeming life it contains, or because of it, Chicago itself is not particularly the subject of lyric effects. The description of the city is likely to be more threatening than it is anything else. Augie recalls that the El pillars are "like a terribly conceived church of madmen" where, in a vaguely Blakean phrase, "worshippers crawl their carts of rags and bones." The insight is Blakean: "sometimes misery came over me to feel that I myself was the creation of such places. How is it that human beings will submit to the gyps of previous history while mere creatures look with original eyes" (*AM*, p. 330). And even more somberly, alone, in the hospital, recuperating from his Bizocho hernia (always the mixture of the ridiculous and the serious!), Augie contemplates Chicago as "the Ezekial cauldron of wrath, stoked with bones . . . you're nothing here. Nothing" (*AM*, pp. 458f.). Significantly, this last quotation is from the last part of the book, where Bellow is particularly concerned with staving off saturnine complication because the light of Augie's innocence has been considerably diminished.

But even in the relatively bright Chicago section this has been a concern. The major recasting in this vein occurs in the Renling episode, where the story of Violet, the runaway adopted daughter of the Renlings, is deleted. The Renlings had opposed her suitor, a graft lawyer. Apparently Violet had more reason for leaving than the affair, since she hated the Renlings anyway. Mrs. Renling's "damnation chats" and general disgust are greater in manuscript and we see Augie saying, "This was when I began to have an inkling of what that disappeared Violet had been up against" (B.1.18). There is also considerable cutting down on Mr. Renling as cynical second best. The final version diminishes the Renlings' shortcomings so that what Augie gives up is seen to be neutral and good. And St. Joe is seen to be largely an attraction, not "Cain's summer pasture" (B.1.18, 138). It is easy not to want to be the surrogate son in such circumstances, more to Augie's credit to resist adoption in the toned-down novel. Most picaros would jump at this chance, but Augie's resistance complicates him upward to questions of identity. Grandma Lausch, too, has some of her rough edges smoothed. She is not quite the "female leopard" (B.1.16) of one manuscript, nor is her "witch-meanness and mental despotism" (B.1.15) made quite so explicit. Both women appear limited in the novel, though not morally dubious.

As shades of the stockyards begin to close upon the growing boy, Augie, like Huck Finn, values people for the humanity they retain and forgives them for the humanity they have lost. Einhorn is the prime Chicago example of Augie's tolerance of moral dubiety. Never mind the amusing freeloading: a man who says at his father's funeral that "the lesson of an American life like my father's . . . is that achievements are compatible with decency" (*AM*, p. 104) but who himself demands kickbacks, tries to get industrial current into a residential block, sets a fire (in manuscript "slave Bavatsky lit it on his orders" [B.1.18]) and generally lacks his father's decency is so shady that he shows the extreme breadth of Augie's latitudinarian nature. (Even the eulogized commissioner is exposed.) Nor is he seen to be wrong. Wasn't it Einhorn who first recognized Augie's essential "opposition," who first formulated for Augie an explicit resistance to determinism? And isn't it Einhorn whose style and swagger transform the narrow quotidian possibilities of immigrant Chicago to a plateau beyond simple moral judgment? Einhorn needs no recasting or substantive editing. His energy disarms criticism.

In both Huck and Augie there is a nocturnal underside to innocence. The comparison, often mentioned, is worth extending:[11] both marginal characters are sensitive, compassionate, effectively orphaned, skeptical, resisting, observant, typically "lighting out," unheroic, buoyant though carrying a weight of suffering, elegaic about nature, with a strong nocturnal streak coming through the daylight of their vernacular delivery. It is the strategy of *Huckleberry Finn* that the reader is more aware of Huck's virtues and vices than Huck himself. There is little of that adolescent immunity in Augie since a greater freight of conscious self-definition comes with genital ego. Yet, as we have seen, Bellow finally chooses to defer to the picaresque convention of comic indeterminacy. Augie has no Tom Sawyer to whom he can defer, but the hokey deference he pays to Frazer and Mintouchian serves the same dramatic function. Since Augie cannot quite simplify his life, it appears that Bellow does it for him.[12]

The nocturnal element is deep-rooted. As we have noted, even at the beginning of the novel it is there. After visiting Georgie with Mama, Augie would take her to a fancy ice-cream parlor "to try to raise her out of her rock-depth of heavy trouble, where, I guess, the greater part of human beings have always spent most of their time" (*AM*, p. 193). Augie's larkiness exists in the face of something like Thoreau's belief that the mass of men lead lives of quiet desperation. Nor does Augie simply consider himself an exception. Spending a night in the lock-up, Augie thinks, "there is a darkness. It is for everyone" (*AM*, p. 175). This darkness of perception tempts Augie in the form of the occasional old friend who seems to have succumbed to it. Jimmy Klein, for instance, tells him "It's all that you want from life comes to you as one single thing—fucking. . . . You live to bring up the kid and oblige your wife" (*AM*, p. 267f.).

Even more pessimistic and more important is Kayo Obermark, a rare instance of minor character transformation in the manuscripts. While in the earliest versions Kayo's negativism is treated as a joke, as it stands finally it achieves a metaphysical dignity. Kayo first appears as a caricature of a philosopher, as a man contemptuous in his manner who is "all for reason and nuts." Despite his yelling that "phenomena and appearances were a trap, how only the good was real, how the flesh was a dream" (B.2.8), he gets upset when there is more meat on Augie's tray at school. He first appears, in other words, as a Bellovian comic contradiction. In the novel, however, he is described as "melancholy and brilliant." His haughtiness and intransigence are still there: "He thought the greatest purity was outside human relations, that those only begot lies and cabbage familiarity" (a precursor of Herzog's "potato love"?). And he tells Augie, "I prefer stones any time. I could be a geologist. I'm not even disappointed in humankind, I just don't care about it, and if there's one thing that's sure, it's that this world is certainly not enough, and if there isn't any more they can have it all back." Not earth-shattering wisdom, perhaps, but not ludicrous.

Indeed, Kayo modulates into noble speech with perception which is to haunt Augie near the end of his adventures: "Everyone has bitterness in his chosen thing. That's what Christ was for, that even God had to have bitterness in his chosen thing if he was really going to be man's God, a god who was human" (*AM*, p. 260). There is a transformation into nobility here; rather than an idealist eccentric, we get in Kayo someone who speaks eloquently on the side of life's essentially heartbreak reality. Augie feels "both drawn . . . and resistant" to Kayo's view, but mainly resistant. Yet the nobility is still there, and some further dramatic undercutting is deleted. In manuscript Mimi is undergoing her abortion nightmare to which Kayo remains aloof. Consequently, Augie feels that "he had to show cause why Mimi deserved what she had and he therefore didn't have to be involved; he could be all justified, a monarch from greater vision" (B.1.22). It is possible that

Bellow dropped this because the personal friction between them was enough to explain Kayo's distance; in any case, Kayo comes off better for it. It is after Thea, after the now faded Einhorn, after Robey, that Augie, "more larky formerly than now" (*AM*, p. 447), looks to Kayo for counsel. Feeling undistinguished and weighed down by a technological culture in which things and spirit are equally real, Augie desires more contact with nature than invention. Kayo then speaks of *moha*, which is a dignified way of naming "the conditioning forces" (*AM*, p. 450) Augie has always tried to resist. The various forms of love are the best resistance, says Kayo, a mellow, if improbable, spokesman for this view. This speech does not appear in some earlier versions and is another indication of Bellow's shift in attitude, his greater susceptibility to quasi-philosophical gloominess. Bitterness in his chosen thing becomes all too real an aspect of Augie's education. The upbeat recasting of the final section only partially mitigates its effect.

The optimism of *Augie March* has been exaggerated by critics who consider going against the modernist mainstream a formal deviationism, *Partisan Review* gone soft. It is clear from the composition of the novel that Bellow was the first to be aware of the loss of power of positive thinking. By definition, the *ingenu* is a character whose expectations exceed his consummations. A good heart can take you only so far in modern conditions. Hence the necessary undercutting of Augie's moral energy, issuing sometimes into obvious, stock ironies, particularly in the last section. The bursts of triumphant vision remain just that; the memorable argumentative dialogues have a quality of monologues juxtaposed. That Augie can summon up an eloquent, bittersweet lyricism at the end, a partial victory of subjectivity in the face of objective truth not exactly triumphant, is consonant with the unheroic quality of the book. Augie remains, by and large, a poet of inevitable balances, the *animal ridens*, seeing the smiling perspective of things. He takes heart in the hard-used Jacqueline, who refuses to live a disappointed life. Speaking through the threatening Atlantic panorama, Augie wants to "beat the dark to Bruges" where he can see "the green canals and ancient palaces" (*AM*, p. 536). Here, as elsewhere in the novel, chaos and civilization struggle to occupy the same subjective space. From Chicago to the Venice of the West, this landlocked Columbus will hope to discover the human.[13]

Chapter 4

Seize the Day

Since there is not much difference between the early and late versions of this short work, many of the changes are verbal, by way of imagistic and figurative heightening. As usual, some of the most memorable utterances—Tamkin's "seize the day" passage, for one—come late. There is a double intensification in revision which suggests no major change in direction of the composition. For all the small changes suggesting a darkening tone, a mounting enervation, there are those which focus on the power of redemptive love; for the negative scenic revisions, there are those suggesting a tenuous, positive effect.

The manuscripts clarify the intention of the final scene, a scene which has troubled some critics. Ihab Hassan wonders how, focusing on the problem of success, the novella "suddenly . . . resolves the question by rising to a more exhalted level of perception." Does the ending consequently seem "rather gratuitous, rather foreign" to Wilhelm's typical concerns?[1] While the revisions—largely verbal here, too—do not speak as directly to this criticism as the entire work does, they do show that there is nothing sudden in the finale, that it is better prepared for, deeper in its emotional texture than Hassan's criticism implies. Keith Opdahl speaks more to the point in saying that "the ambiguity of Wilhelm's drowning, which is both a failure and a triumph, is the central problem of *Seize the Day*" and that Wilhelm's "stature derives most of all . . . from the religious perspective that suffering offers."[2]

The manuscripts also bear clearly on the question of the importance of imagery. This most patterned of Bellow's works has led some critics to interpret it as virtually symbolist fiction. Study of the composition undermines this point of view.

The *Seize the Day* manuscripts are exceptional in being the only ones not at the University of Chicago, and I have described them in detail in the first note at the end of this chapter.

* * *

The novella form excels at the relatively short, dense, psychological flight leading to an explosive climax. Think of *Death in Venice, Mario and the Magician, Notes from Underground, Heart of Darkness,* or *The Pastoral Symphony. Seize the Day,* Bellow's muted bang of a novella, may be seen as a necessary psychic answer to the unearned optimism of *Augie March*. What was most problematic in that novel of more than a little somberness is, as we have seen, the buoyancy with which Augie takes his victimization by Stella. *Seize the Day* undoes the knot of grief and pain, in Bellow's phrase, which more usually, and more convincingly, characterizes such situations. The metaphors of pressure, pain, bursting, the whole Reichian paraphernalia of breathlessness and tics, lead to what is literally an emotional explosion, a catharsis, a denouement, if you will, which is literally an unknotting.

Of course, *Seize the Day* exists primarily on its own terms and not as a reaction to another work, even a work by Bellow. And this work has even more to do with a father-son than a man-wife relationship. Yet in the engaging concatenation of events that constitute Bellow's literary life, nothing is more interesting than the way in which one work leads to the next with, as it seems, a speed of the imagination. Here is truly a career. If *Seize the Day* seems on the face of it a modernist response to the traditionalist exuberance of *Augie March,* if it deals in alienation and the search for the father, it does so with a force that reverses the centrifugal direction of modernism—one thinks of the conclusion of Eliot's "Gerontion" as archetypal, with "DeBailhache, Fresca, Mrs. Cammel, whirled / Beyond the circuit of the shuddering Bear / In fractured atoms"—insisting on a centripetal direction of its own. The story ends not in fragments but with the magnified image of a man. Tommy Wilhelm struggles against the alienation that threatens to engulf him. The last words tell us in axiological certitude of his "heart's ultimate need." What is this need? Bellow speaks of "the happy oblivion of tears" through which Wilhelm "sank deeper than sorrow" toward the consummation of it. Here we see a meaningful suffering affirmed rather than denied, a testimony to its transfiguring, restorative effect; we see a truth as old as the religion Bellow refuses to dismiss. The powerful ending—"the real Russian bang," in Mark Schorer's phrase—of the novella derives from a yearning, a moral certitude, which modernism denies.

Tommy Wilhelm is not, nor was he meant to be, a particularly attractive character. The frequently voiced student (Philistine?) objection—"Who needs this *nebisch*?"—cannot be simply brushed aside. Isn't Wilhelm the victim Bellow wants to delete from his own typology? Isn't Wilhelm's belief that "there's really very little that a man can change at will" (*SD,* p. 24) the all but deterministic reversal of the spirit of Bellow's typical moral strivers?

Most of Bellow's main characters are engaged in the American act of declaring their independence. Tommy's problem is dependence. Though Wilhelm is about Herzog's age, we tend to call him Tommy. Would we call Herzog Moe? Wilhelm may be considered a case of arrested development, a state brought on by a painful relationship with his father. Virtually aware of this Wilhelm says, "it's time I stopped feeling like a kid toward him, a small son," (*SD*, p. 11), the last phrase added in a later revision.[3] It is clear from the penultimate scene of the story that this is a dependency Wilhelm does not succeed in overcoming. Ruined by Tamkin, Wilhelm is abject to his father, reverting to type as the small son. "I should have listened to you. . . . I couldn't agree with you more. . . . You're so right, Father." Like a child playing with matches, Wilhelm gets "burned again and again" (*SD*, p. 109). Yet the most striking image of Wilhelm's dependency occurs in connection with this very Tamkin, this current con man. He thinks of himself on Tamkin's back (*SD*, p. 96). The worried Wilhelm, oh so fully grown, is playing piggyback at forty-seven. As it turns out in the world of financial brass tacks, Wilhelm realizes that Tamkin "made me carry him" (*SD*, p. 105), a weight he can hardly bear.

In keeping with its modernist tendency, *Seize the Day* presents us more emphatically than any other Bellow work with a psychological extreme in character portrayal. Neurosis, sickness is at the center. As Daniel Weiss has observed, the two main characters conform to characterological types familiar to the literature of neurosis.[4] Wilhelm is to the oral-fixation what his father, Dr. Adler, is to the anal. Wilhelm is "childish," masochistic, overweight, tends to his mouth with indiscriminate eat and drink, is irregular, disordered, sloppy, even filthy. Dr. Adler is "adult," sadistic, lean, regular, ordered, neat, even immaculate. Wilhelm fears humiliation, undervalues himself or tends to, is a nonachiever; is, by the conventional money standard, a failure, Dr. Adler is buoyed by vanity, has great self-regard and the regard of his peers, is a professional "success." Wilhelm does not seem to know how to make money or to handle it; Dr. Adler makes money count for him. Dr. Adler is, in short, an ideal figure in the money culture. It has not been clearly enough understood that he is more of a personal failure than Wilhelm in being so. True, Wilhelm's life is such a mess that a certain sympathy is elicited for the old man. And there is some reluctance in giving sympathy to a man in his physical "prime" who is asking support of an octogenarian. Wilhelm recognizes as much in seeing that old men are different, and must, in the face of death, tend to their own needs. They can be forgiven for not taking others into account. Considering Wilhelm's extremity, this is a remarkable insight for him to possess. In such a perception we see Wilhelm's strength—openness, the ability to perceive the other: an ability the anal-retentive, increasingly closed Dr. Adler fails to possess.

But Wilhelm is hardly presented in an heroic light. Bellow describes him in all his neurotic quirkiness. He drinks a Coca-Cola or two before breakfast. Then, at breakfast, rather than juice, he has a large bottle of Coke—the sweetness and sucking involved suggesting the mother he so misses. His smoking also has a peculiarly oral emphasis. He "put the length of a cigarette into his mouth; he seemed to hold it with his teeth, as though it were a cigar" (*SD*, p. 37), writes Bellow in a late inclusion. At breakfast Wilhelm "ate and ate," first his own breakfast, going through all the muffins, then his father's strawberries, "then some pieces of bacon that were left" (*SD*, p. 42). This last is most symptomatic of Wilhelm's lack of control, loss of order—of his being, as Dr. Adler later calls him, a slob. Bellow tries for a heightening of this effect in the writing. Earlier versions (e.g., 8) have orange juice rather than that large coke, and no mention of the additional bacon. Also, Wilhelm's slob quality becomes more vivid in middle versions, as in the description of his jacket pocket, with its "packet of pills and crushed cigarette butts and strings of cellophane, the red tapes of packages which he sometimes used as dental floss" (*SD*, p. 8; not in 8).

The detailed elaboration of pill talk is also absent from the earlier versions. Wilhelm's filth is quickly noticed by the spotless, not to say squeamish, Dr. Adler. In the breakfast scene he views the faint grime left on the egg white by Wilhelm's fingers "with silent repugnance" (*SD*, p. 36; not in 8). Here, as elsewhere, Wilhelm seems the very antithesis of his father. In the battle between father and son, they were made for each other. We must not think that Wilhelm's filth is merely a function of his father's supersensitivity. Recall this case of arrested development rooting passionately for the Dodgers (even Duke Snyder has two strikes on him!), living, the narrator tells us, "in worse filth than a savage" (*SD*, p. 37), in what is another intensification of pathology coming in middle revisions. Related to this, and also coming in middle revisions (not in 1), is Wilhelm's neurotic distaste for water. We are told that "he used an electric razor so that he didn't have to touch water" (*SD*, p. 36) and that "he did not care for the odor of the wall-locked and chlorinated water" (*SD*, p. 43) of his father's health club. His immaculate father, on the contrary, thrives on water, sees hydrotherapy as the answer to all problems; he has the quantified mentality of a man given to the scientific cure of spiritual ills.

This collision of neurotic types would almost be comic of it were not a conflict between father and son in a city where "the fathers were no fathers and the sons no sons" (*SD*, p. 84). But there is something mysterious in this primary relationship which speaks from the depths. This voice makes Wilhelm a nobler character than he appears to be.[5] The psychoanalytic explanation attributes Wilhelm's failure to weakness, and there is much truth to this; but if nothing fails like "success" in American literature, there is a sense in which nothing succeeds like failure. Wilhelm possesses qualities that render him vulnerable, but this vulnerability conceals a strength. He loves not only out of neuroticism, but also out of love itself.

"In his retreat to orality," Weiss holds, "Wilhelm returns to the infantile belief in the omnipotent parent."[6] Weiss bases his statement not on Freud's view of what has come to be called moral (as opposed to physical) masochism as a pathological way of hating (the original sadistic impulse directed against the parent recoils to become parentally derived superego), but on Berliner's view of it as a pathological way of loving. Berliner accepts Freud in acknowledging that masochism comes from guilt and the need for punishment, but maintains that instead of giving up the hated object the person represses the hatred and in adulthood submissively accepts the cruelty as love. Simultaneously the masochist represses any hostile reaction against the loved object because that would also cause its loss. Identifying himself with the hating love object, the masochist turns against himself not his own sadism but the sadism of the parent. He may deny his good qualities, or his intelligence, often to the point of pseudo-imbecility. He displays his unwantedness in a bid for affection. The compulsion to fail, then, is unlike Freud's self-determined punishment for having willed the father's death.

Like most good psychoanalytic explanations this one is illuminating as far as it goes, but it does not—particularly in a writer like Bellow, schooled in psychoanalysis but finally critical of its assumptions—go far enough. Wilhelm's love is not merely a function of his neuroticism; it is a motive as good as, indeed, better than gold. What is latent is not inevitably linked to reductive Oedipal struggle. It may be a revelation. It is one thing to be a masochist and another to be transfigured by suffering. Despite its psychological orientation the central perspective of *Seize the Day* is closer to the religious.

Wilhelm's self-recriminations are not as damaging as they at first appear. The business of America may be business, as Coolidge said (and Dr. Adler probably voted for him), but the business of Wilhelm (certainly in his Jewish, Velvel aspect) is to express the significance of suffering. Critics have too quickly reduced this to pathology (John J. Clayton, for example, to moral masochism).[7] True, Wilhelm himself doubts even his moral superiority to the mercenary Dr. Adler and his ilk, noting in the final version that "they were called to act energetically and this was better than to yell and cry, pray and beg, poke and blunder and go by fits and starts and fall upon the thorns of life.[8] And finally sink beneath that watery floor" (*SD*, p. 56). Though he is wary about indulging in self-pity, Wilhelm touches on something real in his idea of suffering. His envy of his energetic father soon turns into rage, a rage at Dr. Adler's inability to see love. Wilhelm thinks, "If he was poor, I could care for him and show it." And, more emphatically, in a late inclusion, "He'd see how much love and respect I had in me." Love and respect, the ability to see the other, is a casualty of the money culture. To realize this is to suffer, and Tommy bears the burden of goodness. To realize the loss of love, the distortions of the cash-nexus, in the face of mortality—this is what brings Wilhelm to overwhelming tears. This realization destroys mundane considerations, and the tears are, therefore, "a great and happy oblivion." Wilhelm's catharsis, his expression of suffering, is "deeper than sorrow" in that it is in the end an affirmation, "the consummation of his heart's ultimate need" (*SD*, p.118; all of this a late inclusion, not in 5, but in 5c). What is repressed in Wilhelm is not a manifestation of illness but of love.

Seize the Day is as much about love as it is about money. Virtually every variety is present in one form or another, from love of dog to love of God, with every familial variety included. Tamkin speaks of loving a dog or of giving to charity, but then notes that this really isn't love. There is an affection that looks like love but is relatively indiscriminate—the pretender soul, in Tamkin's view; potato love Herzog is to call it—a form of love without content. Is this true of all socially related love, brotherly love as it is called? Wilhelm experiences a manifestation of brotherly love in the Times Square subway station, not a bad place to encounter humanity *en masse*. The place had often been quintessential New York for Wilhelm, claustral and hateful. The graffiti are at once a parody and reminder of moral purity: "Sin no more" and "Do Not Eat the Pig." Here, in the unlikeliest of places, "unsought, a general love for all of the imperfect and lurid-looking people burst out in Wilhelm's breast. He loved them. One and all, he passionately loved them. They were his brothers and his sisters" (*SD*, p. 84). Wilhelm momentarily plays the cleric, blessing everyone in sight, including himself. Though this feeling is fleeting—it lasts but a few minutes—it is authentic. Wilhelm expresses a genuine but fragmentary love. He had himself dismissed this feeling as an almost biological quirk, "like having a hard-on at random," but sees on this fateful day, as Bellow puts it in one of those succinct and idiomatic late inclusions, that he "must go back to that," that it was "something very big. Truth, like"[9] (5c; *SD*, p. 85). Wilhelm, in the final scene, returns to a more convincing expression of the "truth, like," returns to the axiological. His "heart's ultimate need" is the necessity to express communion; this is "deeper than sorrow," a transcendence into moral decency and all the moral attributes Wilhelm calls God. It is deeper, finally, than "brotherly love," the understanding, as Erich Fromm puts it, "that we are all one."[10] As Wilhelm's confusion attests, we are and we are not, but the oneness that inevitably obtains, even in its lack, between parent and child is the deeper mystery. In Bellow's view, then, Wilhelm's love, inseparable from his belief, is not merely a result of his inability to let go of poppa.

In *The Art of Loving* Fromm speaks of the time-honored distinction between mother love and father love. The first "by its very nature is unconditional," the second is "deserved" in that the father represents "the world of thought, of man-made things, of law and order, of discipline, of travel and adventure."[11] Recognizing these as ideal poles—no one has either exclusively—one can see that Wilhelm's parents function in this way. One can see the poignancy of Wilhelm's attachment to his mother, his attachment to "unconditional" love, and how important this is in countering his father's grotesque distortion of the "deserved." "To love one's flesh and blood," Fromm tells us in his tendentiously anti-Freudian way, "is no achievement."[12] Dr. Adler is evidence to the contrary. Discipline is there, but thought has been reduced to profit, man-made things to financial artfulness, law and order to anal retentive hoarding. There is little question here of travel and adventure. In this story Bellow is Freudian enough to think of gold as feces. Dr. Adler's greatest failing is an inability to, in Fromm's words, "transcend concern for myself and see the other in his own terms."[13] He cannot love. Herein lies Wilhelm's unlikely superiority. Weiss begins his essay by saying that the old battlefields of father and son, including "the preference of the kingdom of love over the safe deposit vaults of mammon," no longer "offer a sound footing for waging the conflict."[14] But this preference is to the point in Seize the Day. Weiss says that it is "his own role as victim[15] that Wilhelm accepts in the final scene. There is, as we have seen, more to it than that.

If Wilhelm exhibits a typically Jewish (and Christian) strength in suffering, Dr. Adler, who has no religion, is a victim of his own impregnability. More than any other character in Bellow he is defined by function rather than personal fate, placing on these precisely the opposite emphasis of an Augie March, whose terms these are. Accordingly, he refers to his daughter by function as having "had an important position in Mount Sinai" (SD, p. 31), a bit of information absent from the early versions. Similarly, he values his son quantitatively, falsely bragging that the once affluent Wilhelm has an "income . . . up in the five figures" (SD, p. 36). He has no sense of moral suffering. "I've learned to keep my sympathy for the real ailments," he tells the importuning Wilhelm, like Perls' bone condition (SD, p. 42). When his son comes pleading in the health club, Dr. Adler utters the famous last words of the anal compulsive: "I have set up a rule" (SD, p. 108). Living by rule to the exclusion of heart, he has no instrument to gauge the spirit. "You want to make yourself into my cross," he tells his son. "But I am not going to pick up my cross," (SD, p. 110). Yet it seems that others who have done so have had some influence.

In considering the kinds of love, there remains love of children and of women. The significance of the first is obvious. Wilhelm has the feeling for the welfare of his children that Dr. Adler does not have for his. Ironically, it is they, under his estranged wife's influence, "who did not know how much he cared for them" (*SD*, p. 94). As for the love of woman, there is his long-distance affair with Olive (not in the early 2), but his past love has been and still is a sticking point. His estranged wife Margaret seems to outdo Dr. Adler himself, if that is possible, in the rhetoric of anality. She counts the days of his post-dated check and is eloquent in reducing Wilhelm's character to a quantitative function. "I have great confidence in your earning ability," she confides (*SD*, p. 113). Using quantity as a weapon, "she won't even file a joint tax return" (*SD*, p. 45). The pain is almost comic here, and the woman is not without a sense of black humor. "Every other day you want to make a new start," she berates her unemployed husband. "But in eighteen years you'll be eligible for retirement" (*SD*, p. 112). We may be reminded of Henderson planning an internship at sixty-three. Like her father-in-law, Margaret is an expert at counting, which itself, when overdone, can be an expression of sadism. Dr. Tamkin had noted, in speaking of typical stock market activity, that "counting and number is always a sadistic activity. Like Hitting. In the Bible, the Jews wouldn't allow you to count them. They knew it was sadistic" (*SD*, p. 69). As if to prove Tamkin's theory, Margaret is quite the equal of Dr. Adler in sadism. Unlike Dr. Adler's hers comes from resentment. In an intolerable marital situation, Wilhelm has left her. He thinks of her—and we see things from his point of view—as a resentful sadist. We are told that she "hit him and hit him, beat him, battered him, wanted to beat the very life out of him" (*SD*, p. 113), in a figurative flourish not in the earlier versions. What is here still metaphor is literal in *Herzog*, though no more violent, for that, in its psychological effect upon the central character.

In the same vein is a passage sometimes quoted by irate feminists, a description of the demure woman as vampire, not vamp. During their terrible phone conversation Margaret tells him that she is trying to control herself. Wilhelm then thinks, as it appears originally in manuscript: "He could picture her, her hair cut in graying bangs above her pretty, determined face, and he knew that this was not wholly true, that she was probably sitting quietly enough in the green leatherette rocker near the phone" (5, 11). Once again, the revision is a well-known passage which appears in a late inclusion (5c): "He could picture her, her graying bangs cut with strict fixity above her pretty, decisive face. She prided herself on being fairminded. We could not bear, he thought, to know what we do. Even though blood is spilled. Even though the breath of life is taken from someone's nostrils. This is the way of the weak; quiet and fair. And then smash! They smash" (*SD*, p. 112). Even more than Dr. Adler, his wife drives Wilhelm off the deep end. Like her father-in-law she is an image of rule, order and reason. Her sadism is somewhat more dramatic if no more pervasive. The logical extreme of sadism is murder, here seen as nihilism within the norm. Wilhelm is the victim and seems justified in saying to Margaret, "You must realize you're killing me. You can't be as blind as all that. Thou shalt not kill! Don't you remember that?" (*SD*, p. 112) The nightmare phone booth is Wilhelm's heart of darkness, but in that very darkness he glimpses axiological light, a memory of the ten commandments. Or one of them. In addition to the sixth, he is trying to honor his father as well as his mother, though, unlike his father, he sets no other gods before him.

All but a caricature of the enclosed, sadistic, quantified response is the ancient, loveless Rappaport. With his inability to communicate except in commands, he out-Adlers Adler in grotesque mastery. At his request Wilhelm reads the latest stock figures to him, but notices that "when you told him he didn't say thank you. He said, 'Okay,' instead, or, 'Check,' and turned away until he needed you again" (*SD*, p. 85). "Take me" to the cigar store (*SD*, p. 100), he says imperatively to Wilhelm. Equated with function to the exlusion of pleasure, he smokes a good cigar but, as Wilhelm observes, does not even notice the ash. Generally disagreeable, he becomes irritated at "that woman there" blocking his sight; the woman becomes "those damn guys" (*SD*, p. 90), a casual analogy, it seems, to loss of brotherhood. Ironically, the masterly Rappaport is said to be a bigamist. No woman problems for him. In his anal retentive way, he won't give Wilhelm a drop of advice on investment. But he is voluble on the subject of Teddy Roosevelt. "T. R. once yelled at him, so he loves him," Wilhelm perceptively notes (*SD*, p. 103). Those were the days of an at least benign paternalism. And now? The assymetry of our power arrangement is not lost on Rappaport's acquaintance. "Who controls everything?" Wilhelm reflects. "Old men of this type." Financially flush, physically decrepit, Rappaport stands as an ironic, painful contrast to the big, youngish, good looking but broke Wilhelm, who senses an altogether uncomfortable intimacy. He's "loaded with dough, probably. And I bet he doesn't give his children any. Some of them must be in their fifties. This is what keeps middle-aged men as children" (*SD*, pp. 101f.). Here, as elsewhere, the dependency motif is developed in middle versions.

Rejected by one father figure after another, or at least by one old man after another, the desperate Wilhelm clings to Dr. Tamkin as to a sinking lifeboat. He is vulnerable emotionally as well as financially. Keith Opdahl tells us that "Bellow has said informally that one of his themes in *Seize the Day* is the city dweller's fulfillment of personal needs on strangers. The feelings that usually involve private commitment are now casually exchanged in public."[16] Rousseau really started something. Part confessor, part shrink, mostly fraud, Dr. Tamkin appears to have the sensitivity and insight Wilhelm cannot find in his father. "You want to avoid catching the money fever," he says sympathetically. "This type of activity is filled with hostile feeling and lust. You should see what it does to some of these fellows. They go on the market with murder in their hearts," says Tamkin in a telling metaphor added in the middle revisions. Wilhelm, taken by this, can only respond, "What's that I once heard a guy say? . . . A man is only as good as what he loves (*SD*, p. 10). This late inclusion is a cliché, but a powerful cliché in context, perfectly consistent with the major thematic division of the story as it develops. It is Tamkin who points out the meaning of the phrase, "I'm going to make a killing" (*SD*, p. 69), commenting sagely on the psychopathology of everyday life. He, of course, is in the service of the heart: "I am at my most efficient when I don't need the fee. When I only love. Without a financial reward" (*SD*, p. 66).

So, as they say on the Upper West Side, what could be bad? Everything! Tamkin is rendered in that Dostoevskian satiric mode which Bellow has updated and made entirely his own. He says all the right things, wallows in *Bruderschaft*, has sustained attacks of "the sublime and beautiful," all the while never taking his eye off that self-interested object to a degree that would bring a smile to the face of the underground man. Utilitarian Romanticism lives! Like any good Romantic he says that "I remove myself from the social influence. Especially money. The spiritual compensation is what I look for." He adds, in the rhetoric of spontaneity, that his aim is "Bringing people into the here-and-now.[17] The real universe. That's the present moment. The past is no good to us. The future is full of anxiety. Only the present is real— the here-and-now. Seize the day" (*SD*, p. 66). These words—which even in the middle version appear merely as, "I put myself in the universe, too, and not only in the social life" (*1*, 37)—float weightlessly into the vacuum of Wilhelm's hopes, while they at the same time could pass as a justification for instantaneous, amoral aggrandizement. With Tamkin, Wilhelm is thrust into the role of "a pair of gentlemen experimenting with lard and grain futures" (*SD*, p. 60) (more speculative than the early "stocks"). Tamkin speaks dispassionately of the "elemental conflict between parent and child. It won't ever end. Even with a fine old gentleman like your dad" (*SD*, p. 61). This mixture of elevated tone and actual uncaring is pure Tamkin. It is of a piece with the adventurous stories he fabricates. He is a sort of kitsch Rousseau, telling all, telling the worst, so that he may be redeemed by sheer openness of heart, with the difference, of course, that originality is reduced to venality, imagination to daydream. And who is to say that some of his daydreams are not really facts after all? "Facts are always sensational" (*SD*, p. 65), says Tamkin, a statement to which Bellow and Dostoevsky would grant much credence.

As to his actual stories, well, even Wilhelm does not give them much credence. In a Dostoevskian vein, he tells of his lush wife who committed suicide. "I loved her deeply," he says, "She was the most spiritual woman of my entire experience" (*SD*, p. 95). I should say mock-Dostoevskian because this situation would be literal in him. Bellow, in his turn, uses modernist moral paradox for phoney enlargement, whereas Dostoevsky typically used conventional "Romantic" feelings. Bellow is the master of this for our time, and nowhere does he succeed more brilliantly than with Tamkin. The story about Tamkin's father shows us again the modern "sublime and beautiful." Almost like a Rousseau, "he left us five kids," says Tamkin, "because he fell in love with an opera soprano. I never held it against him, but admired the way he followed the life-principle." Here, too, Tamkin is committed to the higher morality. (Both anecdotal embellishments are not in the earliest version.) Some of his experiences give us flashes of incredulous insight into the bourgeois avant-garde (the nudist dentist), the brutality of real wealth (the Egyptian cotton deal), the utopian mentality in science (working with a Polish inventor on an unsinkable ship, curing epilepsy through psychoanalysis). Still other snatches of incredulity are deleted by Bellow from the final version, like Tamkin paying for the music and drama lessons of many youths, and, perhaps most incredible of all, not charging for treatment. In the stock market, "my mind gets too brutal" for psychological work, says Tamkin. He's really an "ascetic" (5, 93).

However bizarre the tale, you might say that it does not spoil Tamkin's heart of gold. All is held together by an ostensible clairvoyance. His stories are opaque, but a moral does emerge. In his distinction between the real and pretender (social) soul, he speaks with the voice of Romantic truth. As a consequence, as Freud and the Romantics knew, the true soul pays the price in sickness; finally, "it wants to kill the pretender" (*SD*, pp. 70ff.). Wilhelm admits to having guilt, but adds in a grim version of the typically Bellovian wise passiveness, "personally . . . I don't feel like a murderer. I always try to lay off. It's the others who get me" (*SD*, p. 73). Wilhelm is nonetheless taken by Tamkin's analysis, as well he might be, so relevant is it to his own situation. And when Tamkin says to him, in a late inclusion, "don't marry suffering. Some people do. If they go with joy they think it's adultery" (*SD*, p. 98), Wilhelm is rightly struck by what appears to be psychological acumen. The "fantastic" Tamkin "began to surpass himself" with his insight that "some want to love, but the great majority don't" (*SD*, p. 99). This late inclusion gets too close to home, Wilhelm's home much more than Bellow's. In the absence of a real father, Tamkin fills the void, displaying some of Fromm's paternal characteristics—thought, man-made things, law and order, discipline, travel and adventure—displaying them without actually possessing them. Here again advanced ideas are in the service of fraud. Sneaking away from his financial, and moral, obligations, our "ascetic," our man of Romantic, even modernist sensibility, gets Wilhelm to take Rappaport to the store out of goodness. "Don't refuse the old gentleman," he says. "This minute is another instance of the 'here-and-now.' You have to live this very minute . . . . Don't think of the market. It won't run away" (*SD*, p. 100). But Tamkin will, a grim parody of the evanescence of truth.

Many of the manuscript changes in *Seize the Day* relate directly to a darkening of tone, a heightening of enervation. In the writing, this painful tale becomes more painful. But this is a question of emphasis, not of radical change. A close look at Wilhelm's minor personal connections as well as some further major ones makes this clear. For example, absent from the middle versions is Rubin as an intimidating presence. When Wilhelm is aware that "Rubin watched him, loitering and idle, apparently not knowing what to do with himself this morning," he turns to the Coke machine to avoid this vague analogy to his father (*SD*, p. 15). Also absent from the middle versions is the description of Rubin (and, later, the German bank manager) as "the kind of man who knew, and knew and knew" (*SD*, p. 6)—a fine intensification of the general ruefulness. Additionally, the middle versions lack the cardplaying analogy to Wilhelm's "loser" quality: "He had put forth plenty of effort, but that was not the same as working hard, was it? And while the losses were small they weren't gains, were they?" (*SD*, p. 7). One late inclusion adds to the insidious humiliation of Wilhelm. Perls sensed "that he would not lose Dr. Adler's favor by taking an ironic tone with his son" (*SD*, p. 34). Perls himself undergoes a great negative intensification from "a man in his sixties, a retired cigar manufacturer who lived in the hotel" (in early 2) to that "damn frazzle-faced herring with dyed hair and his fish teeth and this drippy moustache" (*SD*, p. 31; in *1*). And Wilhelm wonders, in the bitter tone of the story as it develops late, "Now God alone can tell why I have to lay my whole life bare to this blasted herring here" (*SD*, p. 35). Another late inclusion adds to his isolation by informing us that his sister Catherine does not talk to him anymore. That she has "a B.S. degree" and that his late mother "was a graduate of Bryn Mawr," middle and late inclusions respectively, only accentuate Wilhelm's degreeless isolation. In a small, comic touch of victimization, it is only in the middle revisions that Wilhelm had paid for Tamkin's meal yesterday. Tamkin's appetite grows from "a tomato herring sandwich on pumpernickel, coffee and ice-cream" (in the early 2) to "Yankee pot roast, purple cabbage, potatoes, a big slice of watermelon, and two cups of coffee," in the novella (*SD*, p. 91). Though a comic bit, it is not without its ounce of enervation. And for another ounce, Wilhelm's early search for Tamkin in the lavatory takes on in the revisions the specificity of straw hat, cocoa-colored band, and even "the feet below the door" (*SD*, p. 105).

But the largest instance of enervation, indeed, failure, added (in a middle revision) is the Maurice Venice episode, which appears in an early version (8) only as the "scout had never made him an offer of a studio connection." The masochism of pursuing this non-existent lead—"Like, he sometimes thought, I was going to pick up a weapon and strike myself a blow with it" (*SD*, p. 17)—indeed, the elaborate dark comedy of the whole episode is not present. The marvelous Venice (an art man as con man), 'Nita Christen-berry, the pimply cousin Artie, all contribute to Wilhelm's victimization, sometimes deliciously, as when Venice typecasts the innocuous Wilhelm as "the type that loses the girl to the George Raft type or the William Powell type," the first being the very image of masterful sadism, "that flyweight type with the fists" (*SD*, p. 21), an ironic reminder of Wilhelm's own useless bulk. All of which sinks our hero deeper into the hole.

The descriptions of Wilhelm reflect a similar development. In the begin-ning we see Wilhelm fear that "a huge trouble long presaged but till now formless was due" (*SD*, p. 4), a feeling not explicitly articulated in the middle versions. Similar is the late echoing of the novella's opening: "He was wrong to suppose that he was more capable than the next fellow when it came to concealing his troubles.[19] They were clearly written out upon his face. He wasn't even aware of it" (*SD*, p. 14). The development of chest pain and the rest is also in this vein. The main points of tension, with the possible excep-tion of the phone-booth scene, are the meetings with his father, a tension generally made greater in the revisions in matters small and large. "He lay down the cigar" (*1*, 16) is changed to "He put the cigar butt in an ashtray on the table behind him, for his father did not like the odor" (*SD*, p. 34). "He rapidly struck at his egg" (*8*, 10) becomes "Then he battered it (in his father's opinion) more than was necessary" (*SD*, p. 36). The following expression of general woe is early, but not in the earliest version: "He behaved toward his son as he had formerly done toward his patients, and it was a great grief to Wilhelm; it was almost too much to bear" (*SD*, p. 11). Adler's coldness to his son is not a recent phenomenon. "Dad I couldn't effect one way or the other" (*SD*, p. 115), Wilhelm says (in a late revision), thinking of his Hollywood effort, recalling his father's remoteness even then. A grimly ironic addition to Wilhelm's woes occurs midway in the revisions when his fate is trans-formed from simply not being made an officer in the corporation to being denied his promotion because of nepotism. It seems that some treat sons-in-law better than others treat sons. If Wilhelm's father kills with ice, his wife does with fire. The revisions point to intensified bitchery. "She says okay on Monday and wants more money on Tuesday" (*SD*, p. 48), is a typical middle revision. Her denying him Scissors, a late prop, is also typical; "not that she cared a damn about the animal . . . an Australian sheep dog. . . . They're the gentlest dogs" (*SD*, p. 47). This gentle, large, somewhat ungainly crea-ture is something of a surrogate for Wilhelm himself. Perhaps because of this she keeps the dog from him. Is it any wonder that Margaret is associated in his mind with the lines from Keats' "Endymion" about Sorrow (a middle inclusion)?

Not all the rewriting concerning Wilhelm leads to an intensification of the grim. The revisions focus to some degree on his powers of redemptive love. Again a snatch of famous poetry has a peculiarly evocative effect for him. From Shakespeare's seventy-third sonnet he remembers, "love that well which thou must leave ere long." The middle versions contain no gloss. A late version tells us that "they referred to two and not to one single person" (6, 9). The final version is another illustration of Wilhelm's ability to see the other: "at first he thought it referred to his father, but then he understood that it was for himself, rather. *He* should love that well. 'This thou perceivest, which makes *thy* love more strong' " (*SD*, p. 12). This interpretation is obvious enough but not so obvious for the unlettered Wilhelm. In assuming a certain sympathy for the old, he does more than his father does for the young. For all his faults, Wilhelm is not enclosed. He can be self-critical and does not simply put the blame on his father. The revisions emphasize this as well. In a middle revision, he sees that his father "now . . . looks down on me," but thinks, "maybe in some respects he's right." This is not easy knowledge. "No wonder," writes the narrator, "Wilhelm delayed the moment when he would have to go into the dining room" (*SD*, p. 14). Uneasy their relationship is. When Dr. Adler does not remember the day his wife died, Wilhelm thinks, sardonically, that he would remember the day he interned. But he then checks this tendency with a traditional tenderness (expressed in a middle revision): "Don't quarrel with your own father," he thinks. "Have pity on an old man's feelings" (*SD*, p. 27). Wilhelm possesses in pity a quality like the mercy of the God he implores to let him out of his clutch.

When Wilhelm contemplates Tamkin's doctrine of the two souls, he thinks, in an early revision, that "in Tommy he saw the pretender. And even Wilky might not be himself. Might the name of his true soul be the one by which his old grandfather had called him—Velvel?" Wilhelm's totally secular incarnation leaves him with a moral void the contrary of which can best be elicited by a language or a name reminiscent of an era of deific closeness. Wilhelm—Germanic name (or Dutch), inappropriately suggesting worldly power—yearns for moral certitude, for the truth remaining in tradition. The family is a central ideal in his life, which is one way of seeing the difficulty he has in telling his father off. From him he wants humanity. He does not get it, hence his acceptance of the bogus moral elevation of Tamkin. "That the doctor cared about him pleased him. This was what he craved, that someone should care about him, wish him well. Kindness, mercy, he wanted" (*SD*, p. 73), we are told in a middle revision. But more needs he a divine than this physician. More moving is his yearning, expressed in a middle revision, for " 'My father. My mother'—As he said this there was a great pull at the very center of his soul. When a fish strikes the line you feel the live force in your hand. A mysterious being beneath the water, driven by hunger, has taken the hook and rushes away and fights, writhing. Wilhelm never identified what struck within him. It did not reveal itself. It got away" (SD, p. 93). The line Wilhelm holds is axial.

Wilhelm's nobility resides in his resistance to nihilism. "In Wilhelm's mind," says one middle version describing his thoughts on the dubious cousin Artie, now a professor, "to be a professor and cynical was like being a minister who did not believe in God" (9, 11). For Wilhelm spirituality may be secularized, but there is still such a thing as spirit. A later and final version takes us closer to the moneymen: "No one seemed satisfied, and Wilhelm was especially horrified by the cynicism of successful people" (SD, p. 16). Yes, the line he holds is axial but, in the modern mode of the fleeting and evanescent, the fish got away. Yet Wilhelm is not to be completely denied. His voice is passive but tenacious, and it will have a hearing. When accosted by the old fiddler pointing his bow, a sort of imitation-Romantic-cum-Flaubert-spook, Wilhelm rejects his begging and denies the omen. His generosity serves as immunity to such fatality. Just as the revisions point to a more intense depravity for Dr. Adler, Wilhelm's humanity is enlarged in the writing.

Moving from character to setting, an intensification of the negative again takes place, with the positive additions getting tenuous purchase in the increasing gloom. New York serves as a particularly appropriate location for this developed hell: New York, Wilhelm thinks, "with its complexity and machinery, bricks and tubes, wires and stones, holes and heights" (SD, p. 83; not in the earliest version), the city of impersonal oppression and plugged-in connections, financial and otherwise. Bellow's penchant for the positive uniformly undergoes eclipse when he crosses the Hudson. Almost as much as a city in The Waste Land, Bellow's New York is unreal, a place where one suffers the agony of not knowing "the crazy from the sane, the wise from the fools, the young from the old or the sick from the well" (SD, p. 84; all but the first of these couplings in a late revision). Vast, full of different styles, New York's towers are the new Babel where "every other man spoke a language entirely his own" (SD, p. 83), a parody of the axiological. In this welter simple human needs have little chance. Wilhelm laments, in a well-known passage not present in the earliest version, that the simple desire for a glass of water involves all of Western consciousness, from the Creation to Hitler. Though this idea may sound more like Bellow than Wilhelm, the meaning is clear. The simplest human connections, often the most basic, are lost. The isolation can be desperate and the desperation is not confined to isolation. The parking ticket scene, not in the earliest version, is a simple nightmare; more complicated are the Puerto Rican kids on drugs and the vandals who break tombstones. Even the mild Wilhelm, thinking of his mother's defaced grave, can say, in a middle version, "I could have broken somebody's neck for that" (*SD*, p. 101).

Mainly a story of how the old prosper and the young wither, *Seize the Day* focuses in on the bizarre reality of sartorial splendor in old men, beginning with old Rubin: "he was behind the counter most of the time—but he dresses very well. He had on a rich brown suit; the cuffs embarrassed the hairs on his small hands. He wore a Countess Mara painted necktie" (*SD*, p. 5; a late inclusion). Not to be outdone, Wilhelm displays his "Jack Fagman" shirt. (Wilhelm's father might read something into this, but there really is a men's shop of that name in Chicago.) Mainly, though, Wilhelm is somewhat rumpled, and his upturned coat collar is a minor offense to a well-ordered, well-dressed society. Tamkin is snazzy, if garish, in his "corduroy or velvet shirts from Clyde's, painted neckties, striped socks" (*SD*, p. 83; not in 2), while Dr. Adler buys his clothing from a college shop. Only ancient Rappaport is too old for vanity fair. The old ladies, too, briefly mentioned though they are, add a touch of the bizarre in this sense. In an early description, largely retained in the novel, "the elderly ladies were rouged and mascaraed and hennaed and used blue hair rinse and eye shadow and wore costume jewelry [which] helped them to make life bearable." In a late revision, the last six words are replaced by "and many of them were proud and stared at you with expressions that did not belong to their age" (*SD*, p. 91). The chilling effect is consonant with the general drift of the revisions.

But so is a delicate heightening of Wilhelm's capacity to withstand this drift. In a rather flat, middle-version description of the Hotel Ansonia, we see "the lobby, like the lobbies of all hotels on Broadway in the seventies" (1, 1). This is expanded to include the elevator which, ominously, "sank and sank"; the red carpet; the French drapes; the pigeon alighting on the chain supporting the marquee; and Wilhelm's response to the last: "For one moment he heard the wings beating strongly" (*SD*, p. 4). This fine symbol, suggestive at once of fleeting strength and grounded flight, gives us the essence of the story. Wilhelm's subway vision incarnates the same ambiguity. We see a surge of his will to love, his grounded will. In the subway, after the most somber reflection about New York, in the least likely of places, Wilhelm is seized by an epiphany. There is a Chekhovian, broken-stringed quality to it—this is another fish that got away—but the depth and frequency of such feelings is witness to an unsuspected viability. It is just before Wilhelm arrives at the funeral parlor for the culminating revelation that he, on Broadway in plain daylight, has a redemptive vision of humanity (present in the earliest version). Entranced by the surge of human energy, he sees "the great, great crowd, the inexhaustible current of millions of every race and kind pouring out, pressing round, of every age and of every genius, possessors of every human secret, antique and future, in every face the refinement of one particular motive or essence." It is only in a late revision that we see the expression of this refinement (essentially in 5c): "I labor, I spend, I strive, I design, I love, I cling, I uphold, I give way, I envy, I long, I scorn, I die, I want" (SD, p. 115). The central charge here is positive, the last utterance in particular predicting the driving personalism of Henderson (though also bringing to mind Herzog's skepticism about first-person categorization), serving as a harbinger of possibility, of some eventual fulfillment of desire. The final scene is not this fulfillment, but it is fulfillment of another sort. If New York is hell, it seems that hell has its benefits.

A look at the language of *Seize the Day* reveals both some of the same double intensification, and, as we have seen in other contexts, the fact that a high proportion of the most memorable passages in the work come in late revision. Tamkin's impassioned repudiation of the business class is a case in point. It is transformed from "and businessmen were demented on a number of levels" (1, 31), to "Maddest of all were the businessmen, the heartless, flaunting, boisterous business class who ruled this country with their hard manners and their bold lies and their absurd words that nobody could believe. They were crazier than anyone. They spread the plague" (SD, p. 63). Jeremiah is a prophet who comes in the middle of Bellow's career, but his fulminations are memorable. Even Wilhelm is capable of this sort of perception, as in the scene in the telephone booth, or in his reaction to cynicism, which he considers "the world's business." Wilhelm "had various words to express the effect this had on him. Chicken! Unclean! Congestion! . . . Rat race! Phony! Murder! Play the game! Buggers!" (SD, p. 17). This late inclusion, like the one just quoted, gives us Jeremiah in interior monologue. The rhetoric of accusation embraces self-accusation to some degree. We recall the zoological catalogue which follows a blow-up with his father: "Ass! Idiot! Wild boar! Dumb mule! Slave!" This comes in a middle revision, with "Lousy, wallowing, hippopotamus" following later (SD, p. 55). This language of outrage is balanced somewhat by the development in the language and imagery of love and spiritual resurrection, most notably in the novella's conclusion. Now we only note that there are parodistic elements of these elevated themes as well. "Lard had to go up" (5) becomes, in a late revision, "lard would rise again" (SD, p. 26). Resurrection imagery itself, like its parody, is late. The best comic inversion of the rhetoric of love comes from the lips of Maurice Venice. He is taken by a brassiere ad drawing: "When I saw that drawing, the breath of fate breathed on me" (SD, p. 20), Bellow writes in an inspired late revision. *Moira* has halitosis. This is an instance of the "sublime and beautiful" made commercial. So much for romantic love. In this novella concerned with kinds of love, usually in their disintegrative aspect, Venice also makes his notable, verbal contribution to brotherly love. And Wilhelm falls for it. "This is no bunk," he says. "You become a lover to the whole world. The world wants it, needs it. One fellow smiles, a billion people also smile. One fellow cries, the other billion sob with him" (*SD*, p. 22)—all this in a late revision. Well, Venice is not entirely wrong. And Wilhelm's sobs have gained a following.

Despite these significant changes, the composition of *Seize the Day* reveals that it was very well conceived before it was rewritten—so much is in the first draft—a fact which might have been expected because of its length. The contours of the tale are essentially there at the beginning, and what comes in the revisions, in addition to what has been noted, are points of emphasis, rhetorical enlargement, and imagistic tightness. More than any other Bellow work, *Seize the Day* is patterned, is written in the mode of aesthetic realism. There seems to be a correlation, even in Bellow, between emotional deracination and the polished surface. The most commonly observed example of this surface is the drowning imagery. M. Gilbert Porter has gone so far as to say that this imagery is "the integrating principle of the narrative," and that "each scene in the novel functions as a dimension of the total image,"[20] which is later likened to "a controlling metaphor."[21] A study of the composition, however, shows that the story came before the drowning images and related water images; that far from being a controlling metaphor in Porter's sense, these were added in the revisions as a means of heightening a drama already very much there. Here, as elsewhere, Bellow's foundation is the emotional and moral truth of a situation. The patterned language supports and intensifies this truth. He does not, in symbolist fashion, even in the textured *Seize the Day*, begin with the image and emote his way toward meaning. Of the large number of examples Porter uses to prove his argument, none is in the earliest version of the book, with the exception of the one about Wilhelm not washing his hands before meals; in a forced manner, but in keeping with his drowning motif, Porter describes this as "the hydrophobia of a drowning man."[22] It is more likely the neurotic quirk of a slob. Is Wilhelm's panting laugh, as Porter puts it, "a sound suggesting both panic and frantic exertion to stay afloat"? Does Wilhelm call himself a hippopotamus because it is "an ungainly water creature"? Is Wilhelm's screaming "help" to his father "the hapless swimmer's plea for assistance"? Is the dramatic "slow motion" of *Seize the Day* "appropriate . . . because it suggests the movement of a man under water"?[23]

While the primary meaning of the story is not in the pattern, some meaning is there. And images of drowning are central to it. The meaning is fairly obvious. Unlike Lycidas, it appears that Wilhelm will forever be sunk "beneath the watery floor" (*SD*, p. 56), his living death a contrast to the resurrection of the dead Lycidas. Wilhelm doesn't think of this. He remembers the fragment from English I, a course which has surprising relevance to him now. The two allusions to Lycidas, central though they are, were middle and late inclusions. In the earlier case, the line about the "wat'ry floor" is, at first, "The king sits at Dumferling toune / Drinking the bloud-red wine" (9,

8). The drowning imagery does indeed add meaning. The writing is more intense, the revision a great improvement. As it is when Tamkin embellishes on the Here-and-Now, comparing its glory in a middle version to "a big, huge, giant wave" (*SD*, p. 89), while Wilhelm contemplates his chest weakness. As it is when the troubled Wilhelm hopes for a miracle to save him from the uncertainties of Tamkin: "And what if there is no miracle? Then? Go argue with City Hall" (8, 33) becomes, in brief, "The waters of the earth are going to roll over me" (*SD*, p. 77). The hippopotamus, though, (*SD*, p. 6) does not function as a water image but is an improvement over the original "gorilla" (1; 2 & 8), which would imply too much authority and aggression. The hippo can be aggressive—in a late inclusion Wilhelm himself says he "charged like a hippopotamus" (*SD*, p. 15) in attacking his mother for being against his going to Hollywood. But, all things considered, the change to hippo is just right, the change to a large, sloppy, beefy, ungainly (out of water) finally not particularly threatening beast that has, alas, even a facial resemblance to him ("He saw a big round face, a wide, flourishing red mouth, stump teeth" [*SD*, p. 6].)

Any discussion of water imagery must focus on what many consider its most memorable expression, the climactic paragraph. An especially close look is called for. The earliest version contains no images of drowning either as extinction or as resurrection, though the opening sentence already suggests an experience of transcendence. It reads, "The lights and flowers fused in his blind wet eyes and the music shuddered at his ears. Wilhelm choked his sobs in his handkerchief, and bit his thumb but he failed to check his weeping" (2). Even a late version retains much of the literalness of this description (the handkerchief, the bit thumb) but is enlarged and somewhat rearranged: "Wilhelm choked his sobs in his handkerchief, and bit his thumb through the wet cotton but he utterly failed to check his weeping. The light and flowers fused in his blind, wet eyes and the music shuddered in his ears" (5, 115). This version lasts almost verbatim until the latest revisions and is then followed by the ending essentially in the final version. In a very late version we read: "Wilhelm, bowed, choked his sobs in his handkerchief and bit his thumb through the wet cotton but he was [sic] in every effort to check his weeping. Fresh tears came to carry him even further into oblivion. The lights and flowers fused ecstatically in his . . . (5c). The manuscript is here cut off. Handwritten on the next page is, for the first time, the version which sounds much like the book: "The lights and flowers fused ecstatically in Wilhelm's blind wet eyes, the heavy sea-like music shuddered at his ears. It found him where he had hidden himself in the midst of a crowd by the great and happy oblivion of tears. He sank deeper than sorrow, and by the way that can only be found through sorrow, through torn sobs and cries, he found the secret consummation of his heart's last need" (5c).

The paradox of transfiguration through suffering is now made clear in the language. The first version shows the neurotic, childish thumb in the mouth. The second adds the suggestive lights, flowers and music. The third introduces a note of ecstasy. The fourth breaks through into transcendence. The final version eliminates the oral-erotic, neurotic thumbsicking, leaving the way clear for transfiguration. Bellow writes of an oblivion which is "great and happy." Here we finally encounter the drowning metaphor—"he sank deeper than sorrow"—which serves a similar paradoxial function. This moral paradox is explained in the words which are deleted in the final version as being perhaps too exclusive, too "Russian," too Dostoeskian for Bellow's general sense of things. The meaning is clear enough without them. Maybe life's most important work *was* being done in suffering, as Wilhelm once thought, since there is a purity in suffering that takes it beyond the immediate context. This is further evidence that Bellow does not simply regard his protagonist as a moral masochist. It is another illustration of Bellow's respect for the Hebraic adage that " 'Tis better to dwell in the house of sorrow than to dwell in the house of mirth."

The drowning image, prominent as it is here, is an enhancement of the moral depth of the story, not its motivating force. The final version does accentuate the water image—"shuddered at his ears" becomes "came up to his ears," "it found him" becomes "it poured into him" (*SD*, p. 118). But the change from "heart's last need" to "heart's ultimate need" is even more telling. It speaks of Wilhelm's overriding necessity to relate, to reach for, to affirm the reality of love—brotherly, filial, erotic, religious—in the knowledge of mortality. Simone Weil says that belief in the existence of other human beings is love. Wilhelm has this belief even when the others do not believe in him. Not earning an income up in the five figures, he does not exist for Dr. Adler. (Perhaps the name Adler, "eagle" in German, is another play on the failure of heroism and its inferiority to the unheroic.) But Wilhelm extends Weil's definition of the meaning of love, in that he expresses feeling for that which threatens to destroy him. Wilhelm's only weapon is love, and this is why he is in such a bad way among the money men; it may also be why much informed literary opinion treats him primarily in terms of pathology. To this one must add does love have to be presented only through disintegration, does the lover have to be the victim? Wilhelm must admit that Tamkin knows what he is talking about when he says, "don't marry suffering. Some people do. . . . If they go with joy they think it's adultery (*SD*, p. 98). Augie March, Henderson, and Herzog show that this description does not definitively characterize Bellow's characters. It does characterize Wilhelm, however, and in him Bellow shows how deeply one can go with it. Wilhelm marries suffering, but she is a wife you cannot live with happily ever after. Yet *Seize the Day* shows, as do a number of works of the ethical imagination, that suffering can be more noble than happiness.

Chapter 5

Henderson the Rain King

Given its offbeat character, it is not surprising that *Henderson the Rain King* elicited a problematic critical reaction. Tony Tanner can say that the novel is "enigmatic, its overall intention unclear. . . . It is uncertain to the point of hysteria on the question of individual value. . . . Yet when the book reaches away from negation toward celebration . . . something important . . . is brewing even if we cannot quite identify it."[1] Robert Alter identifies the key scene but finds it lacking: "His spiritual calisthenics with Dahfu's lion do not suggest persuasively or particularly what, in fact, he is supposed to be learning about life."[2] The quest in this philosophical romance is for moral reality and, more particularly, its relation to the growth of the central character about whom everything revolves. Norman Mailer has given us his sense of this reality. Enamored of Dahfu, a black who is "a profoundly sophisticated man with a deep acceptance of magic, an intellectual who believes that civilization can be saved only by a voyage back to the primitive," Mailer laments the falling off of the last fifty pages, the flubbing "of a demonically vast ending." But the manuscripts show even more clearly than the novel itself that, not surprisingly, the primitive in Mailer's sense and the demonic were very far from what Bellow was about, and that Mailer's saying "it is possible that Bellow succeeds in telling us more about the depth of the black man's psyche than either Baldwin or Ellison" is even farther.[3] For Mailer, Bellow was "inching more close to the Beast of mystery than any American novelist before him"—quite a compliment. But for Bellow whatever the mystery is, it won't be a Beast. And it won't be arrived at by that old black magic. For Mailer, then, it is not a question of confusion in the den itself, but a failure to carry his specious clarity to its climax.

From the beginning nearly to the end, *Henderson* is one of Bellow's most rewritten books. Numerous revisions of the first forty pages of the novel show Bellow working at narrative voice and tone. The Arnewi and Wariri sections, so distinct in the novel, are at first not differentiated. They soon are, and numerous plot changes come in the revision. These show Bellow discovering the novel as he wrote it. The Wariri section is relatively easy until the rain-making ceremony, where, as in the climactic lion scene, Bellow's imagination comes to conclusive order. In both sections Henderson's character is enlarged, ennobled as it remains comic. Many would agree with Mailer—though not for his reasons—that the last fifty pages are largely a fade-out, that Dahfu's death is "meaningless" (but is it in terms of magic?), that going back to Lily is an anticlimax. There is even some question as to the rhetorical glories of the novel's windup. Is it as Richard Chase says, "magnificent,"[4] or does it suggest, as Alter holds, a conventional compassion (the orphaned child), an admission of the inadequacy of the story itself "to say fully what it intended to say"?[5] The final upbeat chapters were written in the ease of lyrical solution. Bellow was "very moved"[6] in writing them. Were most readers similarly moved in the reading? Whether they were or not, we see the familiar formal problem of a novelist whose subject is the comic spiritual seeker. The manuscripts shed a unique light on these issues. In addition to showing that not only the reader, but also the writer had some struggling to do before a necessary illumination was achieved, they show, in some ways more clearly than the novel itself, that the dramatic parts of the novel express a meaning far less enigmatic than is commonly supposed.

The manuscripts are virtually a complete set, coming to over 4,000 pages. They contain twelve notebooks (755 pages, B.5.3 to B.6.2) and holograph fragments (about 160 pages, B.6.3–10). There are typewritten fragments (about 460 pages, B.6.10–15); three typewritten drafts, one of them complete (over 1,200 pages, B.6.16 to B.8.7); plus miscellaneous typewritten pages and chapters (about 200 pages, B.8.8 to B.9.12). Much of the above is early material, showing the vast amount of rewriting that was done. A final typewritten draft (373 pages, B.9.13–20) is very close to the novel. There are two sets of proofs with original holograph corrections: the first set shows Bellow's revisions; the second set shows his final revisions (about 260 pages, B.10.1–5, B.10.10–15). These show that here as elsewhere Bellow revised until the last minute, that the final version of a Bellow work was typically not definitively set in galleys.

* * *

Eugene Henderson's three million dollars bring him suffering—with interest. Self-consciousness about the disintegration of family tradition goes with the patrician background. Despite his financial and physical bulk, Henderson cannot help but consider himself a shadow of nobility. Like so many modern heroes since Rameau's nephew—the prototypical, engaging wildman—Henderson is an epigone. Hence, the later versions show his father to be an author as well as a rich, Wasp eccentric, and show the family geneology to include a Secretary of State and Ambassadors to England and France. Each family triumph makes the massive Henderson seem smaller. On the other hand, the disintegration of an ordered world in the face of a chaos of force and numbers, the restlessness and grieving from above, as in Henry Adams, is an appropriate psychological backdrop to Henderson's Romantic yearning. Adams had his medieval France; Henderson has his "primitive" Africa. For Henderson is acutely aware that "nobody truly occupies a station in life any more." Our hero, who in some early versions traces his ancestry back to the "old racial stock of Clotard, Childibert plus the Celts and Gaels" (B.6.18, 156), now sees himself as a refugee from old social wars, a "displaced person" (*HRK*, p. 30). Henderson's relationship to his ancestry is at best ambivalent. If they were builders of America, they were unscrupulous capitalists: pride and guilt are confused, a tradition of gallantry compounded with news of exotic degeneration. The ambivalence is partly resolved in the final version by comedy in, for example, Henderson's wonderful catalogue of relatives: one is carried away in a balloon while publicizing the suffrage movement, one preaches to his neighbors who have to come when he clangs the bell. The service ideal has fallen on hard times. Is Henderson big enough to revive it?

In any case, Henderson's Wasp origin means more as art and psychology than as sociology. Nowhere is the antiphonal development of Bellow's work more apparent than in the movement from *Seize the Day* to *Henderson the Rain King*. One is tight, exquisite, claustral, dark; the other loose, fanciful, airy, dazzling; one is concerned with society, conditionality; the other with the voyage, ideal material freedom; one is a fiction of facticity, in the vein of the novel of manners; the other a fiction of lyricism, a romance. One significance of this novel without Jews is a reaction to the tone, the psychological *vayizmir* of *Seize the Day*. In Henderson we have divorce without murder (indeed, without pain, it seems), money without need, unemployment without guilt, as excruciating passivity gives way to flaunting aggression. Henderson is loaded, not broke, and as a number of patrician American writers since Henry James knew, a few million dollars can make you free to choose. But, of course, in the twentieth century the battery of aforementioned distinctions is not as clear as it seems, and the question of the book is "choose what?"

There are similarities between Wilhelm and Henderson which cannot go unnoticed. If, as his name indicates, one aspires to Wasp distinction, the other almost expires of it. Yet both transfigure themselves through the burden of suffering. For the Bellovian protagonist, grief, sir, can be a species of busyness. But where Wilhelm lives with it, Henderson, like Herzog (who quotes Dr. Johnson on the subject of grief), begins with it but casts it off. Both suffer from (Reichian?) chest pressure, both gain a bursting of the condition which almost sinks them, Wilhelm in his final epiphany, Henderson in his aggrandizing quest to "burst the spirit's sleep." Henderson begins where Wilhelm ends. The bravura and bluster of Henderson's style, the humor of it, the new comedy of self-concern, the ultimate confidence of the "I"—these take us back to the essential difference. For all its airiness and spontaneity, *Henderson* is, as we have seen, one of the most elaborately rewritten of his novels. It seems that when Bellow works close to the social surface, the writing comes more easily. *Augie March* is the most conspicuous example of this. But in *Henderson*, we see the arduous demands of fantasy. It appears that spontaneity, in the completeness of its illusion, must be worked at.

Imagine a novel in which the first forty-four pages were done in seven (B.6.15), the first one hundred sixteen in thirty, a novel without Itelo, without the frog massacre, without an heroic Dahfu, without the Mummah incident, without, that is, Henderson as Rain King (it was first called "Bariri"), without the celebrated theoretical farce of the lion's den, without the death of Dahfu, without the concluding chapter, and you imagine the early versions of the novel. Generally, the best known sections of the novel are the most worked over. As an example, many readers value the first forty pages of the novel above everything else in it, wishing that the intensity of this inspired nuttiness were maintained. There is nothing more worked over than these marvelous pages.

First pages are often a kind of ritualistic settling in for novelists, and Bellow rehearses often the tonality of dissonant, self-ironic, psychological lyricism which is the novel's alpha as well as its omega. Carrying a modern narrative prototype one step further on the road to dislocation, the author gives us a crisis in the life of an already disordered existence. Yet the modernist somberness is undercut by that peculiarly Bellovian amalgam of presto and pain and the stability of a quasi-biblical calm: "the world which I thought so mighty an oppressor has removed its wrath from me" (*HRK*, p. 3). An admirable severity this late note, but it took several drafts to appear. In one early version (B.6.11) little exists of the first two pages but the allusion to "the forgiveness of sins" which redeems even first family bums and the description of his rich and schizophrenic first wife, Frances. This early version (and others) sometimes reads like a scenario: "First wife goes to Europe, or out on the moon, or wherever, and on the way she divorces me," which is later transformed into "Frances and I were divorced. . . . she's now in Switzerland. I was delighted with the divorce. . . . She was like Shelley's moon, wandering companionless" (*HRK*, pp. 4f). The final version is more personal, more spirited and more pointed in its psychological comedy. Some of Henderson's most characteristic quirks—having pressure in the chest, being drunk before lunch, using old currency for bookmarks, breaking bottles at the beach—come in late versions. Henderson is made thereby more vivid, if more painful. Yet this is balanced by the studied carelessness of other late inclusions: e.g., "Christ I've got plenty of children, God bless the whole bunch of them" (*HRK*, p. 4). In earlier versions he simply expresses worry. The final Henderson is more extravagant in his blundering, yet more calm in his recovery. Some of his most memorable utterances do not appear in the early version—"Does truth come in blows?" (*HRK*, p. 23), "There is a curse on this land" (*HRK*, p. 38)—to illustrate from only the opening section. Henderson's most intimate cry, "*I want, I want,*" is there from the beginning, but is given in different ways. By negatives: "it was not the voice of sexual desire" (B.8.4); "a crowd of people? No. Did it want a Jaguar? No. A Burberry coat? A gun . . . ? No, no" (B.8.29). Or by positives: "I want (truth) I want (honor) I want (nobility) I want (completed desires) I want (love)." In one early version (B.5.4), a rather spiritual Henderson tries "thinking, prayer, study . . . a book of poems, or the Bible, or Plato." But the voice will not go away. In the novel Henderson does try reading, but this quickly gives way to chopping wood, fishing, drinking, working, womanizing; none of this, of course, quiets the inner insistence, which remains more powerful for being ineluctable. As the writing proceeds there is an expansion of "I want, I want," which (B.5.13) may be little more than mentioned in early versions. And in support of this there is his violin—not present in earliest versions, gradually expanded in later—it, too, a symbol of infinite longing and the desire to be united with his distinguished father.

    The early versions are also given to a certain generality of description— "Rude health, a big body, an aggressive spirit, I always needed much activity," says Eugene H. Henderson (B.5.3)—a quality scarcely present in the vibrant personal accents of the final version. The later, inimitably personal voice casts out the occasional early solemnity. One cannot imagine Henderson saying (as he does in B.6.11, 11) "The greatest of arts is to know how to speak of the things nearest your heart; my abilities are not of the highest but I deserve credit for what charity there is in me, even if I do not speak with the tongues of angels." In addition to such major matters, many of the vivid minor details of the opening are later inclusions: Lily, moralizing, "turns white and starts to speak under her breath" (*HRK*, p. 7). Hazard gives her a shiner before the wedding. Henderson berates her for "playing chicken-funeral with your own mother" (*HRK*, p. 27). Henderson's pig kingdom with its statues "from Florence and Salzburg turned over" (*HRK*, pp. 20f.), the Sevcik exercises with their noise like smashing eggcrates, and Henderson's finger "indented especially by the steel E string"—such additions help establish the dominant tonality of comic violence. Similarly, little of the gargantuan imagery appears in the early versions. Like Falstaff, Henderson is a much described character, all of the following being lived-into description. Henderson's face is like "the clang of a bell," "an unfinished church," "as long as a city block."[7] His whole body like "an old locomotif," "a giant pine whose roots have crossed and choked one another," "a giant turnip." All this, like the dominant tendency of the book, may seem strange to an age accustomed to instituting downward comparisons. From Dickens' Smallweeds to Eliot's wriggling and scuttling Prufrock to Kafka's Gregor Samsa, literature has been party to an insistent philogenetic regression. There is one such image in *Henderson*, but its use is significantly contrary. Responding to Dahfu's nobility, Henderson uncharacteristically compares himself to a small object. It was as "if a spider should get a stroke and suddenly begin to do a treatise on botany or something—a transfigured vermin. . . . This is how I embraced the king's words" (*HRK*, p. 215). Even in his self-hatred Henderson becomes miraculously enlarged.

Yet there is a certain kind of specificity in the early versions that Bellow does not want—the tendency, sometimes half-hearted, to fall back on the historical cataloguing of *Augie March*. With the Wariri, Henderson "had a rough idea of how Admiral What's-his-name (Commodore Perry) must have felt when he opened a way into barbaric Japan; Kipling and Cecil Rhodes were on my mind too and the old cartoons of cannibal kings in top hats" (B.6.17, 66). He marvels at Dahfu, who can think fearlessly in threatening circumstances: "Did Galileo want to go to jail. Or take the sextant invented by Tycho Brahe (on view in the city of Prague)—did the world ever before see such a dingus? That was primitive for you, I reflected. And yet the angels thought out by Tycho were exactly the angels of heaven" (B.8.24, 352). Here the rhythmic mixture of interrogation and wonder is truly Augie-like, and Bellow sees that they are not Henderson's accents. (There is one image, though, taken over from *Augie*. The Banyuls octopus, symbolizing death, first appears in a manuscript [B.3.13] of *Augie March*. It is never used in that novel, but is a key image in *Henderson*. While not in early drafts [B.6.11, B.6.12], it does soon appear [B.5.13], but in a confused way. Henderson reads the octopus this way: "It said, 'Go to hell!' I clasped my head to keep from fainting"; he concludes, however, "But this forms no part of my story." Our death-conscious hero later realizes that it does.)

The triumph of *Henderson the Rain King* is the creation of a voice, and, as we can see, it did indeed have to be created. Compulsive, self-ironic, beseeching, loud is this voice. A spiritual bully, Henderson is a Jacob in Esau's clothing. Was reality ever more boisterously pursued? The narrative "I" takes us into the intimacy of confession, with the difference that there is nothing more public to the contemporary person than intimacy. The result is our confessional comedy, where the self deflates public judgment by getting there first. To the extent that we are all ill, honesty in confronting symptoms is a cardinal virtue. As the underground men knew, Rousseau's *Confessions* established a new genre of character portrayal, one in which the protagonist brags about his vices. A book like *Henderson*, a novel of character, or struggling to be one, must succeed from the beginning. *Henderson* succeeds nowhere more than in the first forty pages. This explosion of spontaneity was carefully prepared.

Not only the voice, but also the narrative sequence shows careful artistry. The early versions are much condensed. As we have mentioned, in one version (B.6.15) we are in Beventai by page seven. What Bellow does in the revisions is build to a dramatic climax so that the trip to Africa is clearly a psychological necessity. In the early versions there is no mention of Lily in this section (B.6.11). The remembrance concerning Lily—her knocked-out teeth, her worried mother, her forwardness in France—appears to first occur (B.5.10) as a reminiscence in the middle of the lion hunt. It does not stay in this latter part of the novel for long. Similarly, Henderson originally recalls throwing out the tenants, named Wingals, and the subsequent encounter with Darcy the cat, in the Wariri section. Guilty, he hears the lions roar. The Ricey episode is in all versions, but in one early version, at least, there is some question as to whether it is her baby or not. What is wanted here is turmoil, comic remorse, but not that much moral seriousness. Also, in some early versions, Henderson is married to one Gloria (or Selma), described as "a dull woman" despite her lively premarital vagaries. The Lily character, called Joanna, would be a third wife. She courts him, but he considers her too much like him to help him. In short, the final version compresses a widespread sequence of more serious events into more highly concentrated comic disasters, which are at once charged with more aggression and more feeling, creating that jaunty, opening volatility that blasts him off on his quest.

For purposes of compositional analysis, the book falls rather neatly into sections, the next being the visit with the Arnewi, a sequence in which the prose texture is not so rewritten as the first, but in which the nature of the episode did undergo equal change. To begin with, the early versions do not differentiate as much as the novel does between the kinds of episodes in the Arnewi and Wariri sections. In both the central action is an elaborate rain ceremony, the Arnewi's leading to nothing, the Wariri's to rain. Horko tells Henderson (in the middling B.7.13) that "the Bariri and Arnewi had once been one tribe." The early Arnewi versions (e.g., B.6.18) focus as much on one King Banite as on Queen Willatale. He is seen undergoing a ritual martyrdom, the center of a rather lengthy procession which culminates in the sacrifice of a bull. Then a menacing figure, "not like the Arnewi at all," takes the center stage. Troubled, Henderson "suspected these children of

the sun of being children of darkness after all" (B.6.18). But, of course, the
bully is subdued by law and becomes sweet and patient. The later versions
delete any such complication of tone, presenting the Arnewi in their aspect
of untrammeled innocence. Similarly, the procession of Arnewi gods, with
their marks of pity concealing fangs underneath, must be dropped. With the
Arnewi, Bellow does not yet want theological complication. (The gods represent rest rather than motion, Being rather than Becoming, a distinction
which Bellow is content to make in the comparison between Willatale [and,
later, Dahfu] and Henderson.) Henderson's reaction to the ritualistic self-
abasement he sees is ambivalent. First, in the accents of a Yankee from New
York, " 'A lot of good you're going to do yourselves by lying in the dust,' I
wanted to tell them" (B.6.18, 146); but, then, giving way to feeling, he cries
with "sorrow for the Arnewi here and also for the human race, 'Oh, oh!
Mercy! Mercy, Lord, Mercy! We suffer here. . . . Pity! At least for those
that deserve pity! Pity!' " (B.6.18, 147). This last cry recalls, perhaps, Blake's
"The Divine Image," with its invocation of "Mercy, Pity, Peace and Love,"
transcendent suffering being necessary even in a world of innocence. This
Judeo-Christian residue is dropped in the less Blakean final version where
the Yankee Henderson becomes a victim of his own tinkering mentality.

The frog fiasco comes late in the genesis of the book. In what appears to be
the earliest version of the book (B.6.15) there is no equivalent episode.
There is the rain ceremony, but no rain; Henderson, full of pity, but seeing
that there is nothing for him to do, leaves with Romilayu. *Finis* Arnewi
episode. (By page 30 of B.6.15 we are with the Wariri.) In this version,
Henderson notices vultures overhead. In a slightly later version, he asserts
his protective instinct by killing a python. Here the final pattern is already
set, for, as luck would have it, the python is a holy snake and the act
sacrilege; even worse, it's murder, as the snake is Mtalba's late husband,
Itelo's uncle. Perhaps Bellow dropped this—he sticks with it for quite some
time—because the totemistic drama was too farfetched. In any case, he
found in the frog episode a more elaborate vehicle for Henderson's earnest
desire to help, the vestiges of the Wasp service ideal. Not merely protective
courage but Yankee ingenuity—indeed, Faustian engineering—goes in motley as Henderson performs a service which leaves him no alternative but
getting out. An explosive denouement, one might say. Equally undercut is
Henderson's romanticism, his intuition of that special pink light, which
rarely is on land or sea. Henderson's mediumistic tendency backfires as he
buoyantly perceives "some powerful magnificence not human . . . [that]
seemed under me" (*HRK*, pp. 100f.). He is not the one to grasp what one
early version calls "the fringe of the Nirvana" (B.9.2). The frogs do not
symbolize anything in particular, but are a device for getting Henderson out
of Arnewiland in a style to which he is accustomed.

The Arnewi episode, however, is clearly meant to be illustrative, with Willatale remaining, in the final version, the key figure. In one earlier version Itelo says of Willatale, "She do not think. She is very wise" (B.6.17, 96). Fortunately, this College Outline Romanticism is subdued in the novel; the final version gives us a more sophisticated Romanticism. As the novel evolves the contrast with the Wariri becomes clear: Innocence, in a rather Blakean sense, versus a somewhat loosely conceived Experience.[8] The Innocence, in other words, is characterized by an innate caring, by meekness, by the Judeo-Christian moral abstractions (explicit in early versions), and by a sense of metaphysical sadness for undeserved pain and loss. But in their comprehension of vital energy, the Arnewi express aspects of Blake's "The Marriage of Heaven and Hell." The vitalistic "grun-tu-molani" suggests Blake's "Energy is true delight." Willatale embodies Being and coming in such close contact with the omphalos, her belly, induces a kind of high: "I felt as though I were riding in a balloon above the Spice Islands, soaring in hot clouds while exotic odors rose from below" (HRK, p. 74). If there is no lamb here, transcendent mildness in bovine form will have to do. Jungians may get carried away in the balloon, but the odor of the actual should recall them. Anyway, this is pretty high for twentieth-century transcendence.

Why doesn't Henderson, in one version or other, stay—despite the "disaster" and despite the inability to help those undeservedly suffering? Like Melville's protagonist in Typee, he is too complicated for such innocence. "The Arnewi were fine people but I did not belong with them," says Henderson in one early version (B.5.6). He is not strong enough for such uncomplication, in addition to which he feels vulnerable to simplicity of judgment. He cannot tell all to Innocence—"I didn't know where to begin," says Henderson (HRK, p. 77). He needs Experience—which includes difficulty, darkness, images of wrath—to uncomplicate himself. In manuscript (B.7.9, 55), Itelo tells Henderson that the Bariri are "very bad." Henderson replies, "Then there was where I had to go." In another version Henderson says that "You have to know the world and more than the world" (B.6.17, 95). The final version, with its frog disaster, avoids some of the explicitness of such a choice, but it is clear that the world-weary and world-wise Henderson cannot long inhabit the realm of Innocence.

The Arnewi episode takes the shape that it does mostly from rewriting. The wrestling, the cow-shame,[9] the frogs, come, as we have seen, in various stages of composition. The driving lyricism of the book so far owes its refrains largely to the rewriting. Not only the elaboration of the inner I want, the strike, strike, strike, strike, but the "grun-tu-molani" as well comes in revision; as does the haunting, "I do remember well the hour which burst my spirit's sleep" (not in B.8.4), which Bellow takes from Shelley's Dedication to

Laon and Cythna (better known as "The Revolt of Islam").[10] All this makes for an ennobling of Henderson's character, which in some early versions was peevish and imperious. As an indication of the distance Bellow had to come in establishing the right tone, we recall an early version in which an aloof Henderson muses on the Arnewi rain-ceremony: "it didn't have to affect me one way or another how the Arnewi made out, unless I chose to let it" (B.7.9, 37). When Itelo asks Henderson to stay with the tribe, Henderson's reaction is " 'What?' I thought. 'And stay up every night listening to cow funerals?' " (B.7.9, 54). Related to this wrong, early tack is a surfacing antagonism between Henderson and Romilayu. The final Henderson, all yearning, all desire, has none of this melancholy self-importance.

Bellow had a somewhat clearer perception of what he wanted to do in the Wariri section (called Bariri in the earlier versions), at least until the rain-making ceremony. Up to this episode composition was relatively easy, but some changes in the long trek to the Wariri are made. The first of these concerns the scene in which Henderson breaks his bridge. It first appears in the Arnewi sequence, just before the rain ceremony. By transferring this minor disaster to the tense scene in which Henderson and Romilayu, having been ambushed, are made to wait for an audience with Dahfu, the comedy of middle age is intensified. Another advantage is that Bellow, having packed the first forty pages with incident, can break up a particularly flat stretch of narrative with flashback, or intensify present time with past time. Out trot Mme. Montecuccoli, Berthe, the feckless Edward and his Maria Felucca, the Spohrs, and Lily, and Henderson's psychological turmoil eclipses the adventure-story line.

But the adventure comes into its own with the rain-making ceremony, where flogging of the gods involves Henderson in considerable ambivalence. This does not occur so much in the final version, where the pious Henderson will not willingly flog the gods (his rain-king's hand is forced into a formal gesture of metaphysical defiance). Here, as elsewhere, Bellow declines the rebel gambit, choosing to affirm that the gods must be good, must be treated with reverence. But the manuscripts show that Bellow was not altogether clear on this point. In one early version, Henderson, acting with the infectious spirit of rebellion, belts a man on the ear with a stick, who then bleeds. This is a typical Henderson goof, like killing the python or blasting the frogs (B.6.9). More meaningfully in a later version, being forced to beat the gods, Henderson says, "I did it with fear once, twice, and my being caught the motions, and began to turn faster, and then I, too, madly gave a scream and struck Hummat and Mummah. I lashed with all my might. . . . And this great rage grew, and the Amazons and I, out of our minds, flogged the gods until a great thunderclap was heard" (B.5.5). It is characteristic of Bellow to exorcise such murderous impulses—even Henderson has a meekness!—and follow it with remorse: "Now they have had enough, and this is our punishment. We can expect death and deserve death." When Dahfu subsequently tells him that "you have more in common with the Bariri than with the Arnewi," Henderson admits it, saying that he "was horrified . . . should be horrified." Yet, a quirk remains, for "down in the core I'm not. This shocks me" (B.5.6).

Such ambiguity is eventually deleted. But there is considerable early struggling with the idea of poetic justice as there is with the tone of the rain episode in general. One version (B.5.11) tells us that after the rain, Henderson thinks "how witchlike and gloomy it was. . . . I was bitter about it." He is disturbed by the "injustice" of such apparently misplaced fruition: "Do the wicked prosper? That's certainly great news." To compound his alienation, he notes, rather absurdly, that "the curious, not to say astonishing thing and, for me, a little hard to take was that not too much fuss was made over me. . . . After the rain they were all preoccupied with other things."

The final version, however, has little perplexity because, in it, Dahfu's role is, as we shall see, greatly enlarged. Generally, the sinister quality of some of the early manuscripts is deleted; one recalls the sequence in which Henderson, having seen men dangling by their feet from gallows, focuses on "a reluctant figure whose face was framed in a large white frill. Two men in masks come after him in a way that augured no good." The figure tries to retreat, but they gouge, beat, spit, strike him "with sharp pointed sticks." He makes no defense. Dahfu's explanation that this man is Ibono or Obedient, "the man who submits to everything" does not really explain him away. Henderson manifests a strange fascination for this sort of professional sufferer, to the extent that he composes a poem about it: "The lesson of submission! / Submission is oblivion. / Obedience takes the path / laid down for it by wrath. / And follows it to death." Meditating, perhaps uncharacteristically, on motive, Henderson says, "The resonance with which this struck me was unexpected . . . but I knew the truth, that it was far, far less than completely foreign. I was greatly horrified" (B.5.5). Of course, this section had to be deleted—there could be no latently submissive Henderson. It is more of a fascination to Bellow, who knows enough about dangling men and victims, than to this character, reminiscent, for example, of the courtroom scene in Herzog, where a slaughter without ritual is enacted.

Yet there is an attraction to submission or to suffering in so many Bellow characters (Augie, Tommy Wilhelm, Herzog) that critics have sometimes pointed to a moral masochism. Even the powerful Henderson incarnates this quality in his own way. "I am to suffering what Gary is to smoke. One of the world's biggest operations," he tells us (HRK, p. 260). Considered more traditionally, Bellow is often on the side of passive goodness, the strength of what Nietzsche considered weakness; in saying this he is allied to what Nietzsche saw as a central aspect of the Judeo-Christian tradition, with its creation of a "good" and "evil" that ennobles suffering, showing how active apparent passivity can be. It is no accident that the well-known conversations between Henderson and Dahfu on good and evil take place in the novel in this sequence, and that the moral drawn—in darkest, most primitive Africa!—is clearly Judeo–Christian. At the moment, Henderson is rightly "puzzled and angered" by Dahfu's going along with the barbarism he sees, with all his talk about "spectacular goodness" (B.5.5). In the final version the suffering figure is dropped, and much of the puzzlement and anger with it.[11] But the talk about goodness remains and is considerably enlarged.

Uncertain of himself in a strange, and in many ways, hostile land, Henderson wonders at the poetic justice that would grant rain to the Wariri, while denying it to the good Arnewi. (Even the names suggest their moral qualities: the Arnewi are new or innocent; the Wariri, war weary, or experienced.) Remarkably, Dahfu reads his mind. Henderson, elated, thinks, "the world is a mind and all travelers mental travelers" (B.6.15), a sentiment retained in the final version. A transcendental reality is affirmed before which "what we call reality is our own pedantry." In manuscript Henderson then thinks of Marvell's lines from "The Garden": "That ocean where each kind / Doth straight its own resemblance find." How appropriate this poem is to Henderson's frame of mind, with its preference of pastoral to social, its mistrust of achievement, its retreat from womankind, its focus on the primacy of subjectivity ("Annihilating all that's made, / To a green thought in a green shade"), and its doctrine of correspondences. The reference is dropped because Henderson's experience takes him back to Lily rather than away from her (cf. "Two Paradises 'twere in one / To live in Paradise alone"), and perhaps because Bellow wanted the more explicitly Romantic distinction expressed in the novel between the physical and the noumenal, the scientific and the creative. Indeed, Henderson's adventures are to bind him ever more closely to Lily, who finds her "resemblance" as he finds his. Everyone his own poet in the diffusion of Romantic doctrine.

One of the seeming advantages of Experience is that it can express complexity: it can contemplate its anti-self, so to speak. And the muddled Henderson speaks only the language of complexity, arriving at personal harmony through an idiosyncratic dialectic. Like Dahfu, Henderson yearns for the good because his life has made him all too aware of its precariousness. There is a shock of recognition between them, an illustration of the psychic unity or moral universals Bellow intuits. Dahfu knows that bad can be spectacular but good far more spectacular, expressing in a simplified way Bellow's essential view of the modern situation. If Dahfu sounds too much like a high-school valedictorian, Bellow can plead dramatic immunity since African chieftains may sound like that. Nonetheless, Bellow, with all the complexity of postmodernism at hand, sees the necessity of such utterances. In this Africa of western tradition, we reach a simplicity beyond complexity, one in harmony with what one may call traditional western ethics.

The substance of the discussion between Henderson and Dahfu about good and evil is, in its first appearance, part of a Henderson monologue, and its meaning is the reverse of what it is in the novel. Seeing the relation of ritual to result, Henderson thinks that "the gods mind harshness (beating, etc.). . . . 'Beat us and spare one another,' is perhaps what the Bariri Gods would say. But it works out no better than a gospel of love, to judge by the corpses who filled the gallows on this holiday" (B.5.5). This grisly scene as well as the grisly reflections on the apparent failure of poetic justice are transfigured only by a higher moral synthesis. As it stands here, Henderson can only muse, somewhat incongruously, on "Souls that ache with punishment they cannot hand on. . . . This is the great passion, to rid ourselves of blows we have gotten." An enlarged conception of Dahfu shows us the way out of this conundrum.

In the composition of the novel, Dahfu undergoes a transformation. At first, he is associated with brutal Wariri ritual, and it is Henderson who lectures him: "You may hit and torture and cudgel and hang people, but this will not bring the desired result" (B.5.5). Dahfu is soon enough transformed into a benign guru whose power depends on the ability to create at least one disciple. Henderson, all mistrust gone, becomes the disciple. The lesson is that man, who "cannot stand still under blows," needs aggression, even revenge, as an imperfect equivalent of poetic justice. This justifies, in Dahfu's view, the beating of the gods.

Henderson, in what we are to take as an inspired moment, speaks of "some guys who can return good for evil." Dahfu, who is one of these people, agrees that a brave man "shall keep the blow" (HRK, pp. 213f.), knowing that this will always be a minority view. An elevating moral, no doubt, but how much does it have to do with what is actually dramatized in the novel? Is Henderson's aggression more convincing and, by rule of authenticity, more admirable than his "goodness"? This aggression is not to be understood apart from his quest for goodness, for the morally real, and is, indeed, a function of that quest. Yet returning good for evil—for which Henderson himself is not famous—is not adequate to describe this quest. Fortunately, Bellow conceives a way of breathing more convincing life into moral abstraction.

Like many pastoral works, *Henderson the Rain King* shows us civilization uncomplicating itself; commonly the uncomplication derives from a civilized alternative, here manifested as psychoanalytic theory. Since the burden of some psychoanalytical theory is a recapturing of primitive energies, Africa may not be an unlikely place for therapy. In one early version (B.7.3) Henderson actually calls his meetings with Dahfu "sessions," of which he has eleven. If Dahfu is a therapist, he is Reichian rather than Freudian, active, exhorting, judging, voluble in the relationship. Though in the novel Dahfu is a higher blabbermouf', one early version has Dahfu being "too royal to explain very much"! (B.5.6) His role as pundit is literally enlarged.[12]

Dahfu finally emerges as a therapeutic ideologue who preaches a textbook Romantic vitalism as the way back to health. This happens largely in the scenes in the lion's den—the wildest, and perhaps most celebrated in the book, and surely one of the most successful flights into intellectual farce by an author especially gifted in that art. It is, therefore, particularly interesting to know that it did not exist in the earliest versions of the book. For example (B.8.21; B.7.13, 151), some versions have Dahfu rather caught up in the cycle of the blow-for-blow, literally casting his Cain-like brothers out of the palace, all to Henderson's despair. Our hero listlessly goes about his duties as rain king, sprinkling crowds with holy water. Henderson and Dahfu soon go "hunting" and we are immediately marched into the "narrow end of the hopo" (B.7.13, 195) for the end of the story.[13] The climax of the novel is the farce in the lion's den, not the tragedy of Dahfu's death, which is clearly secondary to these scenes and meaningless without them.

When it comes, the earliest appearance of the den scene is quite different from the way it appears in the novel. In manuscript, we see a Henderson whose sense of humor has not yet emerged. "Life is a deceit, a gyp. . . . This is what has put me on the war path" (B.5.13), he says. Dahfu is already psychoanalytic, spouting the theories of Paul Schilder and Wilhelm Reich, insisting that Henderson lie down on the couch as we hear the lion's growl in the background. The trust between them is not yet established—to say nothing of the guru-disciple relationship—and Henderson suspects that "this is where he plays the hoax, turns the animals loose on me and I am torn to pieces." Rather arbitrarily, this is where he thinks of Joanna (Lily) and her failure father, who, drunk, knocks her teeth out on the golf course with a hit ball; he thinks of the party, the snowbank, realizing that this "woman, evaded till now, meant more to me than any other." In the novel this realization comes to him after he makes sense of his quest; the biographical details, of course, come at the beginning, separated from his judgment of Lily by almost three hundred pages. The couch induces moody rumination: "Sometimes, but particularly in the lion's den I would think of the waste of years." This lugubrious, depressive quality must be dropped for an explosion of energy, a sort of psychoanalysis by inversion wherein the analyst actively exhorts, and one's "dream" life is made flesh.

Although Wilhelm Reich is generally taken to be the theoretician to whom Bellow is most indebted in the creation of the new Dahfu, the manuscripts reveal that it is not Reich but Paul Schilder who was the greater influence. Bellow has explicitly said as much in a letter to Jascha Kessler: "It was not . . . Reich who got me going in Henderson but a neurophysiologist named Paul Schilder whose book The Image and Idea (sic Appearance) of the Human Body came highly recommended."[14] Though Bellow had known Reich for some time, we can see that he had not read Schilder until well into the composition of the novel.

Like any post-Freudian psychoanalytic theorist Schilder owes much to Freud, though he conceives of his own theories as being a criticism of Freud. Schilder maintains that Freud's basic attitude, "that our desires try to lead us back to a previous state and merely lead us back to a state of rest," is not a true description of our "inner and outer experiences." Schilder writes: "I insist upon the constructive character of the psychic forces and refuse to make the idea of regression the center of a theory of human behaviour. . . . Freud has been inclined to neglect the principles of emergent evolution (or preferably) constructive evolution, which leads to the creation of new units and configurations."[15] Whether Freud does this or not, this insistence on the constructive character of the psychic forces works against the deterministic tendency in Freud and affords Bellow another opportunity to dramatize his belief that free will has not disappeared before determinism. "It was from Schilder," Bellow writes to Kessler, "that I got the notion that one's physical self really does represent an inner picture, and that we are perhaps somehow responsible for the way we come out. This carries one step forward the doctrine that a man's fate is made by his character." The echo of Augie March is surely intentional, since he is Bellow's first character to be created in the new energy given by the reality of this belief. We recall that *Augie March* gave us a version of free will that was highly qualified by the conditioning factors. Schilder's work gives us a similar view.

When one first opens Schilder's study, one is immediately lost in admiration for the ability of the imagination to transform. One may simply be lost, since Schilder's opening section, "The Physiological Basis of the Body Image," is nearly impenetrable, more of an arcane list than an essay. So we see Henderson quipping, "a term like basal ganglia has always cheered me up a lot. I came across something called Obersteiner's allochiria" (B.8.24, 342). Dahfu is annoyed at Henderson's limpness, at his lack of enthusiasm about "conversion phenomena." In the novel itself, Henderson breaks down over "Obersteiner's allochiria" (in an anthology, here the term is used by Scheminsky), then skips over it to make some sense of what is clearly Schilder's theory.

This theory does strike responsive chords in Bellow, though the first third of the book actually deals with brain lesions. Confronted with the problem of how a paralyzed person thinks she feels sensation in a part of the body where she could not possibly, Schilder holds that sensation may depend on inner activity, the way one views oneself, the "postural model of the body" (60). The reality of phantom limbs in such situations is also to be understood only "when we consider the emotional reactions of individuals toward their own body [*sic*]" (67). Obsessional neuroses show that feeling our body intact is not a matter of course. It is the effect of self-love: "There are forces of hatred scattering the picture of our own body and forces of love putting it together" (166). Yes, we are in some way responsible for how we come out.

Schilder focuses on what he calls conversion, whereby body posture is realized and the cortical activity may bring perception to its final end, action. In this connection, Schilder is particularly interested in imitation, since "when we see or imagine something we change our attitude." The child and the primitive have the advantage here in that their thinking is "full of symbolizations and condensations. . . . It is not only animated but connected with all activities in the universe" (p. 175f.). We are, then, not far from the world of Henderson, where objects of noble imitation present themselves, where symbol is made flesh and takes us, in flashes of elevated farce, into the mystery in motley. Indeed, Schilder states explicitly that the body-image may derive from animals as well as from other human beings, and holds that animism is a phase of general human development. It is, in any case, a phase of Henderson's development. Conversion, which involves energetic change, is not always successful; psychic energy which does not express itself becomes somatic. Henderson's chest pains, his fever, indicate this negative aspect.

The naming of Schilder is explicit in manuscript, though not in the novel. For example, Dahfu responds learnedly to Henderson's question about how thought becomes flesh in the following way:

> I placed at the top of the material I gave you the work of the late Prof. Schilder. . . . To begin with there is a conversion phenomena [*sic*]. You are fearful about a part of your body—that part undergoes a change. Your dread is stomach centred? Your stomach expresses this by an ulcer. . . . A pimple on a lady's nose may be *her idea*. . . . Disease is a speech of the psyche." (B.5.12, B.7.6. The last two statements appear in *HRK*, p. 237)

As psychoanalysts know, Schilder, by contrast to some, minimizes the unconscious and maximizes the volitional, thereby making will a more positive element and adult autonomy more possible than Freud does. True, Dahfu does say, with respect to the lady's pimple, "no blame redounds. We are far from so free to be masters," but adds, "just the same it is done from within us." This "from within us" receives major emphasis in Schilder. Accordingly, Dahfu gives a qualified yes to Henderson's harried question—"do you want to tell me, your highness, that I am the author of my own appearance?"

Grimly, Henderson clings to "heredity, . . . age" as the determining factors. Dahfu does not deny these, but emphasizes the activity of the psyche, an activity which can be "benevolent" as well as "malign." Following Schilder, whom he apostrophizes ("Oh, Schilder, Schilder!"), Dahfu goes into physiological explanation (the cortex, third and fourth ventricles, *und so weiter*), but it is his Romantic idealism that carries the day. Denying that Bergson understood the meaning of evolution, he makes a buoyant estimate of a limitless future: "We have tracked the secret of evolution to its door. The human race may now embark on a new career of greatness. It is a matter of the right model in the cortex. From noble self-conception, noble-beings follow." Dahfu is never quite so buoyant in *Henderson*, but some such visionary fervor is needed to get Henderson into the lion's den and effect his at least partial conversion from pighood to lionism.

In Dahfu's handling of it, conversion is a double-edged sword. If ego-energy is released, it is toward the end of ego-annihilation. On this point the late manuscript and the novel are the same, though the manuscript is somewhat more transparent: "Separate yourself from your lavish personality . . . your great ego. Strive to belong rather to your species, as this animal does" (B.8.22, 317), says Dahfu, showing the ultimate tyranny of animism. Naive, guru-prone, Henderson is swept up "with a longing to do well; my motto being *serviam*. But how to serve? Where?" (B.8.22, 322f.) *A bas* Stephen Dedalus and all those Romantic Lucifers. Yet he must glut himself on the higher impersonality before he falls back into mere character. Dahfu's idealism strikes this comic Faust with a shock of recognition: the "Universe itself may have a psychical existence and Nature be a mentality. . . . Man's mind by alliance with this All-Intelligent is able by freedom to perform certain work, which does not mean miracles" (B.8.22, 349). We have already seen Henderson endorse the idea that all travel is mental travel, that the world is a mind.

What Schilder does is supply the bridge between psychoanalytic theory and Bellow's more optimistic American Romanticism. Henderson's new awareness leads him to recall a source, Walt Whitman: "Enough to merely be! Enough to breathe! Joy! Joy! All over joy!," to which Henderson adds in modern sardonic agreement, "Becoming was beginning to come out of my ears. . . . Time to Be? Burst the spirit's sleep. Wake up America! Stump the experts" (*HRK*, p. 160). Henderson can invoke populist rhetoric to the extent that it confounds modernist intellectuals who predict eternal sleep. And in a Dahfu-inspired rhapsody on the power of imagination and the reality of mental travel, Henderson confirms Romantic doctrine: "The world of facts is real, all right, and not to be altered. The physical is all there, and it belongs to science. But then there is the noumenal department, and there we create and create and create" (*HRK*, p. 167). It is appropriate, then, that Henderson think of Dahfu as "a true artist" (*HRK*, p. 175). This is not the modern artist, with his alienated consciousness and ego-cult; no, it is an older, Romantic conception which shows that "chaos doesn't run the whole show. . . . This is not a sick and hasty ride, helpless, through a dream into oblivion." No drunken boat here, no *poète maudit*, but that earlier pre-symbolist, premodern balance. It is interesting to note that Bellow, who is generally antipathetic to the tradition of the artist-hero, has a hero who is only metaphorically an artist. He is really some kind of psychoanalytic rabbi, a sermonizer, a moralizing citizen. Bellow goes off on what appears to be a Nietzschean tangent in his praise of Dahfu, comparing him to Caesar, Napoleon, and Chaka the Zulu. Typically, the aristocracy named here is not artistic but political, more Hegel than Nietzsche. Dahfu himself speaks for a humbling of the ego through identification with nature, the hero as shrink.

In the den, the tigers of wrath lie down with the horses of instruction, a departure from modernism, where the tigers of wrath are the horses of instruction. Dahfu quotes Blake's aphorism ("The tigers of wrath are wiser than the horses of instruction"), but Henderson doesn't swallow even Blake's tigers whole. Dahfu, after all, is one of those theoreticians who is "triumphantly sure" (*HRK*, p. 236), a sign of certain trouble in Bellow. After this mighty initiation Henderson says, "To tell the truth, I didn't have full confidence in the king's science" (*HRK*, p. 273). One ought not to give Bellow bad marks for not being an orthodox Reichian. Eusebio Rodrigues says, "Though Henderson has had the experience, he probably missed some of its deeper meaning and it is the reader who has to supply this meaning by aligning his perspective with the Reichian slant of the novel."[16] But the novel is not there for the sake of Reichian (or Schilderian) ideas; Bellow's character—with his "limitations" of theoretical intelligence, which are not very limited—is much more important to him than the theoreticians he learns from. And does it really add to our knowledge of the novel to say that Lily "is a Reichian without knowing it"? Lily says, "Maybe I'm not all there and I don't understand. . . . But when we're together, I *know*" (*HRK*, pp. 18f.). Do we need Reich for this knowledge?

Yet the drama of psychic explosion, the numerous physical ticks, the wild psychoanalytic sessions, the preaching, active analyst, the marvelous take-off on character types (and, perhaps, as Rodrigues suggests, on Reich's idea that the total bodily expression can be put in an animal formula) do generally owe something to Reich. In the letter to Kessler, Bellow acknowledges as much: "All the while I was writing of Dahfu I had the ghost of Rosenfeld near at hand, my initiator into the Reichian mysteries." Isaac Rosenfeld introduced Bellow to *The Function of the Orgasm* in 1951, and, Bellow tells us, "for a time I took Reich very seriously." Some of Dahfu's "supreme confidence" reflects Rosenfeld but not Bellow. It is usual for Bellow to see the limitations of utopian solutions; moreover, the differences in outlook and temperament between Bellow and Reich are too vast for these limitations not to have soon manifested themselves. In answer to Kessler's question equating the critical reception of the novel with enemies of spontaneity or the life principle, Bellow writes, "I never for a single moment announced myself as the champion of the life force. Thank you, no. That would be paranoia, right then and there."[17] It was, of course, Reich's paranoia.

Influences, influences, influences; but the work has to be imagined, the inspiration has to come. The scene in the lion's den can properly be said to be inspired. It is at once a celebration and reductio ad absurdum of Romantic iconography, Henderson absorbing the vital spark from noble nature. This nobility is not seen as benign but, in a Blakean way, as energy incarnate. With her eyes of wrath that make Henderson's crotch shrivel, Atti may be considered Bellow's ultimate femme fatale, an updated fantasy figure of the Romantic agony, an indication that the world may be a mind which is not made up. Bellow is not one to leave nature to its own devices. When the chips are down, Henderson falls into Judeo-Christian moral abstraction. Henderson tried to play the lion but is overpowered by the lamb. Henderson helplessly acknowledges Blake's guardian of Innocence, as "God," "Help," "Lord have mercy," "Au secours," emerging as "Hooolp!," "Moo-oorcy!," "Secoooooooor!," come from the depths. De profundis (De Profooo-oondis) is the name for this experience, with music by Handel. Henderson is too much the Wasp, too heavy with a moral sense, to give headlong allegiance to nature. The man of sorrows, despised and rejected, follows him like a doppelgänger (though not in the earliest versions); also following (elsewhere in the book), also from *Messiah*, is the certitude of final moral judgment—"who shall abide the day of His coming!" (*HRK*, p. 84). Henderson is an unlikely believer. Yet when he says, "I believe in Lazarus, I believe in the awakening of the dead. I am sure for some, at least, there is a resurrection" (*HRK*, p. 140), he is not being metaphorical. And "the fighting Lazarus" is probably the Dahfu category that fits him best. The mystical tendency conspicuous in *Humboldt's Gift*, a novel to which *Henderson the Rain King* has been considered an antithesis, is already present in Henderson, who freely admits to being "highly mediumistic" (*HRK*, p. 210). Many of Bellow's characters acknowledge a religious impulse. In the very lion's den of Romantic vitalism, the voice of God is beseeched.

Henderson's Protestantism has an Old Testament, or Jewish, cast. When, besieged with his Sevcik exercises, Henderson cries, "Oh, thou God and judge of life and death," he illustrates familiarity with the Jewish prayer book. True, Henderson is given a certain Wasp distance from Jewishness; witness his satisfaction at staying in hotels which accept no Jews, in his raising pigs in some kind of perverse reaction to Nicki Goldstein (*HRK*, p.

20), in his response to a sunrise (in B.6.11, 58)—"as I am not a Jew, beauty is my Jerusalem." But the voice of Jacob speaks through the hands of Esau. "Mercy . . . justice . . . truth. . . . Thy will be done! Not my will, but Thy will!" (*HRK*, p. 199), cries a rather Hebraic Henderson after he is baptized, Wariri-style, in the mud. Again the moral abstractions, the transcendental dependence, the Blakean Innocence. Henderson is just too old-fashioned to be entirely taken by promises of cure through psychoanalysis: "You get such queer diseases. . . . Who wants? Who needs it? These things occupy the place where a man's soul should be" (*HRK*, p. 83). Psychoanalysis may give us health, but it does not give us this older biblical, moral, Judeo-Christian "soul." Through his drama of character Bellow tries to affirm the reality of this traditional concept. Henderson's lions, it turns out, are not so much avatars of the energy-principle as reminders of traditional virtue. Atti may not be a lion of Judah but she revives in Henderson the command to be noble. Henderson's story is a Jewish plot. Does it surprise the reader that his first manuscript encounter with the crotch-sniffing Atti has Henderson reacting so: "A loud voice within me was sobbing violently—oyoyoy! oy! oy!" (B.5.8). Like Augie and the eagle. What price nobility? (In various places "oy" is changed to, say, "Alas," [*HRK*, p. 182]). Too, a metropolitan Jewish idiom asserts itself from time to time in Henderson's speech, as in his comment to Dahfu regarding the seach for Gmilo: "to think that you are going to be reunited with a dear parent. I only wish such a thing could happen to me" (*HRK*, p. 289). The unabashed filial piety expressed here, and generally, by Henderson is perhaps more characteristically Jewish than Wasp. When Dahfu is killed, Henderson's reaction is, finally, quietistic and traditional, rather than violent and Romantic. In another one of those scenes where a Bellow character has murder in his heart only to have this impulse subdued by more civilized ones, Henderson wants, momentarily, revenge on the Bunam's man: "I'll break his bones. . . . All right I won't break his bones I'll beat him. But I didn't beat him either" (*HRK*, p. 324). Henderson, it seems, learns to keep the blow.

This residue of religious tradition is more a matter of the heart's affections than of orthodoxy, but there is an overlap. Henderson, like other Bellow protagonists, is given to occasional praying. The impulse may be archaic but the prayer at hand is very twentieth-century: "Preserve me from unreal things" (*HRK*, p. 253), pleads Henderson.

The denial of moral imperatives is part of this unreality, part of the spirit's sleep. The irony of the lion sequence is that it, finally, contributes to the creation of unreality. "What," says Henderson, "could an animal do for me? In the last analysis? Really? A beast of prey" (*HRK*, p. 288). And when Dahfu confronts the new lion, Henderson sees in its face "the darkness of murder" (*HRK*, p. 307), the truly inhuman; he thinks, ironically, "that this was all

mankind needed, to be conditioned into the image of a ferocious animal."
Feeling the lion's blast like a blow ("Truth! Blows!" [B.7.4, 445]), he repudiates having given himself over so completely to adventure. It is, after all,
heresy, or at least nonsense, to attribute humanity to a beast. We see here
the usual Bellow movement toward utopian regeneration and the consequent backing off, with much humor along the way. To be sure, Henderson
does learn a posture of nobility, but from Dahfu more than the lion (albeit
from Dahfu through the lion); to this one must add, that even his admiration
of Dahfu is qualified. Dahfu is moving, great but, finally, another dubious
messiah. More clearly than in any other Bellow novel, the conception is
comic. Henderson is a metaphysical fool, full of egotistical bluster, whose
peregrinations, however, do not come to nothing. Though he postures and
even believes in the reality of his posturing (he will be through with his
internship at sixty-three), even this trait is winning in that it describes an
energy that is a welcome alternative to staying in bed. That, it should be
recalled, was the alternative for Henderson.[18] This insight is even more
comic in manuscript where Henderson is a reader of *Oblomov*, "whose hero
didn't know what to do with himself either." Goncharov's weary aristocrat
did not make it out of bed until somewhere in the middle of the book.
Henderson has the Oblomovist's response to *Oblomov:* " I never finished
reading it" (B.5.6). He does move in his own life, however, and, being
virtuous, is rewarded. Part energy, part morality, Henderson's virtue harks
back to a time when these did not exclude each other. Like his Victorian
ancestors, Henderson has defined himself through an ordeal, through a kind
of *bildung*, and has thereby imposed a last-minute asymmetrical shape on an
otherwise amorphous life. He emerges as an improbable embodiment of
Blakean naturalistic balance, "Listen, you guys" Henderson cries out, "my
great excess was I wanted to live" (*HRK*, p. 196); for Henderson, as for
Blake, the road of excess leads to the palace of wisdom, or at least the palace
of Dahfu, daffy wisdom.

Henderson's reward takes two forms. First, Dahfu, Atti, and the "grun-tu-
molani" crack his shell of self-absorption. *I want* then brings on *"she* wants,
he wants, *they* want" (*HRK*, p. 286), in a realization not present in the early
pre-therapeutic versions (added in B.7.3). His final posture of hard-won
calm and harder-won forgiveness (e.g., with Edward and Maria Felucca) is
another manifestation of the post-therapeutic Henderson. He relates to Lily
with a tenderness that comes with reappraisal. The most intricate revision of
the final chapters appears in Henderson's letter to Lily. Critical remarks
about Lily and her snobbish mother are deleted, Henderson's buffoonery at
Charlie's wedding is more complete, an attack on Frances and her Dr. Jung
is dropped, and there is generally more self-criticism. The use of lengthy

italicized passages as a structural device is a late inclusion. It establishes a counterpoint between two voices, one to Lily, the other to the reader, the first largely lyrical and tender, while giving a retrospective view of the narrative, the second alternating between comic and solemn psychological analysis of that striving, restless self. It is this letter which issues into the I-she, he-they harmonies that end the chapter. Is this sense of agreement willed? Is the "love" dramatized? Must it be, further than it is? Given the nature of philosophical romance, personal relationship may be safely subsumed under the category of transcendent subjectivity.

The ending of the book, then, is not a case of Bellow writing himself out of dramatic difficulties but a stroke of boisterous lyricism that is part of the fabric of this essentially lyrical creation. The last section of the book (chapters twenty to twenty-two)—Mailer's last fifty pages—is the one for which there is the least manuscript material. Some of it is the anticlimax of Dahfu's death; some of it is pretty much mechanical winding up (all of chapter twenty-one, for example, which is not in even fairly late versions [B.8.4]). After a false start about three old loonies of a wrecking crew who are manipulated by an operator, and another consisting of a recollection of a gimmicky amusement park job Henderson once held, the right note is reached. Neither the lion nor the pig will quite do for Henderson, but the domesticated bear—"this poor broken ruined creature and I" (*HRK*, p. 338)—seems just about right. "We're two of a kind. Smolak was cast off and I am an Ishmael too" (*HRK*, p. 338), says Henderson. Convincing, up to a point. Henderson is, after all, an Ishmael come home. The lyric flight of the end is a rhetorical triumph, if somewhat put on. Henderson has already acknowledged a deep skepticism about the impact of animal nature on man. So Henderson's being influenced by a bear is a qualified knowledge, and it is presented as such: "So if corporal things are an image of the spiritual and visible objects are renderings of invisible ones, and if Smolak and I were outcasts together, two humorists before the crowd, but brothers in our soul—I enbeared by him, and he probably humanized by me—I didn't come to the pigs as a tabula rasa." Some mysterious influence is at work, but pigs, as they say, is pigs. As we have seen, Henderson moves upward working out that particular beast, which turns out in the end to be *trafe*. The bear tableau succeeds better as retrospective sentiment than as present drama. As for Henderson's final assertion of love, there is a middle-aged, mellow quality to it that may convince because it does not demand too much. Africa has awakened Henderson, so the possibility of love seems natural enough. In a sense, it has washed him clean, renewed him, given him that second, higher innocence through experience, so that the concluding image of man and child appropriately complements, as it supersedes, that of man and bear. That child, that whiteness, that turning of circles, all bespeak an inner harmony that the soul-searching Henderson has won, and that he will certainly need in medical school. After all, he has cast off his violin. With his final skepticism about art and utopian solutions, and with his longing to be "good" in some obvious sense, Henderson is the goofiest of all possible citizen heroes.[19]

Chapter 6

Herzog

Despite the critical acclaim generally accorded *Herzog*, it is seen by some critics to be a deeply flawed book.[1] Complaints usually focus on structure or plot. Tony Tanner notes that the novel, like Herzog's life, "is mismanaged and patternless."[2] And Alfred Kazin shares the not uncommon perception that "Bellow is not a very dramatic novelist." *Herzog* is an example of how "unexpected actions tend to be dragged into his novels—like Herzog's half-hearted attempt to kill his wife's lover—as a way of interrupting the hero's reflections."[3] Kazin is right in focusing on this scene, wrong about its being dragged in. The scene is important, as Forrest Read and Keith Opdahl have noticed. I have argued that it is the central scene, having a clear, pivotal connection to Herzog's ideas and emotions, and that the ideas and the action are related, do form a dramatic pattern. There is a sense of fable, though it is not dramatic necessity conventionally conceived.

The revisions show that the novel is much more selective than is usually believed. I have focused on four kinds of selection: (1) the reworking of the much reworked earlier parts of the novel toward the dual end of dramatizing a severe psychological tension with an evolving, positive ideational counterbalance; (2) the differences between a lengthy fragment, a sort of *Ur-Herzog* called "Memoirs of a Bootlegger's Son," and the Napoleon Street section of the novel; (3) the changes in relationship, tone, emphasis, and conception of key characters; and (4) preparations for the central scene and its aftermath. A critical study of the novel based on the revisions serves to dispel the view that between the beginning and the end nothing happens.

That *Herzog* is one of Bellow's most rewritten novels may not by itself dismiss the charge of formlessness, but it does undermine that point of view. Moreover, the patterning of the novel can be seen clearly in the rewriting even by those who do not at first see it in the novel itself. The clear evolution of the manuscripts suggests that Bellow saw more and more clearly the figure in the marble block.

The manuscripts appear to be even more complete and are even more massive than those of *Henderson*, running nearly 6,000 pages, some of them duplicative. Many parts of the novel are rewritten many times. There are twenty-seven notebooks (nearly 1,200 pages, B.16.1 to B.18.4), half of them early. Also there are some holograph fragments (about 50 pages, B.18.5–9). Long portions of the novel come in the first section of typewritten drafts (over 1,000 pages, B.18.10 to B.19.2), half of these early.

Of special interest is the section labeled "Miscellaneous Typewritten Pages" (nearly 2,000 pages, B.19.3 to B.22.2), which contains short sections of the text. These manuscripts are arranged according to particular sequences of the book. Under "Opening pages of *Herzog*, and Herzog riding to Martha's Vineyard," there are no less than thirty-three entries (393 pages, B.19.3–35), though several of these are carbons. Under "Ramona" there are thirty-five entries (406 pages, B.20.35 to B.21.24), again some of these carbon. Under "Herzog's day in court and his return to Chicago" there are fifteen entries (219 pages, B.21.25–39), some carbon. The "Letters to Dr. Edvig" section alone comprise nine entries (156 pages, B.19.36–44), some carbon. Many of the pages in this entire section contain holograph corrections. What follows is three final drafts (two are copies) with holograph corrections, the first (B.22.3–6) the author's revised copy. Finally come the galley proofs (346 pages, B.23.4–9), with Bellow's last-minute corrections (B.23.4) and galleys with typed-page inserts (B.23.5).

i

Herzog is a triumph of tone, and had to be. When an oblique plot is complicated by an intricate consciousness, when, indeed, plot in the broadest sense involves the uncomplication of that consciousness, narrative voice(s) must give the illusion of absolute pitch. I say illusion because, perfect as the voice appears in the narrative, this was an illusion which had to be achieved. No book of Bellow's came harder than *Herzog;* none gives us more insight into the process of artistic metamorphosis. *Herzog* illustrates how after an author discovers the inner truth of character, the smooth surface may follow. That anxious, fulminating, yet jaunty and even comic beginning, already part of general literary consciousness, seems inevitable, but it was not always that way.

The book deals with purportedly autobiographical material, yet the sense of original crisis had to be recaptured. The earliest draft of *Herzog* begins with a scene which would be unthinkable in the novel. We are introduced to a Dr. Amram Herzog, Professor of Physics, who, familiarly enough, "for the last few days . . . had fallen under a spell, which he did not resist, and was writing letters to everyone under the sun" (B.16.1). We are told that "most of these letters couldn't be sent, but that didn't seem to matter, he wrote them anyway." We cannot imagine the final Herzog mailing letters. And if the tone seems all too casual in comparison with the novel, the dramatic context is even more casual. Professor Herzog, slightly potted, goes for a midnight swim with an equally drunk Miss Thurnwald. Both are soon naked. She swims, Herzog "rolled in the shallows." Lost and confused, Herzog can find neither his clothes nor Miss Thurnwald: "Suppose they had his trousers hanging from the mantelpiece in the living-room and were waiting for nude Herzog to enter? Or suppose even they had found the letters in his pocket and were reading them aloud?" Clearly, Herzog's letters in the final version are not in the same realm as bedroom (or living-room) farce—or not this kind of bedroom farce. They return to the house, she naked from the waist up, everyone there thinking Herzog guilty. In this dramatically awkward circumstance, the recognizable Herzog emerges: "The Professor was not thinking about her at all. He was absorbed in a deeper passion than any Miss Thurnwald, with her green eye shadow and her wagging breasts, could arouse in him. He was writing letters by the score" (B.16.1). In another version Herzog is rather more chivalrous: "It was up to him to spare her the bestiality of a drunken lay" (B.18.11, 72). Miss Thurnwald herself is, variously, someone who used to sing at the Village Vanguard (B.18.5), or who complains about the job competition with young, rich Cliffies (B.18.12). Meanwhile Herzog thinks of his letters. The two strands are incongruous.

There is additional artistically aimless detail. We are informed that this houseguest never went anywhere without a kosher salami, stuck as he has too often been with stingy hearts; and that he loved his breakfast (together with an elaborate description of same). This visit to the Treshansky summer place (the Vane house in *Herzog*) is altogether too relaxed. We see Herzog and Treshansky, a biochemist turned business man, play four-handed Haydn and Schubert. When we are told that Herzog is going back to Chelsea, not as the Treshanskys believe because of Miss Thurnwald but because he wants to be alone to write the letters which bring him out of his depression, we ask, what depression? Though Bellow has the later tone in mind, it is not here adequately dramatized. The building up of an inner tension is here mandated, and this the revisions work toward.

Significantly, the scientist—although "too mixed, too irregular to be a true scientist" (B.16.1)—becomes an intellectual in the later versions;[4] the relative detachment of the early versions gives over to a more appropriately passionate, self-ironic tonality. Our scientist tells us, "If I'm out of my mind it's all right with me." The narrator adds, "But he knew that he was all right and that he was not out of his mind" (B.16.1). The novel does not give such immediate balance and assurance.

One version gives us the trip to Libby's in a plethora of realistic detail. There is no mental turmoil; the meditation about the post-Cartesian Void and politics in the Aristotelian sense (*H*, pp. 92–94) is virtually non-existent (B.18.5). Other versions give us other uncertainties. In one we are given an elaborate description of Libby in her "ripeness" (B.18.18). This is mostly dropped in *Herzog*, where the first signs of old age are emphasized. There is some confusion as to what significance to give Libby. In the novel she is a good friend whom Herzog has helped to defuse her marital difficulties, partly, it is suggested, because she was sensual and attracted to Herzog. The early version puts things rather more explicitly. Herzog somewhat randomly feels that he should have married Libby and "he would, if anything happened to [her husband] Sissler, ask her to be his wife" (B.18.11). When, in the novel, Herzog imagines Sissler dead, he notes cryptically, "*Ideas that depopulate the world*" (*H*, p. 95). It is less cryptic when one considers the manuscript. But this involvement with Libby is scarcely felt even in the manuscript, and the visit is consistently relaxed. In the novel, by contrast, it is not until considerable dramatization of enervated consciousness that he takes the trip to his friends. The visit itself is tense and abrupt, an anticlimax to the inner movement. In his enlarged psychological present, Herzog hasn't got an hour for Libby, let alone a lifetime.

There is a similar tightening in the back to Chelsea section. Much detail for its own sake is cast aside: the window boxes, the Puerto Rican groceries, the super's wife, the undertaker's chauffeur, the lady with two chihuahuas. Nor do we need the smell of dishrag and bugspray in the apartment (B.18.11). And we certainly do not need Herzog aroused by the "thin, sad" cash register girl. Nor do we need a view of the Professor licking his green-stamps (B.18.17, 33b). The reworking of the novel is from a more or less straightforward realism to a tense, subjective lyricism. Here, as in *Henderson*, the establishment of an intimate personal voice had to be dug for, like an oilstrike. Indeed, Chelsea is scarcely mentioned in the novel. Instead we have intensification of the psychological wound. Herzog comes home to a homeopathic cure. Inuring himself to the catastrophe, he rereads Geraldine Portnoy's letter as his heart smolders about Mady and Val. This repetition helps bring a sane balance.

The placing of the letter is itself a stroke worth noticing. Even late manuscripts (e.g. B.22.1) place the letter after the courtroom scene and just before his trip to Chicago. The trials, however, seem to be enough of a blow to get Herzog to fly to save his daughter. The Portnoy letter—with Junie locked in the car by Val as he and Mady argue—would be only an unneeded addition to the already intense vapors. Cast in the earlier part of the book (in B.22.4, 111a), it is quite sufficient to maintain that edge of constant tension, that strain hovering near the bursting point, so necessary to the beginning chapters as they finally appear. The tension is brought to a fine head indeed by the style of the letter and Herzog's reception of it (added in B.22.1, when the letter was moved) and by the contrasts between his personality and its impersonality, heartbreak and university jargon, disintegration and preternatural calm. Geraldine Portnoy's diction— "significant encounter," "pregnant experiences," "tends to be authoritarian," "basically," "actually"—does not succeed in smothering Herzog's resentment in cotton batting. Some minor changes—the last line, for example, from "I don't think Madeleine is actually a bad mother" to "I don't think Madeleine is a bad mother actually"—do her genteel fairness and confidence to a maddening fare-thee-well.

One of the devices used to establish the dissonant, fragmentary rhythm of the dramatized consciousness in the novel is the recasting of epigram. Anxiety about his carelessness and passivity may direct Herzog's subversions: "Waste not the road to hell a watched pot a fool and his money. The meek shall inherit the hearse" (B.20.20, 92). The novel generally presents this wit with more point and more art, giving us a sort of fortune cookie for neurotics or people in trouble. Herzog notes that this game is akin to free association and that "a psychiatrist might have made something of them" (B.16.1). Or perhaps a novelist. One early version has Herzog returning to Chelsea and finding notes on a piece of paper in a drawer: "*Marry in haste, lie down with dogs. An old pot gathers remorse.*" These nuggets of womanly bitterness "were written in a feminine progressive-school (printed and written) hand." Herzog "picks up the game" in masculine counter-anguish: "*A bitch in time breeds contempt. . . . Hitch your agony to a star*" (B.16.4). The sexual distinctions dissolve in the novel, and the game becomes more elaborate. We do not need the clap scare Herzog has in the early version to sustain the blend of comic agony. That would be, again, too broad, too low for the dignified disintegration of the final comedy. More appropriately, Herzog makes ironic use of even biblical authority to unscramble himself. "*Answer a fool according to his folly lest he be wise in his own conceit. Answer not a fool according to his folly, lest thou be likened unto him. Choose one*" (*H*, p. 3), adds the professorial Herzog. Apparently random, these epigrams intimately relate to the movement and tone of the book. *Herzog* moves from an attitude of severe judgment, even revenge, to a tolerance, an acceptance based on an integration of cultural and personal attitudes. *Choose one* suggests the difficulty of the choice which is ultimately made in favor of the latter. "*Death—die—live again—die again—live*" (*H*, p. 3), while having nothing comic about it, is another apparent fragment which actually describes the movement of the book, a movement from death to life, resolving, as it were, the irresolution of the wasteland pattern. *"Grief, Sir, is a species of idleness,"* thinks Herzog (*H*, p. 3), attempting quick Johnsonian dismissal of the postmodernistic gloom. Yet the haze does not lift easily and seems strangely hallowed in the aura it emits.

A number of small verbal changes and minor dramatic developments add to the opening oppressiveness. For example, Herzog's "overstrained nerves" are not as tense as the later "overstrained galloping nerves" (B.23.4, 10a; *H*, p. 27), nor is "the train" as good in this context as "the confining train" (B.23.6, 10a; *H*, p. 27). His clothing purchase is, in later versions, complicated by a near blowup with the salesman (B.22.3; *H*, p. 21) and, on the subway platform at Grand Central Station he sees, in later versions (not in B.18.18 or B.19.14), the "soft face and independent look" of a woman whose eyes "were bitch eyes, that was certain. . . . They expressed a sort of female arrogance which had an immediate sexual power over him" (*H*, p. 34). Here again is one of many instances contributing to an overriding tone. When Herzog writes to Smithers about an idea for a new course, he says that *"people are dying—it is no metaphor—for lack of something real to carry home when day is done. See how willing they are to accept the wildest nonsense"* (*H*, p. 28). The grimness of the cultural description is consonant with the accounting of Herzog's personal condition.

Herzog's first described encounter with the outside world, the visit to Zelda in March, reflects the same tendency. A middle version has Herzog filing an epistolary complaint about the usual slander: *"You shouldn't have repeated to Juliana* [Mady] *what I said about her. And you shouldn't have told me what she was saying. . . . Thanks to her my reputation in Chicago is near absolute zero. That I'm a wild beast, that I'm an idiot, impotent, insane. What can I say? What can I prove? Shall I carry affidavits from women?"* (B.18.8, 38). Things are tense here, but there is some sense of comic recovery. The more piercing version of the letter to Zelda is a later inclusion (not in B.18.18):

> As long as I was Mady's good friend, I was a delightful person. Suddenly, because Madeleine decided that she wanted out—suddenly, I was a mad dog. The police were warned about me and there was talk of committing me to an institution. I know that my friend and Mady's lawyer, Sander Himmelstein, called Dr. Edvig to ask whether I was crazy enough to be put in Manteno or Elgin." (*H*, p. 35)

This is not a reaction to the usual slander but to the threat of enforced incarceration. Hysteria takes the place of the earlier semblance of balance. And Zelda is not merely a witness but an accomplice, who helped her niece by having her husband take Herzog to the hockey game. Herzog's contempt for Zelda extends to a kind of physical disgust. Her dyed hair and purplish lids made Herzog groan. Moreover, there is a cultural disgust. To Zelda's I'm-not-just-another-suburban-hausfrau appearance, Herzog responds, "Your kitchen is different. . . . Your cerebral palsy cannisters are different" (*H*, p. 38). Betrayed, Herzog reflects that Zelda had the advantage of lying out of feeling. The train at this point takes Herzog through a particularly depressing stretch, "Spanish Harlem, heavy, dark, and hot, and Queens far off to the right, a thick document of brick, veiled in atmospheric dirt" (*H*, p. 41)—short vowels, hard consonants and monosyllables doing their special work. In this darkness, Herzog rises to a brilliant bitterness: "*Will never understand what women want. What do they want? They eat green salad and drink human blood*" (*H*, p. 41f.).

The placement of this paraphrased Freudian epigram about the nature of woman shows us something about the nature of the composition. In an early version we see Herzog imagining himself lecturing to students. He says in a Memo to Whittaker, "Listen, my dear boys, they are not all the same of course, but they are considered weak and have the ethics of the weak." Herzog reflects on "the tendency of the social order to protect the weak. Their occasion for strength comes and then—watch out. [Wilhelm had a similar insight.] Their ambling, their lisping. In the restaurant they order green salad, but how often at home they drink human blood. . . . As usual he recoiled from his own excesses. Kindness he had known from women came rapidly to his mind" (B.16.1). A necessary addition, this last turn, but tenderness is not what is dramatically wanted. To be sure, the novel in the long view does make just this meliorative point—makes it again and again—but good will does not possess him at this stage of his tale.

In the much recast first chapters the most important device to emerge in revision is the letters, though they do not appear in this part of the novel first. Even in a fairly late draft (B.19.43) there is nothing of the well-known letter to Dr. Edvig. Almost everything is in dialogue. The new device helps to establish the effect of intense subjectivity, a counter-point to the retrospective objectivity he tries to maintain. So, the relative calm of an earlier version of an Edvig session is broken by, "*you turn out to be a crook too! . . . I was near the point of breakdown*" (*H*, p. 53). And the letter's cultural argument, the defense of charity, for example, against psychoanalytic and Calvinist reductiveness, is a dramatic ordering of hitherto not quite dramatized insights. In all, the scalding, accusatory tone, so appropriate to the essential grimness of the opening, is heightened by epistolary elaboration. The second and third chapters, then, end on a particularly intense psychological note (the Edvig letter, the Portnoy letter and Herzog's reaction to it). The letter to Edvig soars into an empyrean of staccato hysteria: "*You knew nothing. You know nothing. She snowed you completely. And you fell in love with her yourself, didn't you? Just as she planned. She wanted you to help her dump me. She would have done it in any case. She found you, however, a useful instrument. As for me, I was your patient"* (*H*, p. 65). It is instructive to compare this rhythmic crescendo to an earlier, flat version of it. Herzog thinks of Edvig on the way to the courtroom (the first placement of these observations!): "I am out Juliana [Mady] is in. She remained your patient. I left town. It bothered me a lot" (B.17.5). As a character Edvig is perfect for the beginning. Not only is he part of the dupery of the divorce, but, as we shall see, he also represents a version of that modernistic outlook that, along with the divorce, is the other major cause of Herzog's gloom. How different is the tonality here from that of the note he writes Edvig after the murder scene: *"Dear Edvig, . . . You gave me good value for my money when you explained that neuroses might be graded by the inability to tolerate ambiguous situations. . . . Allow me modestly to claim that I am much better now at ambiguities"* (*H*, p. 304).

We are here a long way from the accusation that Edvig fell in love with Mady himself. But the first chapters typically call for the exposition of mean motives. Sandor Himmelstein is another instance of the modern reductiveness. Herzog sees that Sandor's underlying assumption is that

> you must sacrifice your poor, squawking, niggardly individuality—which may be nothing anyway (from an analytic viewpoint) but a persistent infantile megalomania, or (from a Marxian point of view) a stinking little bourgeois property—to historical necessity. And to truth. And truth is true only as it brings down more disgrace and dreariness upon human beings, so that if it shows anything except evil it is illusion, and not truth. (*H*, p. 93)

The earliest version of the Himmelstein scene contains none of this retrospective meditation on his significance, no letters, no place in that downer series of flashbacks that propels him to Libby's and back. It is unrelated to the trip to the Vineyard, taking place after, not during, the trip. In a scene between Brown (Herzog) and Raskin (Himmelstein) we are given a good deal of dialogue and much detail for its own sake. We see Raskin's ashtray with shards of cut tobacco, his foot in a neat leather loafer. As part of this kind of detail, Raskin (called Rubenstein a bit later) regales Herzog with divorce stories, such as the one about the widow who was making it with a young Italian sailor while her husband's coffin was below in the ship's hold. This seems to be Mintouchian country. In one version we are told that Rubenstein "doesn't recognize any such thing as adultery" (B.21.9, 247), though Val is sleeping with his wife. Rubenstein's cynicism ought not to be so blatant, however, and Val must be saved for better things. In the novel an abrasive Himmelstein (Rubenstein) acts as if the world assumes what he assumes, as if Herzog has no recourse in justice and is naive to even think of a custody fight. The discussion of custody does take place even in the earliest version of the scene between them, yet much of the vividness in the dialogue (e.g., the description of Mady at Fritzl's), the bristling give and take, comes later. After seeing Raskin, Brown goes home, where he is still with his child and puts in the storm windows. He appears to be a little late. Mady here is called Lola, because, perhaps, as the popular song of the time had it, whatever she wants she gets. Once upon a time, Brown was the little man little Lola wanted. The final version, then, casts the whole Himmelstein incident more clearly into Herzog's dramatized consciousness as part of his homeopathic cure.

The counterbalance, making positive sense of the experience, comes in later versions with some of the most quoted formulations coming last. Herzog's yearning for recovery into citizen heroism is well known: "The occupation of man is in duty, in use, in civility, in politics in the Aristotelian sense" (*H*, p. 94). Nowhere in the earliest version, it appears in a later version as, "Tell me, Herzog, where is life real? Perhaps in use? In common [sic] In duty. In civility and patience" (B.16.10). In a still later version (B.22.4, 106b) we get everything but "in politics in the Aristotelian sense"; finally, very late, we get it all (B.23.4). Many of the idea letters follow a similar pattern of development. In their combativeness and insight they show us that Herzog is still very much alive and that intellect has its own emotional weight and can be instrumental in dispelling personal gloom.

The letter to Shapiro is a case in point. A somewhat affected intellectual, Shapiro serves to elicit Herzog's contempt for culture without direction, mind without heart, a contempt which covers Mady by extension. Shapiro, out-Wasping the Wasps, says things like "join issue" and "I should not venture to assay the merit of the tendency without more mature consideration." He exhibits a cohabitation with gentility that Herzog finds ludicrous. If this sequence seems to be too much a matter of settling old scores, we recall that Herzog is described as merely sulking. In any case, he evens the score in the main part of the letter. Though one of the most important letters in the novel, the bulk of it (*H*, pp. 74–77) is a late inclusion (not appearing until B.22.3, 87a, b, c). Here, in other words, we see that Herzog's intellectual formulations, so crucial to the fabric of the book, came rather late. Nor is this letter an exception. The greater part of the major idea-letters are late inclusions, which means that many of the most substantial parts of the book were conceived only after it had taken fairly definitive shape. This is a question of moral rather than aesthetic pattern, a question of a writer making definitive sense of his own experience.

The very earliest versions, then, show no letter material; next come the letters of primarily personal grievance (e.g., Edvig) and, finally, the idea-letters (along with a heightening of the idea element in the straight dramatic parts.) As in *Henderson*, the novel was not so much "found" as created. Herzog's most characteristic accent, his truest beseeching voice, was not at all present in the beginning, was not really present, one could argue, until near the end. What starts out as a novel of revenge—an element that is not dropped but is intensified in the first part of the novel—becomes more and more a novel of redemption. Herzog transcends his personal hurt. In *Herzog*, as elsewhere in Bellow, the inner truth may be mental, yet it is a mental and an emotional truth at once. One's life is indistinguishable from one's perceptions. Bellow excels at dramatizing this integration, and the epistolary form enables him to do so with particular brilliance. It is, in point of polemic, not only the solution to a book, but also to much of a lifetime of literary effort.

The letters are central both to the book and to Bellow's career. The argument against "*the full crisis of dissolution . . . , the filthy moment . . . when moral feeling dies, conscience disintegrates, and respect for liberty, law, public decency, all the rest, collapses in cowardice, decadence, blood*" (*H*, p. 74) is *the* argument in Bellow's arsenal. It is the "axial lines" feeling made cultural, and, therefore, intrinsically dramatic in the thick of the constant polemicism of the present. The cast is familiar: Spengler, Eliot, Pound, Wyndham Lewis, Ortega (the wasteland outlook), Sartre and Heidegger (alienation, inauthenticity, forlornness), Burckhardt, Nietzsche (a merely aesthetic critique of modern history)—the orthodoxy of modernism that often issued into cultural, and even political, fascism. Herzog sees this clearly: "*To have assumed, for instance, that the deterioration of language and its debasement was tantamount to dehumanization led straight to cultural fascism.*" Here, as elsewhere, Herzog rejects the dehumanization of ordinary life. The letter is "positive," a ray of light in the modernist gloom, a prediction of Herzog's recovery. This gloom within the gloom itself contributes to Herzog's psychological tension, but at one point well on into the composition of the novel, Bellow seems to have seen a clear connection between Herzog's life and the cultural predicament, one which resolves itself, as I have maintained, in the "murder" scene. His rejection of the wasteland outlook permits him to endure his enemies while he redeems his soul. His personal recovery goes hand and hand with his cultural assault. The novel takes this shape as it is being written.

The very brief original letter to Shapiro (B.18.17) contains a casual allusion to Herzog's review and moves immediately to Herzog's being impressed with the connection between millenarianism and paranoia. The tone is polite. The nightmare edge is yet to come. Herzog does suffer a sense of loss and mentions Juliana (Mady) to him so that "you'll know how great my loss is." There is none of this friendliness, this gentility, in the final version. Although the traits of paranoia are described, clearly Mady's traits, Herzog harbors little resentment for Shapiro, even though he sounds like "The Decline and Fall of the Roman Empire" (B.18.17, 21). With Shapiro, he "wanted to forgive and be forgiven, not to win."

The novel, of course, despite some contrition about his inadequate review of Shapiro's book, gives us a full scale assault. Many small changes show this. "Shapiro was not good-humored although his face wore a good-humored look," is added later, and "His nose was sharp and angry" even later (not in B.18.11). "Natty but dignified" (B.18.17) becomes "He had a dumpy figure, but wore natty clothes" (*H*, p. 69). Shapiro's tight, conservative necktie on that hot day is an addition, as is "That snarling, wild laugh of his, and the white froth foaming on his lips as he attacked everyone" (*H*, p. 70). The sentences, no longer merely Gibbonesque, are "actually Germanic, and filled with incredible bombast" (*H*, p. 70). "The learned conversation" is elaborated into a comic catalogue of learned reference. Shapiro as *parvenu*, but not really as rich as his apple-peddling father, is added. When Shapiro declines the pickled herring (B.18.17) he says, "No thanks. Delightful. But I have an ulcer." In *Herzog*, Shapiro calls it a "stomach condition" (*H*, p. 73), to which Herzog adds, "He had ulcers. Vanity kept him from saying it; the psychosomatic implications were unflattering." There are comic bits to ease the tension—the weight of Shapiro's study, the fear of a hernia from it, the overweight charges, all late inclusions—but the sequence seems peculiarly unrelieved. It seems that the deracination, not to say phoneyness, which may be involved in the process of high acculturation oppresses him to an extreme. When Herzog says, "Culture—ideas—had taken the place of the Church in Mady's heart (a strange organ that must be!)", he means, presumably,[5] that Mady assumes attitudes as if they were garments, as does Shapiro, as does Val. And if one is wearing culture, one will wear what is fashionable. Consequently, one will carry the wasteland view. Hence, Herzog's attack on Shapiro's attitudinizing in the subsequently developed letter. The letter, then, like everything else considered so far, contributes to the down-to-the-bone agonizing that is at once the truest expression and final dramatic effect of Herzog's first day.

Focusing on the problem of nuclear contamination, the letter to Strawforth is a typical day-one transformation. Combining a grim theme with irrepressible flashes of humor (e.g., Dr. Teller's argument that the new fashion of tight pants, by raising body temperatures, could affect the gonads more than fallout), the somberness is again intensified in the revision to include the use of words like "contamination" and "poisoning," a place like Hiroshima, and a negative prophecy of Tocqueville's, darkly interpreted (all revisions occurring in B.22.3). The Tocqueville inclusion is, to be sure, part of the general intellectual heightening, but Herzog's treatment of it is more than that. To Tocqueville's prediction that democracies would produce less crime, more private vice, Herzog adds that he might have said "*less private crime, more collective crime*," implicating thereby the nuclear philosophy of risk. Without explicitly accusing, Herzog seems overcome by darkness: "*De-Tocqueville considered the impulse toward well-being as one of the strongest impulses of a democratic society. He can't be blamed for underestimating the destructive powers generated by the same impulse*" (*H*, p. 50). An even later inclusion is tonally more emphatic: "While in the parlors of indignation the right-thinking citizen brings his heart to a boil" (B.23.4, 18; *H*, p. 50).

After the doldrums of day one, other letters reflect a similar movement but are somewhat different tonally. The letter to Eisenhower is a case in point. Herzog's early manuscript thoughts about Eisenhower display a certain confidence. "The leader of huge armies, chief of state for eight years, can't be a fool, must have tremendous powers. Must" (B.18.18, 128), notes Herzog longingly. But he also notes that "the mutual estrangement of public and private ends" is not dealt with by the report of the Committee on National Aims. The revision of this letter contains great skepticism as to the corporate executive makeup of this committee and greater skepticism about trying to communicate at all with Eisenhower, a man who "hates long, complicated documents," who would "pay no attention" (*H*, p. 161f.) to Herzog's complex, moralistic approach to civil order.

The letter to Eisenhower moves from the theme of diminution of self-hood in the Gross National Product to the expansion of time that industry has brought to private life. This private life, however, competing with technology and other quantitative measures and threats, is driven into "the inspired condition" to assert the reality of self. The ideational considerations here become too refined and original, and the second, newer half of the letter becomes the letter to Pulver. Thus, a further measure of Herzog's disenchantment is written into the book. Yet the letters in this part of the novel—after day one, before the murder scene—though still embattled, are not personally grim, are less strident tonally, more balanced, more positive intellectually. The letter to Pulver is one of the most important idea letters and this may be why Bellow saw fit, at first, to address it to President Ike. However, it is also one of the most subtle, and such confidence was short-lived.

The letter is in none of the early versions, first appearing in B.20.32. By B.22.2, it is essentially complete, except that the end, where Eisenhower is addressed, is crossed out. Herzog speaks to the vogue of negative transcendence, which includes, without his naming it, the new authority of the Marquis de Sade, as in Mailer's appropriation of Romantic criminality in such works as "The White Negro" and *An American Dream*, in which last there is a modern misuse of Dostoevsky. We have seen that a central thrust of Bellow's fiction is against "*'philosophical,' 'gratuitous' crime and similar paths of horror*" (*H*, p. 164). As he adds (B.22.4, 191b) in a final tightening, "*It never seems to occur to such 'criminals' that to behave with decency to another human being might also be 'gratuitous.'* " Such crime is the dead-end Romantic reaction to the threat of a quantified universe, a threat which Herzog feels as well; but he prefers to see himself as an instance of this "age of special comedy" (*H*, p. 163), in which moral insight turns ironically in on itself. "*Good is easily done by machines of production and transportation. Can virtue compete*" (*H*, p. 164)? It can and it cannot, but we need not agree with Hofmannsthal that a word like virtue can no longer be used. For Herzog, virtue exists. So does reason. He notes that in an age in which annihilation is no longer a metaphor, "*Good and Evil are real. The inspired condition is no longer a visionary matter. It is not reserved for gods, kings, poets, priests, shrines, but belongs to mankind and all of existence*" (*H*, p. 165). To the Hulmian contempt for the present ("*We have fashioned a new utopian history, an idyll, comparing the present to an imaginary past, because we hate the world as it is*"), Herzog posits a vaguely Bergsonian "*evolutionary self-development . . . the discovery of qualities*" (*H*, p. 163f.), which would transcend the special comedy. And in a very late revision (B.23.4, 61), he speaks as optimistically as an essentialist can: "*I am certain that there are human qualities still to be discovered*" (*H*, p. 164). The Pulver letter is no lark, but it has a balanced, upbeat content and is not modified by personal bitterness. Herzog has been recalled to stability. This is attributable to Herzog's homeopathic, epistolary cure. It is attributable also to the consolation of Ramona. It is attributable as well to the recollection of his early family life, one of the more memorable sequences in the novel, to the composition of which we now turn.

ii

The Napoleon Street section is a beautifully modulated narrative voyage along the axial lines. Half-sentiment, half trauma, it is a late Romantic recapturing of a spot of time, an anti-modernist illustration of the fact that filial reverie and authenticity need not be mutually exclusive. Bellow shields us from sentimentality by the immediate dramatic surroundings. Mady's introduction to "your sad old story" is exclamatory if, perhaps, elliptical: "Oh, what balls!" Herzog ironically notes (for the second time), "from a favorite source," Blake's "The Marriage of Heaven and Hell," that "*Opposition is true friendship. His house, his child, yea, all that a man hath will he give for wisdom.*" It appears that he has found a friend. Herzog has given up most of Blake's things but not exactly in the sense the poet intended. Still, he has learned wisdom.

Why are we confronted with Romantic theory (in the letter to Dr. Moss-bach) and Romantic character (in the person of Nachman) as a prelude to the Napoleon Street sequence? The Mossbach letter is one which praises Hulme for his attack "*on the introduction by the Romantics of Perfection into human things*"; it sympthathized with his being repulsed by "*the swarming of Romantic feelings*" (*H*, p. 129), while it chastises him for his repressiveness and excoriates his followers for their conservatism and sterility. This ambivalence prepares the way for the appearance of Nachman, an old Napoleon Street friend, a nineteenth-century type in twentieth-century surroundings.

True, Nachman is up against it. The outline of his love affair would do for an opera plot: starving poet in Europe, rich in-laws in America, wife snatched by in-laws. Act I, Paris. Act II, Scarsdale. Act III, Insane Asylum. True, there is a difference between Fountainbleu and the Fountainblue. Yet what Herzog sees in Nachman (or, early, Hillel) is a clichéd poet living a clichéd *vie de Bohème;* or, as Herzog puts it in an earlier and less charitable version, "the artist's life copied out of Jean Christophe, Van Gogh's letters, Starkie's Rimbaud and Rilke's correspondence" (B.18.17, 60 f.). His works are then described as "Jewish American versions of English translations of German Expressionist poems" (B.18.17, 65). In the novel Herzog must say, "*Honestly, I thought you'd be better off in America*" (*H*, p. 130).

The myth of Bohemia, with all virtue resident in art, the myth of the Philistine, with no virtue resident in ordinary life, is a region of mind almost as claustral as Philistia itself. Does living in Paris make you holy? Does living in America make you sinful? Nachman is a Rimbaud *manqué*, forgetting that Rimbaud was, too. Predictably, Nachman's suicidal wife, Laura, in the asylum, wishes to speak of French literature. We are told that Moses "had to agree with what he understood nothing of—the shape of Valéry's images" (*H*, p. 132).[6] In his francophiliated way, Nachman understands nothing more clearly than *épater le bourgeois*. No political idealogue, Nachman proclaims that he is "no Marxist. . . . I keep my heart with William Blake and Rilke" (*H*, p. 133). Blake is added in B.18.17, an indication of Herzog's ambivalence toward Nachman. Blake is Herzog's favorite poet, and Nachman's indict-ment of the "fat gods" is an indictment Bellow himself makes in some of his work, using that exact phrase in his memorial tribute to Isaac Rosenfeld. He thinks feelingly of Nachman and seems to appreciate his characterization of Herzog as "a good heart, a gentle spirit" (*H*, p. 134). Yet "crazy lecturing Nachman" sees nothing remaining in life but a wasteland and his own refusal to touch it. To this Herzog can only counter in sympathetic disagreement. "It isn't as bad as you make out, Nachman. . . . Most people are unpoetical, and you consider this a betrayal" (*H*, p. 134). For Herzog, Nachman is more a part of the modern disease than the cure.

Nachman serves as the free associative entry into Napoleon Street, which incarnates the depth of ordinary life he does not feel. Nachman and Napoleon Street go together in the drafts in that they together embody Bellow's ambivalence toward Romanticism. He rejects the artist-hero saga, particularly in its more extreme modernist manifestations, while holding to the depth of response of ordinary people in ordinary situations, rejects the aristocratic strain or at least subjects it to severe scrutiny and affirms the democratic one. He shows that the ordinary is extraordinary. The letter to Mossbach is a later addition to this sequence and a clear ideational analogy. Nachman, too, introduces Perfection into human things, but the subjective standard of the Romantics remains very much alive—je sens mon coeur et je connais les hommes. The words of Rousseau bear on the intimate feeling of this episode. Our particular prince of the heart—the word Herzog plays with both meanings—knows that there is a mysterious sanctity to the ties that bind. Like the Wordsworthian girl who insists that "we are seven," Herzog affirms his own subjectivity through an intuition of the primacy of family ties. These, in way of wonder, transcend any abstraction. They are the essence of the *amor fati*, Jewish style.

While the modulation from Nachman to the rest of Napoleon Street seems natural, it was in one version apparently not made. After thinking of Daitch (called Ravitch), Nachman's uncle, Herzog cuts it off saying, "There's too much pathos in my memory. . . . One should drive his cart and his plough over the bones of the dead" (B.18.17, 66). The Blakean aphorism is used elsewhere in the novel but not to contain so compelling a flood of memory. In another version the lawyer Simkin-courtroom sequence appears between Nachman and Napoleon Street, but is soon deleted (B.18.18). This would have made little sense as a final version. In this version the Nachman-Napoleon Street sequence is recollected in the boudoir of Ramona as she sleeps. Do these go together? In the novel, more effectively, it is a phone call from Ramona that snaps him out of his tender melancholy.

The Napoleon Street section undergoes an especially interesting transformation in that it was originally a sort of *Ur-Herzog*, a separate piece called "Memoirs of a Bootlegger's Son." Dramatic differences in tone and point of view allow us to see just how "right" the end result is. The Luries live in Montreal in dark St. Dominique Street (also mentioned in *Dangling Man*, p. 85). Young Isaac (or Joshua) Lurie describes himself as "a strange kind. . . . I am of this world and not of it, ancient modern, Old World New World, scientific and mystical," a description which would fit the "archaic" Herzog, as well as Charlie Citrine. Though these polarities, or even these characteristics, are not realized in the early narrative sketches, the observing, sensitive boy of the Napoleon Street section is prefigured.

Bellow's first narrative impulse, usually, is to render things with a rather plain realism, and this work is no exception. We see not only the "blood oranges" that Deutsch (or Daitch, Ravitch) brings home, but also "the tissue paper they were wrapped in" (C.1.8, 3). The apartment is described in some detail. The recollection of St. Petersburg specifies the summer house in Shuvalovo, Finland. Deutsch would take Ike to the Russian bath, and we get a description, to appear enlarged in the more elaborate bath of *Humboldt's Gift*, of the benches, the herring and onion, schnapps, tea, and pinochle. "I was overjoyed when Deutsch brought me here," Ike says. "He would soap my head and rinse and souse me. His kindness to me is a thing to remember. Once he gave me a red hockey stick and another time a little beer bottle souvenir on a chain" (C.1.8, 3). And we get an abundance of family chronicle details.[7] Sister Zelda (Helen) not only has her distinction in piano (as in *Herzog*), but in geometry, geography and history as well. And there are silly, sibling quarrels between them. Isaac plays a scratchy violin and, in one version, has a piety phase, getting up for morning prayers. He is a choirboy, doing "Mi P'nei Chatoulnu" (sic) or "From the Face of Our Sins" (which Himmelstein chants to him in *Herzog*), and a soprano solo of "Selah Lonu." He has a medal in Jewish History. At home there is a picture of Moses holding the tablets (the earliest possible version of Herzog?). The Battle of Verdun and the revolution in Russia are in the news. A harmonica-playing friend does "Tipperary," "Pack Up Your Troubles," and "Moonlight and Roses."

In short, along with the literal detail we get the loving, dispassionate, ruminating "I" of so many nineteenth- and early twentieth-century family chronicles. The events are not perceived by a dramatically realized character whose perception makes them poignant. When Isaac says, "Everybody looks back to his own golden age or his own Garden of Eden. Sometimes I think the golden age is only one's recollection of his youth," the effect is quite different from Herzog's "whom did I ever love as I loved them?" Also, almost everything is stated, spread out on a flat table, as when Isaac thinks of his "youngest brother Bentchka. . . . There was not much philosophy in his makeup. I do not say this in criticism. It is not nearly so important as the fact that we were on earth together" (C.1.8, 2). There is little additional mention of him.

Beginning with Deutsch as an illustration, we can see how in the novel Bellow made something more concentrated and dramatic and at the same time generally less sentimental, more true to the tender anguish of his recollection. In *Herzog*, Deutsch has a spectral tenacity for the protagonist. As an image of aloneness and disintegration could he be a doppelgänger to the fragment of an alienated self in Herzog? In the novel, the avuncular Deutsch is gone. What is needed is not the comforter and friend, the giver of treats, the Russian bath companion, but an image of longing in isolation. It is not relevant that Deutsch "looked like an actor, an athlete, a dancer" (C.1.8,

2). It is relevant that he left his wife and two children in the old country, that he no longer heard from them and was afraid, that he fears their deaths from typhoid, that he sings of his isolation, "*Alein. . . . Elend wie a stein.*" All this is much as it is in *Herzog*. "Was his wife still his wife?", thinks Daitch; but, then, mitigating the pathos of the novel, "He didn't want to see her" (C.1.8, 2). And even further from the intention of the novel, in a later draft of "Memoirs" Daitch admits that he was afraid of his wife now—he'd have to serve her, and he only "used to" love her at that (C.1.11). In *Herzog*, "the project of his life was to send for his family . . . [who] were lost during the Revolution" (*H*, p. 135).

If even any connection between Deutsch and Herzog seems farfetched, in one draft it is a connection made by Herzog himself: "People act as though I had asked them to be my parents. And then I feel like Daitch singing on the stairs, waiting for Papa to come and carry him up. I seem to be making it without the booze. Sometimes I even think that I look a little like Daitch." There is a trace here of Wilhelm's dependency, but it is soon expunged. Mostly, Herzog sees him as a case. The mildly reactive depressive Herzog thinks that Daitch "may have been a manic depressive" (B.20.21, 218). In the novel we see nothing of his manic side. The connection is all but expunged in the novel, where Deutsch is "like a tragic actor from the Yiddish stage, with a straight drunken nose and a bowler hat pressing on the veins of his forehead" (*H*, p. 134). Between "Memoirs" and the novel we have an interesting evolution. Deutsch, in a *Herzog* manuscript, (B.18.18) is described as "a small man but well proportioned, his nose was solemn, straight and beautiful, he had a handsome mouth and straight brows." He wonders about the old country. "Was his wife his wife?" Herzog's self-portraiture gives prominent place to his nasal physiognomy, and he also has cause to suffer about the identity of his wife. But not too much can be made of this. Bellow himself drops the suggestion.

The greater connection is obviously with his own father, a nostalgic connection that goes far beyond nostalgia. No need for unconscious meanings here. The somber lyricism describing Jonah Herzog is the only instance in the Napoleon Street section of an increase in detailed description for its own sake. It sometimes seems that the description has the same fascination for things that we found in *Augie March:*

He did everything quickly, neatly, with skillful Eastern European flourishes: combing his hair, buttoning his shirt, stropping his bone-handled razors, sharpening pencils on the ball of his thumb, holding a loaf of bread to his breast and slicing toward himself, tying parcels with tight little knots, jotting like an artist in his account book. There each cancelled page was covered with a carefully drawn X.

But then we get writing which in the range of its expressiveness would not appear in *Augie March:* "The 1s and 7s carried bars and streamers. They were like pennants in the wind of failure" (*H*, p. 137). Nor would we get the elegaic tone of "his one-man Jewish march," or the repetition of the somber lyricism of "no English, no friends, no influence, no trade, no assets but his still—no help in all the world" (*H*, p. 138). This note of somber elegy reaches its corresponding apogee in Mother Herzog's remark, "I have no servants. I am the servant. *Die dienst bin ich*" (*H*, p. 142).

The elegaic tone, constant in *Herzog*, was at best fragmentary in "Memoirs." The ambivalence there is more often confusion. When the Luries are down on their luck, the young man tells his father reassuringly, "Depend on me"; however, "he looked at me in disbelief" (C.1.11). Soon the young man wonders, "There is no logic in this and yet the fact is common. You are derived from another man, and he is incarnate in you, and you hate each other." Was it any wonder that his "ambition was to become another Houdini." Houdini had all the credentials. Not only had he escaped from a block of ice, a coffin and a grave (the parallel is obvious), but he was the son of a rabbi as well. A sorcerer with *yichus!* Young Joshua practices "magic," symbolic of his wish for the triumph of spirit over matter, hardly a typically Bellovian occupation.

Yes, Pa is at times a less than sympathetic character. Threatening to leave, but liking it when Joshua stands up to him, "Pa was a believer in beating and ruled us by fear" (C.1.16, 20). The emphasis is on near brutality, where in *Herzog* it is on temperament: "In his frequent bursts of temper he slapped his sons swiftly with both hands" (*H*, p. 137). Also, in "Memoirs" Pa is more explicitly profligate, going through the 19,000 ruble dowry of Ma in less than a year (C.1.8). And it is Pa, not Deutsch, who sings the down-and-outer "Al taster panecho mi'meni / I'm broke without a penny / Wich [sic] nobody can deny" (C.1.8). This may be a breach of Pa's dignity as he finally emerges, but, in another sense, the refrain has a haunting relevance to Herzog's own situation, his indigence and spiritual longing. ("Do not hide Thy countenance from us," the translation added later, appears to be fundamentalist, but then it depends on what is meant by countenance.)

Yet when young Joshua first hears that his father is a bootlegger, he suffers sympathetic shock. And when Voplonsky (Lazansky) and Pa are beaten, he reacts very much as in *Herzog:* "It was sacrilege, almost, that Pa should be struck by anybody. . . . My father! Why he was like a king to me, and the image of everything noble and great" (C.1.16). This is the deepest truth in "Memoirs" and the novel's version is an adjustment to this truth; when it comes there, it is not a partial contradiction but a convincing statement: "It was more than I could bear that anyone should lay violent hands on him—a father, a sacred being, a king. Yes, he was a king to us"—this last repetition as if in answer to any of his prior doubts. The novel concludes with a final ascent into the elegaic (not present in an earlier version, B.18.18): "My heart was suffocated by this horror. I thought I would die of it. Whom did I ever love as I loved them" (*H*, p. 147)? Characteristic of his father's elevation, I suppose, is his transformation from "Pa" of "Memoirs" to "Father Herzog" of the novel. ("Mama", curiously, usually remains "Mama", but is also called "Mother Herzog.")

There remain the comparisons between "Memoirs" and the Napoleon Street sequence of the novel involving the showdown with Aunt Zipporah and the hijacking of Father Herzog and his partner. These are in many ways similar, though the Voplonsky sequence, for example, is condensed (from, say, even so late a version as B.19.30), changed from straight narrative to remembrance, focused not on the process of bootlegging but on its effects on Father Herzog. In "Memoirs", as in the novel, Aunt Taube (also Aunt Julie, Sipporah) is a forceful presence who is both threat and promise. One may speculate that she is, biographically considered, the first of the forceful females to make a mark on his impressionable ego. Grandma Lausch, Mrs. Renling, Thea Fenchel, Aunt Zipporah, Mady are a few of the tough mommas. Could his sometime ill-fated attraction to this type, in all her variety, stem from his ambivalence to the Aunt Taube figure, crucial as she was to a momentous childhood incident? And is Herzog's attraction to Mady only the ultimate logic of this psychological set, the weakness for the bitch-eyed maiden, the castiron bluestocking, the castrator, the betrayer, La Belle Dame Sans Moishey? Recalling Aunt Taube's "merciless wit", young Isaac says, "though she oppressed me, I was crazy about her. She was a great show-woman" (C.1.16, 19). But in "Memoirs," as in the novel, Aunt Taube makes her worst accusations (as she denies him money) against her brother, Jacob Lurie, which, considering his vulnerability and his son's attachment to him, might be considered a sort of castration by proxy. With remarkable neutrality of judgment, the novel not only preserves her from castigation, but also presents her in the right. Herzog notes: "Of course Zipporah, that realist, was right to refuse Father Herzog. He wanted to run bootleg whisky to the border, and get into the big time" (*H*, p. 147). Such equanimity comes only with a highly developed genital ego.

Yes, complexity of tone and depth of feeling preserve Herzog from charges of sentimentality, Mady's imprecations to the contrary notwithstanding. We are told that "here was a wider range of human feelings than he had ever again been able to find" (*H*, p. 140), a judgment not present in B.20.40, a judgment characteristic of the elegiac quality of the final version. A subdued lyricism seems perfectly appropriate: "The children of the race, by a never-failing miracle, opened their eyes on one strange world after another, age after age, and uttered the same prayer in each, eagerly loving what they found" (*H*, p. 140). That Bellow came to this rightness of tone through revision is again evident from an early version of this sentence: "Human-kind, these animals which are not animals, opening their eyes from the day of birth on one strange world after another, and finding it *of course!* the right world" (B.18.18, 247). Irony is expunged. The gain in elegaic heightening is countered by Herzog's awareness of the pitfalls of nostalgia. The "I" of "Memoirs" contains neither polarity. Remembering Helen at Haydn and Mozart, Herzog "fought the insidious blight of nostalgia in New York" (*H*, p. 141). It is not until the very late B.23.4, 55 that Bellow gets Herzog to define this ambivalence to his own satisfaction. Commenting on the family saga, Herzog says, "These personal histories, old tales from old times that may not be worth remembering. I remember, I must. But who else—to whom can this matter?" In a sense, Herzog acknowledges that Mady's hardness has some justification. After all, "So many millions—multitudes—go down in terrible pain. And, at that, moral suffering is denied these days. Personali-ties are good only for comic relief. But I am still a slave to Papa's pain." In his attachment to conventional modes of feeling Herzog denies the modernist dehumanization. Yet he can not take the self with Romantic solemnity either: "The way Father Herzog spoke of himself! That could make one laugh. His I had such dignity" (*H*, p. 149). This is balanced judgment. His I did have dignity nonetheless. That all of this is by way of a letter to Nachman underscores the fact that Herzog has these categories in mind, that his most intimate feelings are inextricably bound up with his revision of cultural theory.

If belief in the existence of others is love, as Simone Weil says, we must add that never has love been so minimally yet so irreducibly defined. The definition assumes a universe of indifference, but it is an indifference perva-sive in modernist literature. What the Napoleon Street sequence shows is this belief. Whether these characters are "ordinary" or not, they are char-acters. This faith in the self may be the last viable characteristic of the Romantic. We cannot let it go. As a novel *Herzog* succeeds as much as anything else in conveying belief in character. It is rare in contemporary literature to have such vividness of portraiture.

iii

The enduring quality of the novel depends on an amalgam of idea and character, with character the original inspiration. Bellow's titles conjure up a gallery of portraits—Augie March, Henderson, Herzog, Mr. Sammler, Humboldt (the frequency of Hs indicative, it seems, of some breathless aspiration). Only the "victim" novels have abstract titles: *Dangling Man, The*

Victim, Seize the Day. Many think of *Herzog* as Bellow's most interesting portrait. An account of the genesis of the novel must take the strokes of the portrait into account, beginning with the central character. Since Bellow starts with character, so to speak, we might not expect radical changes, particularly in the central character. Indeed, much of Herzog's character is grasped at the outset. But there are a number of changes in relationship, emphasis, tone and idea. In speaking of beginnings, for example, we have already noted how the right tonality had to be worked for.

Perhaps what is most interesting in the genesis of character is Herzog's relationship to Mady. In the novel patient Griselda Herzog is willing to take the blow. Not quite so in manuscript. In one early version, Herzog's reluctance to marry undercuts his headlong emotional attachment to her in the novel (where a more minimal reluctance is expressed). When Juliana (Mady) "threatened to leave", Herzog "bought a bottle of tranquilizers and took her to the license bureau" (B.18.18, 168). This is put even more clearly to Aunt Short (Zelda) who says, "Juliana realizes now that you never really wanted to marry." He replies, "True, I didn't. But she threatened to leave me" (B.16.5). And when Herzog admits to Edvig (B.19.36, 178), "unhappily, I am domineering", the effect is more implicating than when Zelda makes a similar accusation in the novel. Nor is Herzog especially restrained in the face of Mady's antics. After she overturned a table, Herzog informs Val, "I gave her a powerful kick in the slats" (B.21.10, 246). Val sighs. It may be thought that this gains sympathy for Herzog rather than loses it, but the main point is that Herzog is not above having his. This incident, in a still earlier version, is given a somewhat deeper resonance. "In the bitterness of fantasy, he dragged her by the hair, kicked her, thrashed her, stabbed her, and while he did this he spoke or shouted what was in his heart. 'You used me. You plotted. You hated me. You wanted to kill me.' . . . I did hit her in the country. She overturned the dining room table" (B.17.5). In *Herzog*, such retribution remains checked by a married version of *agape*, which seems to drive Mady even wilder than a beating would. In the genesis of the novel, we see that Herzog was not always above the fray. In one early version, Edvig responds to Herzog's saying that she threatens to call the police in this way: "Obviously she's afraid of you. . . . She thinks you may murder her" (B.17.4). In another version, Edvig applies Herzog's argument for Mady's deficiency of heart in leaving him to Herzog's leaving Daisy. Herzog, feeling a certain guilt, replies that he did not chase after Daisy the way Mady chased after him and that perhaps he did not know what he was doing. Edvig says that maybe Juliana did not either (B.19.36, 113). A note at the end of B.16.6 further undercuts Herzog's integrity. "The reason for the marriage to Juliana was to arrange for the continuation of his blindness and cowardice. Because he knew she did not love him and he took no chance of fulfillment by being married to her. Thus he could continue to be a slave of the world, and within its system of necessity." Such elaborations of motive are far from the novel, where, with whatever irony, Herzog's intentions and actions are high-minded, and he is more sinned against than sinning; it is also far from the dominant direction of the earlier drafts, where such motives are already clearly elaborated. If the function of revision is to arrive at the truth of the character, Herzog's motives are relatively pure in the author's view.

On the other hand we are given a clearer, or at least more obvious glimpse, into Mady's femme fatale attraction to him. Herzog sees that "it was just when all of Juliana's hatred and contempt burned with such ugliness in her eyes that he wanted her most of all" (B.18.13, 34). In the novel, though so inclined, Herzog has too much perspective to support such flat fatality. In another example, when playing basketball Herzog does not make any baskets, and Julie (Mady) scores; he thinks, "It was something like this that made him love her" (B.20.20). More crudely, an early version gives us the streetcorner La Belle Dame: "Oh Rhoda, Rhoda of the Chinese Pogoda, the walls of her halls were adorned with the balls and the tools of fools" (B.18.19). Down uxoriousness! It is all but overcome in the more dignified Herzog of the novel.

Herzog gains in dignity, too, in the revisions of his relationship to Ramona or the ideology she represents. The scene in which Herzog's father throws him out of the house for leaving Daisy, threatening him with a pistol when Herzog asks him to sign a note, has Herzog thinking like Ramona. His head was full of ideas about "Dionysus and Adam, Freud and Taoism, My own kind of religion, my own kind of everything—high flown thoughts about the mystical body, un-neurotic sexuality, preserving civilization by recovering animal nature, drawing more power from the unconscious." In retrospect, Herzog considers himself "A fool! A biblical fool" (B.18.18, 167). The preference of a more or less traditional moral center for the flights of Brown and Marcuse is made in terms of Herzog's own development. Or, as he puts it later in the revision, "I once subscribed to the theory that it was pleasure that gave one strength to be moral, and that only the healthy man could be generous and good, when his senses were gratified. I now believe this is dangerous nonsense" (B.18.18, 213). In the end, his judgment is what it is in the novel. "The great danger," thinks Herzog, "is that in gratitude for making it I may simply turn myself over to Ramona" (B.17.5). There may, of course, be a greater danger; in gratitude for not making it he may turn himself over to somebody else. Be that as it may, it is characteristic of Herzog to be properly skeptical of boudoir Romanticism and to counter it with the idea of civil function, as if, in this age of excess, one had to choose between them. Not that civility necessarily skirts the illusionary. One manuscript version shows us the citizen hero as daydreamer: "I could run the country . . . and do an extraordinary job, too. . . . Herzog in the White House, shrewdly thinking, considering, his heart growing large with desire to serve, to remedy, to establish peace and justice" (B.20.21). But even here abstraction is dissolved by irony as Herzog sits down to pay his bills. Again, the novel is an advance in the seriousness of the central character.

Like the other major characters, Mady is rather clear in the novelist's mind from the outset. Her name, a variation of "mad," is of a piece with the broad, comic nomination of the book, and more part of its essential gaiety than the stately "Juliana." She undergoes, however, little heightening in revision. Some of her grosser qualities are purged. Consider this early description by Herzog: "Dr. Edvig said my violence bullied people but come to think of it he didn't say what was the object of her smashing of china, clawing books, flinging a tureen of stew and a whole watermelon at my head" (B.18.11, 44). In the novel Mady's hysteria falls this side of Gargantua. Her demolition of the car (B.18.15) is also dropped. Though her toughness of language is developed rather than diminished in the revisions, an occasional excess of gaminess is corrected. When Herzog asks her whether she was mixed up with Val, she says, "with the one leg? With the stench he leaves behind him in the toilet. I could never have anything to do with a man whose shit smells like that" (B.18.18, 270f.). This is more effective in the novel, coming as it does from the outraged Herzog. Besides, her contempt for Herzog must stand out in bold relief.

If Herzog, as he says, has the quality of meekness, the ability to take the blow if not the delight in turning the other cheek, Mady has the quality of aggression. In this sense they may be considered a comic version of the Myshkin-Nastasya Filipovna relationship in Dostoevsky's *The Idiot*. As is Nastasya, Mady is finally infuriated at her partner's meekness. Goodness proves to be the last straw. Herzog is attracted, Myshkin-like, to her eyes of doom, but where Myshkin was attracted to suffering humanity, Herzog feels a sexual attraction. Like Nastasya, Mady has been sexually abused as a child. Like her, she is permanently damaged by the brutality of an older male. But Pontritter is her real Totsky. Her father is the brute in her life, motivating her vengefulness with men.

Few characters in Bellow are conceived with such loathing as Pontritter. In manuscript, though not in the novel, Herzog's contempt for him is quite explicit. He says, "I have seen nothing worse than this immense figure of a man with single white fibers growing from his bronzed skull, making mincing steps in his Spanish alpargatas, dancing the samba and the cha-cha-cha" (B.18.9). And Mady's contempt in both manuscript and novel is even more explicit. Despising her father for his bohemian life, his degradation of her mother, Mady clearly is "*not* going to have one of those bohemian affairs" with Herzog. She recalls how her swinging father used to get rid of her: "Here, go to the Automat and buy some chocolate milk and spice cake, and if you open your mouth to Edie I'll kill you both with a hammer." There is, then, some justification in what she calls being "fanatical about conventional things." She concludes, "You and I have to be married in the church" (B.18.18, 149). Pontritter's dimensions are such that, Herzog tells us, his daughter "calls him Cenci" (B.19.16, 21). And revenge she will have.

By the final version, Herzog has overcome his loathing. The description above becomes merely: "He liked Spanish costumes, and when Herzog last saw him he was wearing white duck trousers of bull fighter's cut and alpargatas. Powerful, isolated threads of coarse white grew from his tanned scalp. Madeleine had inherited his eyes" (H, p. 29). And later (H, p. 107) there is an equally neutral description of him dancing the samba and cha-cha with his own "instructress." To be sure, Herzog sees him for what he is. As he "writes" to the pathetic Tennie (Edie), who is testimony to the weakness of meekness, he's *"bursting with the wrongs your daughter did me. The same wrongs you have accepted from Pontritter and forgiven him"* (H, p. 30). Yet, sympathetic sensualist that he in the last analysis remains, Herzog must extend a grudging admiration to a man, even so totally self-absorbed a man, who is going full speed ahead in his later years. The Pontritter who appears in *Herzog* has a marvelous, loud, brusque sociability deriving from his hip sexuality. "This is Adelina," he says of his Filipine dancing friend. "Adelina—Moses. He's laying my daughter. I thought I'd never live to see the day" (H, p. 108). His saying of Mady, "She's got more faggots at her feet than Joan of Arc" seems quintessential Pontritter, but it is a late inclusion (B.22.4, 117), originally spoken by the disenchanted Herzog (B.18.18, 144). Such giving transcends simple contempt.

For that we must return to Mady, who can never forgive her parents for teaching her the ABC's from Lenin's *State and Revolution*. We see Mady's subsequent quest for rules as a parody of the typical Bellow quest for the axial lines. We see, in the letter to Monsignor Hilton, that Herzog and Mady are ostensibly united in being up against the same thing—nihilism. They may be up against the same thing, but they come from different directions, indicating the way in which Romanticism and Christianity (Herzog's subject)—are antithetical. Impatient with Herzog's feelings of reluctance to marry, she exclaims, "Don't give me that line of platitudes about feelings. I don't believe in it. I believe in God-sin-death—so don't pull any sentimental crap on me" (H, p. 166). Did he have to marry a disciple of T. E. Hulme? "She brought ideology into my life," laments the culture-weary Herzog (H, p. 334). Brought it back, he might have said more accurately—after he had spent the better part of his life getting rid of it.

Despite objections to his patent theatricality, Herzog addresses the Monsignor seriously, as between one fundamentally rabbinical temperament and another. Most of the letter does not appear until the manuscript is fairly well on (B.20.8), which is in line with its ideational tenor. Coming even later are some of the interconnected narrative sections, which contain a considerable elaboration of Mady's religious appearance, theatrical Catholicism (hence the special appeal of Monsignor Hilton, named, it seems, after a hotel), and neurotic quirks (e.g., her sharply rising voice and rigid figure *H*, p. 116). The ideational core of the letter is something that a clergyman would easily understand, an affirmation of the ultimate inseparability of fact and value. Again he assaults the modernist mind through an attack on existential assumptions, notably Heidegger's reduction of ordinary life. In so doing, Herzog affirms the American faith in the ordinary, a faith that in different ways inspired the classic American writers Bellow feels close to—Whitman, Twain, and Dreiser.

If Mady brought ideology into Herzog's life, Val brings it into everyone's, in a Dostoevskian sense. His first name, Valentine, speaks for itself; his second, originally Grenzbach—border brook—made some sense, now Gersbach—it just sounds bad. Herzog tells us that "as soon as he slams the door of his Continental he begins to talk like Karl Marx" (*H*, p. 217; inserted B.22.5, 256). This is the sort of satiric intellectual tightening which so often comes in late revision. Val is making what his parents would call a Golden Living blasting the affluent society. Much of the satiric heightening through Hebrew reference comes at about the middle of the revisions. Hence, Gersbach "lecturing at the Hadassah on Martin Buber," his prophetic eye like that of "a judge of Israel" (*H*, p. 58f; not in B.19.43) is not in early versions. Spouting "I and Thou," Val sets his best friend up in a career of cuckoldry, more saintly than his victim since his suffering is greater, "Perhaps the worst part of this was the absence of hypocrisy," quips Herzog, as early as B.16.5: "Grenzbach is not Tartuffe. Tartuffe knew what he was doing." What is most damaging in Val is his weightlessness, a moral posturing without moral meaning. Bellow does not forget that moral weightlessness can support physical vitality, and many of Val's vital mannerisms—his pounding the table, dancing, stumping with the bride—are added late (B.22.4, 119). His hair change, from "blue-black" to "flaming copper," comes early (B.16.6) and carries a similar significance. As for the wooden leg, Bellow shows that stock comic devices can be put to contemporary use.

Ramona, too, is ideological, but she has a body so fine that no idea can violate it. Ramona consoles, but hers are not the consolations of philosophy. (Her name, in an occasional early version Rosette, is reminiscent of the old, sweet love song.) Even in early versions Herzog worries that "Ramona will take me over from sheer weakness" (B.8.12, 11). Her Sag Harbour retreat is metaphor as well as geography. Essentially "right" from the beginning, Ramona picks up some attributes in the composition. In an early version Herzog says that he met a Sybil Weber at a lantern party at the Wadsworth Square mews. She walked with "some impudent swagger as if she had a dagger in her garter belt" (B.19.35, 131), a quality later attributed to Ramona in the boudoir. And in another early version it is Juliana (Mady) who "cooked shrimps [sic] and almonds" (B.18.18, 159). It seems appropriate to associate Ramona with all sensuous gratification, and Mady with none as far as Herzog is concerned. The dish itself undergoes a culinary metamorphosis from shrimp with almonds to shrimp with lemon sauce (B.20.40) to shrimp Arnaud. In one early version, Ramona's kiss—Ramona near her Garden of Eden—gives him a "taste of Eternal Sabbath" (B.17.6). But this is not quite the metaphor for Ramona, any more than her *specialité* would be gefilte fish. Non-kosher, shrimp has the advantages of the forbidden. With Ramona, too, a final intellectual tightening—reference to Brown, Marcuse—is saved for late revisions (B.22.5, 245). Beyond this specificity, Ramona's "meaning" is underscored in later versions. Her voice is a call to pleasure, "not simple pleasure but metaphysical, transcendent pleasure—pleasure which answered the riddle of human existence" (*H*, p. 150; not in B.20.40). The summary statement rising to epigram comes in later revision: "Ramona had passed through the hell of profligacy and attained the seriousness of pleasure. For when will we civilized beings become really serious? said Kierkegaard. Only when we have known hell through and through." (None of this is in late B.20.20.) This is a far more culturally elegant fate than the earlier, she "had been sleeping with everyone, a human turnstile" (B.20.40, 188). Sic Transit Authority gloria mundi. In the revisions, Ramona is given insight along with learning. "Unless you're having a bad time with a woman you can't be serious," she says (*H*, p. 157; B.23.4, 58). Herzog has, overall, an adequate reply to this, but the idea lingers.

Sono can raise no such questions and therein, doubtless, lies her charm. Scrubbing Herzog down in the warm tub, she is everyman's return to the womb of the Orient. Pliant, secondary, amenable, "if he were a communist she would be one too," says an early draft (B.18.12, 83). All this is very fine, thinks Herzog, but alas, "I had to have a woman I could talk to" (B.18.12, 84). Not a bad idea for a professor. Yet Sono is in her way faultless.[8] Curiously bringing to mind Ramona's criticism of him, Herzog writes, "*To tell the truth, I never had it so good. But I lacked the strength of character to bear such joy*" (*H*, p. 169). The last word is, however, his. Once again in Bellow there is a western resistance to uncomplication, stemming perhaps from the biblical idea that moral struggle is more real than pleasure. Sono does not change much in revision, but Herzog's sense of her limited significance becomes comically clear. So long as it has meaning, Herzog, in the Judeo-Christian tradition, is in love with his own suffering. Yet Sono was indeed right about Mady, and there is a distinction between valuing your suffering and pursuing it. Is this last un-American? There is no Constitutional guarantee for "Life, Liberty and the Pursuit of Suffering." Is this yet another instance of the internationalization of American culture?[9]

What seems most disturbing to him about his relationship to Daisy, common flower, was the meaninglessness of the suffering it entailed. In an early version he argues with his first wife about how suffering is not a virtue but a vice when it just keeps coming with "no wisdom, no profit." Hospitalized with pneumonia (in Princeton), Herzog enlarges on his feeling by parodying Shelley. He falls upon the thorns of life, bleeds and learns nothing (B.18.10, 82). Herzog then explodes, rejecting Daisy's mothering and offer of home. He does not have the feeling of being alive with her, yet in one version he writes in a letter to Daisy, "I broke off and escaped, vengeance pursuing, and nearly died of guilt" (B.20.24, 210). Such guilt is effectively expunged from the novel where he has overcome the trauma of separation. Herzog surely does have the feeling of being alive with Ramona, but is aware of the Shelley syndrome there, too. Kissing Ramona goodbye at her Bower of Bliss or Garden of Eden on Lexington Avenue, "he had a taste of the life he might have led if he had been simply a loving creature." But the "inescapable Moses Elkanah Herzog" soon thinks, "I fall upon the thorns of life, I bleed. And then? I fall upon the thorns of life, I bleed. And what next? I get laid, I take a short holiday, but very soon after I fall upon those same thorns with gratification in pain, or suffering in joy—who knows what the mixture is! What good, what lasting good is there in me?" (*H*, p. 206f.).

Like the underground man, Herzog lives on terms of uneasy, masochistic coexistence with his own demanding consciousness. The underground man will not forego this one "most advantageous advantage"[10] for anything. "Consciousness", he says, "is the greatest misfortune for man, yet I know man loves it and would not give it up for any satisfaction."[11] Though bearing the weight of an hypertrophy of consciousness, he can paradoxically say, "I have more life in me than you" because of it. He has individuality, authenticity. Herzog would consider giving it up—or at least forcing it to take a comic cure. Like the underground man, who feels a miserable moral lack, Herzog yearns for a personal incarnation of the good. Unlike him, he has the psychological and moral wherewithal to break out of solipsism; unlike him, he feels that he can move and act: "And what about all the good I have in my heart. . . . This good is no phony. . . . He felt he must do something, something practical and useful and must do it at once" (*H*, p. 207).

iv

This brings us to the dramatic center of the novel, the "murder" scene, with its prefatory courtroom scene. Dropping an elaborate description of Herzog's ablutions and breakfast and talk about the inflated art market, Bellow has the scenes come abruptly after Herzog's talk with lawyer Simkin. Truth comes with blows, says Bellow's Henderson, uttering a truth which extends well beyond the limits of that particular book. The courtroom scene shows us in the mad queen a more likely descendant of the underground man; he "was purer, loftier than any square, did not lie" (*H*, p. 229). His flaunting manner illustrates, in the abstract language of the last revisions, "nastiness in the transcendent position" (*H*, p. 229; B.23.4, 84). What Herzog sees in the courtroom shatters his moral composure. He thinks of the old song, "There's flies on me, there's flies on you, but there ain't no flies on Jesus." Yet his Victorian upbringing and its acculturated moralism seem hollow, self-congratulatory. This was not always the case.

In an early version the letter to Edvig appears as part of the courtroom sequence, with Herzog saying that he happens "to be clear for the time from accusations though having many of the sores . . . of the soul as some of those locked in cells. . . . I've been too clever to be caught." In its problematic insularity this last phrase recalls Asa Leventhal's "I was lucky. I got away with it." We see a composure of sorts, capped by a desire for "the final radiance of final love," and blessed by the famous lines from Blake's "The Black Boy": "For we are placed on earth a little while to learn to bear the beams of love" (B.17.5). This impulse is in contradistinction to "the swindles of desire" Herzog wants to rid himself of. He is very far from his distraught reaction in the courtroom scene as it appears in the novel and the later versions. He will go to Chicago, pick up his father's gun, save his child, murder Val and Mady, and so be it. But even in the early versions this solution is questioned: "So he was flying to his daughter, taking the drug of action. For it was a drug—he knew that. . . . He knew very well, yes, very clearly that June was not being harmed in any direct manner and that . . . he could not really explain why he had come" (B.17.8). Then he reads the Geraldine Portnoy letter (with its description of June in the car), originally placed here, leaving us with an equivocal "Whatever he was going to consider, he would consider on the plane."

Other early versions indicate Herzog's skepticism in intellectual terms: "I wonder what I was doing rushing here. Impulsiveness, immaturity, morbidity, wastefulness, foolishness that looks like generosity, all that schlemiehl nonsense that people take to be the struggle for freedom against bureaucracy-organization, power development. This 'radical innocence' in which I don't believe for one moment and is simply a sign of laziness and limited intellect" (B.17.7). The allusion is to Ihab Hassan's study, which follows perhaps uncritically the alienation line, with its hipster, criminal and ashcan heroes.[12] Bellow, as we have seen, has little use for this typology. Radical innocence is another expression of the fag-end Romanticism Herzog attacks in some of the letters. Another version of about this time counters this immoralism with his own more traditional roots. Thinking of Junie in the car, he wants to kill Gersbach: "But being a civilized man, more or less Jewish, he limited his act to fantasy or imagination and took legal measures instead" (B.21.9, 249). (This brings to mind a remark of Father Herzog's pertaining to his hijackers: "I knew they wouldn't kill me. They were Jews" [B.19.36, 192]. In his refusal to give the physical blow, Herzog is his father's son. "Can you shoot a man?" asks Pappa's clever sister. "Could you even hit someone on the head?" [H, p. 145]. Herzog recalls this soon after he forgoes his own murderous impulse [H, p. 258].)

Still another early version takes us closer to the enervation of the book: "People who do evil are coming to think that they are more authentic and truthful. . . . First I want to find out what they are doing with my daughter. Juliana has a right to prefer Valentine to me. There's nothing criminal about it. But June—a little girl brought up by vulgar liars or even psychopaths" (B.17.17). But the tone becomes uncertain, far too elevated: " 'Though with high wrongs, stuck to the quick' as Prospero says, 'yet with my nobler reason gainst my fury Do I take part. The rarer action is in virtue than in vengeance.' Once committed to the grand project of being, in that special and distinguished sense, human, a man is left with no alternative" (B.17.17). Okay, but better the ironic, nervous comedy of the novel than such high seriousness. Low seriousness is what Bellow is after. In the new comedy a sense of humor is the better part of salvation, and this involves seeing yourself as well as your enemies in proportion.

The novel itself undercuts the element of suspense. We are given preliminary indications of how things will turn out. Writing to Zelda, who had feared for the lives of Mady and Val, Herzog says, "*I'm no criminal, don't have it in me*" (H, p. 41). This proves to be true. Even in his most despairing moments, Herzog says, "if, even in that embrace of lust and treason, they had life and nature on their side, he would quietly step aside. Yes, he would bow out" (H, p. 52). In the end, Mady is associated with murder more definitely than Herzog. Herzog thinks of "the terrifying menstrual ice of her rages, the look of the murderess" (H, p. 63). And when she views him in the police station, her look was made to kill. It "expressed a total will that he should die" (H, p. 301). But the will is not the act and there will be no murder in this novel. So centered in consciousness, even potentially physical explosions are absorbed by it. Radical innocence could not be much more than an elaborate joke in a novel critical of negative transcendence. Herzog, it turns out, is as good as his convictions. The murder scene itself has little but minor verbal revision (e.g., "kill" becomes "shoot or choke," *H*, p. 255; B.23.4, 58). It was "right" from the start.

That this anticlimactic climax is the psychological crux of the book is born out by the instantaneous release Herzog feels. *"The human soul is an amphibian and I have touched its sides"* (*H*, p. 257f). As this figure, borrowed, perhaps unconsciously, from Nietzsche[13] indicates, Herzog's resiliency has passed the test; now he can breathe without chest pains. And the weight of numbers that had oppressed, now releases. It is Herzog's turn to comfort the sick. This he does is the mock-*liebestodt* of Lucas Asphalter and his chimpanzee in a scene which is a *reductio ad absurdum* of reactive depression.[14] Asphalter, as his name suggests, shows that you don't have to be a Romantic poet to be severely depressed. You can be a Romantic scientist, as interesting as macadam. In this scene, Herzog is healthy enough to laugh at heartsickness. "It's one of those painful emotional comedies," says Herzog, perfectly summarizing the meaning in a phrase not present in early versions (B.17.8). He might almost as well be talking about his own love life.

The Asphalter scene provides us with a comic analogy to another aspect of the action, this time ideational. It is a parody of existentialism as dread and death philosophy, as modernist orthodoxy. This parody is a late inclusion. In one late version, Luke does "nudity" exercises to overcome his mind-body dualism (B.22.5, 318); these become exercises in "facing your own death" (B.23.4). "Face death. That's Heidegger," says Herzog (*H*, p. 270; B.23.4, 99). Ironically, what Luke sees in this exercise is Life in all its bulging sensuousness—his fat-assed old aunt saved from a fire, or big burlesque broads playing softball. The lengthy attack on the existentialists with which the chapter concludes—"God is no more. But Death is. That's their story."—does not appear until late (*H*, p. 271–73; mostly not in B.22.6). To this philosophy of anguish, Herzog prefers an older wisdom. In a late inclusion (not in B.22.6) he quotes Blake to make his point: "I really believe that brotherhood is what makes a man human. If I owe God a human life, this is where I fall down. 'Man liveth not by self alone but in his brother's face. . . . Each shall behold the Eternal Father and love and joy abound' " (*H*, p. 272).[15] Despite the awareness of his own shortcomings, the line between potato love and this assertion is a fine one. And Herzog's previously expressed skepticism on the subject indicates that the assertion is authentic only as a polarity of exhilaration. The late revisions here complicate the Asphalter comedy with ideational elements of parody and elegy, and in so doing underscore Herzog's newly established, delicate balance.

If we look at the two most important letters of this section—those to Mermelstein and Nietzsche—we see familiar thematic material considered now with little apparent pain. In a recent study, Professor Mermelstein has stolen Herzog's thunder, but Herzog is above any deep professional envy, insulated in part by his newly found self-satisfaction. More than this, he is not personally disturbed where he may well have cause to be. There is a contrast here with the animal contempt he felt early in the novel for Shapiro and to some extent still feels. The substance of the Mermelstein letter, a defense of *"those of us who remain loyal to civilization"*—there is an almost corporate confidence now expressed in the plural—in the face of *"people playing at crisis, alienation, apocalypse and desperation"* (*H*, p. 316f.) is not new, except for the reference to Kierkegaard. The latter half of this epistle, its most memorable part, seems to be the last revision in the novel (B.23.5, galley 16). Another case of the best, or most quotable (including the fragments above), saved for last. An earlier reference to Mermelstein spoke of Herzog's study as being "about romanticism as the scattered effects of a disintegrated Christian tradition" yielding alienation, where Herzog need "community, consensus, prayer, responsibilities and all the rest of it" (B.21.29, 243f.). This tired formulation is recast, and *"What this country needs is a good five-cent synthesis"* finds its proper place (*H*, p. 207). The argument in the actual letter to Mermelstein—it is not only the situation which is funny, but also the name, with its suggestions of murmur, worm or weasel, followed by "stein" yet—is more clearly about contemporary than Christian apocalyptics. So, for example, a reference to a monograph by Shapiro is changed from "The Roots of Vico in Patristic Literature" (B.17.8) to "From Luther to Lenin, A History of Revolutionary Psychology" (B.22.6, 369). Herzog correctly explains Kierkegaard's position: *"truth has lost its force with us and horrible pain and evil must teach it to us again"* (*H*, p. 316), but then goes on to reject this idea. *"More commonly,"* he holds, *"suffering breaks people, crushes them, and is simply unilluminating. . . . We love apocalypses too much, and crisis ethics and florid extremism with its thrilling language. Excuse me, no. I've had all the monstrosity I want"* (*H*, p. 317). In an earlier version, Herzog's resistence to Kierkegaard ("a marvelous fellow") is not so clearly articulated. He tells us what Kierkegaard means, adding,

> *I do not claim to be an expert in this matter. I don't compare the evils I have known to truly gruesome evils such as we have all heard of. My life is a fairly ordinary one. . . . But what is this truth or seriousness that Kierkegaard thinks Hell must teach us? Is it that eternity must be recovered for the present moment, that that man who fingers all universals must disintegrate?* (B.21.41, 371)

Once again we see how late the final intellectual formulation comes. The point of the Kierkegaard letter(s), finely made in the later revision, is to cast Herzog's suffering in bold relief. He was the man, he suffered, he was there, but let us not succumb to the temptation to consider suffering honorific. It is frequently, all too frequently, meaningless. The morally real can be perceived in other ways as well.

Coming between the letters to Mermelstein and Nietzsche, as a bit of comic relief perhaps, is a letter about the size of the rats in Panama City. Herzog, sounding like a cross between late Faust and Leopold Bloom, thinks of a constructive way of dealing with them. Why here? If the rat is considered a symbol of nihilism, so often the case in modern literature, we see the point of this letter's placement. Having just exposed the danger of religious nihilism, Herzog, in his letter to Nietzsche, for him the master of those whose view is aesthetic, will expose the danger of aesthetic nihilism.

The letter to Nietzsche has the "gaiety" the philosopher admired and is characteristic of Herzog's found equilibrium. Addressing itself primarily to "Nietzsche Contra Wagner," Herzog agrees with Nietzsche's negative re-evaluation of Wagner's music as a histrionic, bogus heroism from below for mass consumption, for "the sick . . . the idiots . . . [the] Wagnerians" (*VPN*, p. 667), and would agree with his judgment that Mozart has the gracious, golden seriousness. Nietzsche saw that living in "a period of reaction *within reaction*" as he did, an "age of national wars," may help "such an art as Wagner's to a sudden glory, without thereby guaranteeing it a future," adding, with some ironic prescience, that "the Germans themselves have no future" (*VPN*, p. 668f). Herzog also speaks of "*that sickly Wagnerian idiocy and bombast*" but chides Nietzsche on his own Wagnerian propensities as manifested in a phrase like the "luxury of destruction" (*H*, p. 309; *VPN*, p. 670). In doing so Herzog questions the clarity of Nietzsche's distinction between the tragic or Nietzchean figure suffering from overfullness, which as a young man the philosopher once saw in Wagner, and the "revenge-against-life" figure suffering from impoverishment. In Goethe we do clearly see "excess" as creativity; in Wagner, most notably in the Romantic Christianity of *Parsifal*, "hatred" as creativity. *Parsifal* is so sorry (yet inevitable?) a conclusion to Wagner's "tragic" art that Nietzsche hopes it is really an elaborate irony. "After all," he says in a funny line, "Parsifal is operetta material par excellance" (*VPN*, p. 674).

Nietzsche's argument about "hatred" as creative force in Wagner is related to the sort of connection that Herzog makes between Romanticism or modernism, on the one hand, and Christianity or otherworldliness, on the other. We have described Bellow's resistance to Flaubert in these terms. It is no surprise that Nietzsche also views Flaubert as the apostle of "hatred" as creativity, "a new edition of Pascal, but as an artist, with the instinctive judgment deep down: '*Flaubert est toujours haissable, l'homme n'est rien, l'oeuvre est tout.*' " (*VPN*, p. 671). Nietzsche laments Flaubert's "selflessness," calling it "the will to the end, in art as well as in morals" (*VPN*, p. 671). In Wagner's case, Nietzsche can only wonder, "Did the *hatred against life* become dominant in him as in Flaubert?" (*VPN*, p. 675). So far so good. Nietzsche himself, however, favors an aesthetic aristocracy and from a diametrically opposite position shows an equal contempt for "the ordinary life," which usually means, in political terms, the assumptions of democratic liberalism. "*John Stuart Mill:* or insulting clarity" Nietzsche quips in *Twilight of the Idols* (*VPN*, p. 513), and, later in that work, "Liberalism: in other words, herd-animalization" (*VPN*, p. 541). Herzog wonders about Nietzsche's invocation of the Dionysian spirit and its power "*to endure the sight of the Terrible,*" the spirit which allows itself "*the luxury of Destruction*" (*H*, p. 319; *VPN*, p. 670). When Herzog says that these expressions have a Germanic ring he is turning Nietzsche's contempt in on himself. For "the Dionysian god and man," says Nietzsche, "what is evil, senseless, and ugly seems, as it were, permissable, as it seems permissable in nature" (*VPN*, p. 670). How these immoralists argue from "nature"! Sade is perhaps the first in modern times. Herzog will not grant Nietzsche his immoralist assumptions, any more than he will grant that "mildness, peacefulness, and goodness" must imply a "saviour" (*VPN*, p. 670). Throughout his career Bellow has been skeptical of the heroic view and even Nietzsche cannot win him over. "*Where,*" wonders Herzog, "*are the heroes who have recovered*" (*H*, p. 319) from the Dionysian luxury of Destruction? Herzog values Nietzsche's immoralism to the extent that it sees through and articulates the falsity of the age, including liberalism as the property of the educated rabble. But the philosopher's high-minded approach to destruction is too much like murder. Great pain may be an ultimate liberator of the spirit, but one must be around to gain from the experience. Love of necessity, even when it is love of one's own sickness, implies a lover. Herzog points to the dubiousness of Nietzsche's arguments and to their peculiar susceptibility to perversion. Implicit is the use to which Nietzsche was put by Nazism, which exhibited qualities that Nietzsche himself despised.

This is made explicit in earlier versions of the letter. "The Nazis asserted the most absolute freedom which only the Dionysian power can claim—the power to endure the sight of the terrible, the questionable, this luxury of destruction" (B.18.9). Nietzsche would have disputed the claim that what he said had application to a state, a military idea, or perhaps anything German. Somewhat more accurately Herzog states in another draft, "you are speaking of some idea of an artist rather than any sort of factual historical existence applicable to the majority of us. . . . I do not wish to test my power to endure the sight of the terrible." Herzog prefers "a different view of Nature, the one, namely, which holds that in us the evolutionary process has achieved a different power, that of self-consciousness, and that Nature looks at itself in mankind. It has entered the mental zone. In this, 'Blood' culminates in 'Mind' and they are not such violent opposites after all" (B.17.8). But is Herzog certain enough even of his own self to stay very long with this optimistic, Romantic metaphysics?

Later in the drafts (B.21.40, 236) Herzog comes back to Nazism. He writes Nietzsche that *"to me Wagner has always been appropriate program or background music for people who are plotting a pogrom. Thus I imagine the Wahnsee Conference [sic] on the Final Solution with that horrible Siegfried on a record, shattering sword after sword."* (The Siegfried the Fearless theme was, in fact, commonly used in Nazi propaganda.) Herzog again questions "the luxury of destruction," expressing, nonetheless, a sympathy for Nietzsche: *"Humankind is in fact losing its ancient forms of personality. Whether a new spirit of destruction should be involved is of course a different question. . . . All of this about new beasts shambling off to Bethlehem to be born is simply nonsense."* He concludes again with the notion that blood may culminate in mind.[16] In sum, the Nietzsche letter is a final critique of modernism, giving some assent to its authority, done with no bitterness, but with a healthy humor. It is all well suited to Herzog's hard-won emotional balance.

For all its concentration of effect, for all its mental depth and psychological turmoil, for all its argumentation and change of scene, the novel takes place in five days, with recuperation at Ludeyville (another joke-name, town of the lewd) being the sixth. This adds verisimilitude to Herzog's conversion to sanity. We come out of the pit with him. He feels confident, happy and wary. In a broad sense, this level-headed view has been present from the beginning. An early draft has the novel title, "Alas and Hooray" (B.18.12). The break with Mady has actually brought him "joy," these last two letters, among others, being written in "tranquil fullness of heart" (*H*, p. 313). Herzog has resisted various temptations to dehumanization, to a wasteland identity, affirming what remains of a moral view. It is appropriate that this "archaic" type utters an almost secular prayer in conclusion. "Thou movest me," Herzog says, explaining his feeling in natural images. "Something produces intensity, a holy feeling, as oranges produce orange, as grass green" (*H*, p. 340). If this is an expression of the attribute of holiness, it is an expression intimately allied to the attributes of Nature. If this is faith, it is faith of feeling, in its way Romantic, a product of the heart recalling Rousseau. But whether he knows his heart or not may not be of the utmost significance. Both of the Romantic and beyond it, an apostle of the ego and a critic of it, Herzog turns to God as an act of the natural man recognizing the limits of Nature. His quest has brought him to affirm the primacy of moral authority addressed as "Thou," or God.[17]

Chapter 7

Herzog, the intellectual milieu

No work of Bellow's deals so explicitly with ideas as *Herzog*, this novel about an intellectual, a typically polemical intellectual at that. An accounting of its compositional contours in this case calls for further definition of ideational contours as they bear upon the novel as meaning and construct.

Herzog's polemical thrust is often directed at what is still called the "absurd." The word gained currency in literary circles partly because of the honorific status of existential philosophy, a "tragic" philosophy that went beyond the bounds of academicism. As analysts of existentialism point out, "absurd" is a new word for an old idea, "contingency"; this is "the traditional technical term for a fact which defies human understanding."[1] Where a traditional philosopher like Thomas Aquinas held that human reason was incompetent to explain the fact of being, and where, in our own time, William James ambiguously described this condition as "metaphysical wonder" or "ontological wonder sickness," Sartre leaves no doubt that contingent being or the absurd leaves one nauseous. It is as if Flaubert's Frederic Moreau had a Ph.D. How the cult of nausea derived from the country of haute cuisine remains a mystery we will leave to future historians of the collapse of civilization to unravel. Be that as it may, the "absurd" has had its modernistic appeal, perhaps most notably in "the theater of the absurd."

The phrase serves as a title of a well-known study by Martin Esslin on modernist drama (Beckett, Ionesco, Genet). What is the absurd? It is the modernist loss of traditional assumptions with nothing—except perhaps monstrous parody—to put in their place. It is Hegel's Unhappy Consciousness in extremis, extremity in extremis. The concept of the absurd is really broader than the traditional concept of contingency in that it posits a world where all facts defy human understanding. Esslin encounters this phenomenon uncritically, as Lionel Abel's review of the book was the first to note. In accents (note especially the first two sentences) that Bellow may have incorporated into Professor Herzog's questioning of Professor Heidegger's fall into the quotidian, Abel says, "Esslin thinks we have lost God. I should like to know when this occurred." He continues:

> Is family gone? At least it is better understood. Is the State gone? But the state seems to require the efforts and adherence of the young, and more than ever. Is patriotism gone? Then who would infer anything from our loss of it? To say that reason is gone is to speak without hope of being understood. An absurd world would be silent; it would not be plied with plays. . . . It is one thing to call the world sad, quite another to call it "absurd.". . .The world can no more become absurd than it can sin, starve or fall down. There are many absurdities in the world; most of them were always there.[2]

Abel expresses an essentialist view that recalls the temper of the fifties, its end-of-innocence tone, its understanding of "negative capability," the phrase from Keats that Lionel Trilling made current in his excellent introduction to Keats' letters. Keats' insight—negative capability is the ability to remain content with half-knowledge "without any irritable reaching after fact and reason"—became almost a doctrine (though Keats in some of the odes could become quite irritable). The appeal of the outlook is its opposition to the ideological; and the absurd, as promulgated by Camus and those influenced by him, like Esslin, is a surrogate ideology. As one critic puts it, "the absurdists' moral revulsion . . . is symptomatic of an apocalyptic impatience for total change, a hope for innocence and salvation, for a new age."[3] What is described here is an aspect of the modernist ideology Bellow has resisted for some time.

This resistance goes farther than Abel's to include a critique of that other continental phenomenon, whose assumptions are consonant with the absurd and may be said to have created it, existentialism. From Bellow's point of view both are squarely in the tradition of modernist ideology. That Bellow has consistently held this position is clear from the composition of *Herzog*. In an early version, Herzog notes that "French e. [existentialism] for all its Marxist pretensions simply promoting existential anguish or whatever they call it to keep society suitably morose." Here existentialism is seen to be a modern mythology inferior to Marxism, which at least saw the light at the end of the tunnel. Retreating from this modernist extremity, Herzog notes with characteristic wishfulness, "Suppose there were joy? (beams of love etc.). . . . I believe in it, because I know nothing else worth all the trouble." Realizing the archaic quality of this impulse, Herzog concludes, "Blessedness of existence at this time must be kept secret, for it will be considered subversive and antisocial." The allusion to Blake's "The Black Boy," particularly the lines "And we are put on earth a little space, / That we may learn to bear the beams of love" occurs in a number of *Herzog* manuscripts. Here as elsewhere Bellow prefers the Romantic to the modern sensibility because it has room for the naive. This "blessedness" of existence is an expression of the incipient Alyosha in him, a cross between Jewish sanctification and Christian grace. Recognizing a Christian affinity in this and recognizing as well, as we have seen, that mildness has little pull with "us," he adds that "as a gospel it [blessedness] leads straight to Golgotha. I've often been backed up to the Cross. My behind is full of splinters, but they've never actually gotten a nail into me" (B.18.11, 67f.). This may not exactly be the Passion, but it is A Pain in the Ass. A price worth paying for certain values.

For Bellow the dread, terror and revulsion of existential anguish is much more convincing than its awe, exhilaration and sublimity. In another early version, Herzog notes that American parents feel

> Romantic defeat, Despair with the big D and the Existential stuff, so that they can give the children nothing but apologies and placate them for exposing them to nothing. I mean Nothing, which is neither a category in logic nor a psychological concept but simply a mental and spiritual disinte-gration from which you're expected to start all over again without illusions or consolations, the Hegelian alienated self in its Unhappy consciousness. No, all that is dead-end Romanticism, and I've always gotten out of it by being a Jew. (B.18.18, 260)

Here again is an oblique opposition of tradition and modernity. "The Exis-tential stuff" yields nihilism, not the strength of disillusion. Yet his belief takes the form of a psychological rather than a religious category; Herzog is not an embodiment of perfect faith or even a defender of the First Cause. He is more involved in the disintegrations of modernism than in the integrations of traditional theology, learning, like Nietzsche, to live with the Void. Ac-knowledging as much, he adds to the quotation about the rejection of the Unhappy Consciousness—"when it suited me—and slipping into and out of Western culture ad-lib. The ghetto could always be a refuge from the di-sasters of Christian history, and that's fair enough for those Jews who clung to their Jewish God. . . . I can't have it both ways, however, dancing with one backside at two weddings" (B.18.18, 260). The abrasive charm of the Yiddish expression amounts to this: it is a question of winnowing the wheat from the immense chaff of tradition. What lives must live in emotion and individual perception; this assumption is a contradiction of tradition, but one within which it must live, if it is to live.

The practical effects of existentialism seem to be stylized misery. And with good reason. Even exponents of the philosophy describe it in a way that makes it another secular version of Original Sin. Heidegger speaks of "the fall into the quotidian," being "thrown into" the world, being "forsaken" as was Christ. The ordinary world is fallen, but the world of art is a state of grace. And Sartre, like a monk *manqué*, speaks of the world being a "varnish" on the surface of Being-in-itself. Robert Olson holds that the basic existential insight is that man is doomed to unhappiness: consciousness is inevitably unhappy consciousness. Olson quotes Dostoevsky to the effect that "Man will never renounce real suffering. . . . Suffering is the sole origin of consciousness." But it is not quite Dostoevsky who says this. It is the underground man, whose vision, unlike Dostoevsky's, excludes the possibility of redemptive love. Suffering without meaning? This is the underground man; but neither Bellow nor Dostoevsky is prepared to go that far with disintegrated consciousness. Like Bellow, the creator of Alyosha and Dmitri Karamazov has not given up on blessedness. Sartre holds a more somber view, saying, in *Saint Genet*, "It is in suffering alone that he [man] can feel himself to be free, because it is the only feeling which can come from within himself."[4] While this may be accurate as self-description, it will hardly do as a description of man in general.

At the heart of Bellow's quarrel with existentialism is the concept of the self. In manuscript Herzog puts it this way: "According to the latest from Paris and London, there is no person. According to Bertrand Russell 'I' is a grammatical expression. According to Sartre there are no essences, and therefore no human nature" (B.18.18, 158). While this is not quite so—there may be said to be "essence" in the sense of the inevitability of the existential situation, the for-itself projecting to be the in-itself—Sartre does deny essence in the sense of God-given soul, a belief to which Bellow finally subscribes. "The idea of God is contradictory," says Sartre, "and we lose ourselves in vain: man is a useless passion."[5] Sartre here expresses the absurdist temperament. He seems to oversimplify the matter of essence by considering it as divine essence, a predetermined nature. But does essence have to be Leibnizian? In his well-known formulation, "existence precedes essence": that is, man, in dreadful freedom, chooses, and his essence is what he chooses, if that can properly be called choice. But there is an essence that has nothing to do with determinism, an essence that precludes it, a mysterious given unique as a face, and that has to do with what "choice" is made. "Existence precedes essence" may destroy Leibniz, but it does not destroy humanism.

As we have seen, existentialism is satirized in the Lucas Asphalter episode. The ideational point can be clarified here. Lucas has been doing exercises to confront his death. Only the backwash of a modernist philosophy could devise such calisthenics. Tina Zokóly is not Heidegger, but both are brought into satiric focus. The idea of pragmatically, hygienically dealing with death is soon enough disposed of, but Heidegger's views require some effort. We recall that Herzog has twice questioned his notion of the degradation of ordinary life, the fall into the quotidian. In *Being and Time* the philosopher holds that confronting one's death breaks the hold of banality and inauthenticity which the quotidian imposes. As in Tolstoy's *The Death of Ivan Ilyich*, the authenticity of confronting death exposes the inauthenticity of ordinary relations. But Tolstoy intended a criticism of class, not of ordinary life as such, as Ilyich's consoling feeling about Gerasim indicates. And unlike Heidegger and other secular existentialists, Ilyich cannot accept his finitude—two points which would make *Ilyich* deeper than Heidegger in Bellow's view. For Heidegger, the fear of death comes from ordinary perception. The willing of death, the affirmation of "absurd" death, the assumption of Being-for-Death is a triumph over mere quotidian life. Herzog seems to be thinking of Heidegger's position in his late, musing letter to Ramona: *"the last question, also the first one, the question of death, offers us the interesting alternatives of disintegrating ourselves by our own wills in proof of our 'freedom,' or the acknowledging that we owe a human life to this waking spell of existence, regardless of the void. (After all, we have no positive knowledge of that void)"* (*H*, p. 314). The first is the existential alternative, with its modern disintegrated consciousness and its final rejection of "ordinary" life in the confrontation with death; the second, Herzog's view, is a tightrope version of community, the citizen hero balancing over the void, a possible nothingness, which in the end can neither be affirmed nor denied. Herzog uses the metaphor of owing, with its typically Jewish sense of obligation to "choose life," in the Asphalter scene as well. Herzog advances his argument as an explicit critique of Heidegger's view of death: without the moral, the political vocation, "without this true employment you never dread death, you cultivate it" (*H*, p. 272). In criticizing the philosopher for his lack of civility, of a sense of community, of ignorance of the other, Professor Herzog is joining a distinguished company. The *Verfallensein* often attends a pathological otherworldliness, the emotional context of Christian asceticism without belief. Herzog describes Tina Zokóly in just these terms, the old *memento mori*, the monk's skull on the table, brought up to date. This sophisticated form of nihilism is contingent upon a reductive, mechanical view or ordinary experience characterized by empty hedonism, guilt and dread. The monolithic gloom of existentialism is based on the typically modern subversion of possibility. Despite these falsifications, Herzog has not given up on serious discourse. "What can thoughtful people and humanists do," he says, "but struggle toward suitable words" (*H*, p. 272). His identification with humanism is much to the point.

Sartre himself has written an essay called "Existentialism is a Humanism" that speaks of humanism in a limited sense: value and intelligibility depend upon the choice of individual persons. But Sartre's more typical, negative evaluation of humanism is given in a scene in *Nausea*. Roquentin is forced to endure the company of the Self-Taught Man, who learned to "believe in men" in an internment camp during World War I. His description of the conversion makes it clear that it is man in the abstract he loves: "All those men were there, you could hardly see them but you could feel them against you. . . . The crush was so great that at first I thought I was going to suffocate, then, suddenly, an overwhelming joy came over me, I almost fainted: then I felt that I loved these men like brothers, I wanted to embrace all of them."[6] This proves to be something of a bad joke when the reader later discovers that the Self-Taught Man is a homosexual. It seems, though, that any form of general humanity attracts the Self-Taught Man. Though a Socialist and an unbeliever, he used to go to Mass for "the communion of souls" (N, p. 155), as if the souls communed with one another. "All men are my friends," he says (N, p. 157). This leads Roquentin to make a sardonic catalogue of ludicrous humanisms, the common denominator of which is its supposed indiscriminateness, "for humanism takes possession and melts all human attitudes into one" (N, p. 159). Roquentin's catalogue is inclusive:

The radical humanist is the particular friend of officials. The so-called "left" humanist's main worry is keeping human values; he belongs to no party because he does not want to betray the human, but his sympathies go toward the humble; he consecrates his beautiful classic culture to the humble. He is generally a widower with a fine eye always clouded with tears: he weeps at anniversaries. He also loves cats, dogs, and all the higher mammals. The Communist writer has been loving men since the second Five-Year Plan; he punishes because he loves. Modest as all strong men, he knows how to hide his feelings, but he also knows, by a look, an inflection of his voice, how to recognize, behind his rough and ready justicial utterances, his passion for his brethren. The Catholic humanist, the late comer, the Benjamin, speaks of men with a marvelous air. What a beautiful fairy tale, says he, is the humble life of a London dockhand, the girl in the shoe factory! He has chosen the humanism of the angels; he writes, for their edification, long, sad and beautiful novels which frequently win the Prix Femina.

Those are the principal roles. But there are others, a swarm of others: the humanist philosopher who bends over his brothers like a wise elder brother who has a sense of his responsibilities; the humanist who loves men as they are, the humanist who loves men as they ought to be, the one who wants to save them with their consent and the one who will save them in spite of themselves, the one who wants to create new myths, and the one who is satisfied with the old ones, the one who loves death in man, the one who loves life in man, the happy humanist who always has the right word to make people laugh, the sober humanist whom you meet especially at funerals or wakes. They all hate each other: as individuals, naturally not as men. (N, pp. 157f.)

The trouble with Roquentin's catalogue is that it itself suffers from a crude indiscriminateness, not to say cynicism. He does not really distinguish between the two humanisms, yet anyone familiar with the revisionist liberal tendency in postwar America knows that this is as important as it is easy (now) to do. The careers of writers and intellectuals like Bellow, Ellison, Trilling and Shils have been founded on this distinction.

Leaving aside Roquentin's caricature, Bellow would clearly be sympathetic to the criticism of abstract humanism as manifested in Marxism and simplistic forms of liberalism, and generally sympathetic to the existential critique of Hegelian abstraction. Revisionist liberalism exists in the service of humanism without illusion. Roquentin's "left" humanist begins, at least, as a fairly close approximation to Bellow's kind of humanism, provided that we add that the socially humble can be psychologically proud. Roquentin, of course, admits to no such recognition and reduces the humanist to caricature. Other snatches of his catalogue germane to Bellow are the philosopher and "the one who loves life in man." Bellow's humanism has defined itself in the collapse of the old, apocalyptic one; it is a humanism with less heat perhaps, but more light, a humanism of civilized possibility. "Whom must you love?" asks Roquentin. "All," answers the Self-Taught Man (*N*, p. 160)—a proposition that Herzog, like Roquentin, would find objectionable. When the Self-Taught Man fails to see that the face of the man at the next table shows a bastard, and says, "how can you judge a man by his face? A face, Monsieur, tells nothing when at rest," Roquentin thinks, "Blind humanists! This face is so outspoken, so frank—but their tender, abstract soul will never let itself be touched by the sense of a face" (*N*, p. 162). The sense of a face, a beautiful phrase. But in what sense is Sartre's protagonist "touched"? The very word implies the opposite of the contempt he feels.

Roquentin is right in taking the abstract humanist to task. How can you not judge a man by his face? Yet who knows this better than the new humanist, better, in fact, than Bellow, who is a master of facial expression. And what does Roquentin's odd construction—their tender, abstract soul— speak of if not the very abstraction he purports to condemn. *They* do not have *a soul*. What are we to make of a man whose championing of individuality does not extend so far as learning his antagonist's name? He remains an abstraction to Roquentin. There is some justification to the nausea Roquentin feels for what might be called the Self-Taught Man's "potato love," but how much credence can we give to a man so pathological that he can say, "a taste of blood in the mouth instead of this taste of cheese makes no difference to me" (*N*, p. 166)? *De gustibus non disputandum? Chacun a son goo?* Roquentin's comparison murders civilization. Even Meursault would not have made it.

The humanism of disillusion can be clearly differentiated from its univer-

salizing brethren. "Potato love" is something Herzog must protect himself
from. Tommy Wilhelm feels a universal love in the New York subway, but it
soon seems to him a bogus affectivity. Yet he realizes that he "must go back
to that" (SD, pp. 84f.) and, in a sense, in the concluding scene of the story,
does—not in the universalizing of love but in the recognition of suffering,
for even his intimate community has dissipated. In *The Victim*, Leventhal's
perception that "everything without exception took place as if within a single
soul or person" is modified by the knowledge that "tomorrow this would be
untenable" (V, p. 151). While falling well short of a Kierkegaardian or Dostoevskian antipathy for theories of humanity considered in the abstract, Bellow's compelling creations are inspired by a principle of individuation, a
sense of personal gain and loss, a sense of face. His heroes often express an
idea of civility and sometimes of community; the latter is sought after but
realized collectively only in wish or gesture or, individually, in a personal
and familial way. Bellow is not usually charmed, and never destroyed, by
collectivist abstraction.

In speaking to Asphalter, Herzog espouses individuality in a context of
brotherhood. Where this collective abstraction is dramatized in the present
tense in Bellow remains a question. Yet Herzog is drawn to it. To be sure,
his is no Comtean belief in a religion of humanity, or in an optimistic
uniting of all mankind in ties of brotherhood. Without believing in Progress, Bellow will not give up on certain Enlightenment ideals. His is the
temper of liberal humanism, which without the optimism of collectivist
humanism, is also without the pessimism of existentialism. Unlike the latter, it posits integrity in the ordinary world. Taking transcendence seriously, it does not, however, assume that existence is a mere shadow of
ontologically prior Being. It believes, in Herzog's words, that Reason exists
and is effective or can be. Fully aware of life's desperation, Herzog stands
with Mill rather than Marx in his political affinities. Like Mill, like Tocqueville, Herzog has in mind the Enlightenment and democracy, on the one
hand, and conservatism, on the other. Like them, like many of the revisionist liberal American writers and intellectuals, he has gone as far in his
anti-Jacobin tendencies as he has in his mistrust of authority—all in the
interests of preserving the narrow and hard-won terrain of individual freedom and of individuality. Like them, he lives in an age whose permanent
feature is transition, making him adopt a psychology of interregnum. In an
essay on Bellow, John Bayley has noted that the "American-Jewish novel
has the obvious but enormous advantage of continuity not only with the
almost pre-fictional tradition of the *honnête homme*, but with the great
humanistic liberal and Victorian novel world of Dickens, Thackeray and
George Eliot. . . . A certain kind of Jewish image today is the product not
of the Torah and the Hasidim but of *Little Dorrit* and John Stuart Mill."[7]

To strike a meliorist balance in dark circumstances, to not give up on the good, to conceive of God as a supernatural sanction of ethical rightness, to believe that there is a moral standard and that liberalism is the best way of realizing it in contemporary circumstances—this nexus of ideas, indeed, the "breakthrough" of American-Jewish writers and intellectuals on the whole, gives the lie to the idea that, in Hegel's terms, the Unhappy Consciousness has put the Honest Consciousness to rout, or, for that matter, that they should be conceived as polar opposites.

Herzog's position vis-à-vis modernism comes into even clearer focus when we look at the traditionalist assault on Romanticism. We have seen that Herzog is unconvinced by T. E. Hulme and his followers. On his part, Hulme had nothing good to say about humanism. "The fundamental error," he holds with apparent lucidity, "is that of placing Perfection in *humanity,* thus giving rise to that bastard thing Personality, and all the bunkum that follows from it."[8] Hulme equates humanism with Romanticism in point of perfection. Assuming, for the sake of argument, that the Romantics espoused what Hulme calls Perfection in humanity—some, perhaps, did, or did for a time; others did not—Hulme's criticism can tell us nothing about the humanism of disillusion, which, as we have seen, is born out of a rejection of various humanisms of "Perfection." One cannot help smiling at Hulme's metaphorical turn. Personality is a bastard thing, an illegitimate cross between man and perfection, as if one would not believe in personality without believing in perfection! In our own day it is almost axiomatic that belief in one precludes belief in the other. Hulme can sound like the Reign of Terror itself. He wants to "destroy all these bastard phenomena" (S, p. 11)—Romanticism in literature, Relativism in ethics, Idealism in philosophy, and Modernism in religion, a devastating and confused list. Suffice it to say, Hulme despises independent subjectivity. Suffice it to say, Hulme has the startling clarity of the pure reactionary.

Hulme is a right-wing Christian ideologist, constructing an embattled and simplified we / they confrontation between the Children of Light and the Children of Darkness. The trouble with humanism, as Hulme sees it, is that it makes that appalling Rousseauvian assumption that man is "good." "A man is essentially bad" (S, p. 47), says Hulme. It is refreshing to find a sophisticated mind who is not afraid to use (or is it aware of using?) the vocabulary of Humanities I. What is wrong with humanism, in his view, is that it refuses to believe in Original Sin or radical imperfection. Life is then the source and measure of all values, "the problem of evil" disappears and the conception of sin loses all meaning. Humanism "distorts the real nature of ethical values by deriving them out of essentially subjective things, like human desires and feelings" (S, p. 48). Tracing our sorry state back to the Greeks and the Renaissance, Hulme maintains that "humanism could have no permanence;

however heroic at the start, it was bound sooner or later to end in Rousseau" (S, p. 62). In saying man is God, Romanticism is the root of an awful lot of evil. But Rousseau said nothing of the kind. Once again Hulme is simplistic. One can know a great deal about imperfection, even make it a way of life, without believing in Original Sin. True, Hulme is speaking of radical imperfection, innate depravity; it may not be naive to think that this does not exist. Admittedly, for the secular humanist—and Hulme, along with Eliot, holds that there can be no other—the conception of sin loses all meaning, yet one can scarcely say that "evil" has become an irrelevant moral category. As an upholder of civilization and humanistic values, Herzog's task as intellectual, as man, is to resist the idea that evil is all there is, that, as Proudhon thinks, God is the evil. Herzog could not accept the notion that humanistic and religious views were necessarily mutually exclusive. If the good is to be found, with or without God's help, it will be through human feelings and perceptions. Herzog speaks to God outside the synagogue, speaks out of feeling, out of personality.

Yes, Romanticism is the root of much evil for Hulme and "the root of all romanticism [is] that man, the individual, is an infinite reservoir of possibilities" (S, p. 116). According to Hulme, Romanticism makes man out to be a god, posits a heaven on earth. Waxing metaphorical, he says, "it is like pouring a pot of treacle over the dinner table. Romanticism then, and this is the best definition I can give of it, is spilt religion" (S, p. 118). In his letter to Dr. Mossbach, Herzog remembers precisely this metaphor, yet it is characteristic of the dialectical resilience of his mind that, while he is critical of Hulme, he gives a measure of assent to the metaphor. "*I sympathize with Hulme's attack on the introduction by the Romantics of Perfection into human things,*" says the revisionist liberal Herzog, "*but do not like his narrow repressiveness either*" (H, p. 129). One early version states that "it has something but not much to do with the way I actually feel" (B.16.12). Herzog can sympathize when Hulme objects "to the sloppiness which doesn't consider that a poem is a poem unless it is a moaning or whining about something or other," objects to Romantics who think that "poetry that isn't damp isn't poetry at all" (S, p. 127). Commenting on this passage, Herzog says, "*He wanted things to be clear, dry, spare, pure, cool, and hard. With this I think we can all sympathize. I too am repelled by the 'dampness,' as he called it and the swarming of Romantic feelings. I see what a villain Rousseau was and how degenerate*" (H, p. 129). But Herzog's recollection of adjectives is perhaps too generous. What Hulme says is, "It is essential to prove that beauty may be in small, dry things" (S, p. 131), precisely the adjectives that his leading disciple, T. S. Eliot, uses as he momentarily rejoices in his discovery of the purgatorial, self-denying, post-Romantic air.

Because these wings are no longer wings to fly
But merely fans to beat the air
The air which is now thoroughly small and dry
Smaller and dryer than the will   ("Ash Wednesday")

Eliot shows that a "small, dry" aesthetic requires a small, dry will. Herzog's partial assent surely does not imply agreement.

Our exhausted Prince of the Heart comes down on the side of Rousseau: "*But I do not see what we can answer when he says* 'Je sens mon coeur et je connais les hommes.' " This statement, from the beginning of *The Confessions*, enshrines the primacy of subjectivity. And for all of Herzog's objections to Rousseau as an individual, he is impressed with him as a type. "*I do not complain that he was ungentlemanly,*" he says; "*it ill becomes me.*" Rousseau is the first of the provincial or petty bourgeois heroes who rise almost magically to a prominent place in the worldly culture by force of will and intelligence, the Young Man From the Provinces, in Lionel Trilling's phrase,[9] who, like Stendhal's Julien Sorel, Balzac's Rastignac, Dickens' Pip, finds a certain historical precedence in Napoleon. We recall Augie March's citation of Napoleon's significance in this regard. It is the "universal eligibility to be noble" (*AM*, p. 29). Rousseau was a creator of the cult of the ego, was a Romantic of feeling but not of thought. The citizen, not the genius, as Hulme might have known and as Professor Herzog might have noted, is his ideal man. And, as has often been noted, in his *La Nouvelle Héloïse* he rewrites *The Sorrows of Werther* with the proper, ethical ending. Rousseau was not nearly so much taken with Perfection in human things as Hulme contends.

For Herzog, the vagaries of the heart remain preferable, in all their ambiguity, to "*bottled religion, on conservative principles.*" Even more emphatically, Herzog deplores the cultural consequences of Hulme's seminal collection of essays. "*Hulme's followers made sterility their truth, confessing their impotence. This was their passion*"—a defensible description of Eliot, Pound and Wyndham Lewis. Toward the end of the novel Herzog seems to be modifying his assessment of Rousseau. He thinks of the line about knowing the heart and is left with some doubt: "his mind detached itself also from its French. *I couldn't say that for sure. My face too blind, my mind too limited, my instincts too narrow.*" He refuses, however, to admit so much authority to disintegration: "But this intensity, doesn't it mean anything?" (*H*, p. 340). The answer is yes. The product of heart is knowledge. Complexity obviates sentimentality here and in his delineation of romanticism in the critique of Hulme. Moreover, that critique is followed by the portrait of Nachman, whose introduction of what Hulme called "Perfection into human things" is seen by Herzog as a living proof of the relevance of Hulme's ideas.

But his memory of the family home on Napoleon Street—the very name, and its shift from St. Dominick Street, indicates the universality of the Young Man From the Provinces as a social type, and Herzog's preference for Romantic to Christian categories—recalls the primacy of the heart.

Granting much more to man's moral agency than does Hulme's version of Christianity, Herzog sees limits to Romantic confusion. It is not accidental to the novel that Herzog is a Jewish intellectual. In opposition to the Romantic, Hulme maintains "that the Church has always taken the classical view since the defeat of the Pelagian heresy and the adoption of the sane classical dogma of original sin" (S, p. 117). One is not entirely certain of what Hulme means by sane. Does this make those who do not believe in Original Sin insane, or merely unhealthy? In any case, one man's heresy is another man's belief, and in identifying the Pelagian heresy, Hulme might as well be identifying Judaism, to which, as theologians have pointed out, there is a close parallel. It comes as a surprise to Christian and secular intellectuals, and, indeed, to Jewish intellectuals (whose bent is often so secular as to exclude knowledge of even the most fundamental Jewish doctrine), that Jews do not believe in Original Sin. One can best quote at this point from a theological scholar, Arthur A. Cohen, the title of whose work, *The Myth of the Judeo–Christian Tradition*, intends to provoke as well as enlighten. Cohen points precisely to the Pelagian quality of Jewish belief. For the Jew "the sin of Adam did not corrupt all mankind. . . . Everything good and everything evil is done by man and not born with man. . . . The Jew is Pelagian since the world, according to his lights, has neither properly fallen nor has been properly redeemed."[10] He follows the Law rather than the Gospel, making "a hopeful estimation of the possibility of human nature before God. The Pelagian commences by affirming that man is not condemned from the beginning; that, if he be condemned, it is through his own works that condemnation is wrought; that, if he be redeemed, it is through his contrition and penance."[11] The Jew is to follow Torah, "sanctify creation, then creation will find favor, and redemption will come to praise it—not rescue it for all eternity." The rescued and the sanctified, says Cohen, "he who is ransomed by faith and he who struggles with the law—will both find their way to God."[12]

Well, Moses (the Law) Elkanah (Praise God) finds his way to God in a fairly Jewish way. True, he is not strong on sanctification, not precisely a devotee of the Shulchan Orach (the 613 *mitzvot* or moral obligations), but his version, and that of other Bellow protagonists, of the *amor fati* conceived as blessedness rather than indifference, is to the point. Somewhat penitent, but not exactly contrite, he is more than anything acutely self-critical. He does utter the classical Jewish *Hineni* (H, p. 310), but in a paradoxically expansive way. He is too steeped in modern consciousness to have the orthodox self-abasement. Though an authority on the sixth commandment, he is not formidable on the seventh. His citizen-hero emphasis on action and community is in the tradition, qualified though it is by modernist ironies, but his emphasis is on the community of mankind rather than Jewish-peoplehood. He addresses God—"Thou movest me" (*H*, p. 340)—but the very terms are Romantic, described in terms of subjectivity, feeling, "a holy feeling" (*H*, p. 340), to be sure. After he says, "Thou movest me" for the second time, an early version adds, "Toward the life of mankind" (B.17.10), as if to underscore the worldliness of his spiritual direction. No such underlining is necessary.

In describing what might be termed Herzog's latitudinarian Jewishness—and latitudinarian Christian outlooks, as opposed to Hulme's or Eliot's, are not far from it—we are describing a religious viewpoint amenable to the tradition of liberalism. In this connection, it is not difficult to see why modernists of a politically reactionary cast were anti-Semitic. As John R. Harrison observes of Lawrence, "like Lewis, Pound and Eliot he believed the whole liberal-democratic tradition to be essentially Jewish in nature."[13] This gives God more credit than He usually comes in for these days, and one might have difficulty gaining the assent of a Hasid on this point, but as Bailie says, the contemporary Jewish writers are closer to Mill than Hasidism, a generalization from which only a few writers might be excepted. For all his weariness of personality, the individual remains the turbulent center of value for Herzog, as it does for liberalism; and Herzog, like the liberal theoretician Hobhouse, has not given up on the idea that society can be based on the self-directing power of personality. In an early version we see Herzog writing to a friend in defense of liberalism: "*Dear Martin* [Seymour Martin Lipset?]: *Is the case for Liberalism really so weak? . . . I wish people would be more cautious about it. By assigning it simply to the bourgeois nineteenth century . . . I'd like to see those very critics managing without*" (B.19.32, 63f.). A mid-century Jew, this Moses is far more beholden to reason than to revelation, spurred on by a spirit of reform but skeptical of utopian solutions and indifferent to the eschatological, which in our literary waiting-for-the-enders is usually reduced to the scatological. He would qualify as one of Eliot's undesirable "free-thinking Jews,"[14] disputing Eliot's assumption that "the disappearance of the idea of Original Sin" means "the disappearance of the idea of intense moral struggle."[15] Eliot wants to "renew our association with traditional wisdom; to re-establish the vital connection between the individual and the race," to fight "the struggle in a word against Liberalism."[16] Well, there are traditions and traditions.

Yet Herzog would see wisdom in Eliot's charge—a serious, crucial one—that instead of morals we have personality, that being one's self "is considered more important than that the self in question should, socially and spiritually, be a good or a bad one."[17] But that one can be good by denying the self rather than affirming it remains doubtful. The movement of Eliot's career is from artistic asceticism to religious asceticism. Herzog resists the message. Hulme's followers have made sterility their truth. It may be thought that they give Original Sin a bad name. One can agree with Harrison's saying that the pessimism of Lewis and Pound is based on a sense of man's feebleness rather than Original Sin, but the distinction is a fine one, and the effect is the same. And Eliot, like other modernists, existential and otherwise, deals in a condition of Original Sin amounting to exile. (The Thomist position, with its meliorist conception of the Fall, is closer to Bellow's own.) We recall Herzog reading from Kierkegaard's *Sickness Unto Death*: *"For dying means that it is all over, but dying the death means to experience death."* Trying to make sense of this, Herzog thinks, as if to tie Sartre and Kierkegaard together, "if existence is nausea then faith is an uncertain relief." As he told Mermelstein, feeling "the power of God as he restores you" by being "demolished by suffering" is part of the doomsday psychology and must be rejected. Not that Herzog avoids thinking about death. Far from it. It is the essential limit. But he considers this, enervated as he is at the beginning of the novel, "probably a symptom of disorder," adding, with Jewish irony, that the "perpetual thought of death was a sin," and concluding, with the Blakean wisdom of Romantic vitalism, "Drive your cart and your plough over the bones of the dead" (*H*, p. 33). Dying is final, but death is not, as we see in his polemic against Death as the god of nihilism: "Death is God. This generation thinks and this is its thought of thoughts—that nothing faithful, vulnerable, fragile can be durable or have any true power" (*H*, p. 290). He resists this as he resists existentialism. His Hebrew invocation of God, "Thou King of Death and Life" (*H*, p. 304) gives a more balanced view, though the slip here—it should be King of Life and Death, as it is in manuscript (B.18.15)—may be an unconscious indication that the deathniks are getting to him.

Hulme's attack on humanism is based on a conception of art that is the very obverse of Bellow's. He comes out for what he takes to be the religious attitude in art: "The disgust with the trivial and accidental characteristics of living shapes, the searching after an austerity, a monumental stability and permanence, a perfection and rigidity, which vital things can never have, leads to the use of forms which can be called *geometrical*. Man is subordinate to certain absolute values: there is no delight in the human form, leading to its natural reproduction."[18] Clearly, this need not necessarily be the essence of art with a religious dimension. Wasn't Blake taken by "the Human Form Divine"? And isn't the author of *Herzog*, so steeped in Blake as he writes? Bellow has always been skeptical about the dehumanization of art, his attack on Sarraute being a conspicuous illustration. For him art must have what

Hulme calls "the trivial and accidental characteristics of living shapes," must have the sense of a face and a body. Ortega y Gasset, who coined the phrase "dehumanization of art" in an essay by that name, holds that "great periods of art have been careful not to let the word revolve about human contents," the nineteenth century representing "a maximum aberration in the history of taste."[19] In Dickens, for example, you get "character" but no style. "Toute maîtrise jette le froid," he quotes Mallarmé sympathetically. "Tears and laughter are, aesthetically, frauds," Ortega tells us. In his view, the Romantic poet had it all wrong: "All the poet wished was to be human."[20] Bellow's humanist art is defined in the face of these arch-conservative proscriptions. He has many links with this nineteenth century, which, in its aberration, was the greatest literary century the world has known.

Bellow's complex relationship to Freud is also to be understood in this context, the context of modernist negation, the delimitation to the point of denial of generous human impulses. In this sense austere Freudianism and austere Christianity—the adjective may be a necessary qualification—are scarcely at odds. We recall that Edvig has written some *"stuff about the psychological realism of Calvin."* And we recall Herzog's reaction to it: *"I hope you don't mind my saying that it reveals a lousy, cringing, grudging conception of human nature. This is how I see your Protestant Freudianism"* (*H*, pp. 57f.). One early version has Edvig, a follower of the Rogers non-directive method, the author of an essay on "Karl Barth and Sigmund Freud" (B.17.4). In another he knows Kierkegaard and has a Lutheran orientation. The point is drawn for us by Herzog:

> The devil was reborn in the Protestant Era, and the Protestant view of sin and of the wickedness of man's heart and the distortion of human aims, the possession of this world by evil, the unreal quality of human actions, the descriptions of work, money, politics, war, society as dark hallucinations, the shadow of a dream—all this could be Freudian as well. (B.19.36, 108)

Well, perhaps it could in one manner of interpretation. The point to be made is that Herzog feels that both represent the idea that "in this world there is no good, no good in human motives . . . man's whole life being in both doctrines a disease. Only, in one case, God may show mercy to those always undeserving sinful . . . betrayers of the divine gift" (B.19.36, 108 f.). When, in another version of the Edvig letter, Herzog inveighs against "the devil in our hearts," he does so against the old Bellovian bugaboo, determinism: "What a man thinks he is doing counts for nothing. All his work in the world is done by impulses he will never understand—sinful to the priest, sexual to the psychiatrist" (B.19.36, 113).

In a recent interview, Bellow tells of reading in Freud about the story of an American doctor who had written Freud after reading *The Future of an*

Illusion (a book that in manuscript [B.20.15] Herzog says he "disagreed" with; "must religion be obsessional neurosis?"), saying that "I, too, at one time lost my faith." As a medical student the doctor had been taken aback when "a very beautiful old woman" was brought into the dissecting room as a cadaver. He could no longer believe in God. Later he recovered his faith and recommended that Freud "postpone a final decision on the existence of God for a time." Freud comments that "of course, what this man saw in the cadaver in the dissecting room was his mother." Bellow reacts strongly to this, "Was it not possible," he asks, "to experience beauty or pity without thinking of your mother, or without the Oedipus complex?" What he is objecting to is the unconscious as a form of determinism. He asks, "What is the unconscious after all? The unconscious is anything human beings don't know. . . . Is it possible that what we don't know has a metaphysical character and not a Freudian, naturalistic character? I think that the unconscious is a concept that begs the question and simply returns us to our ignorance with an arrogant attitude of confidence, and this is why I'm against it."[21] Once again Bellow is insisting on the possibility of purity in human motives and the possibility of moral agency. When we move from the personal unconscious to the collective unconscious of *Totem and Taboo*, Herzog's objection is even more sweeping. He dismisses Freud, Roheim, "primal crime [as] the origin of social order" as "metaphor," saying, "I can't truly feel I can attribute my blundering to this thick unconscious cloud. This primitive blood daze" (*H*, p. 303). The collective conscious, so to speak, in its aspect of social order, gives us the "clumsy, inexact machinery of civil peace." An earlier version adds a then current note of sociological optimism, which is at the same time a denigration of the primal crime theory: "Not everything is dissensus. Overwhelming consensus after all" (B.21.41, 356).

In pointing to Bellow's affirmation of individual autonomy, one is also pointing to his debt to Protestantism, to the line running from Reformation to Romanticism. Herzog can not quite part company with that recalcitrant Swiss Protestant, Rousseau, any more than he can dismiss Romanticism outright or disencumber himself of his own ego. Though we may live in what Herzog once called a "chaos of autonomy," that "cherished inwardness, the gift of Protestantism and capitalism" (B.17.4), is something he is unwilling and, indeed, unable to forego. And if Freud is an influence he must shake off, he is nevertheless an influence. Bellow is so immersed in Freud that much of his psychological comedy is inconceivable without him and the terminology that he made part of everyday speech. *Herzog* and other works of Bellow have an aspect of clinical comedy of which the characters may well be aware. So, for example, a manuscript version has Herzog musing of Valentine in this way: "I am sure he believes he will be an infinitely better father. It is the poor fellow's megalomania. Appealing to Juliana's paranoia.

Which felt contempt for my melancholia" (B.21.31, 250). And Herzog would seem to have some sympathy for the recent vogue of psychohistory, admiring it even though it appears in the work of Egbert Schapiro. Nor does Herzog dispute, though he well might on clinical grounds, the psychoanalytic judgment that he is a reactive depressive. (He is not so depressed, so diminished in his self-regard, as to have his biological needs inhibited for long.) There is much musing on this term, particularly in manuscript, where the source of his insight, Freud's paper on "Mourning and Melancholia," is named. In a letter to Freud, we see Herzog reading, *"stooping over the print in the stacks of the library, my adopted synagogue"* (B.20.40). In another version, Herzog prefaces an elaborate summary of the essay with a note of grudging admiration:

> *As you might imagine . . . I did not read your essay by accident. Man prays in our religion (or former religion) for a "new heart." Radical determinism like yours offers no place for new hearts. But why else would anyone pray or seek light? . . . The depressive is narcissistic. It fears the disappearance of the beloved. Above all terrors it places the terror of abandonment and naked solitude. So with secret hate it cuts off the deserter. . . . You say then that the depressive is often able to state the truth about himself quite reliably and accurately, though he often overstates the case, and you add—it must have been irresistible—that it is odd to think that insight should be the result of disease. . . . But my dear man, I am really very fond of that tart old man, let us go back a bit. Is it possible that some people are born with a greater metaphysical terror than others, with less sheath or with [less] power to apprehend the inhuman and the void.*

Respectful but skeptical, Herzog considers his sickness a form of ordinary consciousness, James' tender-mindedness. After all, bad things can happen to depressives. And the beloved of this particular "depressive" does disappear. Yet Herzog is willing to meet Freud halfway: *"I am grateful to you for certain information, such as that the melancholic is abnormal in stripping his libido so rapidly from the deserting lover. Suffering from love yet intolerably cruel"* (B.21.32, 235f.). The final version retains none of this letter, and only a clinically relevant fragment remains in the first Edvig sequence. As the novel was being written, Bellow wanted to assert more and more an independence from Freud.

As for Freud's epigoni, the manuscripts show that Herzog finds them a source of comic riches. There is the shrink who says that "in three hundred years people will read *Othello* and laugh themselves sick. After the sexual revolution jealousy will be old-fashioned, like silent films" (B.18.12, 23). Then there is the navy shrink who thought Herzog "was sick when I said I had become interested in modern religious literature" (B.19.36, 107). The best such character sketch, apparently left in manuscript because it was too light for the Edvig part of the book, is one of an analyst Edvig recommends, Dr. Harry Seljuk, a self-styled "swinging doctor [who] likes to lean back and talk about his own exploits." He has a philosophical rationale: "life is short, sex is fun, man's reason is just strong enough to understand this." His favorite words for Herzog are "dire" and "grim"; "all too true," says Herzog, "better the house of mourning than the house of mirth, and other Jewish teachings which depress vitality." But Herzog has Dr. Seljuk pegged: he "filled out the modern picture in considerable detail! The mental-nihilist in a power-world, eating, drinking, banking, adding to his healthy substance, under a senseless heaven" (B.17.7).

For all Bellow's fascination with Freud, his rejection in terms of value is final. One early version puts it emphatically: "Freud confessed he laid down his arms before the problem of art. He should have surrendered to all the mysteries of high inspiration, including the work of a moral genius" (B.17.8). These are, of course, strong words. But what of the good? The pure impulse? So persuasive an advocate as Philip Rieff can write, "Freud could not speak of the desire to be good in the same sense that he could speak of desiring what we have to renounce for the good. Surely this is onesided. Aspiration may be as genuine as desire, and as original."[22] Further, Rieff acknowledges that "the Freudian ethic may be liable to an indictment of nihilism. As a purely explanatory and scientific ideal, honesty has no content."[23] In addition, psychological man must be wary of whatever success may lurk in his future, for "openness of character may well elicit more, not less, brutality. . . . The new ethic fears the honest criminal lurking behind the pious neurotic."[24] Rameau's nephew adumbrated these possibilities during the first stirrings of the modern era over two hundred years ago. Freud presents Bellow with only the most brilliant illustration of the modern temper.

Herzog's relationship to modernism is clear enough. His connection to Romanticism, as we have had occasion to see in his letter to Dr. Mossbach, is more complicated. The manuscripts uncomplicate this connection. Herzog has written a book called *Romanticism and Christianity*. While his view of Romanticism is not nearly so critical as Hulme's, he is very critical of its apocalyptic aspect, which, ironically, he considers a carry-over from Christianity. One early version shows Professor Herzog embattled about the Gnostic character Romanticism can take: "Drop a load of brimstone on Romantic self-idolatry. . . . Romanticism is Christianity in modern form. Lawless, apocalyptic, devoid of responsibility, invoking destruction of the old in the expectation of a new birth from the ashes of this civilization of death." There is as much truth to this view as there is to the austere, patrician one of Hulme and Eliot. Yet this is the view most relevant to modern circumstances. For Herzog, would that this were not so, would that the human face of Romanticism, and of Christianity, were in the ascendant. But, he maintains, "it is the violent side of Romanticism that most of us plunge into, not the meaningful heart of William Blake. 'For we are put on earth a little while / To learn to bear the beams of love.' Not that but rather the Brown Shirts and their Final Solution, Götterdämmerung" (B.16.5). Blake, of course, could himself be violent and apocalyptic, but with the spontaneity of the iconoclast, the prophetic voice in the wilderness. When iconoclasm becomes brutality, when the individual becomes the state, when the poet becomes the general, when the apocalyptic becomes the fascistic, we see romanticism distorted into totalitarianism. The sorry history of modern Europe shows that Christianity could be supportive of this shift, as well as opposing. The ceremony of innocence was drowned. Elsewhere, Herzog registers a humanist complaint against what he considers a quality of romantic absolutism derived from Christianity. "It is undoubtedly true," he says, "that with us romanticism is continued mainly by women. Absolute love. Absolute happiness. Absolute power. No details in life. Details are contemptible to the romantic, a legacy of otherworldliness from the church" (B.18.12, 24). He again associates the two in his description of the pathetic Hoberly, who, as Romantic victim, is what a weak Herzog might have been. He rejects the "lowgrade romantic nonsense, the poor man's Liebestod [sic], soiled remnants of confused Christianity" (B.21.9, 266). His resistance to Mady is based on the same juxtaposition. Describing her to Edvig, with whom he has been discussing Christianity, he says, "I think she has a romantic mind. It may amount to the same thing [as a Christian mind, *pace* Hulme]. All that subjective intensity. That otherworldliness. Saviorism" (B.19.43, 201). An earlier version puts it dualistically: "I think she has a Gothic romantic mind. Otherworldliness on the upper level, and dirty pool below. And saviorism" (B.16.6). The indebtedness of our skeptical humanist to the granddaddy of skeptical humanism may come to mind. "Between ourselves," says Montaigne in his essay "Of Experience," "there are two things that I have always observed to be in singular accord: supercelestial thoughts and subterranean conduct."[25] "The voice of Montaigne," we are told, was "always of the deepest personal relevance to Herzog" (B.21.31, 246). This disparaging dual metaphor occurs again when, in manuscript, Herzog speaks of "Romantic individualism" as such, "a bête noir with Herzog, a late union of Christian and Faustian ideals which bred mad wars and revolutions. High apocalyptic dreams above, dung and ashes beneath" (B.18.11, 112). To this he contrasts Hegel, who "believed man's higher development to depend on the state, civil order," an abstraction man must still value.

Herzog makes these last distinctions in a draft letter to General Eisenhower, which, considering the detached, condescending view he takes of him in the novel, is something of a surprise. That he cannot in the end address Eisenhower so seriously is itself an undercutting of the idea of civility and consensus. But, if not the context, the ideas remain intact. "He had been about to explain to the General the views of Professor Lipset that the time of alienation was over for the intellectual. Everyone was on the threshold of integration—the brainy, the black" (B.18.11, 111). If Herzog seems too eager to embrace what is sometimes called the sunshine school of sociology, he is aware of the precariousness of his position, its aspect of uphill struggle in the face of the instant romanticism (yet to surface fully) of the sixties. He sees that "terms like 'the civil state' do not seem adequate to describe the new conditions of consciousness. If the promise of an extended consciousness is that it may put us closer to God, the commoner fact is that this mental development encourages demonism even more than piety toward the world. There are many now who feel like demons, taking the disguise of human beings" (B.18.15, 25). The citizen hero is by definition suspicious of the antinomian Romantic, whose apotheosis is Lucifer—what ever happened to Prometheus?—and whose antecedents include artist-heroes from Werther to Stephen Dedalus. As if in answer to the resounding *non-servium* of the latter, Herzog writes that he is "not a romantic with famished, smoking eyes, the creed of *non-servium* in his pocket . . . but a man who had all his life been making some sort of case" (B.18.12, 117). Of course, rebellion, too, can be a case, but the forensic metaphor implies the imagination of civility. An early version shows Herzog attacking Governor Stevenson for being a political wrong-way Corrigan. He has "the look of a man who gives himself in martyrdom from a sense of duty, and grieves at the loss of his private mental life, and also mocks his own grief—this sort of Byronism, gloominess, romantic sense of Self, just the sort of thing that suits some drunken old professor of Art History going to pieces in a cow college, or a fading queen in the foreign service, but not a leader, for God's sake! An air of uniqueness" (B.18.18, 57). As it appears in *Herzog*, the Stevenson letter is less optimistic about the coalescence of intelligence and power. But Herzog is less hard on Stevenson's self-regard since the former no longer sees it to be Romantic but humanist: "*Perhaps you did contribute something useful in the last decade, showing up the old-fashioned self-intensity of the 'humanist,' the look of the 'intelligent man' grieving at the loss of his private life, sacrificed to public service*" (H, p. 66). Stevenson was, after all, no Romantic rebel. And what, in Bellow's view does contemporary rebellion amount to? Not much. A note in the *Herzog* notebooks could not be more clear: "The big fight against society (Fiedler) amounts to a fight against the bourgeois ideal. It can only produce minor romantic work. There is more

rebellion and horror in the middle-class heart than in the heart of the beatnik. He relieves himself by protest" (B.16.9). Whatever "the bourgeois
ideal" is, one may agree that the beatnik (though not all the rebels of the late
sixties) is a sorry satyr play to the drama that was Romantic rebellion. Herzog
puts it in roughly the same context of judgment: "the present descent into
garbage is the Promethean sublimity of the last century inside-out" (B.17.6).

Though aware of the painful excesses of the cult of the ego, Herzog is also
aware of his indebtedness to it. His consciousness of the heart derives in part
from Rousseau, Blake, and Whitman. "*Must agree in the end with A. N.
Whitehead,*" he notes, "*that the romantic reaction was a protest on behalf of
values. Though romanticism may not survive the attacks of the last few
generations. I have myself contributed. On the inadequacy of the social
ideas of the romantics*" (B.18.5). This, as usual, is a mouthful, but its content
is conventional wisdom. The Romantics preserved the self from the stringen-
cies of scientific rationalism, as Whitehead's *Science and the Modern World*
shows, but the exaltation of the self at the expense of ordinary life led to
excesses of its own. Herzog, however, can value this exaltation in itself. "*I do
not want to sneer at the term Romantic,*" he says, because "*Romanticism
guarded the 'inspired condition,' preserved the poetic, philosophical, and
religious teachings and records of transcendence and the most generous
ideas of mankind, during the greatest and most rapid of transformations*"
(*H*, p. 165). Here it may seem that Herzog has his cake and eats it, for he
lauds the iconoclastic impulses of an inspired condition as he praises it for
affirming tradition. But Herzog is certainly aware that Romanticism did not
leave tradition where it found it, that it recreated it, that it recovered the
visionary. Yet, he maintains, in so doing Romanticism discovered not what
was radically new but what had been obscured. In the *Salmagundi* interview
he says, "Romanticism would have us believe that something startling, daring and new can be found as soon as you purge the film from the inner eye,
or, as soon as you break away from received ideas." But this is Romanticism
exclusively in its modernistic aspect. For Bellow, what is to be found is what
is essentially there: "the important thing [individuals] should discover is
what they are, who they are; that is the novelty, that is what is new."[26]

This skepticism about the radically new brings Bellow closer to classicism
than any pure-bred Romantic can ever get and as close as a Romantic fellow
traveler will ever get. He does, as we have seen, have some sympathy with
Hulme, the author of "Romanticism and Classicism," but less with him than
with the Romantics. In the interview, he acknowledges further attraction to
what he terms classicism in his proposed alternative to romantic originality.
Speaking of Mr. Sammler's wish for coherence through moral imitation, he
says that "Mr. Sammler is thinking of someone like Don Quixote, who said of

course that you can't have anything worthwhile unless you imitate classical models—and that's a classical idea." Is Don Quixote a classical character? A classical work? Are his models classical?

What emerges from this web of terminology is a questioning of the idea of the original or the new as a modernist necessity, as something which assumes that tradition, including traditions of ordinary experience, is dead, that there is no moral center to which to relate, nothing like a moral standard. Imitation, of course, presumes the contrary, and it is an idea which Bellow seriously entertains. But who will Herzog imitate? Or Sammler? And who will determine the models to be imitated? And how can the demands of personality, which in the last analysis are still imperative for Herzog, be reconciled with the requirements of imitation? And does not imitation itself imply an original to be imitated? Rather than literally, he seems to take this as evidence of a lack, as a reminder that there are still people to be looked up to, that morality is still a necessary influence, that one should make the painful admission that there is something—something good—beyond the ego.

Herzog's saturation in personalism has left him, on occasion, sodden. To Ramona he speaks, finally, almost Platonically of "the light of truth," an alternative to "ineffectuality, banishment to personal life, confusion" (H, p. 314). Here, however, he seems to mean not the self as such, but a life which defines itself only in terms of "interpersonal relationships." His letter to God, a problematic correspondent, goes one step farther toward Nirvana. "*How my mind has struggled to make coherent sense. I have not been good at it. But have desired to do your unknowable will, taking it, and you, without symbols. Everything of intensest significance. Especially if divested of me*" (H, p. 326). This from someone with qualified Rousseauistic sympathies. But Herzog values religion as experience not as ontology, as his rejection of symbolism implies. Bellow's spirited "Deep Readers of the World Beware!" piece was an attempt to rescue ordinary experience from the jaws of Being. Herzog's God, in other words, is a psychological necessity. He goes as far as a humanist can go in belief, valuing it as the highest form of emotion, but as literal transcendence, not as cultural anthropology. By Hulme's standard this is still a humanist heresy, but for Bellow a qualitative difference in reality is implied. A manuscript version puts his need for prayer most succinctly: "*it is just as superstitious on the side of knowledge-ability and sophistication to deny real impulse as to believe in primitive hocus pocus, Heavenly Cities, Legions of Gadarene devils and apocalypses.*" He is required to be himself, Herzog says, "but only in accordance with God's will, not in answer to demands of my own" (B.21.41). How one can do this without a more formal, elaborate, ontological committment than Herzog seems prepared to make, we will leave to theologians to determine. Though

Herzog in the end lapses into silence—"Not a single word" (*H*, p. 341)—it is not the silence of otherworldliness. Bellow is not prepared to take this step; but he does not foreclose the possibility. His next novelistic hero is to be a devotee of Meister Eckhart, and the one following him of Rudolf Steiner, two figures, though not approved by the Union of Orthodox Rabbis, who go deeper into the realm of the spirit.

Balancing between the claims of energy and reason, self and selflessness, experience and innocence, it is not surprising that Herzog is a devotee of Blake—"the only writer he could bear reading nowadays" (B.18.16), he says in one manuscript version—the Blake of *Songs of Innocence and Experience*, "The Marriage of Heaven and Hell," and the Rossetti manuscript, with an occasional nod to the prophetic books. Everyone's Blake. So much of the apocalyptic Herzog welcomes. We recall that he has done a chapter on "Heaven and Hell in apocalyptic Romanticism" (*H*, p. 315). There are numerous references to Blake in the manuscripts and the novel—as houseguest, Herzog brings "an old pocket edition of Blake's poems" (*H*, p. 80) to the Himmelsteins—and some references to Bronowski's book on Blake, including a quotation from it which helps explain Blake's attraction. In miscellaneous notes we read, "Revolutions can free him from self-interest: it is the thought which Marx made noble. But they have not then remade man; they have forced him to remake himself. The good remains an end to which societies can give means, but which man must know and make" (B.16.9).

Visionary but not utopian, a psychologist who believes in the soul, Herzog sees a proper balance of Romantic discontent and moral fervor, new spirit and old values, in Blake. Blake's progress from innocence to experience to second innocence, represents, within dialectical shifts, a change of outlook; in Herzog, innocence and experience constitute a continuing dialectic. Blake is the poet of the qualities that attract him to Romanticism. Herzog's chapter on "Romantics and Enthusiasts," which juxtaposes Bacon and Locke with Methodism and William Blake, is about the enthusiastic "reaction against the scientific mode of suspending belief, intolerable to the expressive needs of certain temperaments" (*H*, p. 127), including his own.

Herzog sees in Blake the Romantic awareness of society's repression of self, as in this recollection of "London": "Man has created society to punish him for his desires etc. Marks of weakness marks of woe in every face etc. People consumed by empty duties" (B.18.18). Similarly, he recalls "The Garden of Love": "it's on the social side that the worst brutalities occur, marital slavery, binding the desires with thorns and briars" (B.18.18, 192). Significantly, Blake's poem is an attack on clerical repression, where Herzog seems to see repression intrinsic to the institution of marriage itself (the "marriage hearse" of "London" is something else again), which may be one way of delineating the difference between the 1790s and the 1970s. Yet here

Herzog is pursuing the Blakean idea that energy is true delight, that one must live by "the lineaments of Gratified Desire" ("The Question Answered"), another phrase Herzog likes to quote. Blake, in all his chastity, saw sexuality as an index of one's spiritual condition and he thereby serves Herzog as a reaffirmation of the Romantic vitalist, the principle of naturalistic individuation, in him. Like Blake, he repudiates God as Nobadaddy, inhibitor of delight, dispenser of inevitable sin (B.18.17, 58). Taking the worry out of his relationship with Sono, Herzog recalls (not quite exactly) from "The Marriage of Heaven and Hell," "The pride of the peacock, the lust of the goat, and the wrath of the lion are the glory and wisdom of God" (*H*, p. 188). But even Blake's emphasis on release is subject to Herzog's skepticism: "The poet said that indignation was a kind of joy, but was he right?" (*H*, p. 189) (Again the quote is not exact.) What can be called "biblical" restraint seems even more enduring: "There is a time to speak and a time to shut up."

Valuing the imagination of *Innocence* as he does, Herzog must still go beyond intuitive wisdom to the arduous divisions of self-consciousness, as must Blake himself in *Experience* and "The Marriage of Heaven and Hell." Indeed, the quotation that appears in manuscript as much as any other lines from Blake is the "Motto to the Songs of Innocence and Experience,"[27] which is satiric of innocence standing alone. Herzog has a tendency to use innocence as a shield, as he realizes after being blasted with "truth" by Himmelstein (or, in one manuscript version, by Mady—B.21.9, 261). Moses acknowledges that he puts himself in the hands of these angry spirits: "This is what your masochism means, *mein zisse n'shamele*," he self-ironically quips. As the poet says, "The good are attracted by men's perceptions and think not for themselves" (*H*, p. 86). Rather than go on with the entire poem as he does in manuscript (B.18.18), he comes back to the language of experience: "You must cleanse the gates of perception by self-knowledge, by experience. Besides which, opposition is true friendship. So they tell me" (*H*, p. 86). Blake's wisdom shines through Herzog's ruefulness to show again the indebtedness of this critic of Romanticism to the object of his criticism.

Chapter 8

The Last Analysis

Herzog and *The Last Analysis* came out at about the same time. Though he would not let anyone tamper with one word of the novel, Bellow gave the play over to the stage technicians. As well as being a *succès d'estime*, the novel was Bellow's first real moneymaker. The play was a disappointment. "This shows that prostitution doesn't pay," Bellow quipped half-jokingly. I cite this conversational tidbit to say that one cannot judge the play and its changes as one would any other Bellow work. Change here was sometimes made for the sake of expediency or even sanity by a novelist ill at ease in a collective effort. Criticism of the play, then, will not always be a criticism of Bellow's intentions. This is true even of the final (Viking Press) version, which was in part a salvaging operation.

The play has, in fact, not generated much critical interest. Aside from a few serious reviews—and that of the Broadway version, somewhat longer, less good than the final one—there is little criticism to speak of. And these reviews speak almost as much to the inadequacy of the production as to the doctored play itself. Robert Brustein noticed a sprawling quality, a lack of focus clouding some magnificent rhetoric, rightly saying that the play is nonetheless "rippling with energy and intelligence." He sees Bellow "working out a fascinating theater experiment, trying to combine depth insights with popular American forms."[1] He deplored the ending—Bummidge united with his family—as sentimental, an ending that Bellow changed in the published version. Harold Clurman, less on the mark, saw Bummidge only as "a figment of verbiage," denying a "credible identity"[2] to him, misconceiving either Bellow's psychological intention or the distortion of the central role in the actual performance.

Bellow has said, with only some exaggeration, "I had in mind an old-time farce—just a series of vaudeville scenes with an excuse for a play in between them. Now I look at the play and think someone else wrote it. I never felt that about any of my work before. I recognize only certain passages as mine—the blood ranting!"[3] The *Partisan Review* version of the play, a relatively early one, corresponds to this modesty, not to say skimpiness, of conception. It shows that enlargement was not necessarily a bad thing. Bellow's disclaimers to the contrary notwithstanding, the published version is much better. Yet the compromised quality of the final version gives the manuscript versions a kind of weight in proportion to it that other manuscripts could not possess. What with all the editing Bellow had to do—Lillian Hellman, Bellow said, looked at a long version of the play and remarked, "You have a novel of a play here"—it is not surprising that along with the dross, in no other Bellow work is such a proportion of lively material discarded, in no other work are there as many laughs left out as put in. My essay treats the play as literature. I believe that, all things considered, the published version represents an advance over the numerous earlier versions, which had even greater, in some cases far greater, vulnerabilities.

The essay is organized around four kinds of changes: (1) the development of the main supporting characters in relation to major changes in the character of Bummidge; (2) the deletion of many characters from the early versions for reasons of dramatic economy; (3) the numerous revisions focusing on the character of Bummidge himself, together with a critical account of that character; and (4) the structural revisions. The manuscripts of over 2,600 pages show twenty notebooks in the author's hand representing various stages of composition (424 pages, B.12.1–10). Holograph fragments comprise sixteen folders (about 100 pages, B.12.11–26). There are numerous typewritten drafts which are complete or almost complete (840 pages, B.13.1–17). These fifteen versions show clearly the arduous reworking of the play (two are carbon). Miscellaneous typewritten pages constitute the next section (about 240 pages, B.14.1–22). Multigraphs and photocopies with holograph corrections, some used as acting copies (though not always close to the final version), constitute a series of eleven entries (over 1,000 pages, B.14.23 to B.15.7). There is one set of proofs with holograph corrections (B.15.8).

i

Dated early drafts of *The Last Analysis* indicate that work on the play had begun as early as 1958 or shortly before the publication of *Henderson the Rain King*. More than any other Bellow work it shares its climate of intellectual farce, a medium Bellow has found congenial since the Robey and Basteshaw chapters of *Augie March*. Ostensibly about psychology, it is the least psychological of Bellow's works in terms of representation. The bounds of psychological realism, constant in Bellow (though stretched to their very limits in *Henderson*), are burst. From start to finish, high themes receive low treatment, delicate perceptions are delineated in broad strokes. But never too low or too broad because of the almost inevitable, for Bellow, presence of the intellectual element. The belly laugh of farce is tempered and contained by the smile of comedy. Though none of the characters is given in the way a Bellow character is usually given in the novels, there is, in Bummidge at least, the sort of characterization found in comedy rather than farce. Bellow is fundamentally a realistic novelist, not a farceur or writer of classical comedy, and his best work, the novels, implies a belief in his characters. Farcical though aspects of the play may be, Bummidge is made more serious than the protagonists of farce in that he is seen to some degree as an instance of this belief. Bummidge is ridiculous but in the sympathetic (Don Quixote) rather than the classical (Tartuffe) strain. Like a Don Quixote or a Parson Adams, he is the holy fool mucking through and somehow triumphing in a world of cupidity. Everyone else in the play is given in stock two-dimensionality, though there is a substantial renovation of the typical, with Freudian emphasis.

In place of a chivalric ideal we have heroic honesty. Psychological man is our only romance. Like chivalry in 1600, it, too, is said to be an ossified ideal. The time for comic treatment has come. *The Last Analysis* may be seen as another Bellovian assault on the utopian, in this case the retrieval of that infant mystery that Freudian analysis is designed to recall. To establish the heroic honesty of psychoanalysis as utopian, Bellow makes Bummidge, in point of theory, a throwback to an earlier time, the period from 1910–20, that focused on the removal of infantile amnesia. It was believed that this amounted to cure, recording as it did the then momentous shift from sexual traumata to instinctual sexual development as the etiology of neurosis. Not that this insight has lost much of its importance, nor that psychoanalysis of the Freudian stripe was ever particularly utopian in tendency. But that habit of mind—at last the secret! at last the stripping of the veil of appearance!— pursued more assiduously in various neo-Freudian guises than by Freud himself, amounts to a utopianism of the disillusioned. The play, Bellow tells us in his preface, is "not simply a spoof of Freudian psychology. . . . Its real subject is the mind's comical struggle for survival in an environment of Ideas—its fascination with metaphors, and the peculiarly literal and solemn manner in which Americans dedicate themselves to programs, fancies, or brainstorms. In *The Last Analysis* a clown is driven to thought, and, like modern painters, poets, and musicians before him, turns into a theoretician."[4] Why, Augie March wondered, did I always fall among theoreticians?[5] How, the contemporary American might ask, could it be otherwise? Bellow's description implies a Bergsonian sense of the comic, but Bergson had the classical conception in mind, where Bellow shows that there is virtue in the eccentric. Bummidge is Freudianism as ideology and is therefore ridiculous. The sympathy arises when we see that the norm casting him out is in this case a world of cupidity, a pack of fugitives from *Volpone*. Suffering from humanitis, once called misanthropy, Bummidge may be seen as an Alceste on the couch. Where Molière, in the classical manner appreciated by Bergson, chastened his brilliant eccentric, Rousseau, expressing a Romantic view, saw heroism in Alceste's intransigence amidst what he wrongly took to be a uniform mediocrity. With Bummidge, who has attacks deriving from the perception that being human is suddenly too much for him, Bellow is neither classical nor Romantic. He is postmodern in finding that with which he sympathizes ridiculous. Closer to Molière in the funny bone, he is closer to Rousseau in the heart. For the ridiculous Bummy is only a somewhat farcical version of the comedy of painful self-awareness that we get in his deepest comic works, *Henderson* and *Herzog*. Humanitis is a comic version of the malaise affecting too many of us. It is a modernist legacy. If *The Misanthrope* were written today, Alceste would be only the most brilliant comic representative of the (a?) social norm.[6]

To see how delicate the balance between sympathy and contempt actually is, one must see how Bummidge evolves in the manuscripts. Where in *The Last Analysis* he is a kind of daffy saint surrounded by clear-eyed money-grubbers, in manuscript he can be seen as equally venal to, or even more venal than, his hangers-on. He's a wheeler-dealer with "the Western Mine deal, the Carribean bat-guano deal, the powdered egg syndicate, the lower California call-girl thing" (B.13.3 II). Pamela (Joyce) has so much on Bummidge that she could send him to prison (and one of her lovers is a lawyer). Bummidge has even bribed someone on the program committee of the Eastern Psychiatric Association to get fifteen minutes of closed-circuit air time (B.13.3 I, 2). Furthermore, he offers them a $500,000 gift, which they turn down. For her part, Pamela turns down an offer of $65,000 to leave him. She insists on the $500,000 to stay away and keep him out of prison. Bummidge refuses and we never do learn exactly what she has on him, but it is clearly something. How deep in corruption can we get? Though Bummidge is at first "appalled" at an offer of one million dollars to transfer his insights to commercial television, it is not long before Winkleman persuades him to do such a show. Bummidge demurs, thinking that it is "dirty work," but his friend prevails, and Bummidge sees the bright side: "why they might see it quicker than psychiatrists" (B.13.3 II, 39). So will Bummidge conquer humanitis. CURTAIN. Another ending implicates Bummidge even more deeply, if that is possible, just as it reveals a deeper deception on the part of his retainers. When Bummidge realizes that he has been duped into giving his all before a show-biz rather than a psychiatric audience, he is ready to jump out of the window. He is brought back, however, by the news that his valise with sixty grand in it is missing. Max says that "the thing was done for your best interests," Winkleman speaks of his "commercial renaissance" (B.13.10, 42), and Fiddleman says that Mickey Mantle, Stevenson, and Elizabeth Taylor will fit into the plan. It takes Bummidge about five seconds to decide to go along: "It's true, it's true, I'm corrupt" (B.13.10, 44). But the curtain does not fall yet in this version. When Pamela makes her request for $500,000, Bummidge turns the firehose on them all. He will join the Peace Corps. This soon falls through when he realizes that a security check is needed. His final project is a mission for psychological bums. This version, then, shows Bummidge's tendency to cupidity barely overcome.

There are a number of other examples of his venality. When his performance impresses the Greek movie mogul Mamantakis, to the tune of three million dollars for a three year contract, Imogen warns him against selling out. Bummidge says, "How could you ask me to turn down that amount of money" (B.13.1, III, 28). In *The Last Analysis* Bummidge is such a quixotic representative of pure motive in his professional life that there remains little for Imogen to do but admire. But in manuscript the depth of his venality can go even further than has been shown. In a soliloquy before his speech to the learned society, we see Bummidge "pondering deals." He thinks, "Yes, I am corrupt. . . . I'll form a corporation and buy that mountain in Nevada. . . . We'll wash it away with hydraulic pressure and leave a lake of mud but get out all the minerals . . . millions. And we'll get the government to foot the bill, besides. . . . And when I'm really loaded, I'll fly to Washington to holler about creeping socialism. I'll have another life. Ten, fifty other lives and cheat death at every corner. I have the fantasy of a plane crash in which everyone dies but me . . . How did I get stuck with this monstrous character?" (B.13.2, 19) In *The Last Analysis* Bummidge is no Balzacian monster of cupidity—maybe just a clown of self-conscious narcissism.

Sometimes the mercenary motive needs a lawyer to unravel it. When Bummidge's money bag is missing (he needs it to buy the Old Homestead back in Williamsburg, Brooklyn), Winkleman explains that "legally that money doesn't exist. It was paid by Phil to himself as medical expenses and never reported for taxes" (B.13.1, III, 2). In another version, Bummidge asks Winkleman for five thousand of "legitimate money" for "ten of this." A protesting, relatively innocent Winkleman says, "You want me to get disbarred for crooked dealings" (B.13.5, 59). Nor does Bummidge's complaining about tax money going into military hardware wash the slate clean. Funny and clever his tax scheme is, maybe even useful, but not appropriate to the Bummidge of the final version. In manuscript a furious, relatively moneyless Bummidge searches the Winkleman who exposes his tax scheme. When Imogen then asks, "Philip are you ashamed to search Wink?", Bummidge answers, "Yes, dear. I am humiliated. I hate myself for it. But I'm driven. Don't you understand. I have to eliminate logically" (B.13.1 III, 14). Here is a minor turn on the Dostoevskian malady, supplying the latest, high sounding reasons for bad motives. It is, of course, entirely inappropriate for the final Bummidge. Next he searches Mott. He finds his cufflinks and Mott then comes on with the high-toned doubletalk. Mott tells Bummidge that he took them "to help me get your point of view. To identify with you." Even Imogen is in on the game in this early version. It seems that she hid Bummidge's bag of money because she did not want the real estate agent (of the Old Homestead in Brooklyn) to get his hands on it. She did not want to live in a slum. "Instead," she says, "I was going to spend some of it on things you really want and don't know you want" (B.13.1 III, 19). Bummidge is not the only one to be transfigured beyond cupidity.

One early version of the play begins with Bummidge as a "classic designer"—pun intended—with painting apprentices doing commercial art. (He is steeped in psychoanalysis, but not a comedian here.) One of these is Phillipa, who has lent him $10,350. When asked about repayment Bummidge says, "that's not nice to lend me money which I needed for my major work and then push me for it. I am an artist, not a mechanic" (B.12.12, 11). Phillipa claims that he gets money from women—"you get them in your power, you promise to marry them." He says, "Did I ever say I was going to marry you? Haven't I opened your eyes—saved you from death on Long Island." Here he is a charlatan. It seems he will do almost anything for money. In one version he is seen on the phone with Merkelson "the famous juice man" (B.14.11, 62). Elsewhere he has more dramatic underworld connections, as we discover when he tells the recalcitrant Louis Mott, who insists on having his debt to him cleared up, "I should've let Boston Blackie kill you that day" (B.13.2, 36). Mott goes along with a delay of payment. This sort of coercion is unthinkable in *The Last Analysis*.

Equally unthinkable is his physical coercion of Bella. In one version he takes his decline as a comedian out on his wife. Denying that he beat her, he hears Max set the record straight. Bummidge's response is rich with psychological sophistication or is it sophistry? "Did I really kick her? In the ribs? It's one of my amnesias then," he says (B.13.5, 56). In another early version, after Wink tells him that he gave her a concussion and kicked her in the ribs, Bummidge, not remembering, admits to "neurotic difficulties" (B.13.3, 16). In the final version, it is Bummidge even more than the masculine, self-sufficent Bella who is beleaguered, and the fisticuffs are between Bella and Pamela.

Bummidge, in the early to middle manuscipts, is a fool of vanity, a man who gags with tension before a *Time* interview, though he is indifferent or even hostile to the magazine—and then "confesses" in its pages. He is disturbed that the interviewer is from "Entertainment" rather than "Science" (B.12.8). In one version, the psychodrama itself is attributed to vanity and egotism rather than to the search for the painful truth. "They wouldn't do as I demanded and therefore I wouldn't play at all," says Bummidge, asking to be stapled to the wall in crucifixion. "In sulking I flew back into infancy. It looks as though I must be master or else. . . . I didn't like what I found in life and therefore made up what I did like and commanded all to accept it. . . . I'm confessing. . . . Even in therapy I've assigned parts. I see it now. A law unto myself. All-powerful in my little sphere. So despotic! . . . Please greet me. And welcome me back to the human community, for my long, long exile into myself." But in *The Last Analysis* Bummidge is the opposite of contrite, nor is he hung up on self-accusations of infantile omnipotence. There he is a willing outcast, a Williamsburg Zarathustra breathing the heady air of psychological liberation, a leader indifferent to immediate followers. In *The Last Analysis* he undergoes crucifixion because of the cupidity of others, because of an all-too-human humanitis which issues into the *Noli me tangere* of the second act. True, Bummidge as Christ is itself a source of laughter, but the final version has a different direction, and he remains the improbable center of noble impulse. The delicate balance between sympathy and contempt is maintained.

If Bummidge is essentially sympathetic in the final version, the cast of intimates surrounding him is made generally more contemptible—Imogen excepted. The old age home swindle of Winkleman, Madge, and Max, for example, is a late inclusion. It is as if they were picking up the cupidity Bummidge has dropped in the revisions. Not that they weren't shady from the beginning. Even the early revisions show that they are looking for ways to capitalize on Bummidge. Winkleman is the brains of the outfit, and it is he who convinces the others that there is money in Bummy. In one of the oldest lines in the play he opines, "The public is tired of the old nonsense-type nonsense. It's ripe for serious-type nonsense" (B.12.6). In various versions including the final one, he thinks of show biz possibilities. As we have seen, in some early versions he hoodwinks Bummidge into thinking that a show biz audience is really a meeting of psychiatrists. In one such version, responding to Max's desperation at recovering the money his father has been spending, Winkleman suggests having him committed (B.13.5, 55). The final Winkleman is too polite for this. In some versions, Winkleman has sophisticated intellectual insights into the meaning of Bummidge's doings. He says that Bummidge is "attacking our symbols, which are stable, and wants to substitute the quaking internal dreaming, formless internal man for the man of custom and law whom everybody knows and accepts" (B.12.6). Such nobility (if redundance) of expression is out of place here and even in *The Last Analysis*, where Winkleman's Harvard manner only intensifies his financial shadiness. In some manuscript versions Winkleman is a reader of

Balzac's *The Human Comedy*. But even "the great epic of capitalist society"
has not prepared him for "such a grotesque flight to ruin" (B.12.7, 25) as
Bummidge's. Winkleman thinks that Mott, Professor Louie Mott in early
versions, is conning Bummidge into making a psychological spectacle of
himself. He wants Bummidge to save himself by calling Tsazakis, the Hollywood mogul. "You've gone dead in the box office and you are part of stage
history already. You're getting to be a Ph.D. topic," he moans (B.12.7, 37).
"Why didn't I go into the book business! A little store on 4th Avenue,"
Winkleman laments. "I could sit in the back with an eyeshade and write the
human comedy. Monster nuptials. Greed bigger than the Rocky Moun-
tains. . . . Mendacious that's a good word" (B.12.8, 13f.). The trouble is that
he is part of the mendaciousness and this *weltschmerz* makes him sound too
much like the sporadically idealistic Bummidge. In one version he sounds as
if he is getting humanitis: "Oh, poor Bummy! It's getting too much for me.
I'm going to retire before it's too late and write the Comedy Humane of New
York. Homo homini lupus" (B.13.3 II). In the final version, Winkleman's
Harvard manner and antiseptic coolness leave no room for confusion. This is
a late development. In most of the manuscript versions Winkleman is a salt
of the earth type. Indeed, in one he mocks a nagging television director by
saying, "You better phone the Harvard Club and say you'll be a little late. Or
is it the Young Conservatives of Westchester County?" (B.13.13, 35). An
early version shows us Winkleman as a factotum, yet rich, having made his
fortune in frozen ravioli (this later becomes Max's dream) and real estate
(B.12.4). He is variously described as gourmet and glutton, weighing two
hundred and fifty pounds despite, in one version (B.14.2), being only five
feet two. He is something of a garish dresser, with alligator shoes, Borsalino
hat, Strook shirt. And, in various versions, but not the final one, he courts
Imogen, unsuccessfully. In sum, he is an urban Machiavel made more slip-
pery by the Ivy patina.

   Madge (or Marge, as she is called in early versions) is an even more garish
instance of cupidity from the outset. Winkleman operates, as the phrase
goes, within the law, but even he is offended by her call girl ring, seemingly
an art gallery downstairs (B.12.8). Mother Bummidge (present in early versions) asks with good reason, "Do people have to holler at 3 A.M. when they
look at pictures?" (B.13.1, 16). In one early version, Bummidge has a
daughter named Vivian who paints. When she gives it up she is exhorted to
go on, grade B movie style, by Madge: "Listen, baby, you've got to go on
painting, you understand? You've got to" (B.13.6, 34). If there is an odd
timbre to her voice, it is because she needs the gallery for her call girl
operation. A blithe professional, she can say to Bummidge, "Seymour, I
have to entertain some critics down in the gallery" (B.13.6, 36). We may
contemplate the function of criticism at the present time. Madge, too, is
capable of the Dostoevskian doubletalk. Rationalizing her impending at-

tempted theft of Bummidge's moneybag, she can say: "Why the biggest favor I can do my brother is to rob him. So Pamela can't take him. Then, too, if Bummy should be crazy, I have to have money for a private institution. I'll never put my kid brother in a state hospital" (B.13.2). How sweet she is. If she is disadvantaged, it is perhaps because of her unfortunate marriage. She has married an eighty-six-year-old who is still holding on (B.12.8). In another version, she has married a sixty-year-old who is now ninety (B.13.1). He is a man who could never earn a living. "Have you any idea what Harold has cost me? First his prostate, then the coronary, and his eyes," she moans (B.13.2, 22f.). Madge and almost everyone else fit the classical comic pattern—*le trompeur trompé*. Of course she has for some time relied on Bummidge for financial survival. But there is no response other than incredulity when her once flush brother, now desperate with financial need and idealism, asks her to cover the money he owes Mott. Madge is someone Winkleman can easily appreciate. The lover of Balzac, recalling some of her incarnations, tells her, "You're like Mme. de Marneffe, only she never ran a so-called employment agency in New York. . . . She never used her brother's famous name on a dress shop which the police raided." Madge retorts, "I don't have to read Boozic about life. I *am* it." Winkleman laments the fact that her art gallery shows the paintings Bummidge did "when he thought he was a second Kandinsky" (B.13.1 I, 17f.). He derives a familiar moral from this, one which confuses him with Bummidge, and is long discarded as a Winkleman insight by the time of the final version. "How right I was to beware of such a woman," he says. "How she can use perfume, and paint her nails and have such a soft belly and all the time be such a barracuda. . . . Make Paris look like Mudville. Paris had hypocrisy; we have something worse, sincerity" (B.13.1, 19). (Here, as elsewhere in the manuscript, is an insight which is more appropriate to the concurrently written *Herzog*.) Winkleman, however, must give credit where credit is due. He sees that Madge has a special kind of insight into him: "That woman has your number. . . . She knows that for every buck that passes through your soft little, legal hands, two bucks have to go into your pocket." His clarity makes him rhapsodic.

> Winkleman alone
> With neither child nor kin
> For if I had a twin
> I would do him in.   (B.13.1, 19)

The depth of deviousness here takes a turn too shady for *The Last Analysis* where cupidity will be quite sufficient. We do not need psychological complications from Winkleman. Bummidge supplies us with more than enough. Working in sly tandem by the final version, Madge is the respectable Westchester matron to Winkleman's genteel lawyer.

In Max, cupidity takes an Oedipal turn. Bummidge has the unusual literary distinction—presumably common in ordinary life—of being both Oedipus and Laius. He has *tsuris* fore and aft. If Bummidge is tense about his father sleeping with his mother, he is, in one version, hysterical about his son sleeping with his mistress. In a bit which perhaps ought not to have been discarded, Bummidge feels that handsome Max can get Pamela (Joyce) if he wants (B.13.3 II). But he does not want. In the war between sex and money, money wins. Cupidity routs Cupid. Max wants to get rid of the predatory Pamela and get his share of the pie. The mercenary motive can be all but equally Oedipal. Bummidge complains, "Two years ago I bought Max a cabin cruiser, didn't I. Now he's trying to do me in."[7] Max, it seems, is implicated in Bella's implacable financial demands. "It's my son who's behind this. Because I cut him off, he's going to get Bella's money," he laments (B.13.3 I, 15).

The Oedipal motive, of course, is often free of financial considerations. Max's rage can be purely personal. "We all know what an overpowering stud you are—or were. . . . [You] shipped me off to prep school, though mother begged you not to. . . . You never kept a promise to me in your life. . . . You said on Parent's Day you were coming in a helicopter . . . Then you didn't even show" (B.13.2, 39). Bummidge says that there was an accident. They argue vociferously. Max notices noble emotion in his father's psychological seriousness. He takes advantage of the momentary truce to ask him to lend him money for his Czech-toaster, frozen-lasagna scheme. Bummidge asks *him* for the five thousand dollars he needs. And they are off, much as in the final version. Bummidge calls him, among other things, a "spirochete." And, in the most appropriate of terms, concludes "Go bug your mother" (B.13.2, 40). Max's Oedipal revenge can, on the other hand, take remarkably sublimated form. When wheeler-dealer Bummidge is possibly in trouble, Max thinks, tenderly, that a short prison sentence is just the thing for Dad, with all his distractions. (B.13.3 II). Such tenderness goes hand in hand with his trying to prevent the broadcast and reach his father's money. In one version, when Max tells Madge that if he is disinherited she would want the money for herself, even Madge is offended. She says, "it's like you don't belong to our family. The Bummidges might be peculiar but they're affectionate people" (B.12.5). (In one version, Max takes his mother's maiden name, Triffler—B.15.4.) Peculiar may in her case be a charitable word for it. On his part, Bummidge can hassle with the best of them. When Max, with his hired detective Gallucci, has the goods on the fornicating Pamela, Bummidge threatens to marry her, have a son, and disinherit Max (B.13.2). Between distraction and sublimity, this is not an option for the final Bummidge.

Max's character does not evolve very much. The harsher cupidity is deleted, but the Oedipal aggression remains. In the final version, Max's resistance remains intransigent, despite the six or seven starts Bummidge has given him. He sounds like a "young" rebel from *Mr. Sammler's Plannet*. "His generation is dead," says Max. "Good riddance to the square old stuff" (*LA*, p. 21). The only major shift is the fortunate excision of Max's tendency to intellectual profundity, where he can sound like a crude Herzog: "What's the precious self of his? . . . He's a bundle of weaknesses. He's always been on one kick or another of this sort over his mind. It's *my* adjustment, *my* character, *my* work, *my* feelings, *my* sex life, *my* heart, *my* soul, from start to finish. What's he got that any hamster hasn't got" (B.13.7, 2). And Max hears from Winkleman what he might have heard from Herzog. Commenting on the way his father called the shots, Max says, "I can call mine even better. . . . Because I have a terrific sense of reality. He didn't need it to be a fool." Winkleman says "There's a name for your type. You're what I call a reality instructor. In this confused world there are those who can see clear and call the turns. They think the facts are there to punish fools, and their passion is to drive the lessons home" (B.13.10, 2f.). This is one of several places where the play inappropriately echoes the masterwork written at the same time. An even more inappropriate echo of *Herzog* occurs when Max with Winkleman's support tells his mother to sell the Trilby; he sounds something like Mr. Sammler, Bellow in his deepest skepticism: "These Utopian schemes which seem so exciting often let loose worse evils: Violence, Revolution, Murder" (B.15.6). This is not only out of character, but also irrelevant to the play's concerns. Max's intellectual enlargement attributes an insight to him that he does not possess in the final version where he has been cut to ordinary proportions. With no ideas, no ideology even, he is a sullen, pampered scion of the rich. His get-rich-quick schemes do not sit well with his rebellious demeanor. Already in his mid-thirties, he is clearly going nowhere. "Impeccably tailored, manicured, barbered, he is nevertheless the Angry Young Man" (*LA*, p. IX), writes Bellow in his cast of characters. His context is not social wrong, but the constant slight felt by bourgeois egotism.

Though not one of the group angling to cash in on Bummidge's psychological adventure, Pamela, as we have seen, does quite well in free lance cupidity. Though constantly cast in this role, her sometimes spectacular maneuvers in manuscript are dropped where those of others are not. Since Bella has cleaned him out, there is not very much she can angle for in terms of money, and the final version focuses more on the struggle between Pamela and Bella for Bummidge's person. "The relationship has obviously faded," writes Bellow in the cast of characters. "She does not expect to get much more from him and is tired of humoring him" (*LA*, p. X.). This is a long way from her proposed $500,000 heist. But then there is no hanky-panky she can expose in the Bummidge of the final version. Nearly broke, he has turned into a bit of a *schnorrer*, but he is in his hard-won moral elevation the opposite of a crook. Pamela's motives remain as mendacious as major changes in the writing will allow. Flattery is her way. Desiring marriage when she hears that Bella wants a divorce, she calls him "a force of nature" (B.13.3). "You don't know how overpowering you are to a woman," she says. "Where were you last night," he says. "You're so masterful. You know all the answers," she says. "Bummy I'm behind in my rent dear. I owe the shoe-store, the beauty parlor" (B.13.2, 58f.). They kiss. As in the final version, she tries to get at the keys to his moneybag. He wants to hock the Tiffany anklet he bought her. Questions like "Where were you last night?" or "Who is this Baxter, Pamela?" (B.13.10, 45), which make Bummidge sound like Augie to her Stella, show that their relationship is not above suspicion. If the theme is tiresome, there are still laughs in the extent of Bummidge's original infatua-tion. He swears that she has "never known any man but me" (B.13.3 I, 17). There is also some comedy lost in the deletion of ways in which Pamela has helped to send Bella near the edge. In one version, Bella returns an expen-sive piece of Steuben's glassware that was sent to her by mistake, Pamela (Joyce) having bought it on his charge card (B.13.3 II). In another, Winkle-man reminds him that "while you were playing at the Palladium, you regis-tered at the Savoy with Joyce as Mr. and Mrs. Furthermore; she was seen there naked, by your son, while your wife was at Payne Whitney with a nervous breakdown" (B.13.3 I, 16). The final version gives us a man who is beyond Pamela as well as Bella, a man beyond carnality. What can Pamela do with such a man? In the later versions, for want of anything better, she, too, wants to cash in on the psychodrama.

Bummidge's arduous innocence conveys the idea of a man more victim-ized than victimizing. One way this is established is the transformation of Bella from a good-hearted, vulnerable woman to, in Bellow's words, "an aggressive, hammering woman, large and masculine" (*LA*, p. IX). Just as Bella is softer in many of the manuscripts, Bummidge is harder. He tries to commit her, after which, as Pamela reminds her, she was suicidal. Bella blames Pamela. Toward Bummidge she is contrite, concerned only that people will blame her for his present squalor. More than contrite, she is protective, motherly: "Poor Bummy! My poor scientist. He can't tell a sar-dine from a piranha." And even adoring: "A man like this should have the Nobel Prize for all the good he does" (B.12.6). She even thinks that Bum-midge could have been President. No ingrate she (B.13.7, 24). In one ver-sion, after Fiddleman makes his offer of two million, the wronged wife backs him for his higher purpose (B.12.11). It is not perhaps out of character for a woman so generously disposed (or is she just the fantasy of any divorced husband suffering from a bad case of alimony?) to say at the beginning of their relationship, "I'm a pagan. I love you with abandon" (B.12.3). The harder Bella of the final version gives in to the necessity of a shotgun wedding. As for the consummation itself, she says, "I admit there wasn't much to it" (*LA*, p. 81). In *The Last Analysis* her depth of feeling for Bummidge is nowhere in the vicinity of two million. In the middle manuscripts the ferocious Bella is clearly present, but the ferocity is tempered by a vivid victimization. The familiarly aggressive Bella says, "Where is he, that miserable man! Where is that cheap lay of his! I'll scratch her pancake makeup off" (B.12.11, 63). (For the even more bellicose Bella of the final version the last sentence becomes, "I'll clobber them both. Then let them go on television with bloody faces" *LA*, p. 49). Enter Bummidge rolling a hoop; he is six. Bella is angry with some justice. She complains that while they were living it up in Europe, she had to go to Las Vegas for business where she was taken for the scullery maid and washed dishes (B.13.2, 65). Bummidge never denies this but expresses resentment at her having rented the old Trilby theater for a meat market. Then, too, she has the two million dollars in the separation settlement. Still, the final Bummidge could not be so elaborately and triumphantly devious, the Bella so inordinately put upon. One version fuses her admiration and despair. "He's a great man," says Bella, "I was never good enough for him." Pamela replies, "There are certain things he's not so great at." Struck by this, the lovelorn Bella says, "I think I know what Bummy means by Human-itis. . . . It's when human is suddenly too much for you. . . . I won't take any more pills. No, I won't commit suicide any more. I'll live for the day when you become a hag" (B.15.5, 30). Vulnerable though Bella is here, it will not do for yet another character to steal Bummy's thunder. The human condition is never too much for the final, formidable Bella. In the final version only Bummidge is endowed with such Romantic sensitivities. The final Bella easily holds her own with the mendacious retinue.

Where Bella is made darker in the revisions, Imogen is made more fair. In the early revisions she is Bummidge's carnal companion. Her evolution to spiritual helpmate could not have taken place without a similar development in Bummidge. She is, in Bellow's words, "the utterly credulous ingenue. Bummidge's relationship to her is entirely fatherly" (*LA*, p. X). In the early versions, she is on the brink of unmarried desperation. "Tall, slender, meek, dreary, drooping—about 35," she is far from the nearly angelic darling of *The Last Analysis*. This almost shabby Imogen is depressed because "he keeps saying that he isn't ready for marriage. He is not mature enough yet" (B.12.4). Bummidge is fifty-five. Even here Imogen maintains that "sometimes peoples' motives are pure." She has the sentiment, but it is not her essential character. Though she has other suitors, she has been his girlfriend for seven years, engaged in some versions. She would be his fifth wife in one (B.12.7). Yet she is not as close to his psychodramatics as in the later versions. Some middle versions show Imogen in the process of moral transformation. She used to be a Bunny, but now, "thanks to Mr. B.," she is "a student at Columbia U" (B.13.2, 14). In another version she is getting an M.A. in psychology (B.12.10). Rightfully wary, she had always felt herself victimized by her looks. This is the Imogen who can interpret Bummidge's motives better than he can—the Imogen of calculation. Perhaps there is some justification to the questing Bummidge's reluctance to marry. Clearly, Bellow did some fumbling before he came out with the final Imogen. Yet the Imogen who says, "I never felt I was really myself until I was in that quiet classroom at Columbia" (B.13.2, 14), while a welcome change from still another female operator, creates an unnecessary complication. For example, when Winkleman expresses annoyance at Bummidge's forever playing games, Imogen responds, "Games can be profound. Have you read *Arbeit und Rhythmus. Homo Ludens, Art and Experience?*" Says Winkleman, "My God! have you?" (B.13.2, 50). Winkleman is a male chauvinist, and perhaps Bellow missed an opportunity in developing even a comic supportive theoretician. But most, I think, would agree that Bummidge supplies all the theory we need. By the final version, Imogen has long been simplified as the disinterested, innocent follower. Considering her fragrance this is in itself a tribute to the power of spirit. "You smell like a shipment of nectarines," Bummidge tells her (B.13.5), a sentiment soon transferred to a flirtatious technician. Bummidge and Imogen exist as two unlikely angels. Considering Bummidge's complications, Imogen is the purer, though not more exalted, spirit. "Heaven lies about us in our infancy," says Bummidge, looking at an infant with its diapers full (B.13.8, 12), a Wordsworthian sentiment uttered by the purer Imogen in the final version.[8] She evolves into a comic whiteness.

Most of the main characters, then, undergo changes making for a total effect of greater isolation for Bummidge. But there is one who undergoes a nearly total transformation. Mott, the factotum technician of *The Last Analysis*, is a far more interesting, far more corrupt character in the revisions. Professionally, Mott undergoes a substantial metamorphosis in the writing. He is, variously, an exterminator with an M.A. (B.12.5); a self-made psychologist now in the television business (formerly a grip, he now supervises a crew of technicians—this remains in) (B.13.2); a member of the Purple Gang (B.13.3); a psychology major at Columbia (B.13.7); and a poet who once belonged to a cult, he is ghosting Cy Bummidge's autobiography. Winkleman is Mott's mistrustful rival in early and middle versions. He has a private eye tail Mott. Does he have a license to practice anything? The detective sends to Budapest for information about his Ph.D. but receives no answer. He discovers that he is not licensed to practice in New York but practices anyway, phoning drugstores for placebos. And, shades of Tamkin, with the

$10,000 Bummidge gave him to get the Mental Equilibrium Foundation going, Mott plays the stockmarket (B.14.17). (There is also a manuscript with plot summary notes about a nearly indigent Bummidge investing his last thousands with a charlatan realtor, not Mott. He is investing alone "to prove he's mature" B.14.22.) Winkleman mistrusts Professor Louie's psychologizing; Mott mistrusts Winkleman's business sense. Lasciviousness and gluttony are their corresponding vices: "Compulsive eater! Chow hound!", screams Mott; "Sex maniac! Deviant!" screams Winkleman (B.13.2). Mott does, at one time or another, proposition every woman he lays eyes on. "It so happens you're my erotic type," he tells Imogen, inviting her to his Ansonia Hotel room (the locale of *Seize the Day*). But apparently Madge and the Countess (Bummidge's first wife in early versions) are also his erotic type (B.13.3 II, 10). The latter makes him remember that first girl in the hayloft. "Consequently," says the professor, "a memory of manure awakens in the olfactory nerve" (B.14.1, 46). In this respect Mott does not change much in the final version. "You're my erotic type," he tells Imogen (*LA*, p. 41). "I used to get such a flash when I saw you—in the old days," he tells Madge (*LA*, p. 30). But he is less of a force here because he is far less of a psychological entrepreneur.

In the revisions he is often Bummidge's psychological mentor, often standing in relation to him as Tamkin to Wilhelm. This is not simply a comparison, for Mott is quite Tamkin-like in what he says and even the way he looks. He is Professor Louie Mott, "bald, rather wiry; and has an expression of seeming candor—his brows have an ingenious arch but the eyes are anything but honest." (Wilhelm observes Tamkin's "bald skull, his gull's nose, his rather handsome eyebrows, his vain moustache, his deceiver's brown eyes. . . . He stood pigeon-toed. . . . [His eyes] looked thoughtful—but were they? And honest—but was Dr. Tamkin honest" *SD*, p. 62.) Also Mott is in his mid-fifties and wears a loud suit (B.13.4, 37). Or has a moustache and is bowlegged (B.13.1, 37). In the final version, however, he, like Dr. Adler, "desperately trying to keep youthful . . . wears College Shop clothing" (*LA*, p. X.) He is Tamkin the inventor and benefactor: "though I'm an engineer and chemist and invented a car that wouldn't turn over and air-conditioned the royal palace of Siam, my real calling is to comfort and help people, and take away their fears" (B.13.1 I, 40). He is Tamkin the altruist: "I'll tell you what's my weakness. When I find a human being that needs me, they can't shake me" (B.14.4, 8). Even when stabbed by a paranoid schizophrenic, he stayed with her, as he did with the wife of a South American dictator who ordered he be sent to the firing squad. Mott is Tamkin the psychologist and guru. In one version, trying to explain to Bummidge the cause of his epileptic seizures (his seizures in the final version are psychological and comparatively mild), Mott-Tamkin assures him that:

I studied with Freud and Adler. In India I am a guru; in Japan, a Zen
Master. I know the ancient wisdom of Egypt and Atlantis. In dianetics I
am clear. In general semantics I lectured in Korzybski's place when he was
sick. . . . I have de-inhibited my aims. The libido is forced to inhibit its
aims. I have de-inhibited. I have escaped the destruction-compulsion. My
dead have buried their dead. My blood is amost like chlorophyll." (B.13.1
II, 8)

A naive Bummidge laps this up. Significantly, another version of this speech
is spoken to Sheldon, Bummidge's dumb bodyguard (B.13.12). Mott speaks
the language of a science he claims to rationally comprehend and morally
transcend. Not really Freudian, he poses as a psychological superman. But
he is not above the compulsion to indoctrinate. "The birth trauma is absolutely basic," he says, sounding more like Rank than Freud. He "argued this
out with Freud once when we were spaziering around the Ring." It seems
that Bellow retained this insight in Bummidge's development, for he focuses
on the birth trauma like a Rankian. When Mott discourses on psychological
symbolism he does not seem to be retaining what Freud told him as they
were spaziering around the Ring. For Freud the meaning of the dream
symbol is typically dependent on a particular context, yet Mott deals with it
as a fixed quality, more in the Jungian manner: "Anything ripped, torn or
exploded in your dreams signifies actual birth. Dreams of choking, suffoca-
tion, hanging. Or volcanoes. Or hydrogen bombs" (B.13.1 II, 10f.). Bummidge takes it all in. Dubious or not here, Mott, like Tamkin, is capable of
impressive Bellovian flights of social psychology: "As the machinery of life
becomes more complicated and bureaucratic, the better people, the more
creative types, shrink from it. The people who are at home with details take
over. Either they are obsessives or they have schizoid tendencies. Certain
schizoids love details. . . . The big shots of today are the master clerks"
(B.12.4). Pearls of wisdom for a craving Bummidge.
      Elsewhere the Tamkin-Wilhelm, teacher-tyro relationship is more em-
phatic. Mott tells *him* to "actualize the infantile," to look at the infant, "Pure
Dasein. Without Bewusstsein. It has not learned to hold in. . . . Before
control. . . . Here mankind is the pure event in nature" (B.13.4, 37). In *The
Last Analysis* Bummidge expresses these sentiments. Here a wide-eyed
Bummidge listens, thankful to get the word that he is still alive, unlike the
moribund Winkleman who represents "corrupt civilized time—consciousness plus a gastric compulsiveness." To which Bummidge amenably replies,
"Yes, that describes Winkie very neatly. I've got to hand it to you." Mott
says, "A person like that has a very limited amount of self." A Wilhelm-like
Bummidge asks, "Ah, you mean there are different amounts of self?" And
Mott makes a Tamkin-like, ersatz-Romantic distinction: "Why of course,
that's elementary. There are enriched selfs and unenriched. The self you get

tired of, that's the unenriched, strictly." Bummidge says, "Hell! I should have thought of that myself. It proves what show business has done to my mind." Mott lauds the enriched: "I can picture you when you achieve it. You'll be great. . . . You'll be calm, happy, sober, genital" (B.13.4, 4of.). Mott consequently encourages Bummidge to stick to his psychodramas, though at this point it is impossible to imagine anyone so rubelike involved in anything like a psychodrama. Bummidge recalls a childhood trauma (a brick kids were playing with shattered his father's store window) and then his vaudeville career. Mott says, "Seems to me you have an unfinished potential right there to actualize," and then suggests portentously, "maybe you ought to do the backward acting more systematically." Bummidge is taken by this: "Say, Louie, I think that might be the best approach" (B.13.4, 43). In one version Bummidge even asks Mott where you should begin the psychodrama. "Okay unconscious," says an innocent, Pop version of the Oedipally sophisticated final Bummidge, "do your stuff. Speak you devil. Tell me what's on my mind. . . . (sings) 'married dear old Dad. A girl just like the girl . . . Dear old Dad.' . . . Curse you, you Oedipus complex." Is no place sacred? Not even Tin Pan Alley? (He then repudiates his hangers-on in words we associate with Sandor Himmelstein advising Herzog: "You all want to take away my life, my substance, and put a meter on my nose and tell me how much air to breathe" [B.14.4, 15].) The dramatic coherence here—Bummidge is both naive and aware—sags.

That the final Bummidge should undertake his psychodramatic adventures because of anyone's suggestion or tutelage, let alone Mott's, is unthinkable. He is a passionate, original autodidact, whose very insight leads him into profound isolation. There would be no way of having a superior psychological authority from within his own circle. The difference between the early and late Bummidge is the difference between first and second naiveté. The former is for the young, the latter for the middle-aged trying to simplify themselves. This is why Mott's character had to be so drastically changed—reversed, in fact. Bummidge had to be the egotistical center of the comedy. In addition, Bellow presumably did not want to succumb to the temptation of living on a past success, of doing the same character twice.

ii

These are the more important characters. The manuscripts show that there were a number of characters cut in the writing, some already alluded to in passing. A look at these deleted characters, together with the other excised material, shows that the revision process of *The Last Analysis* is unique in Bellow for excluding as many laughs as it finally includes.

In the early versions, Bummidge has a daughter, Vivian (Annie). She wants to give up her career as a painter (or pianist) and marry her Indian friend Manasi, who works at the United Nations (B.13.4). A possessive Bummidge thinks that his daughter, at twenty-six, is not ready for marriage. "Leave this to me," he tells a friend, "marriage is one of my special fields" (B.12.2). The couple are afraid to tell him of their plans. Bummidge cries when Vivian plays the piano, but Manasi does not like her piano playing (B.12.1). There is some question as to how good an artist Vivian is. Bummidge thinks she is a genuis. "Married!," Bummidge exclaims, "Are you crazy. . . . Yokels get married. Not great performers. . . . As soon as a child is born adultery is born. . . . Save yourself for Mozart, save yourself for Beethoven; stay married to Bach" (B.12.1). In another version Bummidge's mother points out that Vivian does not think she is an artist. Nor is Vivian's sense of Papa complimentary. After telling Manasi about Bummidge's various kicks—vegetarian, nudist, moon-bather, astrology, fish-diet, Yoga, Thoreau, Dianetics, Buddhism, Existentialism and "five different kinds of psychoanalysis"—Vivian confesses, "I think he's dull" (B.14.5, 32). (At his most outraged, Bummidge thinks of her as a "greedy little bitch" [B.13.3, 8].) Vivian also has difficulty with her prospective in-laws. "When he wrote that he was in love with me," she says of Manasi, "his mother went on a hunger strike" (B.12.8). His parents have cut him off—a prince in this version. In another, she is already married to her Hindu prince diplomat. Winkleman, the lover of Balzac, is surprised to see a marriage of love and an exotic one at that. He thought she would go square in reaction to her parents and Balzacian reality in general. In any case, she is now pregnant. Bummidge is one-upped, it seems. But when Winkleman says, "I just saw your father give birth to himself" (B.12.7), the two cannot be certain.

Why is the Vivian business deleted? For one thing, in an Oedipal comedy Max is the more appropriate child. (There are early versions in which Bummidge has a daughter and no son.) Not Bummidge's vanity but the new strain of psychological grotesquerie needs enlargement. For another—and this is true of all the characters deleted—a novelist by temperament and habit had to adjust to the narrower confines of drama. What is expected prolixity and spaciousness in a novel is excess and floundering in a play. What Bellow comes up with, at some cost, is a play so tight that it observes the classical unities!

One cannot help regretting the casting of certain comic bits to oblivion. Countess (Baroness) Thelma Zombrowska, Bummidge's first wife (fiancée in some versions) and Vivian's mother, is another one of these. The Countess is a vain, mendacious, "Balzacian" woman whose advice to Vivian is to get a nose job (B.12.1). She is upset that Vivian will make her a grandmother. For the Countess is in her own eyes a lover of international reputation. Now broke, she has to call her youthful fiancé Pedro in Caracas on Bummidge's phone. Also, since Pedro's mother has taken away his oil refinery, she must borrow money from Bummidge, in one version getting down on her elegant hands and knees to solicit Bummidge who is regressing under a kitchen table (B.12.8). The Countess has loved to the point of amnesia. She tells Vivian of being in the Stockholm underground during the War, married then to "Jean. No, it was Waczlaw. Petrash or Waczlaw." She can remember the name but not the old flame. Perhaps Countess Thelma Zombrowska's amnesia derives from her originally being just plain Thelma who spoke better English way back when (B.14.4). In one version she is called "the so-called Countess Elunoff" (B.13.4, 2), which goes part of the way toward explaining what Bummy the vaudevillian is doing with royalty. She is a woman whose essential wisdom is revealed to one of her own kind. "It is a woman's duty to spend," she tells Imogen. "Every year she should spend one dollar more than her husband makes" (B.13.1 I, 46), which according to today's standards makes her a spendthrift bargain. Winkleman has her number and says, "When you write your memoirs you'll use an adding machine, not a typewriter" (B.13.1 I, 25).

In some of the early versions of this Oedipal comedy, Bummidge's mother is present, an opportunity for limited acting out. In one version Bummidge, putting his head in her lap and guzzling from a bottle, asks, "How about a lullaby?" She begins to sing from the traditional Yiddish "Raisins and Almonds" ("Russinkes mit Mandlen") when Bummidge, ever in quest of the golden moment, suggests breast feeding. "Never," is the reply of his Yiddishe Momma. No Jocasta she. His mother recalls his precocity in the original breast feeding situation: "He was talking already and argued with me about the milk." (This is "explained" in another version where she says, "I didn't wean you until you were nearly three" B.13.1 II, 13.) While this is deleted, Bummidge's perception that he is "ruined" because he was toilet trained early—"He learned shame before he learned joy"—is one comic bit that remains in the final version but in less vivid form. Wishing to "tear the veil of amnesia," Bummidge asks his mother how he was born. Her response to his inquiry is to recall that there are crazy people on both sides of the family (B.12.3). In *The Last Analysis* the kooky family histories and remembrance of weaning are supplied by Aunt Velma, a more neutral and objective observer. She supplies the vivid picture of Bummidge nursing until his feet touched the floor, and of Mother Bummidge's saying that if he didn't want the breast she'd give it to the conductor. In one early version she consoles him about his early toilet training when she says, "It never took. You kept coming home with full pants. Even from kindergarten." Bummidge suggests, "I was struggling" (B.13.3 II, 8). The struggles of the child become the resentments (and the heroics) of the man. When he asks his mother what kind of a child he was, she says, "A fatsy little pudgicle. . . . You were my little momele" (B.14.5, 23). That New Yorkese reduction to cherubic, ice-cream proportions, together with a saccharine sex-change, makes Bum-midge think of Houdini escaping his shackles. The resentment felt by the second generation Jewish-American son toward the over-protective East European mother can, however, be reduced to laughable absurdity. "She crippled me," says Bummidge. "I could have been great, a tremendous, a happy man. She had to rope me with the silver cord, butter my bread, cool my soup, wait in a snowstorm by the schoolgate with galoshes" (B.13.13, 46). Such are the wages of repressive charity.

Vivid in memory and essentially the same in manuscript and the final version, Bummidge's father scarcely appears in the dramatic present. There is a brief description of him as a nondescript old man annotating a racing form. No one seems to take notice of him (B.14.16). "For a fellow with an Oedipus complex like mine to have his old parent around is quite a deal," thinks Bummidge (B.12.7, 23). But the Oedipal effect depends so much more on tearing away the infantile amnesia than on seeing one's old parents on a day-to-day basis—this might bring into question the whole theory—that this was reason enough to leave the literal old couple out of the later versions.

There are some non-familial comic bits worth noting. It appears that Bum-midge owes Twentieth Century Fox one movie on his contract. Bummidge refuses to cooperate, saying that they forced him to make his last movie when he was sick. "The organization aggressed against me," says Bum-midge. "Never have I seen such a case of group psychology and the individ-ual ego," says the follower of Freud (B.12.4). An embattled Bummidge resists the pressures of mogul Mamantakis and his flunkies. Above all, Bum-midge wants something more dignified, more serious. He wants to do *Jude the Obscure*: With some justification the agent tells him that he was not "cut out for tragedy." Speaking what he thinks is Bummidge's language, he offers him twice what he received last year. But the Freudian acolyte turns it down saying, "You see, you can only be happy by realizing a childhood wish. And money isn't a real childhood wish" (B.12.1). Go argue with him!

Other minor characters deserve brief notice. There is Wolkoff, an incom-petent, rich ward of Winkleman's, who, in being constantly at loose ends, prefigures Wallace Gruner of *Mr. Sammler's Planet*. He has spent ten years at Harvard and does not have a B.A. Desperate, he and his friends were going to rescue the Dalai Lama. But he has been rescued (B.14.5). "I'm too old to be a student but I don't know what else to do. I'm almost a geologist, almost a physicist, almost a Ph.D. in political science," he says (B.13.1 I, 38). He writes imaginary obituaries. He is also in pursuit of Imogen. Another minor character appearing in numerous versions is Bummidge's bodyguard, Sheldon. Big, loyal, simple, he is deemed neurotic by Mott because he is ticklish. He is replaced by the lugubrious Bertram in late versions. The latter, an exterminator and not much of a character himself, has the virtue of knowing how to ensnare Bummidge's pests at the end of the play. Squargiallupo, another expunged character, is a minor underworld figure whose job is to spring Madge and her prostitutes from jail when there has been a raid (B.13.1).

Finally, there is something made in manuscript, as there is in the *Herzog* material, of characters and events that will appear in *Humboldt's Gift*. Here Humboldt is called Joey Cottle (once Joe Darling). The story is familiar. Cottle is "threatening" because he thinks Bummidge interfered with his life. He thinks that he had him committed to Bellevue. Cottle is drunk with schemes for getting rich quick. They are not close here. Bummidge even denies that they were pals. "He tried to tell Imogen that I was too old for her," he complains, "that when she was forty, I'd be sixty. When she was fifty, I'd be seventy. . . . Why, he's a blackmailer." Winkleman says, "You interfered with his life. You gave his wife psychiatric advice." Bummidge replies, "She asked for it. You forget what a state she was in. That was after he tried to run her down with the car" (B.13.4, 35). In another version, Cottle accuses Bummidge of stealing his routines and claiming royalties. "He never had an idea in his life except ideas of persecution," says Winkleman in Bummidge's defense. He reports that Cottle wants to settle with Bummidge for a quarter of a million (B.13.13, 23f.). Another view of Cottle shows him calling Bummidge brother and doing him out of a job. "Joey, Joey," says Bummidge. "Oh, I love the guy, and hate myself for it because he's no goddam good. A lousy emotion. Potato love. It makes a patsy of me" (B.14.14, 19). In view of the ambivalence Charlie Citrine feels toward Von Humboldt Fleisher, this quotation has a special interest. Citrine is obviously more generous in his estimate of Humboldt, a character who is almost elegaically rendered. Here, perhaps because of the requirements of comedy, Cottle emerges as one more mendacious character. Included in manuscript is the business of Bummidge and Cottle signing their names on blank checks, like blood brothers. Both here remove their accounts to another bank. This is the yet to be spiritually exalted Bummidge. Still, apparently with justification, he feels morally superior to Cottle. "He's a crooked old drunk," he says, "but we were pals. I still feel the shame of it. . . . It's interesting that I should have such an emotional involvement in him" (B.14.4, 20). As events prove, Bellow's involvement proves far deeper than Bummidge's. Indeed, Bummidge is a man who really cannot be deeply involved in anyone but himself. This is part of the given of the comedy. The Cottle material—quite close in detail to that in *Humboldt's Gift*—is morally problematic and only mildly comic, not the way *The Last Analysis* is comic, and is wisely deleted, not apearing in any later version.

iii

If Bummidge is the egotistical center of the play, it is because he is a fool of idealism. This is his dominant characteristic, and it is present in the manuscripts, contiguous to the largely deleted strain of mendaciousness. Winkleman tells us that he once "picked up a copy of Walden in my house. He had a musical comedy hit on Broadway and he read Walden and disappeared into the woods." Indeed, this relatively early Bummidge "divorced his latest wife because she didn't know who Kierkegaard was" (B.12.5). There is a price to be paid for this integrity. He used to live in Hollywood with two swimming pools; now he is down to a fifteen-minute TV show and does his own commercials. As we know, things get even worse. But what does it matter if he can commune with a bust of Socrates and say, "Know thyself," or quote Montaigne: "I will not cease from mental fight" (B.13.11, 12—Acually, it is "strife" not "fight" and Blake not Montaigne). Some versions are dotted with portentous Socratic snatches. "What is the laughable Thrasymachus?," he asks Bella (B.12.13, 7). Some of this idealism remains in his late transformation to the vatic. Where Bummidge's cupidity is diminished to virtually nothing, his spiritual quality even to the point of otherworldliness is greatly enlarged. Middle versions show his growing detachment from woman, from money. A purified Bummidge is ready for psychodrama. It is idealism that induces humanitis and his self-imposed martyrdom. It is idealism that has made him give up professional comedy. "Laughter comes from repression," he observes. "Nowadays people are so repressed that night and day they look for opportunities to laugh. Everything is a joke. No judgment. People laugh about torture, prison, and murder. They laugh at funerals, they laugh in cemeteries. If you ask them what they believe, they smile and laugh. So it's disgusting, it's a disgrace to be a comedian" (B.12.8, 17f.).

There may be a question here of whether Bummidge is not casting out baby sense of humor with bathwater comedic bilge. Is the Bummidge of *The Last Analysis* too solemn for the Trilby, his comic academy? Perhaps this is why he in the end calls it the Bummidge Institute of Nonsense. He has certainly cast off commercial comedy. He has taken on a sort of Nietzschean laughter at the end that makes him rich and strange. In one version Bummidge says rather too confidently: "Look at all the things I have managed to laugh about. Falling gods. Old neuroses. My own Oedipus complex. Laugh at my former sex life. [A momentous conception!] At Pamela. I can tremblingly announce a tentative cure" (B.13.9, 62). But this is too easy a finale. For while we laugh at all of these things, Bummidge is taking much here with deathly seriousness. Indeed, this is a mainspring of comedy in the play.

Therefore, the transfiguration into a comic version of vatic seriousness at the end is entirely appropriate.

Like Henderson, thinking of medical school as he pushes fifty-five, Bummidge is "nearing sixty . . . still eagerly mapping programs and hatching new projects" (*LA*, p. IX). The main project, of course, is his self-analysis. This is both his major quixotry and the comic focus of the play. He is indeed starting late. Mott, in manuscript, puts this in perspective: "If he starts life over again, he won't be walking till he is fifty-five, talking at fifty-six, he'll start kindergarten when he's sixty and be a teenager at seventy" (B.13.1 III, 2). Coming from Mott it is surprising that we do not envision Bummy swinging at eighty. Of course, it does not work out this way. Bummidge's utopian project does not "work," is not practical, except insofar as it yields him a visionary reality potent enough to transcend and repudiate what is here defined as mendacious ordinary life.

Why does he undertake the project of self-analysis? In one early version Bummidge says, "I had such bad experiences with my psychiatrists I finally decided to do it myself" (B.12.1, 21). Do it yourself—a fine American impulse. But this only superficially explains his motivation. In another version he says that he has been to "Freudians, Jungians, Adlerians, Horney-ites, Sullivans, Rogerses." (One version has him "up late building an orgone box" [B.14.16, 3].) But with a character still "sick—masochistic, narcissistic, paranoid and depressed, exhibitionistic, compulsive, fixated and perverse" he developed his own "existential" method, existential in the sense that "I enact, or re-enact, or re-re-enact" (B.12.5). He thinks immediately of his puritanical father to whom the child Bummidge reacts by wolfing down a Mary Jane candy in the bathroom. He is caught—even here a Mary Jane gets a Bellow protagonist in trouble! Bummidge is really motivated, as is Henderson, by a search for his own identity. Like Henderson, he can say, "at the age of fifty I suddenly realized I didn't know myself. I was two hundred and twenty five pounds of unknown material. [Here he even has Henderson's physical dimensions.] I read the poem—who goes there, mystical, gross, hankering, nude, and I couldn't answer. I was all dressed up with a Borsalino hat and alligator shoes, silk underwear, London clothes. From all this I was estranged. All the things I could identify. But me, the real me . . . with that me I was unacquainted" (B.13.4, 13). Here and elsewhere Bummidge recalls Whitman's phrases without recalling his name. The sentiment, even the accents, were too Hendersonian to be retained. In a similar passage, the unreality of being a Toots Shor celebrity leads to uneasy sleep, and, like Henderson, he "started to think—a man should live and die a stranger to himself" (B.13.6, 22). The quest for reality is on, but Africa is replaced by the darker continent within (as it is even in *Henderson*). The Mary Jane comes up again. The "analyst" explains, "It's you yourself, Mr. Bummidge, wanting to be punished for your illicit desires. Because you wanted to replace your father in your mother's arms. It's not the candy but the sweet of sin" (B.13.6, 33). The Oedipal theme has taken clear shape.

The father, all superego, plays the great role in his analysis. "My father," Bummidge says, "wanted me to be a mixture of a rabbi, a financial wizard, a concert violinist, a chess champion and one of FDR's advisors. He hated children" (B.13.2, 47).[10] All of this subjective enlargement of the old man, yet Madge ironically informs us that "Bummy was bigger and stronger at eight than Papa" (B.13.2, 46). Despite his severity, Bummidge admits that "I had toward him a wild, yearning potato love. Gross love. Earthy. Lumpy love." Usually, potato love could not be wild and yearning; here it is described in relatively neutral terms. But this feeling is transcended by a more authentic one—rebellion, of an involuted sort. "As my father wanted me to be old I stubbornly remained a little child" (B.13.1 IV, 22f.). Not entirely, to be sure, but the logic of his life has lead him in that direction. Still, there remains "ambivalence," the Freudian love-hate. Bummidge is sorry to see his diminished, moustache-shorn father after his heart attack, but the "analyst" takes a harsh line out of *Totem and Taboo:* "An old enemy is going down and the human creature is a violent, snarling heart, laughing, howling and crying." It is coming to terms with society that straightens this creature out. "So his heart is never quiet," continues the "analyst," and "he is a criminal and sinner all his days." (The final version is more personal and professional: "An old enemy and rival is going down. In your heart you also exulted. Maybe you wanted him to live only to see your success." *LA,* p.27) How close this rendition of the Freudian view comes to Original Sin! In the face of this onslaught, the analysand clings to his actual feelings: "Pa . . . how it hurt me to see your strength going" (B.12.5). In *The Last Analysis* Bummidge is more in command of himself. To the more subdued remarks of the "analyst" he responds, "You're a hard-nosed man. Why do you prefer the ugliest interpretations? Why do you pollute all my good impulses?" (*LA,* p. 27). One late version has Imogen complaining about the Freudian paraphernalia (B.13.16, 23). But in the final version it is Bummidge who complains: "It's always Father, Mother. Or again, breast, castration anxiety, fixation of the past. I am desperately bored with these things, sick of them!" The very Freudian "analyst," replies in a late inclusion, "You are sick *from* them. Of course. We are all sick. That is our condition. Man is the sick animal. Repression is the root of his madness and also of his achievements" (*LA,* p. 26). As Philip Rieff (the Freudian whom Citrine attacks in *Humboldt's Gift*) puts it, "we are not unhappy because we are frustrated, Freud implies; we are frustrated because we are, first of all, unhappy combinations of conflicting desires. Civilization can, at best, reach a balance of discontents."[11] We are all ill, man is the sick animal—these are formulations the inevitability of which Bellow resists almost successfully.[12]

iv

No one knows better than Bellow—and no Bellow character illustrates better than Bummidge—the advantages of illness, the nearness of neuroticism
to creativity. Indeed, for the mature Bellow it is often a compositional necessity to start with someone almost out of his mind who achieves stability, even
transcendence, through an arduous reaching for value. A moral critique of
aspects of modernist orthodoxy, in this case Freudianism, takes place. This is
precisely Bummidge's development. Lifting the veil of infantile amnesia
turns Bummidge not toward Dionysius but Christ. What is unresolved in the
metamorphosis will be resolved in laughter. So we are given to believe. A
comedian of the would-be normative, Bummidge speaks in a late formulation of the Pagliacci gangrene, the residue of pain when the laughter is gone
(*LA*, p. 78). In our time this may be the most distinguishing mark of the
all-too-human. Laughter is a health, but health is not the opposite of sickness. Laughter ought to be a triumph of civilized perception over the constant inner chaos that Freud thought of as illness and that Bellow accepts as a
dramatic given to be resolved despite his repugnance to it as a moral norm.

The structural revisions show a carefully orchestrated movement from
chaos to troubled transfiguration. Bummidge's inner turmoil is immediately
the play's focus. The one version of the play that begins with Winkleman on
the couch (!)[13] soon switches to Bummidge (B. 13.3, I, 1). While Bummidge is
totally absorbed in his project in *The Last Analysis*, such clarity of direction
is not present in some early versions. "If I weren't so busy," he says, "I'd
give full-time to this—but everybody's after me for something" (B. 12.1, 5).
In this early version, Bummidge's opening soliloquy is delivered from bed:
"If I could only have stayed in bed, I would have completed my self-analysis
long ago" (B. 12.1, 4), he says. He is suspicious of Poor Richard who attacked
the bed with aphorisms like "Plough deep while the sluggard sleeps"
(B. 12.12). He retains a wise if neurasthenic passiveness. We see a Bummidge who "much resembles Bert Lahr" (B. 12.4), a Bummidge who is more
gross in his perceptions than the final Bummidge. "Oh, how complex my
psyche is," he exclaims (B. 12.1, 8). Complex or not, he does not have so
much room to display it. This version goes from the memories evoked by a
piece of torn lace from Madge's dress, to the session with the "analyst" about
Papa's refusal to let him indulge in a Fat Emma candy, to a rough sketch of
some of the analytic material which later becomes his TV performance. In
other words, much of the play (*LA*, pp. 18–27, 28–73) has not yet materialized. In a different early version, it is a harassed Willie Bummidge who
almost immediately undergoes a willing crucifixion (B. 12.2). This comes
toward the end of Act I in the final version. In another early version, which

goes more elaborately into the self-analysis, the "sounds of Bummidge repelled by life are heard" (B.12.5). Curiously, despite this siege of humanitis, Bummidge's aforementioned benevolence shines through. He recalls his war experience. "Kamerad, nicht schiessen," a captured German soldier says. (Some of this is picked up in *Mr. Sammler's Planet*.) "Get over there Fritz," says Bummidge. There is no shooting; he is another of the merciful Bellow heroes who will not kill. How quaintly tender is the vaudeville song that elicited his recollection:

> Late last night
> By the star-shell light
> I saw you—I saw you
> You was fixin' your barbed wire
> When I opened fire
> If you want to see your Mother in your Vaterland
> Keep your head down, Fritz me boy.

The sentiment is real; except for the song, however, the event is not. Bummidge admits to fabrication, yet remains a cauldron of good intentions. But this incidental tenderness is deleted, and the rhythms of the play are quickly subordinated to his psychological problems.

Much of the revision is concerned with a reworking of his agonizing reappraisal, the analysis itself and particularly, the nub of the analysis, the lifting of the veil of infantile amnesia. "The whole trick," says Bummidge, "is to get back to the preconscious state, before memory, because that's when all the serious trouble starts, from the eighteenth month back, where the great neuroses lie." This early version gives us, by way of getting back, a unique view of Bummidge as a pool player and crapshooter so fat, "I had to have somebody to pick up the dice for me." He thinks, ironically, of Wordsworth's evocation of youth in "Intimations of Immortality":

> There was a time when meadow, grove and stream
> The earth and every common sight
> To me did seem
> Apparelled in celestial light. . . .

He wonders, "Now where did that come from? When did I see meadows? The East River I saw. . . . The flowers I saw were in the cemetery" (B.14.5, 15f.). There is little consolation in his youth. As he works his way back, his earlier recollections are another source of anxiety. He thinks of a song he knew at age five:

> I had a little pony
> His name was Dapple Gray

> I lent him to a lady
> To ride a mile away.
> She whipped him and she lashed him
> She road him through the mire . . . .

An aroused Bummidge thinks, "These people were incredible. Talk about castration fears!" (B.14.5, 21) But should "these people" bear all the blame? From a psychological point of view what is even more significant is that Bummidge remembers the submerged, school-boy masochism of it. Similarly, why, of all his vaudeville routines, does he remember in so many versions the following song:

> Oh I went to school with Maggi Moiphy
> And Maggi Moiphy went to school with me-e-e.
> I tried to get the best of Maggi Moiphy,
> But the sonofagun, she got the best of me.   (*LA*, p. 80)

From Augie's Thea and Stella to Wilhelm's Margaret to Bummidge's Bella and Pamela to Herzog's Mady—this is Bellow's special Golden Oldy. (Though one may also recall Joseph and Iva, Henderson and Frances, Herzog and Daisy.)

The order of recollection more like that of *The Last Analysis* comes in somewhat later versions and is, at first, a chronological one. He remembers back to 1905, his birth, infancy, the brass bed behind the candy store; growing up, puberty; being a tummling waiter in the Catskills; being married, divorced, married, divorced. In his anxiety he yells, "value—value. Give me value" (B.13.1 I, 33). This moral orgasm causes a certain exhaustion. He has an attack of humanitis. Upon awakening, he pursues his analysis with the chronological order reversed, as in *The Last Analysis*, but the remembrances are often different. He is a twenty-two year old vaudevillian playing the Chicago Haymarket ("Maggi Moiphy"); he is taking voice lessons at sixteen and thrown out for incompetence, pocketing his lesson money because Papa would not give him anything; he is badgered by Papa in the Mary Jane incident. "You be a *mensch* or I'll kill you" (*LA*, p. 40), says Papa in one of the oldest lines in the play, unwittingly making like a savage for the sake of civilization. (In a way Papa has the last word. If Bummidge does not quite become a *mensch*, he is at least an *übermensch*.) The final version retains this reverse chronology but, putting the Mary Jane incident earlier in the play, drops the voice lessons and includes his marriage to Bella, which comes later in the manuscript version (B.13.1 III). Moreover, in the final version all of this last sequence takes place on television.

Another important structural difference in the final version is that the primal scene and birth are saved for last, which enables Bellow to carry to its farcical extreme the logic of infantile amnesia. Having achieved this, Bummidge then achieves a psychological apotheosis, making it impossible for him to be touched by mere mortals. The manuscripts show that this transfiguring conclusion was not inevitable. "Full consciousness," thinks Bummidge, "I'm not going to accomplish this. As though I were a savior. I'm too grotesque" (B.12.13). In one version, an uncertain, downcast, poor Bummidge tells Imogen before the performance, "have Sheldon come right back. This may be my last mile and I need my bodyguard" (B.13.2). There is no such thought of defeat in the final version. And his spiritual ascendence in *The Last Analysis*—triumphant if not altogether convincing—precludes the enactment of the kind of situation that is foisted on him in some manuscripts. For example, he is told that he is addressing a learned gathering when he is really addressing an audience of television and ad agency people: "I feel privileged to present to a distinguished audience of psychologists and psychiatrists this demonstration of my own investigations into the secrets of the mind. . . . This is the kind of thing only the learned community will understand—the ordinary showbusiness saphead can never dig this" (B.13.10).[14]

We cannot have the transfigured Bummidge coming in for ordinary pratfalls. Only extraordinary pratfalls will do. Bummidge as Christ-Blake-Nietzsche, the vatic seer, the difficult prophet, the iconoclastic visionary, comes in the last revisions.[15] The heightened literary chorus is an ancillary late inclusion. Elsewhere it is a spontaneous chorus, and most of the lines are delivered by Bummidge (B.13.1). Mother, Sheldon, Winkleman, and Madge speak in character. Rather than historical and critical reference, rather than Lazarus and Bummidge dying of banality, the manuscript gives us still another Oedipal fragment. "I'm a king—emperor. It's the old reality *prinzip*. It collides with the pleasure *prinzip*. (Threatens as he stands.) Don't you touch, Mamzer. I'll give you a slap. (Slap his own hand.) . . . *Thou shalt not!* And keep your hands outside the quilt. . . . (Imitates Mother) No, you filthy boy. And if you don't behave I'll tell popa." Bummidge laments, "And so I must bow my head to the Oedipus complex. Like every son of woman. I carry the cross of flesh" (B.13.1 I, 30f.). In *The Last Analysis* we see Oedipus transcended. Eros is a builder of comic academies. We have typically Bellovian apercus on the nature of contemporary comedy—the social order makes the best jokes—issuing into the Trilby theater project based on the latest psychological insights.[16] A number of manuscript versions end with Bummidge's exhorting sick mankind to manhood (*LA*, p. 97), a note of tenuous nobility that is not enough for the final Bummidge. Nothing less than resurrection will do to overcome his crucifixion. The reader of Kierkegaard says, "I was sick unto death, died, and was buried" (*LA*, p. 98). He awaits his rebirth, and, in a scene reminiscent of "Nighttown" in *Ulysses*, it comes. Bummidge passes out with emotion. Oedipal Max, in a late inclusion accenting the cupidity motif, immediately says, "I've got to see if my deal is still on" (*LA*, p. 99). The phone is now accidentally torn loose so that the illusion of failure may preside. Fair weather friends and family desert him. But then success.[17] Fiddleman suggests television psychotheraphy with "Casey Stengel, Marlon Brando, Artie Shaw" (*LA*, p. 106). But he did not count on the new, freaked-out Bummidge. "All that was familiar is strange, and the strange is familiar," says Bummidge in a campy line true to the identity crisis of all great drama (*LA*, p. 108). ("Now I am alone," he said in another campy line when launching into his opening soliloquy [*LA*, p. 12], a rare borrowing from Shakespeare. Cf. *Hamlet* 2.2.553.) Embracing the *Noli me tangere* and denying his sister, Bummidge is not the person he was. Only the pure Imogen sees that he has been transfigured, and to her he dictates his final, hieratic wisdom, aphoristic, liberated, mock-Orphic, yet, since he is a Bellow character, sensible: "Weeping is the mother of music. . . . Is pleasure the true object of desire? This may be the great modern error. We will revise Freud some more—respectfully. . . . Wouldn't it be better to have a rutting season? Once a year, but the real thing." He now dismisses Pamela with an Elizabethan flourish: "O phantom of erections past, farewell." Bella, too is cast aside: "West Point with a marriage license." And Max, Winkleman and Madge are treated to a Zarathustra-cum-wasteland symbolism of his own: "How does the lonely cactus thrive in deserts dry? . . . It has a mystery to guard. Otherwise, why stand in the sun—why buck the drought, why live with vultures and tarantulas?" (*LA*, p. 111f.). Bummidge repudiates the world of cupidity. It is therefore essential to the play's meaning that he tear up the check Fiddleman proffers. The whole unsavory crew is then caught in the net by the ratcatcher. Earlier notions of reconciliation are discarded for a harder purity. In a mock-Nietzschean ending, Bummidge reflects on the three moralities; from the brutal he has passed through the mediocre and is now "ready for the sublime" (*LA*, p. 118). Is the sublime ready for him?

The answer, of course, is no. Although Bummidge has our sympathy, his sublimity is clearly more posture than substance and is, therefore, ridiculous, sympathetically ridiculous. And yet there are kernels of seriousness in all this corn. Which of Bellow's vintage characters does not reject the mendacious and pursue the noble? It is just that here the polarities are too easily given, given in caricature. But there is enough truth in the opposition for the reader (or viewer) himself to laugh with a residue of pain. More than this, the play's greatest originality is its intellectual comedy, and here Bummidge is seen to be a victim of his noblest intentions. The story is not an unfamiliar one in the contemporary history of mind.

Chapter 9

Mr. Sammler's Planet

Of all Bellow's novels *Mr. Sammler's Planet* is not so much written as aimed, and to a number of late-sixties readers it was aimed in the wrong direction. This polemical work—could anything in the late sixties not be polemical?—aroused considerable counterattack. The attacks focused mainly on Bellow's conservative estimate of the then current radical hopes. The manuscripts show that Bellow never gave a thought to compromise in the writing. Indeed, they show that his inspiration came from what he unswervingly considered the madness of the moment. Changes that were made served typically to intensify his humorous contempt. Surely there was no failure of nerve here, as some alleged, but a demonstration of courage that came short of clairvoyance. Many liked the book as much as some disliked it. It had considerable critical acclaim.

In the euphoria of recent creation, Bellow said of *Sammler* to an interviewer: "I had a high degree of excitement in writing it and finished it in record time. It's my first thoroughly nonapologetic venture into ideas. In *Herzog* and *Henderson the Rain King* I was kidding my way to Jesus, but here I'm baring myself nakedly."[1] A rather rigorous critic of his own work, Bellow was to reverse this assessment, coming to think of *Sammler* as a novel excessively argued. Far from baring himself naked, he came to think that the novel was not personal enough. The manuscripts show the development of the contours of the argument and reveal that while one sort of argument was enlarged others were discarded. But they also show in the development of Sammler a new kind of Bellovian protagonist and in the supporting cast new dimensions in the Bellovian grotesque.

This essay focuses on four kinds of change: (1) the pre-late sixties fragments (Sammler is named Pawlyk here) compared to the novel proper, the subject matter of which did not really present itself until the late sixties; even in the overlapping elements, there is much change in tone, characterization and event; (2) those having to do with his newly found focus on the

Now Generation; (3) those having to do with H. G. Wells and Sammler's Anglophile antidote to the current Francophilia; (4) those having to do with language, which work toward a negative intensification (including ideational heightening). Finally, (5) focuses on the didactic source of all these changes, the challenging moral reality of the book, with an eye toward how the revisions solidified this reality.

Though most of the manuscript material is in the 1969 Deposit, a few relatively short entries are made as early as the 1967 Gift. The 1969 Deposit contains Pawlyk material as well (I.7). These Pawlyk fragments are again relatively brief, featuring various versions of the start of the novel. The 1969 Deposit contains remarkably complete notebook material entitled "The Future of the Moon" (about 980 pages, I.1–4), the novel's first title. It also contains the much revised "first typescript draft" (about 290 pages, I.8–12), here easily labeled because of the relative simplicity and compactness of the holdings. A "second typescript draft" follows (about 290 pages, I.14, II.1) and then a xerox (II. 2–4) annotated by Edward Shils. The uncorrected *Atlantic Monthly* proofs (67 pages, II.5–9) are followed by the Viking proofs (96 pages, II.11–12) with corrections by Bellow (including some changes suggested by Shils). Not in the usual order, the *Altantic* second typescript draft (127 pages, IV.6–7) and galley fragments (76 pages, IV.8–11) follow. As usual Bellow revised into the galleys, the revisions here being more than verbal because of the relative speed of composition.

i

Though once clearly conceived in imagination *Mr. Sammler's Planet* came more easily than any full length novel since *Augie March*—and the whole came even more easily—there are early manuscripts that show that inspiration was not instantaneous. Fragmentary though they are, these versions shed a sharp light on final intentions. It is clear that from the first Bellow wanted a novel that dealt in some way with urban malaise, petty crime and changing sexual mores, all through the mind of a holocaust survivor living in New York (or, in one fragment, Chicago; 1967 Gift VI, 11). But it is also clear, and expected, that much working toward tone, characterization, and event had to take place. For the early fragments give us a story with no pickpocket, no Columbia scene, no Feffer, no Wallace. In short, it was not until the late sixties that the novel's subject matter really presented itself. History was the blow through which the novelist grasped his truth, and this truth was an indictment of the Now Generation.

The early versions begin with old Mr. Pawlyk (Sammler) being mugged as he descends from the elevated tracks in Queens (1967, IV, 19)[2] or as he waits for the bus there (1967, IV, 20; 1969, I, 7). There is nothing here of aesthetic crime, nothing of sexual significance. His money and watch taken, Pawlyk is beaten about the eye and knocked down in "the rubbish and windheap newspaper" (1969, IV, 19). The muggers are two slim, young blacks, one in a "purple windbreaker," another in "a felt hat almost without a brim." A routine occurrence! Having little of the later cultural weight, the incident is given as such. Moral issues are, however, suggested. The "bystanders offer no help" (I, 7, 1), and Pawlyk recalls the public apathy of the Kitty Genovese murder, which also took place in Queens. Something of this apathy is suggested in the novel by the pickpocket's confidence and, later, by the placidity of the crowd watching Feffer tangle with him. But public indifference is not dramatized in the early version. In pre-late sixties fashion, the narrator tells us that "the urban question was the Negro question. . . . The miserable black people were beside themselves in New York." The matter would not be so simply put in the novel. Yet what follows immediately is close to the novel: "The squalor of the Third World, of Ghana, of Brazil, was intertwined with Byzantine luxury. You open a jeweled door and stepped into degradation. You turned a civilized corner and were in a State of Nature" (I, 7, 4). But it is only in the later, extensive revisions that the State of Nature gets its due. And if the statement about "the urban question" shows some uncertainty in narrative voice, compared to the certainty of central-intelligence technique in the novel, even greater narrative voice insecurity is manifested. "Interestingly," says the anonymous narrator, "he told me he couldn't remember falling when struck" (I, 7, 4). But the narrator is not an active character anywhere in the composition of the novel.

What is Pawlyk doing in Queens? Couldn't he have gotten mugged in Manhattan, where he lives? In the novel, Manhattan is sufficient unto the day. In the early versions, he has gone to visit cousin Mary Pawlyk, a survivor "who didn't recognize anyone" (1967, IV, 20). We are told that "to this day she rejected the whole world and sat looking at it offended" (1967, IV, 19). Pawlyk seems to feel a silent communion based on common suffering, though we are told that after his first few years in New York, he "stopped attending meetings of Ghetto and concentration camp survivors" (I, 7B). If Mary is alienated to the point of passivity, Pawlyk has his own special behavior: "He had become deeply objective toward himself, as if he noted from time to time that he still existed" (1967, IV, 19). In the novel Sammler also possesses this quality, a post-bourgeois, post-Wellsian, post-holocaust otherness. His lack of ego involvement supports an almost anthropological detachment well suited to the exotic tribalisms of New York life. Mary Pawlyk is not necessary to his estrangement, and is dropped. Moreover, Bellow imagines events far more dramatic than a routine mugging to define Sammler's "objectivity."

9. *Mr. Sammler's Planet* 211

But Pawlyk still has an attenuated attachment to Wells. What appear to be the very first words of the manuscripts show him breaking with his scholarly past: "Pawlyk did not want to explain to Rosa [Shula-Slawa] why he had dropped his 'studies.' Attempts to explain would have led to confusion if not disintegration. Since he had a strange mind it was best to have continuity in strangeness" (1967, IV, 19). But Pawlyk's mind is perhaps not so strange. As the novel makes clear, there is good reason for him to discontinue his studies. This opening description attributes a more lurid, almost Herzog-like subjectivity to the old man than he possesses. Pawlyk is not so much strange as estranged, and, given the facts of his life, not very estranged at that. His typical stance is a near distance from people—people who generally appear more estranged than he. That he is working on his "Polish memoirs" (I, 7, C. 22) is an early touch that implies more self-involvement, more continuity in strangeness, than he has in the novel. These experiences of chaos are, to be sure, eminently worth recording—Bellow records them in the novel—but Sammler himself does not have the will to literary expression.

As in the novel, his daughter Rosa is eager for him to pursue his Wells study, which, in one early version, is "an analysis of his thought" (1967, IV, 19) rather than the more appropriate memoir. While Shula is recognizable in the early Rosa, with her pale face, "kinky" hair, "odd . . . decisive" thoughts, "irrational" eyes, cheap wig, devoted manner (1967, IV, 19), while she is "something of a nut" (I, 7, A, 8), even "grotesque" (I, 7, B, 9), she is not as kooky as she is in the novel. So, for example, she borrows the manuscript on the moon; she does not steal it, to say nothing of attempting to justify the crime. (She borrows it from a South African. There is no Lal in the early versions.) She does not collect rabbis and observe Ash Wednesday. Furthermore, she has an element of self-conscious rationality that is later dropped. "Rumkowski is nonsense," she tells her ghetto-brooding father (I, 7, C, 6). She is less innocent, more explicitly aware, making "an emotional and stormy thing of these 'civilized' memoirs of his, and she was afraid he would write his 'barbarous' memoirs instead" (I, 7, B, 8). Nor is she so strange that she can not be a following companion for Angela at the hairdresser and gym (I, 7, C, 11). Above all, Rosa is sometimes given a seriousness, a judiciousness, that contradicts the odd qualities and that is therefore omitted in the later versions. Gruner, for example, thinks that Rosa's "mind went beyond his own" in questions regarding human values (I, 7, C, 13). One version projects Rosa as "angry . . . sardonic . . . skeptical . . . responsible" (I, 7, A, 5), annoyed that her father would travel to Queens alone. "Rosa might be odd but she was decisive," we are told in a context that implies maturity, not the reverse (I, 7, A, 7). She is stunned to learn that her father wishes to move to a hotel. (In the novel we find him already moved in with the Arkins, who are not in the early fragments; he moves because of the tension of bearing with his daughter's oddity—e.g., the bathtub hen walking over his books and documents.) The novel gives us no such subjective complication. Finally, the later inclusions work toward comic extremity. There is Shula picking up "eight for a dollar rubbish bargains" (*MSP*, pp. 53f.; not in I, 2). There is Shula baking Sammler's shoes in the oven to dry (*MSP*, p. 274; not in IV, 17). There is Shula stealing manuscripts.

If Rosa had to be simplified into a finer extremity, a more definite grotesqueness, so did Angela. Despite her blatant sensuality, one version presents her as "intelligent, goodhearted" (I, 7, A, 26), which would hardly describe the Angela of the novel. Unhappily married, absorbed in an affair, Angela is, in these early versions, a serious woman of art, escorting her uncle to galleries but mainly interested in her career as a director of plays (IV, 20, 26). Angela is one of two Gruner daughters. The other is not mentioned. Ostensibly generous in time spent with Rosa, her will is toward other things: "she could always reflect on her wardrobe, or do her isometric exercises under her dress, keeping her magnificent belly in condition" (I, 7, C, 15). Her visits to Pawlyk, who lives in a student hotel near her psychiatrist, are motivated by authentic involvement. Physically, the early version is certainly the familiar Angela, "her cheeks bursting with color, her hair dyed with streaks like raccoon fur . . . white net stockings . . . bas de poule, as the French called them . . . Arabian musk" (I, 7, C, 24). As Pawlyk surmises, "her generation had a mission, which was to free pleasure from its connection with sin" (I, 7, C, 25), in itself not a bad idea. The problem is that this mission may take excessive, seedy forms. Angela is having an affair with a stand-up comic, a married man and father of four who earnestly talks about teachers and psychologists. Though Pawlyk takes a dim, patrician view of this ("Why did Nero love actors and singers? Or Byron prizefighters?" [I, 7, C, 25]), though Angela is a woman too sensually advanced, the excesses of her life are muted and serious talk can take place between them. Pawlyk even likes her. "Her frankness was not exactly to his taste, yet he liked even that about her. He had great respect for vital power in every form" (I, 7, C, 26). Sammler could never think this. In the later versions the tensions between them are too exacerbated for such amiability. As the book is written, it moves toward negative intensification. The cult of vitality is enlarged (e.g., Horricker) only to be rejected. For her part, the Angela of the novel looks askance at Sammler, rejecting his traditionalist request for deathbed forgiveness as "too hokey," even for her father (*MSP*, p. 306; not in 1967, IV, 17). The early versions, on the other hand, show Angela diffident, even contrite. She felt "a little [that] he looked down on her . . . and somehow, too, she shared his judgment on herself—a judgment which, very reluctantly, he could not dissemble." But what exactly is this judgment? It, too, illustrates a confused amicability: "Someday her kind of life must stop, must change. And really he was saying to her that his own opinions were wrong whenever they were too austere. One musn't be severe with flesh and blood." Not precisely the point of *Mr. Sammler's Planet*, though some of the critics would have liked it to be. In the early draft, Angela reciprocates this generosity, thinking that though she could hear this from her analyst, it was deeper coming from her uncle, "perhaps because she loved the old man. By her confidences she tried to draw him out. She wanted him to know her. She wanted also to know him" (I, 7, C, 32f.). In the light of the late-sixties reality, this perspective is radically altered.

Gruner, too, is less tainted with the element of moral dubiety from which almost no one in the later versions is quite free. There is no mention of his being a Mafia abortionist. He is in the wholesale meat business, which, in his eyes at least, incurs its own kind of guilt. Gruner is the kind of man who is sensitive enough to feel his own moral shortcomings. He feels a certain guilt at just making money and "in meat, by taking life." In addition, he feels guilty about being a survivor, at not having demanded that FDR do something about the camps. He made, we are told, "a great and unhappy success" (I, 7, C, 12). Hence his sensitivity, his altruism, his insistence on life expressive, in some way, of moral obligation. That West Street meat-packing area that Sammler is so fond of is Gruner's place of business in the early drafts. His transformation into a Mafia abortionist is only another instance of the element of moral weightlessness.

Pawlyk is much like Sammler, but with some differences. Brought up in a patrician manner, he was once "very cold to the family and other bourgeois institutions" (I, 7, A, 2). He would have been a "privatdocent in Cracow if the Poles hadn't been such anti-Semitic brutes" (1967, IV, 19). In the war his wife is "shot to death in a Warsaw street," his daughter renamed and hidden in a village (I, 7, C, 12). (In another early version, as in the novel, Pawlyk is the lone survivor of a mass grave [1967, IV, 20, 10].) When Rosa asks him to read the book on the moon that she borrowed, he answers, "What the devil have I got to do with the moon," which, in another manner, is essentially his point in the climatic discussion with Lal. Rosa replies that what interests Wells should interest him. "Yes," he replies, "I see. All right, I understand the connection" (I, 7, B. 12). Though one wonders just what this understanding means since he has given up his Wells memoir and is working on his Polish memoirs, which would have an opposite emphasis. We do get a sense of Pawlyk's sensibility when he ruminates about his own tastes. He likes "Polybius and Tacitus, and liked . . . calm, leisurely novels, Trollope, Gottfried Keller, Tolstoi's *Family Happiness*. He avoided the literature of crisis. . . . He liked *The History of Mr. Polly* quite a lot." His tastes reflect a wish for normalcy. We are told, in addition, that "he didn't care for *The Time Machine* or *The Island of Dr. Moreau* with its monsters, cannibals and animals surgically transformed into men. Did he need fantasies of horror? Why couldn't he choose a nice, harmless, dignified sort of work, a gentlemanly memoir of a distinguished British intellectual. Why must he be drawn back to unbearable subjects of which even a superhuman intelligence could never make sense?" (I, 7, C, 22f.). In the novel Bellow finds it easy to integrate the somber aspect of Wells with the contemporary scene, a scene that is easy for this connoisseur of chaos to comprehend. And there is no mention of the benign Mr. Polly or the other "leisurely" books. This full-blown, dark conception of the contemporary was not in the early fragments.

ii

For Bellow, the late sixties was a case of nightmare as inspiration. He is in this sense indebted to Living Theater, Dionysius '69, the philosophy of the Beatles; and to Adorno, Marcuse, and Norman O. Brown, whom Sammler finds "worthless fellows" (*MSP*, p. 37). As Sammler sees the assault at Columbia,[3] he is a victim of the cult of infantile gratification made political: "Who raised the diaper flag?," he asks. "Who made shit a sacrament?" (*MSP*, p. 45). Moral judgment is not obviated by the knowledge that one was arrested at the stage of toilet training. In her experimenting with the polymorphous perverse, Angela gives us a more sophisticated version of the cult of the child. She makes infantile impulse adult routine. It is the one thing, other than common parentage, that she shares with her brother. "In Angela's expression," we are told, "as in Wallace's there was something soft, a hint of infancy or of baby reverie. The parents must have longed overmuch for babies and so inhibited something in their cycle of development" (*MSP*, p. 158). Though he deplores the result, Sammler relies on the terms of the analysis.

Wallace, of course, is the late sixties writ large. His appearance in the manuscripts coincides with its late-sixties flavor. He may have been arrested at the stage of toilet training, but he should have been imprisoned. His originality consists of being a professional youth. He will oppose everything that is adult. If Sammler is trying to affirm an indestructable minimum, Wallace is against roots. "Roots are not modern" (*MSP*, p. 245), says the new Oedipus with some justice. If the bursting of his father's cranial network is too obviously paralleled by the bursting of his pipes at home, the Oedipal drama escapes him. Growing up implies the ability to feel guilt when guilt is in question. A suburban Oedipus, he can only conceive of his fate as a revolt against affluence: "All I see is ten thousand a year, like my father's life sentence on me. I have to bust out while he's still living" (*MSP*, p. 245). It may be thought that the triviality of his self-expression is not adequate to the moral seriousness of the book (another example: his desire to tell his dying father about his exciting plane crash) or, perhaps, not truly representative of the moral seriousness of the affluent rebels. Yet irresponsibility was also the order of the day, and Bellow successfully defines this aspect of revolt without pain as a flip rejection of any established values. If his father is a Zionist, Wallace has a sudden, short-lived passion for Arab culture. If his father is American middle-class, Wallace is enamoured of Castro, whom he considers a "bohemian radical" who has "held his own against the Washington super-power." Wallace, of course, has "ideas about revolution" (*MSP*, p. 246). As a rebel against the straight, Wallace seems to have neither function nor sex. Oppressed with the details of living, overwhelmed by the chaos of events, Wallace flies into the utopia of the definite in his business venture with Feffer. His partner is precisely right in saying, "It's divine. You think you're a new man" (*MSP*, p. 111). The only facts Wallace cannot master are the facts of life, which is why he faints in a New York movie house watching *The Birth of a Child*. And why, like his sister, he cannot acknowledge death, even his father's. The siblings act as if they were unfettered, oblivious to conditionality. In short, Wallace is a "Dostoevskian" conception. A mitigating factor is that society, too, as in *The Possessed*, has its "Dostoevskian" aspect, is also given an element of duplicitous contradiction as Sammler realizes in contemplating the sex life of barbarous-rich New York.

Yet Bellow's "Dostoevskian" emphasis is on the rebellious young. Nothing illustrates this more clearly than amplification of Wallace's love of Castro, that "bohemian radical." Castro is, of course, anything but that; he is all brass knuckles and no backtalk. But middle-class youth in army fatigues fighting the war against Batista in 1968 on Broadway are bohemian radicals. Sammler sees the phenomenon as the influence of modernism, a triumph of the aesthetic view, giving us

> more actors, apes, copycats . . . more fiction, illusion, more fantasy . . . this imitative anarchy of the streets—these Chinese revolutionary tunics, these babes in unisex toyland, these surrealist warchiefs. . . . They sought originality, they were obviously derivative. And of what—of Paiutes, of Fidel Castro? No, of Hollywood extras. Acting mythic. Casting themselves into chaos, hoping to adhere to higher consciousness, to be washed up on the shores of truth. (*MSP*, p. 148f.)

None of this remarkable passage is in the relatively late IV, 16 or IV, 1, indicating again how often Bellow's memorable formulations, particularly cultural or intellectual ones, come to flower in the late revisions. This is radicalism as aesthetic transcendence, the radicalism of the Now Generation.

The phrase "bohemian radical" does not originate with Wallace or his peers. It originates with Marx's *The Eighteenth Brumaire of Louis Bonaparte*, his attack on the bourgeois king. His well-known claim, borrowed from Hegel, that "All great world-historical facts and personages occur, as it were, twice; the first time as tragedy, the second as farce" comes from this work. Bourgeois revolution is an aesthetic imitation of revolution, with costumes and rituals substituting for class distinctions. For Marx, these bohemians are economic parasites. The rumbling in the streets of the sixties, like the chaos after 1848, is an illustration. Bellow makes use of this most non-Marxian of Marx's works—a work that, as Harold Rosenberg has said, could have been used by Marx "to disprove his theory that the class struggle can be relied on as the motor of history,"[5] indirectly suggesting what may be part of its appeal to Bellow. Without grinding Rosenberg's Marxist ax, Bellow would see much in his saying that in being the study "of a spurious event, it goes to the heart of our epoch of false appearances and aimless adventures. It is the political complement of nonplot theater, art made by chance, avant-gardism without a program or message."[6] If we consider "our epoch" to be the late sixties, Bellow would seem to be in complete agreement.

But in considering even Marx's most congenial work, Bellow cannot refrain from emphasizing its inadequacies. Without actually naming *The Eighteenth Brumaire of Louis Bonaparte* (he does name it in manuscript) he refers to it just before the passage about aesthetic imitation we have quoted. Marx insisted, thinks Sammler, "that revolutions were made in historical costume, the Cromwellians as Old Testament prophets, the French in 1789 dressed in Roman outfits. But the proletariat, he said, he declared, he affirmed, would make the first non-imitative revolution. . . . He was as giddy as the rest about originality. And only the working class was original. Thus history would get away from mere poetry. . . . It would be free from Art. Oh, no. No, no, not so, thought Sammler. Instead, Art increased, and a sort of chaos" (*MSP*, p. 148). As far as Sammler can see, the myth of proletarian revolution has been put to aesthetic uses. When Sammler mentions Marx again it is once more with a rather critical eye. In manuscript Sammler notes that Marx "loathed bohemians; in *The 18th Brumaire* his attack on Louis Bonaparte is really an attack on political movements organized by political gangs" (IV, 12, 143). Sammler pejoratively adds, "his ideological hashish was very potent" (*MSP*, p. 213). Sammler's metaphorical point, like Raymond Aron's, is that Marxism is, or was, the opiate of the intellectuals. But Marx saw clearly through bohemian radicalism.

The Now Generation is open to the familiar Bellow charge of utopianism, a more exotic, despairing variety here than in dull Utilitarian, Marxist-Leninist Russia. Sammler thinks this as he contemplates Angela's postlapsarian lap, a lap of luxury indeed. Sex as salvation does not seem to work for her and Wharton. Desperation shows. D. H. Lawrence's vision of Mexican redemption through the primitive seems to have backfired, turned seedy. This, then, is death as the void. There is no question of death as appropriate end, meaningful conclusion. Her father's death is one "now" that Angela missed and that Wallace did not even come near. This is the personal climax of the novel, and it is a drama of absence. Adhering to Sammler's request for forgiveness would have meant acknowledging a moral standard non-existent in her world-weary eyes. In touching Gruner with the halo of disinterested- ness, Sammler comes out for middle-class virtue—family feeling, private property. (Though he does not go so far as to endorse monogomy, not with Gruner's geometric wife.) Sammler has come full circle in disillusioned wis- dom from the youth who had taken the "Marx-Engels-private-property- the-origins-of-the-state-and-the-family" line. After all, for him, revolution ends in nihilism. The current American revolution involved "sexual nigger- hood for everyone," which Sammler sees as a utopian enterprise. This is underscored in a manuscript version that continues, "Prehuman, of another era, of the dawn, before the fallen world knew good and evil and was inno- cent of the Tree" (IV, 16, 32). So much perfection Bellow denies, without insisting on the fallen world. The prevalence of this utopian impulse under- mines his own remaining humanistic assumptions. Sammler, with a bow to Max Weber, thinks that "this liberation into individuality has not been a great success. . . . Hearts that get no real wage, souls that find no nourish- ment. Falsehoods unlimited. Desire, unlimited. . . . with hair, with clothes, with drugs and cosmetics, with genitalia, with round trips through evil, monstrosity and orgy, with even God approached through obscenities?" Old-fashioned enough to use the word "evil," Sammler rightly identifies the evil genius behind this, the Marquis de Sade (*MSP*, p. 228), recognizing that his followers do not have claim to the blasphemous subversion of this philo- sophe gone mad.

But if Sade can be seen as an extreme heir of the philosophes, he may more easily be seen nowadays as a tortured version of the Romantics, the originator of negative transcendence, an apostle of energy and impulse. In *Philosophy in the Bedroom* he presents a surrogate who espouses the ideas of the French Revolution. "Revolutions do end up in the hands of madmen," thinks the wary Sammler (*MSP*, p. 218), though in Sade's case, during the Terror, it was the other way around. It is a curious irony that the only conventional sadist in the book, Sammler's wife-beating son-in-law Eisen (meaning Iron), is an artist, "like many another madman," one manuscript version has it; "it's the idea that anybody's suffering is worth a fortune in creativity. That being sick is a great property" (IV, 139). Eisen is a caricature of Romantic transcendence, "rising and rising to heights of world mastery. By the divinity of art. . . . Hurray, Eisen, flying from peak to peak" (*MSP*, p. 168). With his gruesome colors, he is the end of the aesthetic line. He asks,

"How can art hurt?" (*MSP*, p. 171). Later he provides an answer. In the world Sammler sees, the Romantic is reduced to travesty. In this respect Eisen approximates the Now Generation, and Sammler thinks of him as a voice in the loud, aesthetic *carpe diem*. Nor is Sammler alone in rejecting the morality of impulse, for on this point Lal agrees with him. Thinking of the chemical order of the universe, Lal transposes to the social chaos. The wisdom of the *cigale* and the *fourmi*, he notes, has been reversed. The reference to LaFontaine's fable reminds us that civilization has been built, among other things, on renunciation or the willingness to forego immediate gratification when higher purpose was involved. Wallace and Angela tell us that there is no such higher purpose. This is the message of the Now Generation.

What Sammler sees is the backwash of modernism, residues and retentions, renewals and oblivions. Only the decadent and extreme is notable when the norm is extreme to the point of pathology . In this nihilistic setting the criminal is in the air. Consider the scene in which Eisen smashes the pickpocket. In one version Eisen is considered a "reasoning madman, artist-type" who "makes mortuary life-studies" (IV, 17, 226) and, more ominously, "Homicidal maniac: Artist-type" in a later one (IV, 7, 272). In the novel, Sammler simply exclaims, "You're crazy, Eisen, crazy enough to murder him" (*MSP*, p. 291). This is a portrait of darkness on darkness, for the ominous pickpocket "was probably a mad spirit. But mad with an idea of noblesse" (*MSP*, p. 294). He seems to be a character out of Genet. Sammler himself, we recall, is implicated in the pull of violence. He remembers that just before he pulled the trigger the Nazi said, "I have children" (*MSP*, p. 139). He acknowledged an unexpected joy in killing without pity. Of course, these were extenuating circumstances, and most of his life stands opposed to such activity. Sammler killed but did not murder, and what he did cannot be considered criminal. Though, thinking of the murder of the pawnbroker in *Crime and Punishment*, he concedes that "horror, crime, murder, did vivify all the phenomena, the most ordinary details of experience," that "in evil as in art there was illumination": he sobers himself up with the recollection of Lamb's *Dissertation on a Roast Pig* (*MSP*, p. 11). More to the point, "Sammler didn't give a damn for the glamour, the style, the art of criminals. They were no social heroes to him" (*MSP*, p. 10). This is his first reaction to the pickpocket, who, like Genet, wears a single, golden earring. What is even more ominous than the pickpocket is the moral weightlessness that makes him possible, a weightlessness that threatens to undermine Sammler's confidence in the moral stability of even a man like Gruner. Contemplating the lack of "resistance to the glamour of killers," Sammler attributes it to the fact that "the middle class had formed no independent standards of honor. . . . Having failed to create a spiritual life of its own, investing everything in material expansion, [it] faced disaster" (*MSP*, p.

145). Gruner's actions eventually meliorate the heaviest of Sammler's thoughts. Duty, obligation, decency, family feeling—these, too, are, after all, middle class. And even crime has its redeeming moments. In comic distortion of Dostoevsky, Shula justifies her stealing Lal's work for her father by saying, "For the creative there are no crimes. And aren't you a creative person?" (*MSP*, p. 199). With arguments like these even Sammler cannot help feeling a slight tug toward the moral vacuum. Though he can save himself, he cannot avoid the almost universal psychological extremity; for example, his own philo-paternal, sexless daughter, a casualty of pain, and his mis-paternal, oversexed niece, a casualty of pleasure—one the sadist's object, the other the *femme fatale*. Perhaps the pathetic, elderly Bruch, a marvelous nut, speaks most clearly to the disjunction between the moral and the physical, growing up and aimless sensuality. Masturbating in public over visions of sensuous arms, while at the same time pursuing "a highly idealistic and refined relationship with some lady" (*MSP*, p. 59), he plays alone in his room with toys he buys at F. A. O. Schwartz, an ironic comment on the revolution of the children in a century accustomed to disproportion.

iii

Sammler's Anglophile tendencies surface as an antidote to the extremity of the current Francophilia. Angela, we recall, has had "a bad education. In literature, mostly French" (*MSP*, p. 11). French literature, in almost every case, is seen as modernist, whether it be Baudelaire and Rimbaud breaking through the confines of circumstance or Genet through the confines of convention. (Feffer identifies the man who assaulted Sammler at Columbia as "a poor man's Jean Genet. Buggery behind bars. Or being a pure Christian angel because you commit murder and have beautiful male love affairs" *MSP*, p. 109).[7] "British," on the other hand, is civilized, sane, the possibility of a middle way. It is the value of obligation even over impulse. Sammler is "British" even to the point of disliking open declarations of affection, a difficulty he has with Gruner. But in admiring his surgeon cousin because "he did what he disliked," Sammler is emphasizing the superiority of obligation to impulse. After all, there is "Elya's assignment. . . . That's why he has such a human look. He's made something of himself" (*MSP*, p. 303). The metaphor implies ethical fulfillment, and this is what creates a human face.

Although he has put aside his memoir, the great British example for Sammler is H. G. Wells, a figure whom Bellow takes quite seriously. What attracts Sammler is precisely Wells' British quality, his belief in a politics of civility. But history was the shock that destroyed the dream. In Sammler's view, Wells was himself "Utopian" in the sense that "he didn't even imagine that the hoped-for future would bring excesses, pornography, sexual abnormality" (*MSP*, p. 72). He thought only of a better race. Wells was a scientific humanist believing in progress and reason, in civilization. As an honest reader of Wells' fiction, Sammler must add, "Wells had many dark thoughts. Take a book like *The War of the Worlds*. There the Martians come to get rid of mankind. They treat our species as Americans treated the bison and other animals, or for that matter the American Indians. Exterminations" (*MSP*, p. 210). This is an interesting interpretive turn, which attributes to Wells the theme of imperialist guilt, or the guilt of establishing civilization (including mechanization).

Wells is a man of words and a man of ideas, and there is a good deal of grappling with the writer and the figure as the novel evolves. Just what Wells did mean to Sammler is something that had to be established. First, Wells is of interest as a social type, one of the "Olympians of lower class origin" (*MSP*, p. 111). The manuscripts go into great detail about this. We learn that "according to Orwell, Wells was the most influential writer of the period from 1900 to 1920, the one who meant most to the young. . . . A poor boy . . . he became rich and powerful through words. One can take it back to Jean-Jacques Rousseau" (IV, 12, 142). One can, and one does, but the final version deletes a lengthy sociological treatise on this phenomenon.[8] Wells is fascinating in his rise and admirable even in his decline. As Sammler notes, "one thing in Wells' favor was that because of personal disappointments he at least did not demand the sacrifice of civilization. He did not become a cult figure, a royal personality, a grand art-hero or activist leader" (IV, 12, 144). He kept, as it were, a stiff upper lip, not succumbing to flamboyant Romantic posturing. It is typical of the Bellow protagonist to think of the art-hero in this negative way.

As for the art itself, it was not of the self-conscious aesthetic realistic sort. As an Edwardian, Wells could hardly avoid a sociological bent. His famous quarrel with James shows how impatient of the aesthetic view he could be. "For him," writes Walter Allen, "the novel was essentially a medium of ideas,"[9] concluding that he gave up for mankind what was meant for the novel, to mankind's ultimate loss. One version shows us Sammler lamenting a related aspect of Wells' development: "A man like Wells did not choose the way of art. He preferred to be a spokesman or explainer, or encyclopedist. I don't care much for his educational works, *The Work, Wealth, and Happiness of Mankind, The Shape of Things to Come, The Science of Life, The Outline of History*. They are gabby books. The words have gone bad. It is spoiled language" (IV, 12, 143f.). And when Sammler thinks of *God the Invisible King*, the one Wells that Shula has dipped into, doubtless for its title with its suggestion of paternal omnipotence, he says that he "just couldn't read it. Human evolution with God as Intelligence. I saw the point, the rest was garrulous" (*MSP*, p. 199f.). A reader might say that when it comes to garrulousness, Sammler is something of an authority. Bellow has acknowledged as much, saying that the book was too much of an essay.[10] Of all his works this one gives the most centrality to dramatized argument. This is, of course, what didactic fiction does, and however didactic, it is a novel primarily motivated by character. Even so, certain adjustments must be made. We cannot have Sammler attacking spokesmen and explainers. Nor is he the most logical champion of "the way of art." Which is why a manuscript reference containing Sammler's critique of Wells' story of the one-eyed king in the Country of the Blind is also deleted. ("Not a good story," thinks Sammler. "He labored it. A good story does not grow from a thesis" [IV, 17, 168]). In any case, the treatment of Wells even as idea skillfully parallels the more palpable social and psychological realities of the novel.

The most notable illustrations of this are the allusions to one of Wells' best known works, *The Time Machine*, which, we recall, Sammler rejects in the early fragments as a fantasy of horror. It seems that he has learned a wisdom in adversity. As Sammler observes, between the flower children and Wells' Eloi there are distinct resemblances. Wells' traveler tells us that their "hair [was] uniformly curly . . . the eyes were large and mild . . . there was a certain lack of interest I might have expected in them."[11] Their minds were on the intellectual level of five year old children. "Brightly clad people"[12] who are "strict vegetarians,"[13] one came "laughing toward me, carrying a chain of beautiful flowers altogether new to me, and put it about my neck."[14] The traveler "never met people more indolent or more easily fatigued. . . . They would come to me with eager cries of astonishment, like children, but like children, they would soon stop examining me and wander away after some other toy."[15] He observes "a close resemblance of the sexes"[16] and finds "them engaged in no toil."[17] In their way representative of a "Golden Age," they "spent all their time in playing gently, in bathing in the river, in making love in a half-playful fashion, in eating fruit and sleeping."[18] Here then are Sammler's babes in unisex toyland, or even universityland, an aspect of the late sixties. Woodstock prophesied. Wells sensed this developing overripeness, the spoiled, middle-class children and their imitators seen in the extreme logic of fantasy. With a disillusionment that parallels Sammler's, the traveler laments that "the great triumph of Humanity I had dreamed of took a different shape in my mind. It had been no such triumph of moral education and general co-operation as I had imagined."[19] Even more than Sammler's, his vision turns to blackness. The flower children, a shadow of artistic impulse, are subject to "something inhuman and malign."[20] Centuries of privilege have turned the Eloi into "fatted cattle" for the predatory Morlocks, in a fantasy linking social guilt and fear. Sammler remembers this work of Wells' more vividly than any other. In one version we see that though "Sammler had never had a high opinion of Wells' novel *The Time Machine* . . . he had to admit that Wells had anticipated these half naked boys and girls in the Eloi, those hedonistic mindless herds nourished on Arcadian fruits by their brethren, the cannibalistic Morlocks." He adds, by way of mitigating his judgment of the Eloi, "Nature was their goddess, yes, but something else had reached them" (IV, 17, 203). The final version of this passage is not so charitable as to include, let alone enlarge on, this "something else." Sammler looks askance at the local "natives of somewhere," adding, in a description reminiscent of the tough-minded appropriation of the same figure in Trilling's *The Middle of the Journey*, "innocent, devoid of aggression, opting out, much like Ferdinand the Bull. No *corrida* for them; only smelling flowers under the lovely cork tree. How similar also to the Eloi of H. G. Wells' fantasy *The Time Machine*. Lovely young human cattle herded by the cannibalistic Morlocks" (*MSP*, p. 106). Sammler does see something positive, if not in the Eloi themselves, in the traveler's impulse to reach out to them. He remembers, from another science fiction fantasy, that Captain Nemo, 20,000 leagues under the sea, played Bach and Handel on the organ, "Good stuff, but old." Similarly, Wells' traveler fell in love with an Eloi maiden. "To take with one," Sammler concludes, "whether down into the depths or out into space and time, something dear, and to preserve it—that seemed to be the impulse" (*MSP*, p. 136). Sammler values impulse insofar as it is conservative.

But Sammler's involvement with Wells' science fiction, like that of most people, derives from a sense of imminent catastrophe. This accounts for the popularity of *The Time Machine* and *The War of the Worlds*, whose "dark thoughts" (MSP, p. 210) are also recalled by him. The second title gives us war as a metaphor for the unknown but only too well imagined. The second book, like *Mr. Sammler's Planet*, deals with a central character whose papers on "the probable developments of moral ideas as civilization progressed"[21] seem irrelevant to the contemporary realities of warfare, genocide, universal destruction. "It was the beginning of the rout of civilization," we are told, "of the massacre of mankind."[22] What we see in Wells' science fiction and its progeny, the reason for its particular appeal, is the democratization of the imagination of disaster. You do not have to possess the sensibility of a Henry James to feel such intimations. Wells' book does not end with total destruction. Like Sammler, the central character survives. And he hears moral wisdom from a Cockney, wisdom which is close to that of Mr. Sammler. "There's books, there's models," says the Cockney, adding, in a Wellsian turn, "not novels and poetry swipes, but ideas, science books."[23] When the central character, after the Martian holocaust, comes to see his wife, she says simply, "I knew, I knew,"[24] a last-ditch affirmation perhaps unconsciously echoed at the end of Bellow's novel. We see some light in the darkness. It seems, though, that even "English" Wells is not proof against the darker, destructive possibilities. Yet civilization must be affirmed. This is very much the world of Sammler.

iv

"The luxury of nonintimidation by doom" (*MSP*, p. 134)—this phrase perfectly captures the old survivor's uneasy equilibrium. His world has come near the edge, and once it toppled over. He survived with a special vision. For him the moon is "a white corroded pearl" (*MSP*, p. 105) and "the sunlight," as he speaks to his recalcitrant niece, is "yellow, sweet. It was horrible" (*MSP*, p. 300). He recalls that "the sun tried to rise" (*MSP*, p. 140) when the Poles turned on the Jews after the war. If there is that light in the darkness, it is refracted through the heavy gloom of history.

The light imagery is not merely a figurative flourish. The rewriting of the book shows Bellow enlarging on its intrinsic gloominess, a mood appropriate to the enervated consciousness of its central character. Numerous illustrations point this up. "Buses were bearable, subways were killing. Must he give up the bus?" is added late (*MSP*, p. 5; not in IV, 16). "The subway" is changed to "the grinding subway" (*MSP*, p. 6; not in I, 1). Gruner's admonition to Sammler not to run in Riverside Park is another late addition: "I don't want you to be mugged. When you're winded from running some crazy sonofabitch jumps out and cuts your throat!" (*MSP*, p. 84; not in IV, 16). The revisions plainly work toward intensifying Sammler's vulnerability and isolation. Sammler experiences a nightmare moment when he calls to the crowd to separate the black pickpocket and Feffer. In one version there is no appeal at all (I, 4), in the next "His appeal [to "some of you"] was disregarded" (I, 5). In the novel we see the fullblown nightmare: "But of course 'some of you' did not exist. No one would do anything, and suddenly Sammler felt extremely foreign—voice, accent, syntax, manner, face, mind, everything, foreign" (*MSP*, p. 287; not in IV, 17). The impact of this event induces a state of self-alienation. He is psychically floored, a man out of his time: "Sammler was powerless. To be so powerless was death. And suddenly he saw himself not so much standing as strangely leaning, as reclining, and peculiarly in profile, and as a *past* person" (*MSP*, p. 289f.; not in I, 5). His Columbia lecture reference to the Browning Society anticipated this deeper sense of isolation: "But there was no laughter, and he had to remember that Browning Societies had been extinct for a long time" (*MSP*, p. 40; not in I, 1). The verbal assault on Sammler is made more uncanny by recasting in the passive voice. He is interrupted by "shouting" (IV, 16, 36); this becomes "a clear loud voice. He was being questioned. He was being shouted at" (*MSP*, p. 42;

not in IV, 16). His recollection on that occasion of Wells's *Cosmopolis*, "a service society based on a rational scientific attitude toward life" (*MSP*, p. 41) is seen as the manuscripts progress, variously, as an "ingenuous scheme" (I, 1), an "ingenuous, silly scheme" (IV, 16, 36), and, finally, an "ingenuous, stupid scheme" (*MSP*, p. 41). This adjectival switch indicates as well as anything else in the composition Sammler's disenchantment with the politics of civility.

The darkest of his *obiter dicta* are also late inclusions: "Revolutions do end up in the hands of madmen. Of course there are always enough madmen for every purpose" (*MSP*, p. 218; not in I, 4). One can see why this Bellow character says so. An even harder wisdom comes with his saying, "It is a dangerous illusion to think one can do much for more than a very few" (*MSP*, p. 228; not in I, 4). Has Bellow, then, given up on politics in the Aristotelian sense? Gruner may embody the civil heart, but civility is itself a concept which implies more than personal relations. Sammler, at any rate, must settle for smaller gains. His experience has been too painful. The revisions intensify this pain, even in the physical sense. When, toward the end of the war, the Poles came shooting "as soon as it was light enough for murder" (*MSP*, p. 140), Sammler hides out only to appear in Zamosht wild "gaunt, decaying, the dead eye bulging—like a whelk" (*MSP*, p. 140; first appears in the very late II, 12, 42). Even the searing recollection of his orignal escape from death at Nazi hands is made more intense. "Oh heart-bursting! Oh vile!", he exclaims, thinking of his crawling out from the mass of dead bodies (*MSP*, p. 141; not in IV, 1). The very act of his "burial" is rendered more vividly, down to "The thick fall of soil. A ton, two tons . . . a sound of shovel metal, gritting" (*MSP*, p. 273; not in IV, 17). Is it the sound of the end of civilization? Sammler himself would deny that it was.

The negative intensification involves virtually all of the characters, even the "good" ones. So, for example, the kindly Gruner, is indirectly part of the process: "Some, many, would go on with business to the last breath, but Elya was not like that . . . not finally ruled by business considerations. He was not in that insect and mechanical state—such a surrender, such an insect disaster for human beings" (*MSP*, p. 260; not in II, 4). And Feffer's handling of the Columbia affair seems almost to have been a betrayal. "He brought me to speak" (IV, 1, 93) is changed to he "abandoned me" (*MSP*, p. 99). Sammler's admonition of Feffer is added late: "You shouldn't have left. I was your guest. Too late, I suppose, for you to learn manners" (*MSP*, p. 108; not in IV, 1). Even the openminded Lal, defending Pentagon expenditures as such, is put off, in a late version, by American corruption: "Unfortunately, the results are mostly and usually corrupt, making vile profits, playboy recreations and building reactionary fortunes" (*MSP*, p. 217; not in I, 4). His reference to "the great Calcutta killing" (*MSP*, p. 216; in very late II, 12, 36 for the first time), the genocidal Moslem-Hindu riots, is another figure in the carpet of atrocity. When Sammler says to Lal, "It really is a frightful moment" (*MSP*, p. 215; in very late III, 1, 64), he is underlining what has already been expressed.

The description of a Now Generation type like Angela reinforces the pattern of corruption. "Millions of corrupt ladies, Sammler saw, had fortunes to live on. Foolish creatures, or worse, squandering the wealth of the land" (*MSP*, p. 178; not in IV, 1) is late. Even her father's judgment of her becomes more severe in the revisions. "You see a woman," he tells Sammler, "who has done it in too many ways with too many men. . . . And she looks. . . . Her eyes—she has fucked-out eyes" (*MSP*, p. 178; not in IV, 16). His suggestion that if she isn't Frenching an orderly she may be "in a daisy chain" (*MSP*, p. 178) comes after IV, 1. Commenting on why Angela and Wharton have split, Wallace says, "She's *done* him. Who's next" (I, 4, 7). This later becomes, more appropriate to the swinging sixties, "why she let that twerp in Mexico ball her fore and aft in front of Wharton, with who-knows-what-else thrown in free by her" (*MSP*, p. 187). *Pace* D. H. Lawrence.

At times the language is reordered for the sake of intensified ironic thrust. The description of Wallace is an example: "Wallace was a handicapper. His latest passion or rather a revival of one. He was a gambler. He was also a mathematician. He might, Dr. Gruner said, have been a genius in mathematics, physics, astronomy. He had stunning gifts. But he was a kinky fellow" (I, 2). There is one minor change having to do with point of view. It is, appropriately, Angela who says, "He was a kinky cat" (*MSP*, p. 88). Sammler would not say kinky. The rest of the description is rearranged to build to an ironic point: "Wallace nearly became a physicist, nearly became a mathematician"—added after I, 2 in brackets—"[nearly a lawyer (he had even passed the bar and opened an office, once), nearly an engineer, nearly a Ph.D. in behavioral science. He was a licensed pilot. Nearly an alcoholic, nearly a homosexual.] At the present he seemed to be a handicapper" (*MSP*, p. 88). Here, too, there is some negative intensification per se, as well as the rhetorical heightening. The repetition of the incantatory "nearly," the addition of more and darker quirks, the saving of the *coup de canon* for last—all make the passage better and grimmer. What is the wisdom of my son, the handicapper? Wallace tells Sammler that his father has "about a two percent chance to live" (*MSP*, p. 98; not in I, 3).

There is one tantalizing, negative variety of late inclusion that might be called laughable hedonism, a mode of description in which Bellow's enjoyment almost transcends his moral censure. Angela and her friend Wharton are prime illustrations. "The soft challenge of her female endowment in motion" (IV, 16, 16)—this would seem to be good enough for Angela, despite its suggestion that she has been incorporated. But Bellow will have it less neutral, more sensuous: "her flesh in motion—thighs, hips, bosom displayed with a certain fake innocence. Presumably maddening men and infuriating women. . . . It was all in Angela's calves, in the cut of her blouses, in the motions of her fingertips, the musical brass of her whispers" (*MSP*, p. 78). It is not for nothing that Sammler is an admirer of Zola. Overripeness is all. No appetite left unsated, no whim even: "If Pucci didn't have what she wanted, she ordered from Hermès" (*MSP*, p. 67; not in I, 2). It would seem that Angela cannot be outdone in Narcissism and decadence. Yet her lover, or ex-lover, gives her stiff competition.

The elegant Wharton Horricker, younger than Angela and mod, a third-generation Jew who in name out-Wasps the Wasps (it appears that he was named after a business school!) and in body out-pagans the pagans, has his up-to-date apartment-gym, with its instantaneous op and pop art and its Narcissistic "prevalence of mirrors" (*MSP*, p. 68). Romantic egotism finds extinction in Sparta. Perhaps the clearest indication that this is indeed the house of Narcissus is the reverential treatment Wharton gives his locks, that "crisp long hair with a darling curl at the back. . . . You could play sacred music while he had his hair cut." How secular can spirituality get! Wharton is a man who will never undervalue appearance. "Once when he thought [Angela] improperly dressed, he abandoned her on the street" (*MSP*, p. 68, not in I, 2). There is a certain hilarity motivating this description, but it is not devoid of contempt. Angela's "musical brass," Wharton's gaudy interior—both suggest the triumph of the aesthetic view. When Sammler watches the black man struggling with Feffer he notices a special elegance to the pickpocket's clothing. Sammler sees a criminal "with a belt that matched the necktie—a crimson belt! How consciousness was lashed by such a fact" (*MSP*, p. 288; not in I, 5). It is moral consciousness getting a message from aesthetic consciousness, or what remains of either in tangential communication.

Given the moral air of the novel, its intellectual revision has limited play. In *Herzog* the intellectual heightening was often humorous and elevating, where in *Sammler* it is more nearly straight deflation. The attack on Arendt, for example, is there from the beginning, but its cultural point comes late: "This woman professor's enemy is modern civilization itself. She is only using the Germans to attack the twentieth century—to denounce it in terms invented by Germans. Making use of a tragic history to promote the foolish ideas of Weimar intellectuals" (*MSP*, p. 18f.; not in late II, 2).[25] Similarly, the aesthetic judgment Sammler makes of Eisen's work becomes increasingly corrosive in revision. Eisen is seen as "an insane mind and a frightened soul. . . . By using color he robbed every subject of color. Everybody looked like a corpse, with black lips and red eyes, with faces a kind of left-over cooked-liver green." Naturally, he has found a place in New York. Sammler thinks of him a "a cheerful maniac. Now so many highbrows have discovered that madness is higher knowledge" (*MSP*, p. 64f.; not in I, 2). Sammler laments this dehumanized art as he laments the general discrediting of moral life. Here, too, an important intellectual formulation emerges in revision: "As long as there is no ethical life and everything poured so barbarously and recklessly into personal gesture this must be endured" (*MSP*, p. 235; not in I, 4). No ethical life—this is the problem for Sammler. Has he, then, no "positive" suggestion of his own?

Positive and negative assertions in Bellow often exist in near equilibrium, yet the positive assertions of this novel are more qualified than those in any other Bellow work thus far. Humanistic, liberal affirmation seems not to survive the novel's air. One rather obvious example of this is soon deleted. In one version Bellow begins Chapter III with a burst of buoyant lyricism for which there is just no room in Sammler's world, as he seems to recognize even as he writes:

> In its sombrest tunnels the soul heard syllables hinting at release. It was the prophecy of amplitude and a bigger matter even than the idea of personal expansion that ran through Europe after the rise of Napoleon. In one work it was the Revolution, it was the new state of mankind. Of course, the moral and intellectual decay of New York at this moment was [so] wide, deep and massive that the Revolution was eclipsed. (I, 3)

This is surely the most abortive of Bellow's affirmations. This is not the novel to embrace humanity, let alone revolution. Some mixed assertions in the work are not so disparate. Thinking that the Broadway carnival is an attempt to rise above the common life, Sammler wonders, "And what is 'common' about 'the common life'? What if some genius were to do with 'common life' what Einstein did with 'matter'? Finding its energetics, uncovering its radiance." One might say that this has been the central thrust of Bellow's fiction, that he does often, even to some degree in this novel, dramatize these energetics. To the extent that Bellow speaks through Sammler here, the remark takes on a poignant quality, as if "some genius" could succeed where Bellow himself can only think wishfully of doing so. "But at the present level of crude vision," concludes Sammler in the negative, "agitated spirits fled from the oppressiveness of 'the common life' " (*MSP*, p. 147; not in II, 1). In all fairness it can be said that Bellow has never fled from this task. Yet when Sammler feels "we are an animal of genius. This was a thing he often thought. At the moment it was only a formula. He did not thoroughly feel it" (*MSP*, p. 305; in very late III, 1), Bellow seems to be speaking through him. The positive is qualified nearly to extinction in these remarks, though even here some element of further equilibrium is added. The word "thoroughly" does not appear until after the very late III, 1, indicating that there is still some such feeling left, however diminished it may be. Indeed, the language and imagery often form a vocabulary of diminution, of small recoveries and saved remnants. "The luxury of nonintimidation by doom"—this is a survivor's affirmation. "The pain of duty makes the creature upright" (*MSP*, p. 220; in II, 1, 165)—this is a hard, Stoical wisdom, but ethical wisdom has often posited a world as difficult as Sammler's.

v

Ethical wisdom, a reawakening to traditional truth, is what Sammler wants, still clings to. But if we have to look to contemporary physicians for the morally exemplary, the state totters. If Gruner is a brick, he is a cork brick. He is goodness at a remove in a book that deals with intimations of the ideal. Sammler likes him because in being a doctor he did what he disliked for a higher end. But it is also possible to do what one likes for a higher end. Too, he was a Mafia abortionist—not a sterling credential. Above all, in our dramatic context, he was not a very good father—a point never brought up in the book. No good father could have children so unrelated to him. But goodness can exist anywhere, as we may infer from Gruner's elevation. There is an eighteenth-century munificence as well as a Jewish sense of *mitzvot*, pleasure in fulfilling moral obligation, about him, with his "undisclosed charities . . . [and] stratagems of benevolence" (*MSP*, p. 283). He is, as Sammler says, on the old system and undoubtedly has genuine family feeling. As such he really is a ray of light in the gloom. And no one but Sammler seems to care much when this ray is extinguished.

In Gruner we see decency intact. The novel dramatizes diminished virtue. In a very late passage which seems to have in mind Hemingway's rejection of moral abstraction in *A Farewell to Arms*, Sammler thinks: "It was not the behavior that was gone. What was gone was the old words. Forms and signs were absent. Not honor but the word honor. Not virtuous impulse, but the terms beaten into flat nonsense. Not compassion; but what was compassionate utterance? And compassionate utterance was a mortal necessity" (*MSP*, p. 261; not in IV, 7). Sammler then, in taking Gruner's illness with all possible seriousness, exemplifies the compassion he believes in. Under the aspect of mortality, Sammler's quiet goodness asserts itself. There is something traditionally religious about this, and, considering the world of appearance Sammler is up against, the ideal becomes a moral necessity.

How is the moral to realize itself? Sammler comes to a solution novel in its antiquity. Contemplating the "imitative anarchy of the streets," imitation deriving from style, he thinks of imitation deriving from morality:

"Better . . . to accept the inevitability of imitation and then to imitate good things. The ancients had this right. Greatness without models. Inconceivable. . . . But choose higher representations" (*MSP*, p. 149). Sammler wants to go from the current originality to convention so that the soul can dwell in more stately mansions. He does not deny the uniqueness of the soul, but he cannot accept the contemporary forms that the cult of originality has taken. What we have is the imitation of originality. What was sublime in the Romantics is ridiculous in the postmoderns.

The Roman Stoics, too, had this idea of imitation, in this case of the sage. What would the *sapiens* do? Like these Stoics, Sammler seems to have little confidence in the criterion of Greek Stoicism—What will my reason tell me to do? Sammler is perhaps too willing to subordinate his self to the powers that Be. He leaves us with the engaging idea of imitation, but does not adumbrate its problems. What actually is the connection between the self and the subject imitated? Can one under such circumstances be said to have a self? And, for all its problems, isn't the belief in the self irreversible? Can one imitate good and really be good? Doesn't this split imply that the saint or sage be removed from the divine average, to say nothing of the mass of mankind, in splendid isolation, in impressive resignation? Isn't there the danger of patrician complacency, patrician contempt? And hasn't Bellow devoted the best energies of his career to combating such patrician contempt deriving from the religion of art? Isn't the liberal humanist rightly suspicious of such self-abnegation?

Sammler's quest for moral certitude issues in a striking if problematic figure: "It is sometimes necessary to repeat what all know. All mapmakers should place the Mississippi in the same location, and avoid originality. It may be boring, but one has to know where he is. We cannot have the Mississippi flowing toward the Rockies for a change" (*MSP*, p. 228; not in I, 4). Here, then, is one of Bellow's positive formulations coming late in composition. Describing the moral life in geographical metaphor is itself significant, an indication of—or is it a wish for?—permanence, for something abiding in the nature of things. The essentialist speaks here. Of course, we could never know where we are, never know the accuracy of maps, if it were not for the originality of explorers.

Moreover, there is something even more abiding than nature for Sammler—God. Indeed, Sammler "wanted, with God, to be free from the bondage of the ordinary and the finite. A soul released from Nature, from impressions and from everyday life." Having been so abused by the real world, the old man desires only the ideal: "What besides the spirit should a man care for who has come back from the grave?" Old, androgynous, half-blind, Sammler is a Tiresias of the Upper West Side. His moral judgments carry the weight of objectivity, his prophecy the integrity of disinterestedness. He has come back to tell us all. But Sammler can not be as ascetic as he may wish to be: "mysteriously enough, it happened . . . that one was always, and so persuasively, drawn back to human conditions" (*MSP*, p. 117f.). He is, after all, a Bellow character.

But Sammler is a Bellow character with a difference. Though a number of his characters issue spontaneous, lyric prayers, Sammler is the first Bellow character who can be considered religious in outlook. There is a more real world for him than the phenomenal, a world of moral perfectability. Considering the scrawls on plate glass of an empty shop near the hospital, Sammler takes them to be eloquent of "future non-being. . . . But also of the greatness of eternity which shall lift us from this present shallowness. . . . Another future in which the full soul concentrates upon eternal being" (*MSP*, p. 89). These thoughts are all present from the beginning of the full-length manuscripts. Bellow, who for so long has given us the energetics of the ordinary, now give us a character who is something of a supernaturalist. Not that this is a radically new element in Bellow as such: there are Herzog's prayers and his religious tendency; there are Henderson's prayers and his admission that he is highly mediumistic and attuned; there are Tommy Wilhelm's prayers, too. All of these characters have been receptive to the spiritual music, but none of them, not even Wilhelm, thought of triumphing over a world of mere appearance. The stage for Charlie Citrine's dedicated apprehension of the spiritual is set.

What Rudolf Steiner does for Citrine, Meister Eckhart does for Sammler. Anybody who can get off a plane at Kennedy and read Eckhart as soon as he gets to the city, as Sammler does, may safely be described as spiritual. But what, exactly, does Eckhart say? The words seem familiar, for Eckhart has imitated Christ. He says, "Blessed are the poor in spirit. . . . See to it that you are stripped of all creatures, of all consolation from creatures. For certainly as long as creatures comfort and are able to comfort you, you will never find true comfort. But if nothing can comfort you save God, truly God will console." This is a severe doctrine, one which Unamuno agonized over. It is both Christian and Stoic. A parallel between Christianity and Roman Stoicism has often been noticed. Seneca was a favorite of the church fathers. Much later, he and Marcus Aurelius had an impact on the skeptical Montaigne, who, like a contemporary admirer, Bellow, sought ethical seriousness without dogma. We are accordingly told: "Mr. Sammler could not say that he literally believed what he was reading. He could, however, say that he cared to read nothing but this" (*MSP*, p. 253f.). Sammler, then, is one in the line of Bellovian feeling believers. "If he had all the answers," Bellow has said, "he would have been the religious man he wished to be. In reading Meister Eckhart he was feeling his way. He was only beginning to acknowledge the first stirrings of religion."[26] Though he feels only stirrings, those he feels are more otherworldly than any yet felt by a Bellow character. If Sammler literally believed Eckhart's words, the novel would be a refutation of the humanist stance Bellow has loosely maintained up to this work. It seems that Bellow has some feeling for them, too. Sammler's withdrawal and quietism, his flirtation with Original Sin, is a polar opposite of the noisy embrace of humanity Bellow attempts in *Augie March* and, to some degree, the fiction that follows it. This embrace has never been, could never be, an easy one, but various faces come shining forth as a result of the effort. Maybe this is what Sammler means when he says that "it is a dangerous illusion to think that one can do anything for more than a very few." Maybe, but what a difference in emphasis!

Perhaps Bellow succeeded too well in creating an old man who is out of it. Someone closer to the action could have seen that the young in the late sixties were not only contemporary American versions of Dostoevsky's possessed—although some were, like Pytor Verkovensky, modeled on Nechaev—but people with a legitimate sense of grievance. There really was a Lyndon Johnson, a J. Edgar Hoover, a Mayor Daley, a Julius Hoffman. Then again, there really "was" an Abbie Hoffman, a Bernadine Dorn. Bellow is right in presenting us with the startling reality that Sammler sees, not only right, but also courageous, considering that this was written at the height of the great turmoil and in the teeth of much trendy and cowardly posturing. But one cannot help wondering about the strategy of a writer with such gifts for humanistic possibility in presenting us with a character so alone that the younger generations seem to him a form of strangeness. Bellow has said that the novel "was a sort of an exotic report on life in the United States; it was not condemnatory."[27] But if Sammler is looking at the natives with anthropological detachment, he can do so only by holding his nose. There is, it seems, a decisive shift of emphasis. The politics of civility has been transformed into the consolations of religion. Of course, civility and religion need not necessarily exclude each other. But in Eckhart they do. Sammler's interest in imitation, archetypes, and mandalas raises him above history, enabling him to approach a Jungian world Bellow once rejected in favor of historical personality.

Sammler does hedge his transcendental religious thoughts with more homely, ethical ones. "A few may comprehend," he says, "that it is the strength to do one's duty daily and promptly"—his toilet training must have been formidable!—"that makes saints and heroes" (*MSP*, p. 93). He contrasts this with the general Romantic chaos about him: "Most have fantasies of vaulting into higher states, feeling just mad enough to qualify" (*MSP*, p. 93). But what is Sammler doing when he says, "very often, and almost daily, I have strong impressions of eternity," if not some modest vaulting of his own? Yet his impressions have mostly to do with man in his ordinary aspect.

Sammler says that though he would not "mind if there were nothing after death," he "would miss mainly my God adumbrations in the daily forms" (*MSP*, p. 237). Thinking of the time when justice will come, he muses that "when we had an earth of saints, and our hearts were set upon the moon, we could get into our machines and rise up" (*MSP*, p. 237).[28] This tribute to the vaulting power of spirit is positively Hasidic in its optimism, but it is not so different from the desire of the Yippies to raise the Pentagon two inches off the ground by the force of *their* virtue. Be that as it may, religion does serve Sammler as a stay, a positive alternative and a way of seeing. He can see Gruner's goodness: "Remember, God, the soul of Elya Gruner. . . . He was able to do what was required of him. . . . He met the terms of his contract" (*MSP*, p. 313). In a typically Jewish way, Sammler recognizes the beauty of moral obligation, a concept and a metaphor that go back to the Covenant. God, who created man in his image, is, after all, the first and major source of imitation. Gruner, finally, is a righteous man. But is he a saint? The day of justice has not yet come. And when it does, no man who goes to medical school because his mother wanted him to will qualify for that position.

There may be a fatality in Sammler's having been named after Arthur Schopenhauer, a philosopher whom he has read and remembered. Considering Schopenhauer's emphasis on self-denial and withdrawal, on contemplation and asceticism, on the opposition of the noumenal and phenomenal, there may be something in a name. He is a good philosopher for a bad time, as those in post-1848 Europe knew. Like Sammler, he wished to penetrate the veil of Maya, of appearance, to get at the reality behind it. Sammler recalls that the seat of the Will (or Cosmic Force) in man is, according to Schopenhauer, the sex organ. He immediately thinks of the pickpocket's exposure: "He drew aside not the veil of Maya itself but one of its forehangings and showed Sammler his metaphysical warrant" (*MSP*, p. 209; not in I, 4). Through asceticism and withdrawal, through being an historical victim as well, Sammler has at times penetrated the veil to find not Schopenhauer's Cosmic Force but the realm of the mystics.[29]

Chapter 10

Humboldt's Gift

The familiar Bellow tension between aspiring self and resistant world, spiritual seeking and material finding, issued into a story of a poet engulfed by the contradictions and a friend straining to reconcile them. The antitheses here are so sharp that they can be held together—when they are held together—only by a comic perspective. This tension, so extended here, is a rich one in Bellow and carries him through novel after novel with great élan until he finds himself two-thirds of the way through the writing. Then comes the problem of winding up or ending on which many critics, including Bellow as we have seen, have commented. While the tendency of his work is to move toward wry or lyrical affirmation, the question of authenticity arises, and it is nowhere more apparent than in *Humboldt's Gift*.

The manuscripts reveal, remarkably, that the novel was a fusion of two separate novels, one about Humboldt and New York, one about Sweibel and Cantabile and Chicago. Knowing this (or not) some have been tempted to say the first is rich and the second poor, but I believe that this is a temptation to be resisted. The first came into full being only by comic juxtaposition with the second, and it is not without reason that Bellow thinks *Humboldt's Gift* his funniest book. Wanting for a long time to write a novel based on Delmore Schwartz, but floundering in the attempt, the idea clicked when the two novels were made one by the perception of a narrator who evolved as a character in the writing. This final narrator, Citrine, has lived a life that is a tale of two cities, New York and Chicago; culture and anarchy, you might say, except that culture veers toward anarchy and anarchy toward culture. The novel about Schwartz did not become a reality, Bellow has said, "until I got into some of the characters around him; they took the book over and it became interesting and possible."[1] Roger Shattuck, in a minority report, finds that the Cantabile plot comes close to overshadowing Humboldt; he is one of the readers for whom no element reconciles Citrine's "soaring and slumming selves."[2] Bellow's strategy is a daring one, but surely his instincts were right through much of the book. Yet the exhaustion of Charlie Citrine and the shaky form his affirmation takes seem intimately related and point to a gap between the ideal and the real so wide that it can only lead to an unconvincing denouement. Humboldt's gift, for example, is supposed to be comic poetic justice, but it may more easily be perceived as a boomerang. Trying for the celestial, the balloon springs a leak.

The manuscripts show Bellow in the process of a frequently successful fusion. It follows that much of the comedy came in the revisions. The philosophizing, especially the mysticism—sometimes part of the comedy— came, generally, late in the revisions. There are five major areas of revision that show Bellow trying to straddle the contraries, a high-wire act between here and there with an occasional splat: (1) Citrine; (2) the Chicago characters; (3) the New York characters, including a brilliant but excluded, related but virtually independant manuscript section pertaining to Zetland[3] (Isaac Rosenfeld); (4) Humboldt and the struggle for the right opening voice to capture him; and (5) important deletions and shifts of emphasis pertaining to the dual nature of Humboldt and Citrine.

The manuscripts of *Humboldt's Gift*, though not complete, are among Bellow's most copious, running about 6,000 pages. Upper West Side rumor has it that Bellow dictated the novel, but the abundant handwritten material of the notebooks shows that this is not the case. Rather he improvised orally on already written material. Bellow has explicity confirmed this: "I didn't dictate *Humboldt* to Karyl Roosevelt—I dictated the Jerusalem book to her, and the 'notes' [of *Humboldt*] were very full. . . . I had already worked up the notes—I had a draft and, yes, I also 'improvised.' Henderson, too, was written that way, with more improvisation. Dictation has the effect of putting one's 'voice' into the book. Most of my books are 'voice' books (as distinguished from 'eye' books)."[4] So *Henderson* actually had more dictation than *Humboldt*. This discredits the mean suggestion that dictation implies that the novelist can no longer write.

Listed under 1978 Gift, some manuscripts date back to a period ten years before that. The manuscript material, catalogued in a fairly random way in this case, shows fragmentary holograph material (about 60 pages, 7.1), typewritten drafts (about 500 pages, 7.2 to 8.8), thirteen holograph notebooks (9.1 to 10.6) and eight holograph fragmentary drafts (about 250 pages, 10.7–14), a complete typescript draft (almost 800 pages, 11.1–11) close to the first printed edition, an earlier typescript draft (about 560 pages, 12.1–8) another draft with Bellow's corrections (about 200 pages, 12.9–11) individual typescript drafts containing sections of the work (about 1,300 pages, 13.1 to 15.20), typescript fragments of shorter passages (about 400 pages, 16.1–16). An "early" section entitled "Orlansky Story" includes six holograph notebooks (17.1–6) and further typescript (about 350 pages, 17.7–14). These are not the only manuscripts in which Orlansky appears. A section called "Zet-land Story" contains eight holograph notebooks (18.1–8) and typed pages (about 680, 18.9 to 19.17), almost enough material for a separate novel. Fragments and copyedited manuscripts, including a substantial fragment in which Humboldt is called Delmore (20.1) come next (about 450 pages, 20.1–7). Then there is a copyedited manuscript (775 pages, 20.18 to 21.8). Finally there are the sometimes heavily annotated galleys (266 pages, 21.10–11).

i

Written over a period of eight years, *Humboldt's Gift*[5] was a vortex in search of a center. In all those years there was a constant element, the character of Humboldt. What was not constant was the way Humboldt was conceived, the person doing the conceiving, and the precise ambience of the conception. At the same time there was another novel being written. We are fortunate in having Richard G. Stern's account of the process:

> It began as most of the books do, *out there*, with an event, a feeling about an event. Bellow's old friend, the poet Delmore Schwartz, had died in squalor. Bellow had seen him on the streets some weeks earlier and could not face him. He began a memoir . . . which, in a month, turned fictional, became a subject, a story: it was important who remembered and why. The book was written over and with different centers, once or twice without them. Meanwhile—lucky, I think—Humboldt and Humboldt's world grew. (He is the largest second banana in Bellow's fiction.) . . . Bellow had also worked on another book, "an easy, funny book," based somewhat on the life and stories of his old pal . . . David Pelz, a Gary contractor, health freak, and bon vivant. . . . Pelz's character and misadventures melted into the book about Humboldt, and another deeper Bellovian narrator came along to hold the two worlds together.[6]

One way of seeing Bellow's uncertainty regarding his central character is the striking variation in Citrine's professional status. Not that a distinguished man is necessarily wiser than a hack—indeed, the Chevalier's idiosyncracies are in part a deliberate refutation of this notion—but the implication is that he may well be and, in any case, he would be in a position to know Humboldt as an equal, an important condition in the establishment of a final voice, the voice of a friend. The earlier versions of the work usually give us a Citrine who is not the distinguished historian, successful playwright, Chevalier; he is likely to be a failed playwright (*Von Trenck* has failed), a minor scribbler who makes his living as a hack biographer or even, in one version, in advertising (7.7). Little or nothing is made of the creative aspect of

Citrine's life. Much is made of his hackwork. At its worst he writes the lives of Americans for junior-high-school textbooks (8.1), or becomes a vanity biographer, an appreciator of the "silly conceited people I was sent into the sticks to write about. . . . All these inventors of waterproof-processes, manufacturers of toilet seats, all those theosophists and operatic divas and tenors, fighters for planned parenthood" (7.6). (Theosophy in this context shows how far from his mind Steiner was in the early stages of composition!)[7] One version has him teaching Commercial Law in the high schools for eight years; holding a degree from John Marshall Law School in Chicago, he passed the bar exam on his second try.

But Citrine is usually an editor, a respectable one. In one version he is a consultant to encyclopedias and biographiccal dictionaries, "rated highly as a technician-trouble shooter, incomparable at editing, doctoring and salvage work, getting fat fees for it" (17.1). He may even do occasional rewriting of presidential speeches—a job that elicits Humboldt's power envy (7.16)—or interview Lippman, Kennan, McLuhan, and Erikson on television. At its best, Citrine's entrepreneurial self takes the form of Editorial Director of American Biographical Archives, where he hopes to rival Sir Leslie Stephen's *Dictionary of National Biography*. Citrine the struggler, in other words, often alternates with the man who has arrived. There is even early mention of Citrine as distinguished historian, whose book, *Lincoln, Stanton, Andrew Johnson*, was praised by Denis Brogan "as a model of American character studies" (7.23, 12). Even so, he remains primarily an editor who writes unproduced plays. In a later version he is distinguished enough to receive a $30,000 advance to do a book on Robert Kennedy, with whom he spends ten days at Hickory Hill. He never does write the book (15.16, 228). Another, earlier version has Citrine "supposedly" working on two books, *Twenty-Sixth and California*, a study of the criminal courts, and *Charismatic Politics Under the Kennedys* (10.7). If the books are never finished, the implications are clear. First, Citrine is here something of a personage. It is he rather than Humboldt who says, "Es schwindelt" (10.7). Second, Citrine's sublimations are likely to be political. And his politics liberal, which for Bellow is another name for essentialist: "He had the liberal temperament. At the bottom of such a temperament there was always a secret bargain with the social order, with Capitalism. . . . Capitalism was only a bad name for the way things were" (17.10, 76). Since he is a personage, Citrine's views are known, and he must pay for them. "Often," he tells us self-ironically, "in enemy lists of liberal-humanists dead on their feet, my name turned up." He does not seem upset by this and is confident in his achievement. "On the whole," he tells us, "I was thought to be very good" (16.10, 55). We are a long way from the early hack.

Occasionally, Citrine emerges on an even more exalted level as a sort of

Herzog, an intellectual historian of great scope whose project is unfulfilled. His favorite daughter and perhaps her husband, he fantasizes, will bring it to completion. What is the project? "A very personal overview of the Intellectual Comedy, the peculiar flowering of the modern mind since the time of Leonardo" (10.10). Assuming the same "personal" view, this would surely need his son-in-law and probably his grandchildren as well. Far from being a hack, Citrine is here an ambitious intellectual. The novel gives us the original rather than the hack Citrine. This development is necessary in the convincing establishment of a narrative presence suitable to the intimate portrayal of Humboldt, himself a formidable, complex, difficult original.

A similar movement occurs in Citrine's view of art, original portraiture. Early in the drafts he struggles with his Organization Man identity. Well-known enough to know Huggins, he reconstructs Huggins' dismissive sense of him: "just a bit stoney—square, loved his comforts too well, didn't want to be bothered with subtleties, hard mental work. He had copped out, gone back to the Midwest, never quite made the grade in the East. Orlansky [Citrine] had some ability. Had risen quickly. But though the organization was somewhat intellectual it was an organzation." Huggins has a much harder time in the novel, where his dismissiveness can not be so convincing and where it may be seen as a form of New York provincialism. But here Citrine must acquiesce to some degree in the negative judgment. "He was," he admits, "what Rosenberg called an Orgamerican," (actually "Orgman," an equally ugly formulation)[8] or liberal sellout, like David Riesman in Harold Rosenberg's view. But even here Citrine cannot take very seriously "those excommunicating formulas of the highbrow church." Though Citrine agrees that he "had gone away from the spiritual frontline trenches" (7.14, 8), he takes this to be an advantage. Almost alone in his generation he "had not been stuck back in the Thirties, the Forties, Fifties. Desuetude (he liked the word) and obsolescence had not been his fate" (7.14, 15). Since this confidence? smugness? does not even ring true for the artist-historian of the novel, it certainly does not for the glorified hack of the early manuscripts. There may even be some question as to what he is doing and why he is known in the milieu of Village writers and intellectuals. What is needed is a deeper Citrine, a private rather than a public character, one devoted to real rather than official portraiture. This is understood by the early expense-account, corporate Citrine, who expresses a significant dissatisfaction. With all his glossy publication connections, he cannot take his mind off Humboldt (here Jonas Hamilcar). We see here a clear prefiguring of the final Citrine, a man, in his own description, involved in politics but not political.

His view of Humboldt is not uncritical. Early in the manuscripts Citrine expresses a typical ambivalence. He "himself had given up on the artist's life. It was no capitulation or, as imbeciles called it, a sell out. . . . In

America the art-life was a freak show. Transcendent things, freedom, pas-sion, love, divine madness—yes. Shabbiness, postures, buffoonery, idiocy—no!" (7.13). Though Citrine is not referring to Humboldt here, he is express-ing the kind of double judgment necessary to an apprehension of Hum-boldt's life. It is one thing to say it in summary, another to apply it to a life. The evolution of the narrative persona bridges the gap. The advance in complexity of voice is to be accompanied by a credible success in the artistic world.

Citrine will not be shipwrecked on the shores of Lake Michigan. He will not do what the alienated artist is supposed to do, what Humboldt did; yet he may appear to be doing so. In a middle version he notices that by moving back to Chicago he has "deprived [Denise] of an interesting life. . . . And I myself, as she saw it, had come back to disintegrate in Home Town bore-dom. Such perversity only the Death Wish could explain." Citrine tran-scends this situational irony in knowing that "my life was a Chicago matter and would yield up its secrets only in this city." He says this well aware that these secrets may be far from elevating. Curiously he then thinks, "Edgar Allan Poe would expound his theories, would explain Eureka to drunks in taverns. Active minds become desperate in these mental deserts" (9.1). This is unexpected because Citrine implicitly compares his own life to that of a *poète maudit*, which is what he does with Humboldt. But the comparison in Citrine's case is limited, since the juxtaposition of Citrine and Chicago is essentially comic. He can sympathize with Humboldt's fate, but he cannot empathize with it.

At times Citrine can sound like the artist-hero, even in, especially in, the Chicago context. "I wanted to write a book about Chicago," he says, "a sort of poem" no less. "The great Doughty had answered when he was asked why he had gone to Arabia that his purpose was to rescue English Prose. I could not say such a thing with a straight face. And yet I must say some such thing, because it is the truth." To be sure, he is not as messianic as Stephen Dedalus, but he does feel the call: "This embarrassing pretentious ambition must be confessed at last; I [am] ashamed to speak of it, but my life makes no sense if this is not admitted. I had told Humboldt that this was the one thing I may have been destined—even providentially destined to do" (10.9). It seems that in the twentieth century every writer must make a bow to artistic heroism, even if one's pants split in the process. Citrine's sentiments are elevated enough, but this is not what is wanted for his voice as it develops, one which is as world-weary as it is worldly-wise. Indeed, the weariness of his wisdom, the wisdom of his weariness is such that art is less relevant to his pursuit than religion.

Though there is no mention of Steiner or anthroposophy in early, pre-*Sammler* manuscripts, it is clear that Bellow thinks of Citrine as religious. A manuscript note reads: "Kept himself available for his true vocation: the praise of God," adding with some sobriety, "This was what made him such a nervous person" (9.2). Herzog's middle name was Elkanah, and Citrine's might just as well have been. In both, the search for Halleluliah is necessary but enervating. And well it might be. God and Chicago are about as harmoniously fitted as the Virgin and the Dynamo. One early version does show the young Citrine indifferent, even hostile, to religion, an apostle of Nietzsche and Rimbaud. Recalling university days, he thinks that "if I saw in Szathmar the fateful image of the limping Byron and his airs he saw in me the twisting, skinny dark boy so eager to form clubs and read papers on *The Antichrist* or *A Season in Hell*" (15.17, 51). As the novel develops it is for Humboldt, not Citrine, to be the apostle of modernism.

Another early reference indicates Citrine's final religious direction more accurately. He here has a vision of brotherhood based on a Dostoevskian dream: "But when (or if) these true bonds increased, when these millions coalesced in fraternity, when the State, as Dostoevsky had desired and advocated, became a Church or the Church a State, the Kingdom of Darkness receding, everybody uniting in one communion of universal love, then my kind of existence would be unnecessary. Something better than the Comical Subject would stand between heaven and earth" (15.17, 37). Sympathetic to such visions of fraternity though the Bellow surrogate is—one thinks, for example, of Wilhelm's vision in the subway—there is no other place in manuscript or final version where he entertains explicitly reactionary, albeit visionary, fantasies. The political liberal in him precludes the extremes of a Dostoevsky. Yet the early manuscripts give us a character, not unusual in Bellow, for whom prayer comes spontaneously. "I gave thanks of a sort," Citrine tells us. "My ancestors after all had the habit of muttering prayers and blessings all day long, over every crust and shot of schnapps and I've inherited the tendency. . . . I muttered—Chimerical man, glory and scum of the universe, vessel of truth, cloaca of doubt and error. An odd prayer, but unbidden" (14.16, 32). Odd it is not, but is it a prayer? Or a fragmentary apostrophe to his own sense of the mystery and to his own need for elevation? Whatever it is, it predicts his need to wrestle with the cosmic ambiguities in a tone of implied gratitude. One of the differences between the early and late version is the greater precariousness of Citrine's religious impulse in the former. He can even say in one early version, "about Higher Things, I was just an imposter" (15.17, 60).

It is not until his discovery of Steiner—in the middle versions, developed fully only in the later ones—that Citrine's religious impulse takes something like wings. An early manuscript reference shows the difference. "Sons of greenhorns were made to embrace the USA," says Citrine. "I had taken it into my head also to be a marvelous person. Why not! I would be marvelous.

If there had been Thrones, Cherubim, Seraphim, Powers and Dominions my heart would have been satisfied. But as the world was devoid of divine persences I made my own bid to be marvelous" (14.6, 4). In Steiner there are just such celestial presences, and the later Citrine is receptive to them. The thrust to be a marvelous person, ironically undercut in *Herzog*, is a matter of the past for the accomplished Citrine, who came, saw, conquered, and konked out. Boredom may be a kind of death, but death, Citrine believes, will not be boring.

Yet the religious tendency of Citrine even in early and middle manuscripts may on occasion go beyond humanism to anticipate the later Citrine's mysticism. He recovers childhood, "states of extended reflection and feeling, of pure affection, pure interest, of idleness, invention, vision (Blake's vison or Traherne's). From this came the strength to cope with the world, and the faith that it would be worthwhile to do so." He refers to the religious rather than the naturalistic Blake, to the metaphysical Traherne. His search for transcendence is not, then, politically Romantic. Citrine tells us that it was "never done for the 'radical I' the antinomian, self-infinitizing, hedonistic self 'against society,' etc." What then is its motive? "The object," he points out romantically enough, "was always to stir the imagination so that it would reclaim the world from infuriating and barren abstraction. This was Citrine's 'politics.' The external world had become empty. . . . In captivity to the collective representations and in the idolatry of Appearances. In the 3rd phase (1. Innocence 2. The fall into Experience) God gave Saul 'another heart,' so that he prophecied" (9.5).

This kind of utterance represents a decisive shift in Bellow to a genuinely mystical mentality. Citrine's "politics" here bear no relation to Herzog's politics in the Aristotelian sense. It is Citrine, not Renata, who says of Chicago in an early manuscript, "Without O'Hare, sheer despair" (10.5). The world is seen at a considerable metaphysical distance. Citrine speaks of reclaiming it, but he seems indifferent to the idea of community, of civility, We are moving toward the final Citrine, who recalls his "early and peculiar sense of existence—sunk in the glassy depths of life and groping, thrillingly and desperately, for sense, a person keenly aware of painted veils, of Maya, of domes of many-colored glass staining the white radiance of eternity, quivering in the intense inane and so on" (*HG*, p. 3). The casual, Arnoldian undercutting of the Shelley in him does not alter the central thrust. The child is father of the man. Citrine's laughing distance from the ordinary life he remains up to his ears in is at times so attenuated that it approaches alienation. One must admire Bellow's honesty but wonder about his direction. There is a certain dramatic advantage gained. For Citrine such spiritual distancing was necessary for a clairvoyant assessment of Humboldt's mysterious soul, and for his own.[9]

ii

The unity of *Humboldt's Gift* hinges on the incongruities of spirit in a material society. The worlds of Humboldt and Cantabile are comically juxtaposed. It took the Citrine of the middle to later versions to see the humor and without humor there is no connection between these disparate worlds. The poetic character, living everywhere but at rest nowhere, he is himself in both worlds if not quite of them. Rather like an elderly Augie March, he touches all sides, and nobody knows where he belongs. Marginal everywhere, he is always reaching for the center of his soul, where he finds a sense of rich incongruity.

The reviewers "didn't seem aware that it was a funny book," Bellow has complained, with justification, it seems to me.[10] A key to the humor is that the joke is often on the Chevalier. "Charlie is not really successful," Bellow has said. "Charlie is a man who, by having success, has excused himself from success. Charlie is like Julien Sorel in *The Red and the Black*. When he gets to the top of society, there is nothing to do but shoot Mme. de Renal and get his head cut off. That's exactly the Charlie position in the book. That's why he'd rather hang aroung with card players and bums and tramps." There is no late Romantic sentimentality here. "It isn't that he thinks they're more genuine," Bellow says. "No, everybody's equally genuine or false. It's just that he thinks they express the ludicrousness of the position."[11] Whatever one thinks of Bellow's view of Julien Sorel's motivation in the murder and trial scenes of *The Red and the Black*, it is significant that he compares Citrine to a man who has tasted the fruits of the world and found them wanting, a man whose energies are converted to the unheroic. If a Bellow surrogate is going to be an artist or part artist—even this identity he must straddle—he will not be an artist-hero. He will be the artist in his unheroic dimension. No special fate, no precious dawn, no tantalizing bird, no passionate program, no martyrdom will be his. Given typical American conditions, and Chicago will supply these in abundance, Luciferian pride is ridiculous. Humility may be more like it, or at least a saving humor. And Cantabile is there to teach their uses.

A character in what Richard Stern refers to as the novel about Pelz, Cantabile evolves as a central figure in the fused novel. His shadiness is documented in early versions. In the Army during the Korean war he sold a truck full of gas to the North Koreans. Deserting the Army he lives in East Germany for a while. He then gives back half of the profiteering money in return for a short, two-year prison term that he serves in Leavenworth (1967 Gift, 6.9).[12] In other early versions, he is a "juice man" who lent out money at 100 percent (7.13), bragging that he served time in Leavenworth (9.2). Cantabile's rougher edges are eliminated in later versions. In addition to his flaunting criminality, Cantabile is, in manuscript, involved with a charter-flight outfit, a dehydrated vegetable venture, silver speculation, outbidding a Japanese competitor in Ecuador. (Only his toilet disinfectant business is retained in the novel.) He is Bellow's familiar wheeler-dealer made criminal.

Cantabile's educated wife is not bothered by all this. She "took in these boasts with deep contentment. She was one of those 100 percent wives who have the secret of translating a husband's brainstorms into measureless inner peace" (9.2). The actual dramatic presence of wife Lucy is cut after the early versions. The main scene cut is a dinner at the Cantabile's attended by Renata and Citrine that was "so awful that it was comical," a cosmopolitan feast that misfires in the kitchen (9.2). Does Cantabile's Ph.D. wife outrage credibility? This question had occurred to Bellow in manuscript and he answered it there, as he does in the novel, in the negative: "There was nothing so exceptional here. Highly educated women were excited by scoundrels, criminals and lunatics, and these criminals, etcetera, were drawn to culture. Diderot and Dostoevsky had made us familiar with this. It was positively old hat" (9.1). Offhand, one might wish to call for a point of clarification, but the compositional point is clear enough. Yet even Bellow detects an implausibility in Lucy Cantabile sufficient to have her appear in the novel as a point of reference but not a character. Cantabile's mistress is more probable than his wife.

Still, Cantabile's attraction to culture, such as it is, is believable in the topsy-turvy normalcy of Chicago. The particular hold he takes of it, though, had to be ascertained. In manuscript Sweibel says that he went to a "cow college," asserting that "he said he had to meet you—the writer. What he really wants probably is to write a book" (9.5). His wife, a writer, maybe; Cantabile a writer, no. What is possible is Cantabile as cultural entrepreneur, or is it profiteer? He wants to tape readings of Citrine's essays and articles and rent them to colleges and universities—the Bobby Kennedy piece, the Houdini piece, the piece on bores (10.11). What is possible is the presence of a force representing brute Chicago that wishes to rub shoulders with artistic and intellectual achievement, while the very center of such achievement, Citrine, is nearly exhausted by the attempt to make sense of a life intimately bound up with that same brute Chicago.

Citrine is, paradoxically, rejuvenated by the sheer force of being of a man who personifies the extremity of the city. Cantabile, Citrine tells us, "may have been trying to act the desperado, Billy the Kid, Ivan the Terrible, but the result, the effect (on a distinct mind) was to bring back the happy world of innocence" (10.12). For a criminal, Cantabile's acts take a remarkably aesthetic turn. The smashing of the Mercedes, not present in early versions, is Mafia-style action sculpture, a symbolic act figuring a rough poetic justice. The culture-conscious Cantabile is positively torn by the act. "You son of a bitch," he frantically yells into the late-night phone, "Look what you're doing to me" (*HG*, p. 37), reminiscent of Gersbach pained at having to take the wife of his best friend. In one manuscript version Citrine wonders, "Why did he batter my car? To endear himself to me" (10.14). Charming, but the final version will not go so deeply into depth psychology.

If the smashing of the Mercedes was motivated by endearment, the stall entrapment had to have been motivated by *caritas* itself. Somehow this is a wrong tack. The stall scene is brutality asserting its authority. The authority of culture perceives the significance of the act. What it perceives is brutality made aesthetic. "This might have been a sign that his vital endowment or natural imagination was more prodigal and fertile than mine," Citrine speculates (*HG*, p. 83). Cantabile's tour-de-force is the construction site scene, his transcendent arena, where high, overlooking the city, he floats Citrine's contrite fifties into the dark. This is the latest turn on the gratuitous act, extortion with the purpose of getting nothing tangible out of it for oneself. With his alligator shoes, raglan coat, and ermine moustache, our steel-beam transcendentalist resembles the elegant pickpocket in *Mr. Sammler's Planet*, another instance of imaginative brute force whose actions speak louder than words. The wonder of this relationship is that Cantabile looks up to Citrine even as he abuses him. Citrine had to be enlarged into a figure of reputation, had to be big enough to envy, for this to be dramatically convincing.

The scene at the baths is in early manuscripts, but the scene at the club is not. The plushness comes later. With it comes another portrait of the criminal in Langobardi, the authentic Mafioso. Bellow's treatment of him is hardly that of the popular imagination. The thing about Langobardi is his stylishness, again a courting of the aesthetic by the criminal, the aesthetic of the bourgeois eye. Citrine meets him on a high sartorial plane, perhaps too comfortably. Though he notices the lining of his coatsleeves, he does not see the blood on his hands. Bellow has had a certain sympathy for the *goniff*, the operator trying to assert his being in a tough economic system, but not for the professional criminal. It seems that the propinquity of brute Chicago, in all its aesthetic splendor, has lulled Citrine into a judgmental lapse. One can't quite see a Bellow surrogate chummy with a murderer. One feels a certain sympathy with Denise at this point as she remonstrates about a man who gets along better with hoodlums (including Cantabile) than with his psychiatrist, professor and architect neighbors. Citrine does not dispute her point; in one middle version he says it himself, adding, very dubiously, "All the hoodlums want is to be gentlemen, softspoken, courteous, non-vulgar, their shirts made to measure in Hong Kong, their holidays spent at Lake Como. It's the businessman who has the loud mouth and behaves as he thinks gangsters behave" (9.6, 9f.). One need go no further than Sweibel or brother Ulick to see that Bellow's feelings about businessmen are more complicated.

Sweibel is pure Chicago, to Denise's regret and Citrine's delight. A businessman, he started out as an actor. In Sweibel material conditions have not entirely won out over style. Although he knows Ibsen and Brecht, his style is motivated by nature. In his dandified gymnast's appearance, he is physicality made aesthetic. With Sweibel at one pole and Humboldt at the other, Citrine has plenty of middle ground for both physical and mental gymnastics. Early versions present Sweibel in the first person, an unlikely tack for a Bellow novel, considering that his interior is mostly exterior. Sweibel is better perceived than revealed. Still, what is Carbon City, Illinois, his Chicago area residence, without culture? "In a dream," Sweibel tells us, "I saw Igor Stravinsky." He tells Stravinsky that he is from Carbon City and that he is a contractor. Stravinsky promptly asks him to write a libretto (17.5). In one version Sweibel is not only conversant with modern theater, but he has also tried playwrighting. This is consistent with the practical American need for self-improvement. Why should improvements happen only to basements and attics? But Sweibel feels the pressure. "I may be the biggest reader in Zorro, Illinois," he tells us. "But it is a hapless outlook. First my mind is swayed by MacLuhan, and then by Konrad Lorenz, then by Robert Ardrey and Leakey digging in the Olduvai Gorge. But over the years I have come to accept Jungian psychology, the archetypes, the collective unconscious, the anima, the mandalas. At the same time I am in the siding business" (17.5). Sweibel's ironic self-consciousness allows Bellow to forego satirizing the practical idealist. Worldly wisdom sits better on Sweibel's broad frame than book wisdom. In the novel, the sophisticated narrator derives much from Sweibel's version of the former, while he is cool toward his version of the latter. "Down-to-earth George is not without myths of his own," Citrine says, "especially where women are concerned. He has Jungian views which he expresses coarsely" (*HG*, p. 40). An even more blunt Citrine says, "George is not stupid except when he proclaims his ideas" (*HG*, p. 59). Citrine remains Sweibel's friend, evidence of his remaining love for Chicago and its environs.

Sweibel is especially important in terms of composition, the novel about him having fused with the one about Humboldt to make *Humboldt's Gift*. Most of the Cantabile plot is from the Sweibel novel. The details, somewhat varied, are spectacular. For apparent default on a poker debt, Cantabile throws cinder blocks through the window of Sweibel's place of business. In one version Cantabile calls to say, "I am sad for you now Georgie. Look what you made me do (1967 Gift 6.9). At Cantabile's request they meet at the old baths on Division Street. Cantabile comes toward Sweibel with baseball bats. Sweibel thinks, "he might maul my Mercedes Benz with the bats, in his fury" (20.17, 56). (The mauling of Citrine's Mercedes was a later addition.) He then takes George into the toilet and makes him smell his stink. To restore family honor in the eyes of the mob, Sweibel is made to confess to columnist Mike Schneiderman and again before a "fence" of expensive items. Then comes the construction site scene as in the novel, except that it involves Sweibel rather than Citrine. That these things could happen to a man like Citrine strains credibility in some readers, yet America is asymmetrical enough (in ways that the novel describes) and Citrine odd enough in his social preferences for almost anything to happen. Indeed, this asymmetry is what makes the novel crystallize.

Sweibel was advised not to pay his debt by Gollam, a writer who goes to Saigon to write about graft and whores. George thinks of him as "a famous artist," of Cantabile, as he does of Citrine in the novel, as "a prick with a pen" (20.17, 62). Cantabile gives a socio-literary critique of Gollam that would be beyond him in *Humboldt's Gift*. "He knows as much about low life as the squares he writes for," says Cantabile (20.17, 62). Cantabile knows that Sweibel and Gollam "make the rounds" together: "Arlington . . . the fights, hockey, old jazz joints, skid row, the Shamrock, hob nob with old drunks and criminals." He says, "That's how Gollam gets his kicks. We're his material and his subject matter. He describes us and pities us." Sweibel says, "You've read his books, I see." Cantabile replies, "I've tried" (20.17, 67). (Elsewhere, Cantabile suggests that Gollam was at the poker game "so he could show off and prove he had genuine underworld connections" [20.16, 65].) In another version he sounds even less like the final Cantabile. In a section entitled "Arpeggio not Cantabile?" an earlier Cantabile comments that in Europe Gollam is billed as the historian of Chicago's gangs and rackets. "He knows no more about these things than the rest of us," says Cantabile. "His real achievement is his mastery of the rhetoric, which gives the illusion of thorough familiarity with the jail, the clinic, and all the romance of whorehouses and addiction. The facts are much better known by any cop or ambulance attendant" (1967 Gift 6.9). Insightful, no doubt, but this sounds more like a well-known Chicago writer on another well-known Chicago writer than it does Cantabile. And would Sweibel, at the Playboy Club for his visit with Schneiderman say, regarding the stupendous view, "Man has conquered the vacancy of the mid-continent" (20.17, 69)? One of the difficulites with the Sweibel novel was the establishment of a voice. We do not need Sweibel or Cantabile for cultural generalizations and literary insights. Much better their common coarseness, as in *Humboldt's Gift*.

Another part of the Sweibel novel that is excluded is the new-lover-jilted-wife story. That would be redundant in *Humboldt's Gift*. Automatic adultery as a plot requirement is one of the sources of boredom Citrine did not consider. Apparently, Bellow did. Still, random screwing proceeds at such a furious pace it staggers credibility if not morality. That Gumballs Schwirner, for example, who supplies Cannibal Pinsker with legal strategy through Denise, would be cohabiting with the fiercely virginal Mrs. Citrine is harder to believe than Steiner's nonsense about the lotus position. When Sweibel, in an early version, sees a psychologist about his wife, the good doctor says, "If I were your Rosie, I'd make you live with the consequences of your actions" (1967 Gift 6.9). He proposes that she get a lawyer, appropriate George's funds and lock him out of the house. George thinks this is funny. But the last laugh is on Citrine.

Another important Chicago portrait, though not from the Sweibel plot, is brother Ulick. Delineated in the later versions, Ulick is to appetite what his brother is to spirit, a sort of gourmand. He wolfs down candy, smoked fish, loquats, persimmons, and chicken molé the way his brother devours major reputations. Coming from the ordinary, both have a vivacity, a need for transcendence, that transfigures it. Both undergo a crisis of heart, Ulick's physical, Charlie's spiritual. Ulick is the battered body, the substance of the Chicago of which Charlie is the lacerated soul, the essence. But what is such a place without the substantial? Like his brother, even Ulick would find it boring in such circumstances. But just as Charlie is drawn to Ulick, essence to substance, emotion to action, ideas to money, so Ulick is drawn to Charlie. What is remarkable about their talk is the extent to which culture has permeated cash. Ulick finds his brother's books unreadable, his brother's plays incomprehensible. But he wants his children to learn languages, and he wants his painting of the ocean, the unmediated ocean. "Even he was no longer all business," Charlie notes. "What did a seascape devoid of landmarks signify? Didn't it signify elemental liberty, release from the daily way and the horror of tension? O God, liberty" (HG, p. 421f.). It also may signify, traditionally, release from more than the cash nexus, release from life itself, immortality, infinity, the unknown journey. But that this desire for release should take aesthetic form in Ulick is the wonder. "To think that we should be brothers," Ulick muses aloud. "It's positively a subject of a poem" (HG, p. 385). The transplanted Texas wheeler-dealer is not without his own sense of wonder. Indeed, the business culture has taken an aesthetic turn. Ulick thinks of big money in art as something ominous, his well-to-do writer brother as something humorous, capitalism tempting art. Though this may have come as a surprise to some, the writer's venality was not necessarily exposed. And whoever said that poverty was an honorific? As in *Augie March* and *Herzog*, there is an almost mystical sense of family connection underlying the brothers' relationship. Thinking that he may die on the operating table, Ulick tells his brother to marry his wife in that event. He has already spoken to her. "She'll do what I tell her. So will you," he says (HG,

p. 398). Charlie's depth of feeling does not blind him to the tyranny of good intentions. Intellect and money can meet on intimate terms but cannot lie in the same bed.

Szathmar is another Chicago character who shows the world of money and culture in delicate imbalance. In the novel he is a friendly, somewhat shady, lawyer friend of long standing, a reality-instructor in the vein of Sandor Himmelstein of *Herzog*. Always eager to indulge intellect, he sets Citrine up with Renata for their first assignation. Citrine remembers the chubby, schoolboy poet Szathmar once was as Arse Poetica. Szathmar's character evolves in manuscript from that of a sinister man who uses culture to that of an amiable one who envies it in a friendly way. A middle version has him talking Berdyaev's language. He talks about freedom and suffering. "It was shown by Dostoievsky," he says, "that the intellectual's rage for freedom, existentially speaking, was also the sin of Pride" (16.3, 50). (Citrine, the wise skeptic, counters: "What does this *Existential* mean? . . . What a crappy word. I hear it all the time on WFMT when they're advertising that Bohunk Savings Bank" [16.3, 50].) At the same time Szathmar confirms Denise's worst suspicions by taking half of the profits of a front-load real estate deal. We are in the realm of Dostoevsky, all right, the realm of idealistic duplicity. Various versions show Szathmar as a seducer of Denise-before-Citrine. Citrine knew the routine that culminated in a candlelight dinner and quotations from Berdyaev's *Slavery and Freedom*, chapter one. Why chapter one? Because he never got as far as chapter two. Szathmar is judged to have the peculiar American hypocrisy. "Because he became an American Businessman," says Citrine, "he had the sanction of national usage to lie and also to keep his sentiments pure, to say, 'my friend' or 'I love' while thinking something quite different. But unaware! He was spared even the knowledge of lying" (16.3, 57). Morally weightless, he is also crude in the manner of Cantabile. Throwing a party for the Chevalier to drum up law business, Szathmar berates Citrine for never having been in a threesome, for never having been reamed. How can Citrine pretend to a knowledge of his contemporaries (14.8, 44)? This early Szathmar is a colleague of stock manipulators and Mafiosi. In the novel Cantabile assumes this role. Would Citrine be on old-buddy terms with a scoundrel? Szathmar remains the worldly manipulator verbally abusing his idealist friend to protect him from the grasping, mercenary motive. His kindness is witness to the balance he has struck between money and culture.

When Pierre Thaxter comes to Chicago he is delighted to face the criminal element so serendipitously. He appears to have no inkling of how well suited he is to this environment. "Was Thaxter a crook?", Citrine wonders. "I couldn't answer" (9.2). Thaxter, morally dubious if not a unique white-collar criminal, is still another turn on the axis of crime and art. He is well qualified for an aesthetic appreciation of Cantabile. The manuscripts show that Thaxter's criminality is toned down in the writing. For example, it occurs to Citrine in the museum that Thaxter "was calculating how these masterpieces might be stolen" (15.5, 147). Such obvious criminality is not possible for the Thaxter of the novel. Thaxter's moral dubiousness is not a matter for contempt but for amazed enjoyment: "He had been a Benedictine novice, a cryptographer, a professional hockey player, a drag racer, a foreign correspondent . . . on top of it all, Thaxter was a Tolstoyan" (15.5, 145f.). Where does he get the "chartered . . . private jet from Minnesota when he wanted to catch a basketball game in New York" (15.6, 138b)? Where his lush Palo Alto setup? Partly from Citrine, of course. Thaxter is a comic analogue to Humboldt, a lovable misfit, a swindling man of letters, a publishing scoundrel. "Stay away from values," warns the value-cherishing and value-ridden Citrine (*HG*, p. 359). Thaxter's aristocratic veneer masks a need for money as obsessive as his need for culture. In this novel where crime and culture are ironically joined, there is a moral euphoria with respect to negative judgment. Citrine is the most tolerant, perhaps the most passive—from pp. 111 to 168 he is lying down, like Augie, like Bummidge, like Herzog, getting some of his best insights in that position—certainly the most spectatorial of Bellow's personae. What brings it off is the wisdom and humor of the persona. Citrine had to evolve into a character who had reached a pinnacle of professional triumph in imaginative work to express the irony of mind in a money society and then view it with equanimity. For Citrine, Cantabile and Thaxter are worth the high price.

Is Denise worth the even higher price? Totally absent from the early versions of the work and not really enlarged until the later versions is Citrine's marriage to Denise. The early versions show him married to Tinka (or Lettie or Erna), a different kind of woman. Nothing of a killer, like Denise, Citrine tells us that she "already saved my life once by artificial respiration when I stopped breathing" (17.5). He describes her as an old socialist but square (8.1). "Systematically solicitous," she "sewed blouses, knitted scarves and sweaters, baked, sent baskets of fruit, little notes of acknowledgement, congratulation, condolence. She was the good gal—unassailable. She represented the power and dignity of the common life. . . . She might be a dumb-sock, but she was a good soul" (7.14, 10f.). But in various versions they are either separated or divorced. So much for the power and dignity of common life. Tinka is reminiscent of Daisy in *Herzog*, as is her straight-laced Hoosier milieu, down to her American Rube brother with his Hudson that had a blind on the rear window. "Tedium was our medium," quips Citrine (10.8). With Denise he graduates from tedium to boredom, a more desperate spiritual condition. But the reversal in marital situation, from shafter to shaftee (let's live with this coinage as a word somehow expressive of the grotesque comedy of Chicago divorce courts), brings Citrine more in line with the madness of American normalcy, more in line with the reality Humboldt experiences in a psychotic way. In the divorce courts Citrine is a paranoid with enemies. The reduction of the personage by the tough facts of Chicago's reality instruction provides a comic version of the paranoia theme. Had Citrine been the early sickly hack rather than the health nut Chevalier, the separation would have been far less amenable to a comic perspective.

In the writing Denise represented two possibilities: late-sixties radicalism and the divorce courts. The first of these became irrelevant to the novel as it developed. Radicalism was not the problem; respectability was. In a middle manuscript Denise calls Boss Daley "an evil man. . . . We've got a small Police State in Chicago and you know it." Citrine responds that "Forty percent of the force is Black. . . . And if it were really a Police State you wouldn't be able to scream 'Kill Whitey' as you did at the Rally for Huey Newton." Denise replies, "You let the Establishment trot you out" (9.1). (In the novel this kind of baiting is left to old Huggins, the figure of youth as virile radical.) Denise is also associated with the new sexual radicalism, at least aesthetically. Citrine takes a dim view of the art in her house, "the inflamed phalluses painted by her friend Donato. . . . I grinned grimly at the six-foot cunts and snaking red headed phalluses of Donato, repeating for the nth time, *le mauvais goût mène aux crimes*" (14.17, 37f.). The aphorism, from Stendhal, shows the typically Bellovian association of moral disintegration with aesthetic irresponsibility. The details are fine, but they are not Denise.

More relevant to Denise is the way she is part of the Establishment, the way she is part of contemporary upper-middle-class Chicago. In this connection a more intriguing deletion is an episode in which Citrine takes Denise (called Abigail here) to see her former maid Aretha, whom she says she has missed. They drive to the slum in a Detroit car, not the Mercedes. It turns out that Aretha is prepared to shorten Denise's hems (9.6).[13] Elsewhere, an economical Denise bargains with Citrine for half of what a Humboldt letter in her possession might be worth in cash (9.1). A shrewd Denise points out to him that he has given the government half a million dollars in ten years and that he is now in the seventy percent tax bracket. But most of all the respectable, upper-middle-class Denise (called Deborah) "had Bluestockings up to the throat . . . a blue body stocking" (17.6), and is part of the comedy of the man who has arrived and is met by the woman who would like to. In the novel, though, Denise is less the true Bluestocking than she is the respectable matron who pursues status through knowledgeability. But her deep, quirky husband is put off by the obviousness of her pursuit. More than knowledgeability, more than money, the respectable, culture-oriented Denise wants to capture her important husband with all the ultimacy of Ahab pursuing Moby Dick. And, as with Ahab, there is the suggestion that she has lost the low, enjoying power. Her offer to drop the whole thing if he comes back shows how fantastic the normal can be.

Less conventionally ambitious, more at home if sometimes restless, Renata is Chicago made erotic. Possessing the spirit made physical, she is an apparent virtuoso of the obvious. In a state of inspiration, Citrine gives new meaning to the word sexagenarian. But can a sixty-year-old man still think of women as "bims" and "broads"? While it is nice to see a man his age making it with his young palooka, it gives one pause. It is like having an eight course dinner at eleven o'clock. Not wrong but flatulent. In the writing, Citrine recognizes as much. He can see himself as "an old lecher trying to please a floozie . . . a Venetian comedy pantaloon spending the last of his money on this beauty, this baby, this carnal artist." What does the wise man learn? "The uses found by the younger generation for lips, teeth, toes, tongues, fingertips, backsides" (9.1). There is not one flower without style or meaning in that crannied wall. But, to ask Tennyson's question, does it help Citrine know what God and man is? Apparently not. Citrine is aware of this. So he cannot marry her, or even pursue this question passionately, except as Bellow's farcical version of the modernist what-might-have-been in his trip to Madrid.

Renata (first called Cynthia) evolves somewhat in manuscript. Some of the early and middle versions show her in a light less flattering than that of the novel. "She is a great baby and something of a modern moron," thinks Citrine, adding, "of course I seldom told her what I really thought. Her reactions were too disappointing" (9.3). He notes in another version that "Denise was a far more intelligent woman" (9.1). Not present in the novel, this kind of negative judgment would explain his resistance to marriage there. In the novel, though she is a sexual object, she is an aesthetic object as well, "a Rothko design" (HG, p. 211), a source of wonder and beyond contempt. She is always an object in the novel, miraculously so, the object made subject, his Chicago lover. She is a force, a style, but not, he judges, a value. She makes Citrine think of Ahriman, "potentate of darkness"[14] (HG, p. 212) rather than Eros. Citrine thinks her "cheerfully nihilistic": but her nihilism, "since she had so much vitality to spend, was not of the depressing kind" (9.2). As with Ramona, a normally moralistic Bellow persona suspends judgment on this subject. Renata's vitality, like Ramona's, is of a particularly engaging kind. Sexuality aside, Citrine makes a similar judgment of her mother.[15] And even more significantly, of Cantabile, not to mention the other aggressive types that he seems to attract, a disinterested man in a world of Machiavellians. Vitality is akin to force; when it is not engaging, it is disarming. A good Chicagoan, a friend of Sweibel, Citrine himself possesses vitality and thinks of playing the ultimate raquetball game before the Ark of the Covenant. In regard to athleticism, Renata's vitality is actually toned down. Some manuscript versions describe her as "very strong," routinely doing fifty sit-ups, fifty push-ups and chinning on a bar (9.1). Had that quality been enlarged or even retained, she would have had little need to persuade Citrine to marriage; she could have abducted him by brute force, a Chicago kidnapping. Short of that, Renata was nonetheless "one of the new breed of young people" in whom "the 'resurrected body' of certain modern thinkers" could be seen (15.5, 131). This aspect of culture Chicago can effortlessly absorb.[16]

In short, the Chicago milieu presents culture as comedy. Citrine's Chicago identity goes beyond culture as he considered it in his New York incarnation. There is a residue of soul that he must contend with in all seriousness, and for this he needs a religious or quasi-religious solution— anthroposophy. "Reading Steiner had an effect," says Citrine. "One felt wiser, sounder. Chicago and its events lost power. One of these days I was going to take the offensive" (10.10). After he and Cantabile are arrested and fingerprinted, Naomi Lutz' daughter helps him get the ink off his fingers, and he is sensitive to her touch. Embarrassed, Citrine wonders "when . . . will I rise at last above all this stuff, the accidental, the merely phenomenal, the wastefully and randomly human, and be fit to enter higher worlds" (*HG*, p. 290). But one of Bellow's major virtues as a novelist, conspicuous in *Humboldt's Gift*, has been his power to record "the merely phenomenal," or what he calls elsewhere, even more unforgivingly and unforgivably, "this deluded human scene" (*HG*, p. 373). In this kind of statement Bellow has lost contact with Chicago and his Jewish roots as well. His readers, though not Steiner's, will find consolation in the tentativeness with which he embraces the scientist of the invisible. We have seen nothing so questionable in Bellow since his espousal of Reich, long renounced. Small wonder he does not tell his friend Durnwald about it. "I was afraid to tell him," Citrine notes in manuscript. "He would have been stunned by my latest madness" (10.17). Citrine's view of Steiner becomes increasingly serious and less defensive in the writing, though he is not without reservations about it even in the novel. Steiner is a subject for the Citrine of sophisticated ironies. There is no mention of him in the earlier manuscripts. It is a way for the man of the world to go beyond irony. But it is a road Citrine is not fully prepared to take.

iii

Chicago is a typical American city, New York an international one, a cultural capital. In reworking the novel, Bellow enlarges on the Chicago characters and scenes and cuts down radically on the New York ones. Lengthy sections on Village life in the early fifties are completely excluded, though, of course, the parts concerning Humboldt remain and are refined. The New York character is likely to be steeped in culture though this does not necessarily make him any better as a man for it. Where in his younger days Citrine went to New York to gain the great world, in later years he goes to Chicago to escape it. The manuscripts reveal that along with the marvel of Village life embodied in Humboldt, the splendor and misery of it, there is a side with few redeeming features. Various sketches produce something like a rogue's gallery.

There are, for example, Ablove and Sharfer, editors of a leading leftist literary magazine. Ablove is "ponderous, pale, Sam Johnson looking, radical-orthodox—as the Jews to God, so the proletariat to Marx, and as rabbis to small Russian synagogues, so Ablove to village intellectuals." It is noted that Ablove has introduced various modern writers. After Citrine describes him this way to Humboldt, the poet says, "I'm disappointed in you this time." Why? Were his sterling qualities glossed over? No. "You've missed about ten essentials," Humboldt says. "What about the social climbing, the craze for upperclass gentile women, the big, declamatory fist, the ideas lifted from Wyndham Lewis, the funny deals with publishers?" (9.4). For his vaguely Chinese-looking co-editor, Citrine will need no help. "He's Miaow Tse Tung," he says of Sharfer, "the revolutionary kitty-cat. Silly, also canny, weakly, hypochondriac, overpsychoanalyzed." Sharfer "has delusions that the GPR is seeking his life because he was one of five hundred signers of a statement about the death of General Krivitsky" (15.11, 184). A brutal scene takes place when Humboldt and Citrine visit Ablove and Sharfer in the unglamorous office of *Avantgarde*, the magazine in question. Pressed by money needs and by paranoia, Humboldt, an editor, wants a one-third share in the magazine. "You'd be scheming day and night how to split us," Ablove says. Humboldt accuses them of profiteering with money from the State Department. (There were certain "little magazines" that received CIA money, funneled through other organizations; it does not follow that any profiteering was done.) Offended, an irate Ablove says, "Do you want me to tell your wife whom you've been sleeping with?" Humboldt replies, "So you've switched from poetry to blackmail." Much later, Ablove tells Citrine that Humboldt "was really a very misanthropic and cynical person who took you in by his kidding, his routines, his wide-ranging mind, his mad sense of fun, his charm, all camouflage for gloom, envy, hatred" (15.11, 186f.). It may be hard to say who comes off worse, Ablove or Humboldt, but that the New York literary scene can be cutthroat is easy to see.

Humboldt does not come off well here, but he is generally more sympathetically drawn vis-à-vis typical New York intellectual idealogues. Citrine thinks that the art critic Gumbein, a man big enough to fill a phone booth, would take a dim view of the solicitude of Huggins and himself regarding

Humboldt. He would accuse them of being "sentimental babies. 'False consciousness,' he would have said. Why should we afflict ourselves with recollections of a failed and crazy poet! . . . a man who had missed the world-historical place and moment completely." Citrine must admit that "in a way I agree with this hard judgment. His later work was not worth reading." Yet Citrine's reason is hardly that of a modernist idealogue. "I wish," he says, "Humboldt had not been so familiar with Freud, Marx, Wittgenstein and Whitehead. He became damn dull" (9.5, 18 f.). Commenting on Gumbein's harsh judgment, Citrine reverses its terms: "Humboldt had laid himself open to it by being, like Gumbein himself, an intellectual heir of the critical tradition of the nineteenth century, more mental than expressive. I blamed him for yielding to the influence of the Gumbeins" (14.3, 19). Good advice to an artist, perhaps, but where would criticism be if it took these words seriously? What primarily concerns Citrine is the way in which a critic like Gumbein casts things in an ideological mold, perverting personal judgments with the instant wisdom of Marxism. He notes that "Gumbein had already decided that my feelings were those of an undeveloped person, of a mind which had not done the hardest lessons of modern history. I had looked carelessly into the greatest visionaries of the century. I hadn't studied my Marx" (14.3, 15). As if these visionaries would prove Marxist doctrine! In the Dostoevskian manner, Citrine presents the left ideologue as personally unsavory. Gumbein is an aging, ailing adulterer and cheapskate to boot. "He had himself become a wealthy critic and he was terribly stingy. He made scenes about the electricity bill with his wife. This," Citrine notes, "the girl friend had told me." Bizarrely, "she was part of the intimate family circle" (14.3, 15f.).

Gumbein is the Establishment radical, not quite so untrustworthy a character as the Establishment conservative. Some early versions show a youngish Citrine looking for a job at *Time* magazine. One tends to forget how much the writers of that generation were children of the Depression. "An unemployed generation revered jobs," Citrine tells us. "And such a job, too. Seventy-five bucks a week, in those days a fortune. Even twenty-four, on the WPA, had seemed a lot," he says, alluding to the Writer's Project. He adds, "And then, too, the glamor of being employable, the very thought—allied to madness—of having a place in the social order . . . stirred all the nerves of the heart" (17.10, 72). But these "comically high" expectations come to naught. At *Time* he is interviewed by Whittaker Chambers, so named in manuscript, and described to a fare-thee-well down to his rotten teeth. "In his own poor person he had experienced history. Passing through Hell. The suffering servant of God . . . having suffered etcetera, and gone through the dark night of the soul he was not a man to be corrupted by power. Besides he was now a Quaker" (17.10, 72). Chambers is in charge of the part of the magazine dealing with Education, Religion, Art, Theater, Film, Books. Citrine wants a job as a movie reviewer, yet is asked the following question in the interview. "Kindly answer," Chambers says. "The first fact of significance about Wordsworth is that he was a dash, or blank, poet. A . . . ?" Citrine (Orlansky) says, expectedly enough, "a Romantic poet." To which Chambers replies, "Sorry Mr. Orlansky. . . . There is no place for you in this organization" (17.10, 74). Here Citrine is victimized by an ideologue of the Right. He is told that "according to Chambers Wordsworth is horseshit, all except *The Excursion*" (17.10, 74). Chambers, in other words, subverts the Wordsworth of the Great Decade to the religious, abstract Wordsworth who saw man's reason as abject and vain apart from the "high truths" of "solemn institutions," expressing, ironically, a position that would have had some appeal to Citrine as he later develops, the world weary Citrine of spiritual inclinations. But what strikes him in the office of *Time* is the ideological distortion of Chambers' view. "That's the mark of the thoroughly untrustworthy man," thinks Citrine, "to have a special theory of everything. For this end others must non-exist, supporting one's uniqueness." Where is individual judgment, humanist latitude? He concludes with a mixture of accuracy and sour grapes: "probably Mr. Chambers did his country more harm as an editor of *Time* than as a Russian spy" (17.10, 74). Still, his account of Chambers in *Biographia Americana* was perfectly sober, evenhanded.

As one might expect, Citrine's portrait of a woman intellectual is done in kinder strokes. Though this may be because she never really makes it and is more of a Village type than anything else. Rosabelle Magruder was born in the Bronx. Her father was "a butcher by trade, and meat-wholesaler under the lofty tracks at W. 125th St." (17.1), a memorable locale for Bellow, appearing in *Mr. Sammler's Planet* as well. A brilliant woman, she is nonetheless a Columbia Ph.D. dropout. She turns to political life, attacking the old-age-home racket. She works for Bobby Kennedy, who "was not a natural liberal [but] had to learn it all because he wanted power. But he was a much better man than these other jokers in office" (17.8, 101). Rosabelle goes so far as to try to run for office, outlining her campaign plans to Citrine's amusement and disgust. "Rosabelle, please stop, I am suffering," he moans. "How I hate these contemporary moments. We are getting nowhere by this kind of being" (17.8, 111). What, presumably, is a mind like Rosabelle doing in the nuts and bolts department? His most poignant memory of her, typically, concerns her private life, her life as a lover. Men visit her who for social reasons would not be seen with her—too ugly, too queer. Not of special fascination in herself, her victimization gives rise to a passage of fulminating eloquence.

It seems that one arrivist, Leroy Chutnick (elsewhere Krupsky) is the man she still carries a torch for. "Up from [the] slums of Philadelphia to become

Czar of the avantgarde art world . . . he discussed everything with her, his Machiavellian articles, his putsches, the rigged reputations and gallery swindles." Chutnick is "bald, ruddy, measured, deliberate, squeaking." He is presented in the Dostoevskian manner. Considering him a con man, Citrine adds that "I don't think I ever heard him . . . pull anything without reference to a very high standard. What he likes to call 'revolutionary morality.' Or else 'a tragic sense of life.' " Chutnick "stole freely from everyone. But on the other hand he would tell you that there is no creativity without theft. Citing Hermes in Greek mythology, a god who swiped things. But believing in radical bluntness, bolshevistic hardness, he told Rosemary she was too ugly to be seen with. . . . He had to be seen with rich beauties, from whom he borrowed money." Does Chutnick live with remorse? No, "some ten years of psychoanalysis purged him of all sense of guilt" (7.4). Chutnick, and some of the other intellectuals described, is in Citrine's eyes one of Julien Benda's intellectuals. Citrine reflects on Benda's description of a class "betraying their vocation for politics, going over to social interests, being opportunists, careerists, finaglers, giving up pure thought, justice, disinterestedness and taking sides, hustling for power, influence and comfort" (16.15, 254).

Well! It is a matter of some significance, though, that none of these portraits appears in the novel (there is brief mention of Gumbein, but in a neutral context). Brief to begin with (except for the affectionate portrait of Rosabelle), they are forgotten as Bellow has more interesting things to do than satiric getting even. The one Village intellectual portrait that is retained is the more complex one of Huggins, satiric, to be sure, but a character who is especially well suited in turning that avenue into a two-way street. Such characterization is not simply a matter of the novelist's temperament. In intellectual life, of course, the satiric barb is a way of life. What would a novel about intellectuals be without some bloodletting? What would any novel be?

From the beginning Huggins is not spared. He is taken down for his "mouldered Leninism" (7.6, 343), for being considered "in some New York circles . . . a fool, a pest, absurd . . . On any question of [the] day he loved to hold the most outrageous opinion he could put together" (7.14). (Still, he "would rate a notice in the Dictionary" [7.20].) His utopian vision of "a society purified of all corruption" is seen as one of the lesser forms of "Christian Enthusiasm" (7.24, 43). Constant in his description is the suggestive striping on his shirts, like the Maypole at Marymount "when the devil-worshipping, sex-crazed Puritans went dancing in a secret glade" (10.9). Most memorable is Huggins' progenitive slide-trombone performance at the Truro swimming party, his member waxing and waning astride a log relative to his interest in the lady or the politics (10.9).[17] Huggins creates an acid balance, so to speak, between Citrine and himself. So Citrine is seen to be somehow associated with Boss Daley, with Illinois, where people still think the earth is flat. Citrine is taken to be an apologist for the American system of government, "a front man and stooge, practically an Andrei Vishinsky" (*HG*, p. 321). In some manuscripts versions Huggins can't quite figure out what Humboldt saw in Citrine. He is put off by Citrine's attacks—"I used to have i-i-ideas, and now I had only buttons" (*HG*, p. 323). And when Citrine generously says that he will go personally to Waldemar so that Humboldt's papers can be retrieved, Huggins cracks, in his inimitable manner, "I'm sure you'll be irre—ree. You'll be irresistable" (*HG*, p. 325).

Possessing neither high-powered intellectuality, nor tough careerist impulses, Demmie Vonghel is the one New York character who is not an intellectual, though even she bears marks of cultivation which would be foreign in his Chicago lovers: respectable, ambitious Denise; sexy, worldly Renata; sweet sentimentally remembered but not sentimentally perceived Naomi. Still, Demmie's gentility and classical training hardly make her typical Village. She could have happened in Chicago or even Kansas City. Perhaps it is her neuroticism that makes her typically New York, though on this count Chicago is a worthy Second City. As his lover, Demmie is essentially independent of the pattern of mentality that otherwise characterizes Citrine's New York.

There are traces of Demmie as early as the manuscripts of *Henderson the Rain King* in a portrait of Selma, an early version of Henderson's first wife. "She was my sort of woman," says Henderson. "She had been a juvenile delinquent." She stole from department stores. Her mother took her to a reformatory, showed her girls her own age (fourteen) scrubbing floors and said, "Feel your knees, and then decide if this is the life you want." She stopped stealing and became a leper buff out of fear (B.6.11, 19). Kleptomania and leper colonies, transformed, find their way into the portrait of Demmie. Her money-making, missionary parents, never elegant, are not so satirically drawn in the novel as in some manuscripts. One middle version has it that her daddy was "Mencken's Boobus Americanus. His parlor rug was a huge green copy of an American Express check" (15.10, 102f.). The final Demmie has neutral, if unusual, ancestry. The main differences in composition concern Demmie herself. In one middle version she is pregnant by Citrine and wants her unborn baby. "Charley you are a shit," she says. "You'll share your life with nobody" (15.11, 213). In various versions Demmie does not die in a plane crash. She goes to Mt. Coptic by railroad (10.3). She does, however, die. She takes an overdose of pills and alcohol when Citrine refuses to live in her apartment and moves to the St. Regis (to be nearer the theater) (12.3). In one version she says, "You'll just kill me Charlie if you go. . . . I warn you" (16.6, 210). Such a turn of events would involve him in past guilt when he is already up to his ears in woman trouble. By having her die in a plane crash he can remember her as an ideal love.

Not all of Citrine's portraits of Village literary intellectuals are acerbic. Humboldt, of course, is drawn with much affection, even love. Equally so is the portrait of Elias Zetland (Konig or Honig in early versions). The portrait of Zetland is very extensive in manuscripts, running to about one hundred pages in larger fragments and through numerous revisions generally. Never before has Bellow worked up so much material in the manuscripts of a published novel only to exclude it. Who is Zetland? He is easily identified as Isaac Rosenfeld, though at times he is a composite figure of Bellow and Rosenfeld or Bellow himself. Both Zetland and Citrine take the symbolic journey from Chicago to New York. For Zetland and his wife Lottie it is a momentous shift. "They had reached the World City, that was what it was. Where the resonance of all behavior was deeper and where everything had a more precious bearing" (18.9, 41). A buoyant, youthful estimate, one with which the anonymous third person narrator is in essential sympathy. Why shouldn't they feel that way? Haven't they got "rid of . . . Chicago, the most boring city in America" (18.9, 40)?[18] Zetland lives on hack biography and reviews, some adjunct teaching, his Fuller Brush route (Citrine does this last in the novel). The Zetlands live, variously, in a small West Side apartment, whose tub-flap converted into a kitchen table (18.9); in Laurelton, Queens, for the kids; or in a small, dingy but animated Greenwich Village flat. Their Village apartment in particular overflows with pets, visitors, children, books—an amiable mess. Though he came to New York to study philosophy at Columbia as a graduate fellow, "after he started reading Melville he could never become a Ph.D. in Philosophy" (18.9, 43). We are told that "the real business of his life was with comprehensive visions" (18.9, 44). Though he "had it in him to be purely rational, far from all idleness, playfulness, another *M. Teste*" (18.9, 37), his artistic temperament prevails.

Zetland is a particular sort of visionary, vulnerable to abuse, Franciscan (in one version the Chicago Zetland "made a little money mopping floors at Billings Hospital but he shared it with clinic patients, brought them sandwiches" [18.2]). The narrator notes, portentously, that "the most melancholy and most despairing are in that way often the most generous" (18.9, 37). Thus the duality of Zetland's character is established, idealistic and depressive, a companion to the Bellow surrogate, who appears either as anonymous third person narrator telling the story from Zetland's point of view or as Citrine (Orlansky) telling the story in the first person.

As door-to-door Fuller brushman Zetland listens to many family tales of lonely ladies, "He wasn't seeing them," says the narrator, "he was seeing Dostoevsky's Poor Folk, being a Russian Christian. Or else his head was full of Wordsworth's Leech Gatherer." The narrator feels that "his ideas were too literary. Even when he was feeling . . . so low, so dull, he was thinking about John Stuart Mill's emotional crisis; he was thinking of Matthew Arnold who said he was now thirty years old and three-fourths iced over; of William James who had a similar episode" (18.9, 47). Zetland yearns for the light but doubts the importance of the person. He thinks sympathetically of Valéry who "would rather read technical books than fiction or even history," who was against "psychological self-indulgence and autobiographical exaggeration, [for] lives were boring, all but a few" (18.9, 48). Depressed, bored, Zetland has no will to live: "I don't believe what I thought I believed, and I don't love what I always said I loved. I've had no affects for anything. I feel schizophrenic. I have destructive fantasies. Living in a nightmare. Nothing is anything. . . . Life as we've made it isn't worth living. I'm sorry for these children Lottie and I brought here. Posterity is a mistake" (18.9, 48). These are strong words for a man known for his kindness, known for his special sense of children. The narrator records Zetland's suicidal desperation: "He prayed at moments, Dear God send me life, but if no life then death. If you *are* a God, why is this life?" Zetland's condition adumbrates Citrine's idea of boredom as spiritual emptiness, a second death.

Zetland's sorrows are expressed in the presence of Village intellectuals who supply an ironic counterpoint to such suffering. The Village in the fifties was not Wetzlar in the 1770s, and even then nobody found it possible to put up with Werther for very long. But the wry Village context deflates the effusions as if it were the expected thing to do. "Don't overdo this Dostoievsky-Gogol stuff—all this spleen-swallowing, sneaking Jesus, love-hate routine," says one Arlo Hahn. "Forget it. Try Samuel Butler instead, why don't you. Trade a few punches with the human condition. It won't kill you" (18.10, 51). One of the sources of Zetland's depression is the vanity biography he is working on, *A Son of Orpheus*, which is a parody of the belief he wanted to have in soul and love. Another Village friend, Crocker, a Harvard Business School Marxist, tells him, "You got a bad dose of life-is-meaningful." He urges him to cast off "the old tyranny of the Good and step away from the metaphysical police of Moses and Mt. Sinai" (18.10, 52). Hahn laughs off Zetland's "feverish ideas about salvation . . . the Jewish vertigo" (18.10, 84). He perceptively notes that "Zet is disillusioned with Communism, Stalinism, but of course he's still a revolutionary" (18.11, 38). What form does his radical impulse take?

Reichianism. He goes to a therapist in Queens. While some of the Village crowd consider this ridiculous—"He's going to Queens for fucking lessons" (18.9, 19)—Citrine (Orlansky) does his best to take his old friend seriously. He has lived through his various phases, having had little interest in his logical positivism, more in his Marxism, a great deal in his Tolstoyan-Gandhian phase, less in his Reichian phase (8.1, 115; 8.3). Zetland "never did things by halves," says Citrine. When he turned to Reich "he became an extreme Reichian" (8.1, 115). He made his own orgone box (Reich would not have approved). When Citrine complains of a headache, Zetland insists on his taking care of it with an orgone shooter, a metal funnel contraption worn like a turban (which he also made). For Citrine, "the whole matter seemed . . . like the second coming of the irrational" (8.1, 118). "He had talents," thinks Citrine, "absurdity was one of them" (17.8, 75). Zetland's wife thinks he is "a riot" (8.1, 118). Unorthodox, original, Zetland has a toughness of self that is most at home against the grain. His "spectacles were meek; he, under them, was obdurate. . . . He drew fire, it was deliberate; he was a provocateur; he preferred to be misunderstood. Being thought a lunatic did something for him—it thickened the vault, it deepened the silence, purified his isolation, enriched his sick soul by aggravation" (17.4).

There is, of course, seriousness in the Reichian view. "Real history," for Zetland, "was the result of civilized control (read madness) on the natural creature. The other history, given by intellectual tradition, was simply distortion. Mankind was affected by an emotional plague" (8.1, 115). Only a natural, not a supernatural, redemption was possible, a partial redemption. Zetland takes as gospel a phrase like "the prison of this flesh" (18.9, 19). Redemption from the unlived life is needed. Zetland's innocence, his talk of a "sacramental perception of nature" (19.4, 47), provokes the illusionless Village intellectuals. These avant-garde Villagers are more receptive to his rejection of Freud, about whom the narrator says Zetland was "entirely correct," for both Freud and Pascal built on a "radical hatred of the self [as] the indispensable first step." The longtime analysand was like "a tooth which the dentist had been treating for the same length of time. Overtreated. Saved perhaps, but desensitized" (19.4, 48f.). Therapy was the release: "In the truthfulness there was a shock, something like a dive into the North Atlantic ice, frightful at first, but followed by the mad bliss of the blood, the Maine water first burning the body and then become as luxurious as silk" (18.9, 58). Zetland is opposed to psychoanalysis because it was "discourse, a verbal therapy. He rejected the biographical concept implicit in Freud," the narrator tells us. Besides, "in the matter of words, he could run rings around an analyst." But Zetland's main point is that "one must cut through to pre-verbal infancy" (18.9, 58f.).

The Reichian therapy is meant to do just this. Of great interest in the manuscripts is the dramatization of such a session. One suspects that some or much of this aspect of Zetland's portrait is derived from Bellow's own experience, since he, too, under Rosenfeld's influence, made the trip from Freud to Reich. Unlike Rosenfeld he was not convinced for long, if he was ever really convinced at all. The Reichian therapist is not impersonal and vaguely affirmative. On the contrary, his purpose is intrusion and provocation, breaking through the character armor into a reality of primal yells. The patient, it seems, must be naked, symbolic of total disclosure in a system where mind and body are one. The analyst is free to prod, poke, even hit to get the necessary response, the welling up from within. It was not uncommon for Zetland to return from a session with black and blue marks.

In a long, nearly hundred-page, fragment entitled *Charm and Death*, Zetland sees himself in the office of Dr. Sapir: "In this white cell, naked on the couch, clothing out of reach, you gave up your defenses, line after line" (18.9, 4). On the couch Zetland thinks of the line from "Prufrock," "to spit out all the butt ends of my days and ways." Although "he didn't like Eliot much, he didn't respect him, [he] involuntarily . . . quoted him." He wonders how he can restore "true breathing," thinking that "it had to be relearned." The sessions parallel in a number of ways the ones involving Henderson, Dahfu, and the lioness in *Henderson*. Zetland thinks, "Observe the animals—in their respiration the whole body was involved, belly as well as chest" (18.1). Zetland is described as "a crank, if you like. Rejected, despised, a man of sorrows and acquainted with grief," recalling the lines from Handel's *Messiah* so haunting to Henderson. In accents similar to Dahfu's, Dr. Sapir exhorts Zetland to unrepress himself by symbolically pummeling the couch: "Batter it, Zetland! Come on, come on, strike out. . . . Hit! That's it. Hit! Find your rage." Zetland even assumes a physical posture similar to Henderson's: "Zetland was on his knees. His pounding fists, his walloping arms were eager. . . . He had zeal. His face was blind. His teeth showing." Sapir shouts, "Strike, strike!" (18.10, 95). Dr. Sapir wants to go beyond verbal discourse in Zetland's case especially, for this is, in his reductive view, precisely the formidable part of his character armor. The therapist tries to avoid discussion. Sapir is a crusader against "inflexible organisms, hardened inflexible minds, murderous minds." Does Zetland qualify? Hardly. Yet one can cast a retrospective glance at certain Bellow characters who do—Dr. Adler of *Seize the Day*, for example, another work that shows Reichian influences. When Sapir says, "The dying loathe the living. They cannot forgive them" (18.10, 60), it is as if he were speaking of Dr. Adler, who embodies physical and cultural death.

Perhaps the most provocative technique Sapir uses is verbal degradation. On the level of exclamation, he calls Zetland a pig. Further, after asking Zetland to "behave as if there were a woman under you on the couch," he exclaims, "Nothing! Nothing there. Disgrace . . . you haven't got it there" (18.10, 88). But such an exclamatory judgment must lead to discourse. In a similar situation Zetland says, "You mean I've never had real sexual feelings?" Sapir says, "No." Zetland asks, "What have I had?" Sapir answers, "Certain neurotic moments of high excitement with a sexual tinge." Zetland replies, "I don't see how you can say that." Sapir insists, "Come, admit it, what has it been? Wax fruit. Paper flowers." Zetland replies, "And the girls . . . the women I've loved?" Sapir says, "You haven't loved." A perplexed Zetland asks, "Then what happened?" Sapir's reply—"Very faint shadows happened"—is sexual platonism of a high order. Sapir adds, "What most people call sexual intercourse—an absurd occurrence. In the degenerate word fucking. What is fucking? an interpersonal disaster. Clutching, tearing, blind aggression, terror, mutual violation. This is the debased sexuality of civilized people—so called." This scene, hilarious in its specificity and its implications, might almost have come out of *The Last Analysis*. But here Bellow plays it straight, a rare instance in Bellow where a rich comic situation is not taken for one. Zetland, insulted, nonetheless thinks that "there was enough truth in what Dr. Sapir said to keep him from leaving." Besides, leaving would only be succumbing to your character armor, wouldn't it? Dealing with a Reichian is like dealing with a simplistic Marxist. Only the initiate understands the so-called contradictions, in Marx's term. Dr. Sapir lays it on the line: "With that structure you are not capable of love. Only of fucking—a disgraceful, obscene, totally destructive act. You must admit that. You must confess your impotency. You are not literally impotent. They used to say that the fear of God is the beginning for us here" (18.10, 65f.). Why Zetland does not equate Reich with Freud and Pascal as a man who begins with contempt for the self is not clear. Sapir himself unwittingly points to the similarity.

Zetland is well aware of the ideological cast of Reichianism, and its peculiar ritual. "The way I'm treated on this couch, and the way I accept it," he thinks, "there's something totalitarian about it, and brainwashing, like a preparation for the Moscow Trials, like being talked into confession" (19.8, 98). He is, at times, all but fed up with "the party-line, the crap." But it seems that Zetland must choose between ideology and madness, since, for himself, "art had not worked." In his desperation he espouses therapy. It has to work. More than this, "it really seemed to him as though Dr. Sapir's therapy (rough, yes, desperate measures) was making him sane" (18.1). When he is assaulted in the Reichian manner by Sapir, Zetland sometimes cannot help thinking of revolt. "Suppose he said to Dr. Sapir, 'you are a cruel maniac. You are a sadist,' (as conceivably the man was) . . . then," he thinks, "he could leave with his old self-respect." But apparently he does not want his old self-respect. This would mean a continuance of "his false ways" (18.10, 68). So he grimly reconciles himself to ideology. A certain irony remains—the irony of having to work at spontaneity. Of the strange therapy the narrator notes, "this was how a bookish Jew-Man would recover the primordial" (19.2, 97). Another irony: redemption from the bottom. A Jewish solution? Hahn calls Zetland "a kind of saint in the making . . . an inspirer, a saviour." To the list of modern saints (political, revolutionary, artistic, economic, decadent, nihilistic, psychological), Zetland adds the sexual saint (18.4). Another Village character calls him, absurdly enough, "the Dante of sex" (19.5, 24c).

Zetland's ideological bent takes unwittingly humorous form, not only in the sessions (where the narrator is too deeply involved to see the humor), but at home as well (where the narrator does see it). In his effort to free all impulse, he advises his young son to feel under a little girl's dress: "Touch her. Let her touch you" (18.10, 79). An advocate of unihibited sex play for children, he also breaks with tradition in refusing to have his son circumcised. Too traumatic. And he has let him nurse as long as he liked (19.11, 142). For Zetland, "the sign of a good disposition [which he does not always show], of being on the side of life and willing health, was that you loved children and made every sacrifice to save them" (18.19, 16). Tolstoy, John Dewey, above all, A. S. Neill were essentially of this opinion. Zetland's libertarianism can be understood, in part, as a reaction to his paternalistic, repressive father, a man "who wanted him to be all marrow, no bone. He caged him in a reprehending and punitive silence; he demanded that he dazzle the world; he never approved of him" (18.9, 32). The Commisar, General Bruin, Ozymandius, Zetland called him. For Zetland, the spontaneity of childhood is to be literally retained in adulthood. At a gathering of serious intellectuals, Zetland and Lottie play jacks on the floor, under a table, laughing and kissing merrily underfoot. "This was noted with a certain Mitteleuropa grimness by the guests" (19.11, 140). To the delight of child and adult, Zetland is a marvel at imitations. "He was a steam-iron, a time clock, a tractor, a telescope; he sang Don Giovanni in all parts and voices" (18.2). Again Bellow shows an affinity for a man reminiscent of Rameau's nephew in his mimetic capacities, originality and spontaneity.

All clowns reflect a certain desperation and Zetland is no exception. He is "very hostile toward conventional married life," thinking that "no relationship between a man and a woman could endure longer than five or six years" (8.1, 118f.). He likens the stewed admen lowered dead drunk at their stations for their waiting wives to the "Deposition from the Cross" (8.1, 119). But he is married to Lottie, a person capable of instinctual gratification. She is more than this, or she is a transcendent expression of this: "She was his contact with the heart . . . with the sympathies and the darkness (the unconscious and, incidentally, all that was not Jewish)." Looked upon by some as a saviour, he himself felt that "he was being saved." Fed up, bored, an instance of Sartre's *nausée*, Zetland, the narrator tells us, had the "sickness unto death . . . until it was coming out of my ears." The narrator's view is familiar to any reader of Bellow: "That culture to me [is] as banal as babbitry, and almost as commercial" (18.3). Zetland, as we have seen, does something to combat the sickness with which he feels himself infected. But for all his

Reichianism, for all his "Tolstoyan, Ruskinian, Gandhian purity," one morning "he wanted to hit Lottie with an axe, and cut Constantine's [his son's]
throat and then hang himself in the toilet from the shower-nozzle, kicking off
from the stacked works of Wilhelm Reich and A. S. Neill." His wife has
bruxism, an indication, Zetland believes, that she is not getting full gratification. "In recent weeks," we are told, "he was a washout" (19.10, 99). The
narrator shrewdly notes that "primitivists never had their own share in the
primordial," adding, "it was his fantasy that Lottie was thrusting, thrusting,
gasping with some furious stud" (19.10, 100). Zetland struggles with "this
pathological jealousy of his" (18.8). Still, when bloodily assaulted by a Penn
Station crazy, he will not violate the rules of open marriage by walking in on
Lottie for help (19.11, 162). His physical disabilities (a skin disease, bad
eyesight), his rejection from the Army, contribute to Zetland's malaise.

In a novel about Humboldt, Zetland was dropped. The visible sky can
hold only one comet at a time. One valetudinarian literary man, one brilliant
case, was enough. In addition, as we have seen, Humboldt had to be juxtaposed with Chicago for the character of Citrine to have evolved. In some
manuscripts, Humboldt and Zetland do know each other but are usually
indifferent acquaintances, or even at odds. It seems that the friction between
them was too insistent to do anything but complicate an already complex
relationship between Humboldt and Citrine. "You're upset about Humboldt," Rosabelle tells Citrine. "I hope you realize that he said mean things
about you. He was not one of your best friends. He thought you liked Ezra
Konig [Zetland] better, and they were rivals" (8.1, 100f.). Too much push
and shove might only obscure the central complication. The strained idealism of Humboldt and Zetland would also have been in some ways duplicative. Citrine thinks, "Ezra Konig certainly did have a grandiose idea of his
life [with his] blind pursuit of chimerical ideas or dreaming one's time away
in delusions." Somewhat more august, "Von Humboldt Fleisher absolutely
was sold on the grand homme belief of Baudelaire. Priests, poets and soldiers, men who sacrifice themselves, and for the rest the whip" (8.1, 112).
Even here Zetland's passivity and Humboldt's aggression figure promi-
nently. On his part, Zetland makes a Reichian critique of Humboldt. He says
that "Humboldt was like a huge storage battery, charging up. No adequate
sexual discharge." Citrine, "preoccupied, nodded. He knew the system.
Terrible stasis, Humboldt had. No flexibility. The somatic armor of the
forehead." Zetland draws the moral: "You know what's the matter with
Humboldt, he's on the make, too much. He's not pure in heart" (17.8, 76).
While Citrine thinks something like this in the novel, he has great pity, great
sympathy for Humboldt's stained purity. And Citrine's judgment of their
personality clash is partial to Humboldt. He maintains that Zetland "was
jealous of Humboldt's fame. Humboldt was accepted as the real thing. Konig

[Zetland] was too eccentric, unorthodox for Eastern intellectual society. But in addition Konig had an envious nature" (17.8, 77). On his part, Humboldt laughs at Reichian therapy, considers it "disgusting" (18.8). In his place he puts Joyce, quoting "God is a shout in the street," "History is a nightmare from which I am trying to awaken," "Nothing is anything," "It's all the same." Zetland's response to this is negative, and here Zetland is clearly Bellow speaking:

> I don't believe in any of that stuff. My real belief is in a much simpler state of human existence in which human beings are kind, not a bunch of metaphysical amateurs. I really hate all this ornamental soul-sickness and exhibitionistic self-disintegration. . . . There is no ethical community and we are badgered by ghosts to wake up again to duty, to feeling, to good, to avenge the murder of innocence, but it is all a dream. All a dream unless we recover the power to experience our natural life. (18.8)[19]

Hence Zetland's (Citrine's) sometime, residual sympathy for Reich. "I don't have the sex doctrine for the sake of sex," he says. "Just the reverse. I want to be free from oppressions that have their root in this pervasive sex preoccupation" (18.8). A clever reversal, but one that finally does not convince Bellow himself.[20]

iv

The character of Humboldt presents sufficient complication to warrant a separate discussion. Indeed, a central problem in the composition is how to view Humboldt in all his complication. Is he a genius? a disaster? a martyr? a con man? all of these things? Should he be viewed with sympathy? contempt? both? And, whatever the answer, from what point of view can such discriminations be made? I said at the outset that the character of Citrine had to evolve for the character of Humboldt to be appreciated, for the necessary ambivalence to be dramatized. It seems that the mellower Citrine becomes—the more worldly, the more spiritual—the more discerningly Humboldt is drawn.

Generally speaking, the earlier descriptions of Humboldt are acerbic, neutral to negative; the later ones forgiving, elegaic, neutral to positive. Citrine compares Jonas Hamilcar's end to that of Poe, "a textbook death for an American poet, with its feeling of sacrifice, of crucifixion." Citrine "sometimes felt tired of all these sick victims. At least he had a strong desire to put Jonas down and to blame him for his failure and death." This despite his feeling "very tender towards the dead man" (7.13). Citrine goes so far as to question Humboldt's major premise. "Poetry was a sad mistake," he says.

"Poetry? In this day and age? You must be kidding" (7.23, 17). Or, somewhat less negatively: "A poet in America? A Polynesian in Finland! The thing is feasible, but tough" (9.6, 1). (Before we are too hard on Citrine, let us remember that some of the best modern American poetry springs from similar perceptions.) These typical early perceptions are complex enough but not generous in tone. The early judgments can be penetrating. Citrine muses about Humboldt's impressive variety of jobs and connections, noting that "he had, however, chosen the starving poet bit. Or the insulted and injured. Apparently functioning best when he had grievances. Denying success for the most practical of reasons, namely, that he was more vigorous when down on his luck" (7.1). Here Humboldt sounds something like Zetland the provocateur. Sometimes Humboldt is given in a very negative way: "That he liked me, his jealousy made clear. He warned me against anyone I had a good word for" (7.1). There may even be virtual contempt in Citrine's judgment: "Humboldt's idea of success was total nonsense. He had the most boring delusions about it . . . Napoleon youth, the conquest of power, the godlike artist. He used to brood about the Great Gatsby and other sacrificial American heroes" (7.6, 10f.). And it does not add to his luster in Citrine's eyes that he "descended through Baudelaire, Rimbaud and Eliot" (7.1) or that he threatened him with a lawsuit for embezzlement when they met ten years ago (7.2). Pathetically, "Humboldt had only the *idea* of being calculating and at bottom was clumsy and genuinely improvident. Whatever he planned or thought he planned, thinking he was Nero fiddling, Humboldt was really a fiddler who Neroed" (7.23, 9). For all of Humboldt's nasty disclosures, not to say slanders, "when you came down to it . . . the lawyers were too cagey for him. There was only one lawsuit, after all, that went as far as the courtroom, and that was the suit against Magnasco. That lawyer must have been a real ringer. The others, on examination of the facts, couldn't see their fee clearly and dropped the case" (15.17, 45). The description of Humboldt may be very dark: "He was a schemer, filled with envy. Really he was. He was misanthropic. He was sinister. He had it in for children" (14.16, 37c). But Citrine recalls his bigness of soul. Yet the hard judgment persists. When Huggins comments that Humboldt will have "many pages" in *Compendium*, Citrine's biographical enterprise, the editor thinks, "the truth of the matter, however, was that Jonas H. would never make the grade. He was not important enough. I, Orlansky added, will not be important enough either" (7.14, 9). There is none of this severity in the final version.

In addition, several incidents emphasizing Humboldt's smallness are diminished or not found at all in the novel. We are told of a speaking engagement at which Kathleen is sitting on the platform with him. "She had to be up front on the right or he wouldn't go on. . . . People interpreted this sentimentally," Citrine says. How touching, the poet and his wife. "She supposedly carried poems in the crumbling brown portfolio. But he knew his poems by heart, and those were legal papers, telephone bills, letters from the bank he spread out on the lectern" (7.6, 20). The paranoid poet will not let her out of his sight. Of course, much of Humboldt's murderous rage toward his wife is dramatized in the novel. It could not be otherwise. But it is fascinating to see what was too tawdry to be included. One such excised scene, recalled at a dinner party, reveals Humboldt attacking a departmental secretary of an upstate college with a hammer (9.2). Another shows us Humboldt as addict. We know from the novel that he carries a Merck Manual around with him bound in black like the Bible. In manuscript he is treated by "a mastoid specialist put out of business by antibiotics. . . . Mastoid surgeons, accustomed to big fees, with children in private schools, and trying to hold on to 'principal,' to their own investments, became corrupt" (7.25, 41). This doctor would take cash only and would not put the hypo and needle together until the money was in his pocket. Katherine was going to call the police, "but Humboldt arranged to meet his doctor in the lobby and would get the shot while rising in the elevator. The doctor would ring the bell leaving Humboldt propped against the door. The usual hour for this was 6 A.M."

Though the portrait of Humboldt in the early manuscripts is grim in these ways, we have seen that ambivalence of judgment is there from the beginning. There is an unalloyed admiration for Humboldt's perception of the good and the beautiful. Citrine fondly recalls how his friend, on a trip to Chicago, "responded most to the old neighborhood. The silvered boiler rivets and the blazing geraniums got him" (10.10). Again, he recalls discussing *Crime and Punishment* with him and how Humboldt "was much moved by Sonia's reading of the Gospel to Raskolnikov, and ranked *Crime and Punishment* itself with the Gospels" (8.4, 53). He recalls how the humanist Humboldt, lecturing at a party, said: "Civilized people humanize. . . . Like the idea that if you can catch the eye of your enemy and exchange a human look with him, beyond all social ideas, man to man, he will not have the heart to shoot you. That's how Tolstoy saves Pierre's life in *War and Peace*. . . . A nice thing when it works, but how often does it work? I don't say never. . . . Without such ideas, however, life isn't human. Not civilized. Not worth living" (7.1). This insight, from a part of the manuscript written before *Mr. Sammler's Planet*, is incorporated by Bellow in that novel and may be yet another instance of "Humboldt's" influence. His insights can be liberating, elevating. Citrine can be moved even by his paranoia sublimated into humor, as in Humboldt's poem about the hanged rats of the mad husband of Catherine the Great. (17.18, 4). He also likes the poem quoted in the novel about the lion's "meal of blood" as "living good," which also exhibits a sublimated paranoia. (Citrine comes to terms too easily with the murderously aggressive quality of the imagination Humboldt sings.) Then, too, Humboldt can be memorably funny in his mistrust. About his country neighbors he whispers: "Arson," or "Incest with his 12 year old daughter," or "Sodomy with goats," or "Ku Klux Klan." Humboldt's energy, his sense of life as performance, usually transcends psychological shortcomings. Consider this description: "He passed from statement to recitative, from recitative he soared to aria, and behind him an orchestra of intimations. Before your eyes, the man composing himself" (9.3). Once again qualities of Rameau's nephew[21] emerge in a Bellow character. But where the nephew hardly transcends cynicism, Humboldt does. Citrine remains deeply attached to his comic friend because of Humboldt's idealism, failed though that may be. To a considerable extent, "the memory of big wisdom, of beauty order and perfection drove him deeper into Harlequin routines, into 'barbarism,' in Santayana's word" (16.13, 132). The author of *Von Trenck* says, "both Humboldt and Von Trenck were of a human type I adored—the endearing-wrongheaded type—" admitting that "the play was written under Humboldt's influence" (9.5). Humboldt makes an indelible impression on Citrine's art as well as on his person, for all his difficulty.

A look at different beginnings of the novel show in detail how the right tone and point of view in the description of Humboldt were achieved. Early manuscripts seem to bear out Stern's recollection that it all started as memoir. A fragment entitled, "a report from existence,"[22] begins: "My friend the poet Delmore Schwartz died last week in New York [1966], presumably of heart failure, in a derelict's hotel in the Broadway area" (20.1, 1). He had not seen him in ten years, but two weeks before he died Bellow did see him in the street and avoided him. The memoir has little of the quiet evocativeness of the novel's beginning. Where the retrospective Citrine is excited, Bellow is here matter of fact: "We were first acquainted in the Village. He was a youthful celebrity then and I had published a few worthless stories and stayed afloat in New York with the help of editors" (who gave him reviews). Delmore was

receptive and polite, said nice things about my stories. . . . He seemed to understand that although I envied his luck, his friendship with leading intellectuals, his public recognition, I also admired his talent and liked him. I had come to visit the successful poet, to see how the thing might be done, to observe his style, to hear how he spoke[23] of Stevens, Eliot, Cummings, of Harvard and the scholars, New York and the critics, to note his tone toward the great. I had come with a jealous and skeptical heart but I was 26 years old, from Chicago, a zealot, devoted to literature. I was

wary and guarded, but I could be moved—I was moved greatly by him.
But he said some odd things too. (20.1, 3f.) [E.g., noting quite seriously
the significance of the day of his birth.]

This voice, disillusioned, matter-of-fact, respectful, with an eye on the main
chance, is less the proper setting for the exotic jewel that is Humboldt than
the voice finally arrived at, talky, sensitive, grateful, ironic, emotive:

> I had read *Harlequin Ballads* enthusiastically. I was a student at the
> University of Wisconsin and thought about nothing but literature day and
> night. Humboldt revealed to me new ways of doing things. I was ecstatic.
> I envied his luck, his talent, and his fame, and I went east in May to have a
> look at him—perhaps to get next to him. . . . The bus windows were
> open. I had never seen real mountains before. Trees were budding.

And, to cap off the sense of euphoria, the late inclusion, "It was like Beethoven's *Pastorale*" (*HG*, p. 1f.).[24] Striking the right note of youthful enthusiasm
took some doing. One earlier attempt errs on the side of generosity: "I said
in my thankful heart, 'This guy is *it!*' At dawn I jumped into Lake Mendota in
my underpants" (14.2, 2). In this context Citrine can sound like Augie
March: "On the river from sheer gratitude, he could have put his arms
around Humboldt and kissed him for talking about art, for opening the door"
(17.1). Citrine soon sheds most traces of the innocent.

  The opening brightness is soon dissipated in the writing by Humboldt's
envy of Citrine's success and subsequent wealth. But "money wasn't what I
had in mind," Citrine says. He adds, in a late inclusion (not in 14.4), "Oh
God, no, what I wanted was to do good," do some serious writing. In an even
later inclusion (not in 14.2), this desire takes on the spiritual cast of the
novel, with Citrine's desire to do good issuing from his childhood awareness
of painted veils, of Maya, of domes of many-colored glass staining the white
radiance of eternity (*HG*, p. 3). Humboldt needed the more appreciative,
idealistic Citrine, a man himself accomplished but a bit far out, an alter ego
of the spirit in a world where money and power exact their formidable price.
This condition, in Bellow's view, while it has particularly intense contemporary American manifestations, is not unique to our time and place but essentially in the nature of things.

  No Bellow novel was harder to start than *Humboldt's Gift*. We have seen
some of the possible beginnings. There were others. One early version
begins with a June dinner in Chicago with Magnasco, who asks Citrine
whether he will do a portrait of Humboldt. "No," says Citrine forcefully. Yet
"the very strength of the denial proved that once more I had been overtaken
by Humboldt" (17.11, 1). A related version sees Citrine thinking along

similar lines in a somewhat more advanced part of the manuscript: "I began to think of proposing to Philip Dunsimore [Thaxter] that I should substitute my recollections of Von Humboldt Fleisher for the 'Boredom' essay. To run in several installments in *The Species*" (*The Ark* in the novel). But for this version of Citrine boredom may be the better choice. "I thought I had meant what I said to Magnasco," he says, "that it wasn't worth doing. But now I began to think that I didn't have enough worth to do it" (14.14, 40f.). The radically different tonality of the final version immediately dispels these doubts, though it does not dispel boredom as a subject.

In another version Citrine is forced to reconsider Humboldt as a subject at the urging of the Cantabiles. The tone is again different. "Cheerful, I dig into my files. I piled notebooks letters diaries and manuscripts on the coffee table" (9.1). Much of his reminiscence of Humboldt, the New Jersey hinterlands episodes, for example, is told, as it were, to Mrs. Cantabile. "You *asked* for this! O Mrs. Cantabile," Citrine exclaims. With a flip, playful assurance he says, "Picture it, dear Mrs. Cantabile . . . stick with me and you'll write a thesis such as no would-be hoodlum's wife" (9.1). In another version Cantabile gives Citrine "a long list of questions about Humboldt and his work." Mrs. Cantabile wants written answers. Citrine won't do it. He also declines a tape recording chat with her (13.12, 126). Clearly what Citrine had to say about Humboldt transcended graduate student inquiries, was far too personal for that kind of discourse.

Some of the beginnings, some of the subsequent developments of point of view, are even more improbable. In one such, Citrine tells us that he is from "the sticks, from Cleveland, thirty-five years old, a lawyer. My father has been called out of retirement temporarily, to look after my practice and let me make my bid to conquer Broadway with my first play. To exchange Euclid Heights for Sutton Place? Or a pretty melancholy wife for an Angela? Highly unlikely" (16.8, 3). An Angela? Yes, Angela Gruner "whose doting and wealthy father is a meat wholesaler at the Hudson River of 125th St." She is arty, "interested in theater, and as the old man makes [sic] her an allowance of fifty or sixty thousand she occasionally buys into a show, and she is one of Trenck's financial backers." *Humboldt* and *Sammler* are thus tied together. Though Citrine does not notice her, she calls him. He sees her in her home "among antiques, in Pucci trousers, barefooted, cheeks bursting with color, hair with dyed streaks like racoon fur, eyes a beautiful sexual dark blue." He tells her of his troubles with the lousy director, the awful lead actor. "We ought to get my Uncle Meyer down to the theater," she says. They "spent the evening talking about Pawlyk. A far more interesting man than Trenck" (16.8, 4).[25] Interesting enough to have a novel written about him! (Pawlyk, it will be remembered, is one of Sammler's manuscript names.) The fragment ends here and may well be the place where Bellow puts aside the already substantial novel about Humboldt to work on *Mr. Sammler's Planet*.

In another pre-Sammler fragment, Eddie Goodkin, author of *Von Trenck* and a man with a heart condition, sees a pickpocket operating on a bus. His heart behaves strangely. He notes the number of the bus and goes to a sidewalk booth to phone the police. The instrument is smashed. The booth smells of urine. He goes home, noting the security equipment in the lobby. He takes the elevator up—"Old Ted was on duty" (1967 Gift, 6.1,9). No nightmare lobby scene, no black pickpocket of sartorial splendor. He goes up to his apartment and describes the pickpocket to his wife and kids. That's it. Angela in this version is the morally weak Angela; fashion, Happenings, high-camp movies, group sex, and orgies occupy her life. More sympathetic than in *Sammler*, "there is also the unusually devoted daughter." And Montessori. And the projected kindergarten in Harlem. Meyer Pawlyk is "under her special protection" (1967 Gift, 6.1, 12).[26] So he should not rot in his hotel room, she takes him to museums, concerts, plays, rehearsals, including those for *Trenck*, which fails.

Some beginnings are marred by an immediate takeoff into abstraction. Citrine thinks of the money he has made and that poor, dead Humboldt has not. He thinks of capitalism's sense of humor in so gracing him, knowing that "this was exactly the sort of subject Von Humboldt Fleisher would have loved to discuss." We then get an interesting, undramatized reflection:

> I have always thought of Capitalism as a monster, a scaly giant thing out of Pilgrim's Progress. Dr. Milton Friedman the famous free enterprise theorist who lives in the neighborhood would not be interested in my visions and projections. These grand specialists and leaders of thought are anyway difficult to get into general conversation. It's one of the disappointments of contemporary life. Geniuses of all sorts, convinced in their hearts that they are the glue which holds the social or even universal substance together, each offering a public persona—take it or leave it. Speak to me of mathematics or of Federal money policy or pass by. (14.16, 1)[27]

Citrine goes into a short disquisition on how artistic talent is converted into property, into another on Marx's dim view of the man of letters and his up and down career in capitalist culture. All of this unfocused generality is dropped for a concentration on Humboldt, Citrine's initial inspiration and proper beginning.

As it finally appears, the beginning is a tempered elegy, with retrospective youthful effusiveness present but not out of hand. The expansion of snatches of dialogue makes Humboldt more warm, on the one hand (he comments on Citrine's "large emotional handsome eyes" [*HG*, p. 2; not in 10.1]), and more threatening on the other (he says, "who the hell is Citrine to become so rich. . . . After making this dough why does he bury himself in the sticks? What's he in Chicago for?" [*HG*, p.2; not in 14.2]. And, more harshly, in a later inclusion, "He's afraid to be found out" [not in 13.5]). But the soulful, final Citrine sees that "to be loused up by Humboldt was really a kind of privilege" (*HG*, p. 4; not in 14.4). The elegaic sweep of the first pages is partly established through Citrine's account of Humboldt's exotic upbringing, his wild, rich, failed father, the affluent Chicago interlude, the abandoned, mad mother.

Often in manuscript this is given in Humboldt's first person, creating a sense of embarrassment instead of wonder. In one version Humboldt says, "Of course my sister and I had a dotty mother and Pa ran away to save his sanity." Then showing pictures from an album he speaks of Rumania, the cavalry, Mexico and Pershing, Pancho Villa, the Edgewater Beach Hotel, and the Pierce Arrow (17.4). In another version Humboldt recalls that at Wrigley Field he took a foul ball away from the chauffeur, who had caught it. "I pulled rank. I was the Little Prince," says Humboldt. Citrine notes that "he became gloomy at this memory. A class wrong, a terrible injustice" (17.11, 135). Another version has "poor, loony mother" giving Humboldt instructions to spy on his father at the Edgewater Beach Hotel. "I was to find out where he kept his money, the numbers of safe-deposit boxes, the names of the banks," Humboldt says (15.11, 222). Never mind the girls. Omitting the sordid, Citrine actually glamorizes these events in the novel: "there were lovely John Held, Jr., girls, beautiful, who wore step-ins" (*HG*, p. 4). The spying business is one bit of early embarrassment that finds its way to the novel. Even the mellow Citrine could not do a whitewash of the makings of a manic-depressive. But in the "I"-narrative earlier snatches—nowhere is the narrative given in Humboldt's first person for very long—Humboldt is the gloomer. For example, he says of Henrici's: "I went with the old man's mistress. Similar to Kathleen. I know what those quiet, fair, lovely girls can do, the kind of pain they can cause, the kind of pain they *want* to cause." Citrine then berates Humboldt for being self-victimized by the "stupid romantic platitude that intellect wastes people's sexual power. That's the Thomas Hardy idiocy about Yeobright. Moravia in *Conjugal Love* has just turned that crank again" (15.11, 122). In the novel Henrici's becomes another aspect of Humboldt's youthful glamor: "Humboldt ate devil's-food coconut-marshmellow layer cake at Henrici's. I never saw the inside of Henrici's" (*HG*, p. 5). There would be no shortage of occasions for Humboldt to expose his inadequacies.

As a psychologist, Citrine could hardly gloss over the origins of Humboldt's shortcomings (particularly in a fictionalized life of a writer whose main claim to fictional fame is a story about the disaster of having such parents, "In Dreams Begin Responsibilities"). But at this point in the novel Bellow is reflecting in a mood of mellow elevation. Citrine thinks of Humboldt's poems as Platonic, displaying "an original perfection to which all human beings long to return" (*HG*, p. 11). Consonant with the opening tone is Citrine's reverence for the fine talk of the Village, where Humboldt shone. "He was simply the Mozart of conversation," Citrine says in a late inclusion (*HG*, p. 13). There is a pleasure of cataloguing, an energy of nomination in the opening section that recalls *Augie March*, but bent to the description of an intellectual poet. These descriptions dramatize Citrine's original excitement, that Augie-like excitement at times. But Humboldt soon speaks of his enemies, and Citrine soon realizes, as Augie never does, that "this hemorrhage of eagerness would weaken me" (*HG*, p. 14). In the quick, nervous juxtaposition between past and present of the opening pages, Humboldt's picketing of Citrine's successful play soon follows. The ingenuousness of the Bellow protagonist is here retrospective. To give still more of an idea of how much this beginning was written, one need only say that the early versions of the novel (e.g., 7.1) exclude everything I have alluded to as "beginning." They start with a description of Humboldt's death, which is not given until page fifteen of the novel.[28]

v

The beginning of the novel is not the only part to undergo major changes. Whole episodes were deleted. In early manuscripts much is made of Humboldt's funeral. In some versions Citrine refuses to go near Riverside Chapel. In others he declines doing the eulogy, for the same reason—the funeral would be an occasion to "hear American society accused of madness, depravity" (7.6). In one version Citrine notes, "Old Left and New Left personalities would be there, importers of stale French ideas for the American culture market" (7.24, 23). Citrine thinks that on this sad occasion the old Village crowd "might be considering certain ideas, 'ritual,' for instance, or 'superstructure,' or 'mystification and ceremonialism,' something to do with death-observances. After thirty or forty years of mental or ideological confusion, they were 100 percent unfit for ordinary occasions of life" (7.24, 24). Worse than this, the funeral takes on a late-sixties aspect, something out of *Mr. Sammler's Planet*. Like Sammler, Citrine observes the odd, "aesthetic" types, "like Hollywood extras mingling at lunchtime, on the lot—Watusi warriors, cowboys, pirates, Confederate generals having a beer with King Kong and Major Barbara." Not as hard as Sammler, Citrine concedes that "costumes need to be displayed. Occasions are necessary. The expressive longings of mankind" (17.1). But he will not concede much. That Jasper

Stems, the anti-Semitic, Black Power poet who did not know Humboldt, is speaking at the funeral outrages him. Moreover, Stems is a mental light-weight with "all that D. H. Lawrence stuff about the death of the white consciousness" (17.10, 77). He is disturbed that Huggins has turned "the thing into a rally" (7.24, 39). He is equally astonished that Ronald Vernick (Magnasco), whom Humboldt tried to kill, has been instrumental in arrang-ing the whole affair.

In another version the "funeral orgy" is given over to "Maoists, Castroites and Fanonists. . . . One professor of English who later joined Gay Lib spoke of fink poets like Wallace Stevens who had made their peace with the sys-tem—executives of the Hartford Insurance Company." But, Citrine re-flects, "Humboldt admired Stevens. It's not too much to say that he had loved him" (14.18, 35). Besieged with such nonsense, in self-defense Citrine imagines a eulogy: "He was great . . . his conversation . . . made you feel the sweetness of life" (7.24, 26). Yet the other, difficult Humboldt haunts his memory. The remainder of his speech would have a reconciling, Platonic resonance: "We are still here . . . going about in the same old light, the only light we knew. Where things are difficult, twisted, vivid, but painful. Mostly unintelligible. . . . We don't know beginnings and we don't know endings. And we don't know eternity. So what can we expect except this disgraceful condition?" Citrine realizes that "the mourners would never stand for such stuff." One may ask, why should they, even those who are not apocalyptic revolutionaries? Citrine, however, has the latter in mind: "They would grumble; they might even stand up to object; about knowledge, or about eternity, or yelling, 'What the hell do *you* know about eternity!' " (7.24, 33). A fair question, a tough exclamation. Citrine is concerned that they would start a riot, that the coffin would be overturned. This would be disgraceful, but it pertains more to the late sixties as seen by Sammler than it does to the contemporary reality perceived by Citrine. Humboldt deserved a larger context.

Also deleted are Citrine's recollections of his early family life. He remem-bers Papa dying; he was still alive when his son reached the hospital. Some-how he refuses to go into the room, and ten minutes later Papa is dead. "Did he die knowing that I was at the door unwilling to come in?" thinks Citrine (7.16, 4). Mostly he remembers Papa not being the breadwinner. That was son-in-law Sussman, who delivered soda and beer. "Papa peddled table-runners and small carpets but brought home very little. He had no mascu-line authority. . . . [Momma] didn't care for him" (8.6, 46). There is a photo of Papa, circa 1898, as a Russian private, but "all Papasha ever fought was the maggots in the meat-ration" (17.3). Citrine thinks, "a fellow like Papasha could fill a revolutionist with passion. Restore the dignity of this man!" (17.3). In these early sketches, however, it is not the son who is adversely affected, but the wife. "Why did I think of Moma [sic] and Von Humboldt Fleisher together?" wonders Citrine. "Both lived in states of agitation. Both were nutty and in different degrees creative. Both made personality a sort of racket. Each pursued power by means of magnetic exertions" (8.6, 55).

The picture of Momma is even more grimly drawn: "she was a natural misanthrope. It wasn't just that she loathed sex. She loathed mankind. And she [was] frantic with rage against the *particulars*. A born Existentialist. . . . And it was all Papasha's fault because he was not a good provider" (8.6, 56). Later, when he visits Momma in an old age home, he notices that she "suffered vigorously in the Moscow Art Theater style. All along I've been convinced that the success of *Trenck* owed much to the deep impression she made on her children when she quarreled with Papa." But that is not all. There is also the son-in-law. Momma acted the artistic lady "waiting on the proletarian boor in his Commisar's Cap." At the nursing home she recalls, in words reminiscent of Mother Herzog, that she was "the *dienst* of my daughters" (10.8). In a number of Bellow works, the author must cut down on his tendency to remember, on the enormous lure of childhood. Humboldt's family history is central and quite enough. Citrine, to be sure, has his persistent memories, but Bellow wants to emphasize his worldly perceptions rather than his filial pieties. What is appropriate to the subjective world of Herzog would be indulgence in the relatively objective world of Citrine.

The Princeton episode is the oldest in the book, having roots as far back as the manuscripts of *Herzog*. In this sense *Humboldt's Gift* can be said to have been over fifteen years in the incubation. In an early version of the novel Citrine tells us that Humboldt pins the following verses on the office wall:

> God should have lowered the boom
> On me in my mother's womb.
> Even suffering is full of it.
> Birds have departed my West.
> Get the hell off my chest.
> Even suffering is full of it.
> Get the hell off my back.
> Black, black, black, black, black!
> Even suffering is full of it.

Citrine notes that these lines "comprised a comment on things he had once given his heart to with perfect piety, sacred things" (20.1). Giving up on suffering must have been a hard thing for this Jewish devotee of Dostoevsky to have done. In the *Herzog* manuscripts these lines, and very close approximations to them, are quoted several times. They are usually said to be co-authored by Vic Koppel (Humboldt) and Herzog; sometimes another colleague has helped in the composition. But the tone is not always solemn.

Sometimes it is more of a jaded, Princeton office caper. The bulk of the Vic Koppel episodes are, however, tonally similar to *Humboldt*. Herzog and Vic are Jews at Princeton on non-tenure lines (B.16, 2). Vic wants in on a permanent basis (B.19, 34). Vic is described as someone who has knocked down his wife twice and who once tried to run her over with his Chrysler. He is victimized by Pinelli, a detective who wants him to believe in the fantasy of his wife's adultery. There is money in it for him. Vic reads his own adulterous ways into his wife Mary (B.16, 2). Fearing for her life, Mary wants to leave him (B.18, 10). Vic is institutionalized at Bellevue (B.18, 7). Herzog is filling in for a man who was awarded a Fulbright lectureship to Constantinople; but he "wouldn't be here at all if I hadn't broken with Daisy," his first wife (B.16, 1). Another Princeton character—Briggs in the *Humboldt's Gift* manuscripts, Driver in the *Herzog* manuscripts—is a well born Wasp who takes his wife's leaving him in a George Hoberly manner. He does not make it to the final version of either novel, except as a transformed George Hoberly in *Herzog*. So much for the *Herzog* manuscripts.

Sewell, Ricketts, Longstaff, the main contours of the Princeton episode, appear pretty much as they do in the early *Humboldt* manuscripts. Worth noting, however, are some late changes in what Citrine thinks about Humboldt's manuevers and in what Humboldt thinks of Citrine. Feeling sorry for his turbulent friend and for himself and "all of us," Citrine thinks of human beings as "banished souls . . . longing for their home-world. Everyone alive mourned the loss of his homeworld" (*HG*, p. 125). This could not have been said until the later drafts. Not that moody yearning has been absent in Bellow even years before. When Humboldt tells his friend, "You're always mooning in your private mind about some kind of cosmic destiny. Tell me, what is this great thing you're always working on" (*HG*, p. 122), he might be Clem Tambow talking to Augie March. But in *Humboldt's Gift* the idea and vocabulary of the spiritual is much more developed. When Humboldt says, in a late inclusion, "I think you may be psychologically one of those Axel types that only cares about inner inspiration, no connection with the outer world" (*HG*, p. 122), one cannot help noting the irony involved. Bellow's central thrust has been against the Axels, the aesthetic idealists who would let the servants do the mere living for them. Has his hold on life become so tenuous in his anthroposophical incarnation as to sustain such a comparison?

A look at the tonality of some of the late inclusions dealing with Citrine's spiritual identity indicates the contrary. Even his rejection of "the plastered idols of the Appearances" is made in words that come strictly from that world: "the painted veil isn't what it used to be. The damn thing is wearing out. Like a roller-towel in a Mexican men's room" (*HG*, p. 16). Again, he says that "Humboldt wanted to drape the world in radiance, but he didn't have enough material" (*HG*, p. 107). This is not exactly the vocabulary of

Meister Eckhart, whom Citrine, like Sammler, reads. Such language indicates rather a comic grasp of transcendence. Citrine confesses his skepticism about many of Steiner's props: Moon Evolution, fire spirits, Sons of Life, Atlantis, "the lotus flower organs of spiritual perception or the strange mingling of Abraham with Zarathustra, or the coming together of Jesus and Buddha. It was all too much for me." What, then, remains? A psychological attachment to a death-transcending vocabulary and even a literal belief in some dear, gorgeous nonsense. The heavy Dr. Scheldt interlude appears late and then in a structurally ironic context. Cantabile is abducting Citrine and a willing Thaxter to shady Stronson's.[29] Perhaps the funniest expression of spiritualism in the Chicago context, though, comes when Judge Urbanovitch, a City Hall hack with his eye on the object—money—sympathizes with "the problems of intellectuals" who "may get into special preoccupations that aren't lucrative." But he understands that "this Maharishi fellow by teaching people to turn their tongues backward past the palate so that they can get the tip of their tongue into their own sinuses has become a millionaire." The Judge advises Citrine that "many ideas are marketable." Citrine, however, does not laugh. He retains his equanimity by virtue of anthroposophy. His spirit disassociates itself: "It left me and passed out of the window to float a bit over the civic plaza" (HG, p. 231). Presumably, it had the good sense to float back.

When Citrine goes far out, earth goddess Renata is usually there to bring him back. "You'll wind up with bare feet in the Loop carrying one of those where-will-you-spend-eternity signs" (HG, p. 320), she predicts. And, in another late inclusion, she reads the final verdict: "you don't spend years trying to dope your way out of the human condition. To me that's boring." Citrine has paid for his transcendental flights. "I believe in nature," says Renata with good cause. A woman of the contemporary world, she thinks that "when you're dead you're dead, and that's that." And she is a woman willing to act upon her insights: "that is what Flonzaley stands for. Dead is dead" (HG, p. 430f.). This is not the only thing he stands for. He stands for marriage and money in the bank (Renata has no quarrel with death as profit) and, for all Citrine'e spiritualism, these forces seem to carry the day. The high seriousness of Citrine's quest is thus undercut by a counterpoint of constant comic deflation. Making death comic was daring (though Bellow had already done so in Henderson and Herzog). But, like the Humboldt's gift sequence, this one exists largely as comic pattern. The deeply felt writing on Humboldt and on death are not done justice by these clever unwindings.

Bellow makes a humanist's case for the spiritual, and his confession of faith is a preference of the Romantic to the modern view. This, too, like so many of his important mental formulations, is expressed in a very late inclusion. "I had a strange hunch," he says, "that nature itself was not *out there*, an object

world eternally separated from subjects, but that everything external corre-
sponded vividly with something internal, that the two realms were identical
and interchangeable, and that nature was my own unconscious being. Which
I would come to know through intellectual work, scientific study, and intimate contemplation. Each thing in nature was an emblem for something in
my own soul" (*HG*, p. 356f.). Citrine remains, then, an optimist of sorts, a
tender-minded man in an age of tough-minded rationalism. His metaphysical bent allies him not surprisingly with Goethe. However, thinks Citrine,
"my late friend Humboldt was overawed by rational orthodoxy, and because
he was a poet this probably cost him his life" (*HG*, p. 363). Yet Citrine's
latest discovery about Humboldt, and a very late inclusion, is that "Humboldt really believed that human beings were supernatural beings" (*HG*, p.
363). This last had to have been late because Humboldt's "gift," as it appears
in the novel, the scenario-letter on which his friends may make money, does
not itself appear until relatively late. The final line of Humboldt's letter—
"Last of all—remember we are not natural beings but supernatural beings"
(*HG*, p. 347)—is not included until very late. Without enough confidence in
the soul, Humboldt at the last still found it necessary to affirm the supernatural. This may be taken as part of that deus ex machina quality of the latter
part of the novel, including the "gift,"[30] which a number of readers have
considered a falling off from the novel's earlier intensity. But if Citrine's
Romantic metaphysics is seen as solemn, Bellow is the first to undercut his
own solemnity. Typically, Citrine's expression of Romantic faith occurs in a
context of structural irony. In the midst of these lofty reflections there is
Thaxter and his expensive schemes. And in the midst of Thaxter's lofty
sentiments, Renata has her gourmand, footsy orgasm.

Given the endless ambiguity of Citrine's relationship to Renata—can body
and soul live happily ever after?—this novel could not have ended happily in
the conventional sense. The disjunction between the ideal and the real, the
world dreamed and the world observed, increasingly problematic in Bellow's fiction, reaches what must be a peak in *Humboldt's Gift*. As often as not
Bellow has viewed this disjunction as a critic of the ideal, particularly in its
ideological manifestations. When, however, the ideal expressed itself as
soul, metaphysically, Bellow found it easy to becomes its instrument. What
is new in *Humboldt's Gift* is the extent to which a stark opposition has
developed between ideal and real. Where modernist ideology is still present
in Humboldt, it is there mainly as a tarnished remove of a deeper brightness. Humboldt's authentication of the supernatural is, as we have seen, a
last-minute revision and, it seems, a wishful afterthought. For Bellow, the
disjunction between dream and event, wish and action, has frequently
issued into the comic or lyrical tentativeness of a novel's end. *Henderson*
and, to a lesser extent, *Herzog* end in lyric flights; *Augie March* in a comic

recessional issuing into a lyrical conclusion. *Humboldt's Gift*, too, incorpo-
rates both elements. There is, with many funny turns, the long, familiar
unwinding—the victimized lover, the caring for the child, the rumble of
concluding complication. After the success of the Caldofreddo script, after
Thaxter's kidnapping, after Citrine's crying over having to leave Roger (all of
these events late inclusions), we may all need some theological first-aid.

The final lyricism shows a subtler hand, a hand strengthened in revision.
The burial scene is marked by the broken singing of Menasha Klinger. In
manuscript, Menasha, called Jeremiah Shklar, boarder, machinist, singer,
punch press operator with a deformed nose that needed surgery and cal-
loused palms, has a wish to sing at La Scala. Citrine would like to discuss this
comic situation with him, but he is dead (15.17, 57). In art, if not in life,
resurrection may occur. Menasha is brought back for the later versions,
where Citrine feels a particular affinity for the Coney Island resident: "He
and I obviously held permanent membership in some larger, more extended
human outfit, and his desire to stand in brocade and sing Rhadames in *Aida*
was like my eagerness to make it with Renata or to collect my bequest from
Humboldt." The words past the last comma are part of an already late
manuscript (12.6), but they are replaced by, "far beyond fellow intellectuals
of my generation who had lost the imaginative soul" (*HG*, p. 332). This last
Steinerian flourish indicates how late the expression of Citrine's spiritual
ambition often was. What follows in this very late inclusion shows why
Menasha became important. "Music drew me toward Menasha," says Citrine. "By means of music a man affirmed that the logically unanswerable
was, in a different form, answerable. . . . This was such a man's assignment.
I, too, in spite of lethargy and weakness, was here for a big reason" (*HG*, p.
332). The final revisions, then, underscore the direction of Bellow's quest.
Menasha's music is valued more for its fulfillment of a moral obligation, an
assignment, than it is for its aesthetic satisfaction. Menasha, in a croaking
voice, sings "In questa tomba oscura," fulfilling something of his ambition as
Humboldt is about to be reburied. Even more appropriately, though less
relevant to La Scala, he sings "Goin' Home." Weak in voice, off-key, but
"terrably moved" (*HG*, p. 486), Menasha is reminiscent of the homely Jacqueline of *Augie March*, "as hard used as that by rough forces" (*AM*, p. 536),
who sings and urges Augie March to sing to ward off physical catastrophe.
Jacqueline is not moved by the singing as such but much moved by Augie's
"La Cucaracha," which reminds the poor woman of her dream of Mexico. As
Columbus' imprisonment didn't prove there was no America, Humboldt's
burial didn't prove there was no God. And didn't prove there was.

If politics in a novel is, in Stendhal's words, like a pistol shot at a concert,
anthroposophy is like tear gas. This may be one way of bringing back the
larmoyant. Be that as it may, Bellow is too instinctively the novelist to give

himself over definitively to the absolute. In notes for a lecture, Bellow speaks of Valéry's hostility to novelists. Valéry "often says there is no principle of necessity in the facts they offer. Other facts can easily be substituted. In a novel things are entirely too relative to interest him." Bellow notes this insight with disapprobation and comes to the novel's defense. "The novel," he says, "is the highest form of human expression so far attained. Why? Because it is so incapable of the absolute" (10.12). These words, written during the composition of *Humboldt's Gift*, suggest that however far out Bellow will go in quest of his version of the absolute, he is, above all, the novelist and will always be right back. For, to paraphrase his favorite poet Blake, whether or not eternity is in love with the productions of time, it has to learn to live with them.

Chapter 11

Bellow's short stories

Bellow's gifts as a novelist may lead one to feel that the story form could not be much more than a five-finger exercise for him. Do we not, when he is at his best, behold a teeming panorama, a weight of social facticity, a soul who needs at least three hundred fifty pages to define himself? The dramatization of mental suffering in conjunction with the comedy of culture does not lend itself easily to brief illumination. Moreover, the aesthetic realistic mode, which is virtually what we mean—or used to mean, not too long ago—by short story, the Flaubert-Joyce-Mansfield-New Yorker ironic cast, is essentially what Bellow repudiates. What kind of short story, then, does he write?

Mainly variations on a basic type. Not unexpectedly, Bellow is especially given to the character sketch, which may take a variety of guises. It may literally be a monologue, as in "Two Morning Monologues," "A Sermon By Doctor Pep," "An Address by Gooley MacDowell to the Hasbeens Club of Chicago," and other, little-known pieces. These are sketches, but "Leaving the Yellow House" and "Mosby's Memoirs" show how character sketch can become story of complicated inner illumination. Despite the great differences in development and technique, despite the different voices, all of these character stories sound like Bellow, constituting something like a mirror image of his novelistic development. When such a story does not sound like him (e.g., "The Mexican General"), it is because the strategy and tone are derivative. Other character stories, as it were by antithesis, represent a working through of themes and tonalities inimical to a soon to be asserted major direction. In "The Trip to Galena" Bellow finds a thematic dead end; in "A Father-to-Be" the mode is more that of aesthetic realism than Bellow's own. Still others in which the character element is subdued, and which might not be identified as typical Bellow for that reason, are among his more distinguished stories. "Looking for Mr. Green" and "The Gonzaga Manuscripts" remain forceful, original conceptions that focus on situation. The first dramatizes an insight hitherto unique in Bellow, and illustrates just what a man essentially a novelist needs the short story for; the second is a story derived from the discarded, "political" section of *Augie March* and is a story, as is "Yellow House," for which there is elaborate manuscript material. These are considerable achievements, and, along with works like "Yellow House," "The Old System," and "Mosby's Memoirs," show that Bellow can be near or at the top of his form in the short story. "Yellow House" and "The Old System" are triumphs of a purely personal perspective; "Mosby" mines a vein more typical of his longer work, another instance of culture and ideology working as a form of self-deception.

Bellow's first published stories establish at once the ambience of the early work. Mandelbaum, the "I" of the first of "Two Morning Monologues," prefigures the dangling man. Urban, isolated, self-pitying, he is a soul in search of employment. He is also looking for a job. Taunted by a resentful, money-bound father (cf. Leventhal, Tommy Wilhelm), consoled by a passive, remote mother, he expresses as clearly as any early Bellow character the psychological funk that is the hallmark of alienation. His father, not without some justification, is intensely annoyed at the presence of his grown son home at eleven o'clock in the morning. Five years of college, all that money—he should be doing something better than reading Dick Tracy. So unbeknownst to Mandelbaum—a comic wrinkle here, but lost in the humorlessness of the whole—he advertises in the paper for a job for his son, using his son's name. This is a particularly acute pain to the son, a man whose family deidentification is so great that he "can't remember a time in my life when I didn't swallow saying it."[1]

Mandelbaum sings the urban, autodidact blues: "I know a great deal about myself. . . . I'm very nearly sunk." The combination of insight and powerlessness is not new. In early Bellow it yields a peculiarly claustral quality. Our hero looks out on "the same alley, post in the alley, tin plate on the post reading 666. Same for Dapple Gray, Walter Scott, *The Counterfeiters*" (p. 231). In this image, facticity mocks subjectivity and the history of the novel from Flaubert to Kafka is subsumed. Literature has not been a release for the son, any more than business has been for the failed father; toting overalls and trowel, he can remember that he once owned the house he now pays rent in. Nor does the unglamorous, unthreatening mother help much. Though she sometimes kisses the son goodbye on his way out to look for a job, Mandelbaum says that "Ordinarily she is as strange to me as though she were dead or nonexistent" (p. 232). Mandelbaum, before the publication of *The Stranger*, has problems rather like those of Meursault.

Mandelbaum's principal activity is, in a sense, art; he *imitates* looking for a job. But the actively mimetic has its limits, and he becomes a connoisseur of enclosed landscape, "all in two colors, sand and gray." There is not much chance of rejuvenation through nature, not to this last of the sun scholars:

"Just before we creep under the elevated lines it appears for a moment. Not much hope for it, I remark to myself. If it outlives me it won't be for long" (p. 232). The psychological depression is given a willed, cosmic dimension. Is there any wonder that his one wish is to have been "one of the first draft numbers. . . . Perhaps I should become a volunteer" (p. 230). Like the dangling man, he sees in regimentation an at least nominal ordering of inner chaos.

Where the portrait of Mandelbaum is done in the terse strokes of aesthetic realism, the one of the gambler, in the second of the monologues, gives us an aria on impotence abstractly rendered. Bellow's portrait of the gambler, unlike Dostoevsky's, is not a dramatization of obsession but a lyric on power and loss. The gambler is in the same psychological predicament as Mandelbaum. Gambling is an attempt to control chance, manipulate the wheel of fortune. But failed gambling? Our gambler admits to the supremacy of chance: "Close my eyes and pick, I may as well. It turns out the same; mostly sour loss. System is nothing and to try to dope them is just wasted. . . . The card is dark always; the dice to the last role." Gambling does not bring control but a fated defeat. It imposes a false excitement on an aimless life, affirming the American Oblomovism characteristic of much of Bellow's early work. But if beggars have their superfluities, idlers have their superiorities. Like Leventhal, the gambler feels that he got away with it. In his smart shoes and smooth pants, he views the "sucker scraping the griddle," thinking, "I couldn't put in his twelve hours. . . . To get around it counts. Slipping through" (p. 234f.). Having neither Mandelbaum's desperation nor his incipient conscience he would not fantasize the Army as ordering principle. Here, too, he got away with it, "in the Grand National for peacetime privates. But that I expected. It would have been funny to come out a loser with so many fall guys in" (p. 235). What we have in the gambler is a flip superiority to contrast with Mandelbaum's self-lacerating contempt. His life has none of the pathos of the manic Dostoevskian thing, but merely the sourness of failed calculation. What is notable is the aesthetic rendering of his failure: "That's how it turns out. Money owing, rent postponed, hole in your glove, one egg, cheap tobacco. Then you hear the swishing in the heart like a deck riffled, and the stains grow under the arm" (p. 236). This is not notable enough, however, and in this sketch Bellow is performing very minor work.

Bellow's next story, "The Mexican General," displays an uneasy balance between originality and influence. Rarely noticed, it is a story about Trotsky's assassination, an event which, we can see from all that manuscript work about Trotsky in *Augie March,* seems to have amounted to a preoccupation for the young *Partisan Review* writer. But if the voice is Jacob's, the hands are Esau's. The rendering of the political violence is done in an indirect, understated, ironic, "sensitive" manner that owes something to Hemingway—even to the extent that the prose occasionally sounds like a translation from the Spanish. This is the only instance in Bellow where Hemingway's positive influence is apparent. The story is told from the point of view of Citrón, the one who is sensitive, the one who understands everything, the unheroic hero whose decency defines itself as a reaction to false heroism. The Mexican General himself is also out of Hemingway, the man of false public front who reduces the military uniform to caricature. In Hemingway, though, even the phoney generals have something to do with battle, but since this is Mexico, our general is merely a phoney bureaucrat.

When this general embarks on a retreat, it is to a resort town. He comes with his entourage, consisting of three "nieces" (the euphemism recalls Hemingway again) and two lieutenants, one of whom is Citrón, the other Paco, whose function is to elicit Citrón's gradual revelation of the story. Psychologically aware, Citrón sees that the general measures success by the number of people he has the right to despise. This false, self-indulgent leader, this chip in the historical wind, is contrasted with a truly world-historic figure who is gradually revealed to be Trotsky. "Everything about him was of much consequence and all based on principle," says Citrón.[2] Trotsky's assassination turns into a major political coup for the general, via the public relations route: "there already was the whole business with el Jefe's pictures right in the middle as though it had all taken place for his sake" (p. 190). Even worse, Trotsky's body is handled in the morgue by the photographers "like a slab of beef" (p. 193). Here, albeit somewhat too explicitly, is the Hemingway contempt for the publicity aspect of historical events. Here, too, the Hemingway-cum-Tolstoy "making things strange." For three days the general sits on platforms, directs the placing of wreaths, consoles the widow. His assignation with a "niece," a woman he does care for in his fashion, ends the story with a sinking modernist irony.

"A Sermon by Doctor Pep" is Bellow's first brilliant short fiction, anticipating that dazzling aura of energetic reference of the more stellar autodidacts of *Augie March*—Einhorn, Robey or Augie himself. And not anticipating it in time by much, since later in that same year (1949) the first of several published chapters of *Augie March* appears. Indeed, "A Sermon By Doctor Pep" and "An Address by Gooley MacDowell" are monologues that belong as certainly to the release of *Augie March* as "Two Morning Monologues" belongs to the inhibitions of *Dangling Man*. Dr. Pep, as the name indicates, is a Professor of Energy. Lest this august title plunge us too quickly into the rapids and cataracts of Romantic vitalism, let us establish at once that Pep's energy is rooted in conscience rather than impulse, morality as style rather than style as morality. Not that Dr. Pep doesn't have an aesthetic manner of his own. To be sure, Westside Rococo was never more in evidence in Bellow's Chicago (or New York) creations. But the ornateness, as in a house of worship, redounds to the glory of a moral impulse.

Half-theologian, half-lay analyst, fully unemployed, he sermonizes out of the pulpit; the locale is Bughouse Square (an Elysian Field to which a certain aspect of the urban populist imagination consigns all ideas), adjacent not to a church, but to the Newberry Library, of which Dr. Pep is an habitué. "Easter isn't far away," notes the Doctor, thinking of renewal: "the dead-looking are resurrected off the sidewalks and sent to be gandy-walkers with little blue flowers of Montana, where the birds chirp like the sound of scissors and snip the air into beautiful streamers, and the butterflies drink up what is left of the porcupines who passed on happy in their sleep."[3] It is clear that whatever else he is, Dr. Pep is a poet, one with a benign grasp of love and death. But, gimpy and old, Dr. Pep is not himself eligible for the resurrection of the section hand. "Natural selection has been rough on me," he muses. Nevertheless, he is fully capable of lecturing on his subject, which is the "Health of the Person" (p. 458). This is no subject for mere biology or fads. "I'm talking of nutrition plain and simple, and the deep causes of good and bad health," says Dr. Pep, immediately flashing into brilliance: "I began with hamburger meaning to explore why the shape of the creature is ground up." Why? So as "not to give an evidence of the living and a hint of obligation to reverence and indebtedness" (p. 488). This is one of the ways in which the civilized man is less human than the primitive one. A guilt abides in carnivorous modern man. As Dr. Pep inimitably puts it: "Does that make cold tallow out of the fat which should be the grease of love? I believe so." Man is not a creature who can get away with it. Bad conscience remains because "things have to be accounted for in full by a demand of our nature" (p. 488). This guilt transcends class barriers in that the welfare of the common man rests on beasts just as the welfare of the great rests on common man. One must feel, radically, the weight of all suffering. Dr. Pep's exemplar is, appropriately, the late Dr. Julius Widig, the physician and Bughouse Square speaker who wrote *Reefer Rosie, The Tragedy of a Girl Bum*. When arrested during World War I as an anarchist and thrown into Joliet "he kept up his noble heart by healing the jailbird venerealees." For this goodness, "he came out healthier than Ponce came out of the Florida swamps, nearly killed by his quest for elixirs." Dr. Widig embodies a Judeo-Christian paradox: "It was the miseries of other men that did him good" (p. 456). Dr. Pep and his colleague, then, are caricatures of Bellow's central literary impulse, the dramatization of the good. Not hypocrites, like Dr. Tamkin, but men whose idealism is on the far side of utopia, whose best impulses are not quite separable from the ludicrous. Indeed, when Dr. Pep, anticipating counter-argument about instinct (don't cats eat fish? isn't it natural?), argues that we are "creature and more, having hopes of brilliancy . . . embracing every-thing with infinite desire," he transcends himself to arrive, paradoxically, this side of paradise. A tiny masterpiece, "A Sermon By Dr. Pep" gives us the first of Bellow's inspired, wacky poet-orators.

While "The Trip to Galena," "Looking for Mr. Green," and two unimpor-tant stories intervened between "Sermon By Dr. Pep" and "Address by Gooley MacDowell to the Hasbeens Club of Chicago," the latter is so clearly a companion piece to "Sermon By Dr. Pep" that it is best considered with it. Not quite as successful in its verbal panache—there is only one Dr. Pep!—the later monologue is motivated, too, by an idea: the mind is too much with us. Once again Bellow presents in caricature, yet with some essential sym-pathy, what he elsewhere takes quite seriously. "It's true, fellows, that I used to be very intelligent," says Gooley, "and now don't know but what I should give it all up."[4] It's not just his creeping senility, but the creeping senility of a civilization. There is wisdom literature aplenty, but, as Gooley observes, "we are not free to use it, that is why the advice is a loaded burden" (p. 226). Moreover, it is precisely mental consciousness that is the burden: "as you get better by the correction of intellect you may lose your nature, and have less and less to say because what your nature prompts your betterness turns down, so you become silent and are otherwise in danger of becoming better than you can afford" (p. 226). Yes, in the democratization of culture Romantic doctrine is food for thought at the Hasbeens Club. Civil-ization itself, like a character in late James, is notable for what might have been. Despite this, despite its most spectacular failure (the holocaust), Gooley will not withdraw entirely from mind. Nor, finally, in more serious incarnations, does Bellow.

These monologues burn with a gemlike flame deriving not from an idea of art but from an idea of character, a willingness to honor self-definition where one finds it—and one does find it. This willingness, this casting out of vulgar denigration, achieves its real release in the gargantuan thrust of *Augie March*. Bellow has become a master of the isolated voice. The novel would present us with more than characters talking essentially to themselves.

"The Trip to Galena" presents us with a paradigm of Bellow's moral pro-gress. Excerpted from a discarded novel called *The Crab and the Butterfly*, it concerns itself with the meaning of a gratuitous impulse to smash some-one's skull. Interestingly, it is a Bellow surrogate named Weyl who has this impulse. The story takes the form of a conversation between Weyl and his interlocutor, Scampi; the setting is a Chicago hospital, where Weyl recuper-ates from a breakdown. Weyl is an early Bellow type, one which derives from the underground man, the healthier-than-thou sicknick. His trip to Galena was a trip to respectability and might just as well have been a trip to Hell. His sister, recoiling from a harrowing affair with a gangster, finds her will to love in the bourgeois Neff family. Subsequently, like Augie with the Magnuses, Weyl has the opportunity to marry a factory and, like him, prefers not to. The Bartleby echo applies more to Weyl than to Augie in that there is in him no innocence to mitigate his break with bourgeois life. Yet both Bellow characters cry out for a worthwhile fate, "for which a function is a substitution of a deeper despair" (*AM*, p. 516). And for this reason, Weyl regards his gifted sister's compromise as a sellout. When the skeptical Scampi rightly questions Weyl's shaky self-esteem the latter rises to the occasion in a central Bellovian self-analysis that is halfway between the self-laceration of the dangling man and the self-exaltation of Augie March. If, like Augie, Weyl is "in a campaign . . . in the name of what was worth doing," unlike him "I never had any idea that what I was doing was worthwhile."⁵ Like Augie, Weyl says, "I'd take up anything I thought feeling had stayed in" (p. 782), but, unlike him, he does not find anything. And, very much unlike him, he is bored, suffering from being "energetically bored, melancholy" (p. 791). Chronologically beyond *Dangling Man* and *The Victim*, Bellow is also beyond finding in this cast of mind the symbol of a special providence. His hero says, "If there's anything I hate, it's that romantic Hamlet-melancholy. I despise it. I despised it in myself. . . . Being sad is being disfigured. . . . It's a platitude and an indecency." Maybe so, but this shift into buoyancy is always hard won, and the truth may be platitudinous. But not indecent. In a statement Bellow is often to make again, Weyl attacks those who "have a practical hammerlock . . . on this life they personally consider not good enough" (p. 792).

Weyl's problem is not that he attacks fashionable negativism, but that he has, apparently, nothing to put in its place. His mind is ominously full of violent portents, which culminate in the gratuitous skull-fracture he inflicts on someone as his "personal act of war" (p. 793), an act which, in his somewhat deranged, obsessed mind, relates to the mass murder of the holocaust. Weyl finds the amenities of Galena a charade in view of the one virtue he has attained—psychological honesty: "Nobody takes that seriously any more, the dance of conduct. . . . We're more and more in the open about our natures, nearer and nearer to the original personal quality in people." The risks are great, however, and predictably harrowing: "if we've murdered, it will be because the original nature is murderous; if not, because there's something redeeming in the original thing and a reason for all the old talk about nobility. But before we can have conduct, everything will have to be proved all over again" (p. 788). Weyl is clearly an intellectual at loose ends, dangling closer to the orbit of the murderous than the noble nature. Knowing what we do about the former in Bellow, we can see how fundamental a paralysis this work represented and how necessary it was for him to cast it off. Weyl is an instance of the negativism he resists. He lacks the liberating tone, and that tone would come only with the creation of Augie March.

Coming shortly after "The Trip to Galena" and shortly before most of the separate chapters of *Augie March* were published, "Looking for Mr. Green"[6] inhabits the limbo between the pervasiveness of conditionality (Kayo's *moha*) and the possibility of identity. A classicist in the Depression, George Grebe is fortunate to have found a job delivering relief checks. The former University of Chicago Fellow is teased by his immediate superior, a man with a law degree, about "the last things" and "the fallen world of appearances." What are these distinctions compared to twelve dollars more a week?

The story takes place during the Depression in the black ghetto of South Chicago, where the Platonic categories have their ironic relevance, the weight of urban facticity figuring vividly as ontology as well as sociology. The quality of this facticity is reminiscent of the Platonic *doxa*, characterized by sensory flux, transience, knowledge at a remove. Trying to find Mr. Green is something like trying to corner the reality by pursuing the shadow. If the story suggests an updated Plato, it suggests, similarly, a Kafkaesque metaphysical futility. Grebe asks Green's janitor where he can find him and is told, "I don' know all the tenants, leave alone the tenants' tenants. The rooms turn over so fast, people movin' in and out every day" (p. 139). To which Grebe later adds, "sometimes there were as many as twenty people living in an apartment. . . . In some places the beds were used in shifts" (p. 143). Transients *are* transience in what is indeed a fallen world of appearances. Where the play with philosophy implies the loss of reality, the abrasion of the flux, the sociological dimension adds loss of identity. "You knew people, but not names. The same man might not have the same name twice," says the Italian grocer to the inquiring caseworker. Heraclitus has nothing on him. Reciting the familiar catalogue (murder, incest) without sympathy, the grocer informs Grebe that "nobody will tell anything." In the darkest cave of a ghetto, Green is at the remove of a remove of a remove.

As are all of us city dwellers. The history of Chicago is not unique: "Numbers had given the place forced growth, enormous numbers had also broken it down. Objects once so new, so concrete that it could never have occurred to anyone they stood for other things, had crumbled." This is true of the naturalistic city, where numbers are mere integers devoid of an inner amassing harmony. Reality is circumscribed by facticity. Is this true of all cities? "Rome, that was almost permanent, did not give rise to thoughts like these. And was it abidingly real?," as it were, a Platonic city? The question remains a question, as it must for modern man. On the shores of Lake Michigan flux holds sway: "in Chicago, where the cycles were so fast and the familiar died out, and again rose and changed, and died again in thirty years, you saw the common agreement or covenant (things stand for something by agreement), and we're forced to think about appearances and realities" (p. 155). In the world of appearances what is real is what people consent to have as reality at that time. But there is a force in appearance beyond consent, an eternal demiurge indifferent to ideal forms and mere appearances alike. Looking at the ruined part of Chicago once rebuilt after the Great Fire, Grebe describes it this way: "it wasn't desolation that this made you feel, but rather a faltering of organization that set free a huge energy, an escaped, unattached, unregulated power from the giant raw place." Man's fate, thinks our humanist, is to impose civilized pattern; man's fate, in this sense, is to have a function. He knows, that "to feel this energy and yet have no task to do—that was horrible; that was suffering," adding—a typical Bellow protagonist in that he has had trouble with function—"he knew what that was" (p. 154). Now, as check deliverer, he performs a serious function, if only at a considerable remove from his avocational interest and even at a remove from Mr. Green. The metaphorical Platonism of the story is insistent, but Bellow inverts the Platonic process, making ordinary humanity the object of his search. Finally, at the end of his tether, Grebe gives the check to a drunken, naked "Mrs. Green" who mutters about her orgasmic reality—bare facticity, all vegetative and appetitive in the classical lingo. She merely "stood for Green, whom he was not to see this time." Grebe must settle for the Platonic shadow, the Kafkaesque under-castellan. Despite the sense here of ontological descent, the classicist remains undaunted: "it was important that there was a real Mr. Green whom they could not keep him from reaching because he seemed to come as an emissary from hostile appearances. For, after all . . . he could be found" (p. 160). Yet Mr. Green remains at the end of the story, an illusion, perhaps an illusion *perdu*.

But all individuality is not lost. Witness Winston Field, the black welfare recipient whose identity is as clear as his social security card and his naval discharge papers. Not only does he have an identity, but he also has a program. Quite rightly surmising that "as long as they can take it away from you they got no respect for you," he envisions a time when all black men will contribute to the making of black millionaires. Behind the consensual reality is Field's *idea*, redolent with a rough-and-ready ghetto version of Plato's allegory of light: "That's the only sunbeams, money. Nothing is black where it shines, and the only place you see black is where it ain't shining" (p. 153). Not precisely Plato's point, but a distinction which has its own ontological validity. Field is a Yankee, not very different from a captain of industry like Yerkes who, in conceiving the El, got the many to pay, understood the value of agreement. But even this success reveals the lesser Platonic reality of the remove: "what a scheme of a scheme it seemed, how close to an appearance." Grebe shrewdly sees that Yerkes gave money to astronomers "to find out where in the universe being and seeming were identical. . . . Yes, he wanted to know what abides" (p. 155). The deeper longing must be satisfied. Yet I have called the Platonism of this story metaphorical, for the thing above all others that the Platonic forms do not comprehend is conditionality, and conditionality is what the story is about as much as anything else. Grebe is left with nagging questions that won't be answered easily, if at all, by a classical terminology. If one thinks of what abides, one must think the following: "What about need . . . that keeps so many vast thousands in position?" Even "the fallen world of appearances" (the phrase makes Grebe wince, but Citrine is later to take it quite seriously), especially that world, does tease us out of thought as does eternity: "Why is the consent given to misery? And why so painfully ugly? Because there is *something* that is dismal and permanently ugly? Here he sighed and gave it up" (p. 156). Content with half-knowledge, he senses that finding the answer to this will be harder than finding Mr. Green. Nothing utopian here, but a tempered, small integrity survives bitter winter in the windy city, city of flux. Written while *Augie March* was being composed, the story stands as a refutation of its energy of celebration, but not as a refutation of the book itself. For parts of *Augie March* present us with views of Chicago that Grebe would have little trouble recognizing.

Augie March's charming fantasy of fatherhood is an indication of his will to live; "A Father to Be," a story also concerned with this fantasy, is an indication of the contrary will. Written after the novel, the story anticipates the painful weight of *Seize the Day* and recalls the claustral quality, mitigated by aesthetic release, of Flaubertian-Joycean realism. Like *Seize the Day,* which is written about the same time, it is one of Bellow's clearest statements about the meaning of money. On this point, if on this point only, Bellow plays the orthodox Freudian. Gold is shit, the pursuit of it—as distinguished from the necessity to make it—strongly indicative of anal retentive meanness (also Dostoevsky's view). If there were anything to it, children would value it for its own sake. Rogin, an erstwhile thirty-one year old research chemist affianced to Joan, is encumbered by circumstantiality so heavy that the quantitative problems bring on the qualitative or psychic reactions. There is such a thing as being too responsible. If a Leventhal was wrong in not feeling responsible enough, Rogin is, at least financially, overcommitted. His dream of striking it rich through a chemical coup, his synthesis—a synthetic albumen which is going to revolutionize the egg industry—is more elusive than Herzog's.

We meet the dependable Rogin at the coming of the crisis, as he falls "into a peculiar state." Putting his younger brother through college, partly supporting his aging mother, paying his wife's dental, department store, osteopath, doctor, and psychiatric bills, it is no wonder that, with the crescendo of Christmas, "Rogin almost went mad" (p. 122). Who says that men have it good in our society? A nice tension arises. Since lucre is filthy, making a living is shitty, and who is he to complain about his wife's mental health? Bellow does not explore the enormous comic possibilities of this situation, but plays it straight. Hurting, Rogin "loved her too much to show his suffering. He believed she had a marvelous character, always cheerful, and she really didn't need a psychiatrist at all" (p. 122). Again, no ironic twist intended.

But the problem is larger than defining the degree of neurosis. Money does crush people, through health and in sickness, till death do us part. Rogin reflects on a "clear idea": "Money surrounds you in life, as the earth does in death. Superimposition is the universal law. Who is free? No one is free. Who has no burdens? Everyone is under pressure." At this point, the resilient Rogin feels buoyant—everyone is in the pressure cooker, making for a community of overcoming. But this equanimity in the face of financial pain cannot be long sustained. In the deli—for this, too, Rogin is responsible—to buy supper, he sees that the owner, an inevitable product of New York commercial culture, is "toughened by every abuse of the city, trained to suspect everyone" (p. 124). Yet he has not been dehumanized; something of humanity has prevailed: "in his own realm, on the board behind the counter, there was justice. Even clemency." The suggestion is that his Jewish heritage still serves this storekeeper well. Also, in the story—this, too, is typical New York—is a Puerto Rican who can't speak any English but who is dressed as the complete cowboy. Hard material circumstance generates the lavish dream. There is no judgment made here, as there is in *Mr. Sammler's Planet*, but judgment soon comes. Rogin himself is beyond the lavish dream and on the subway home the commercial culture crystallizes as nightmare. Resisting financial determinism, Rogin sees that "to think of money was to think as the world wanted you to think; then you'd never be your own master." Something in Rogin recognizes a counterforce: "When people said they wouldn't do something for love or money, they meant that love and money were opposite passions and one the enemy of the other" (p. 126). An interesting perception, but it only adds to a smiling superiority in Rogin. What good is the perception without the feeling?

Rogin's real position is made clear by his recellection of two dreams. In one, an undertaker offers a haircut and Rogin refuses. He's not dead yet. In the other, he had been carrying a woman on his head. How's that for burden? Rogin's malaise takes living shape in The Man on the Subway, whom he contemplates with underground (no pun) man loathing, particularly when he observes his "detestable blue-checked coat . . . his rosy nasty face" (p. 130). The man is a dandy, but "of respectibility," not counter-respectability. A precursor of Dr. Adler, he incarnates bourgeois narcissism: "he seemed to warn people that he wanted no difficulties with them, he wanted nothing to do with them. Wearing such blue suède shoes, he could not afford to have people treading on his feet, and he seemed to draw about himself a circle of privilege" (p. 128). The man resembles his wife, and, remarkably, his hated father-in-law. Fearing the self-pitying worst, Rogin reverts to the gloom of the dangling man, a tonality Bellow had ostensibly bypassed in doing *Augie March*. "To suffer, to labor, to toil and force your way through the spikes of life . . . to struggle under the weight of economy, to make money . . . only to become the father of a fourth-rate man of the world like this, so flat-looking with his ordinary, clear, rosy, uninteresting, self-satisfied, fundamentally bourgeois face." Clearly, things are tougher than Shelley knew. Bourgeois, here, as in Dostoevsky, is a spiritual category, and Bellow contemplates The Man on the Subway much the same way Dostoevsky contemplates Luzhin. They share virtually every essential characteristic, above all, that combination of self-satisfaction and anal-retentive meanness: "He was so pleased, with all he owned and all he did and all he was that he could hardly unfasten his lip. . . . He wouldn't give anyone the time of day." The speculative Rogin shudders to think of him as the norm forty years from now. In contrast to this money-centered inhumanity, "Man's personal aims were nothing, illusion."

Rogin concludes with a melodramatic pessimism which, more than any other passage in Bellow, recalls the lyric speculations of the turn of the century American naturalists—with some recent sociological twists:

> The life force occupied each of us in turn in its progress toward its own fulfillment, trampling on our individual humanity, using us for its own ends like mere dinosaurs or bees, exploiting love heartlessly, making us engage in the social process, labor, struggle for money, and submit to the law of pressure, the universal law of layers, superimposition! (p. 129f.)

It's just too much, and Rogin wants out of marriage to preserve what little individuality is left him. The figurative content of this interior tirade, with its institution of downward comparisons, so unusual in Bellow, only underscores real trouble. On his return home Rogin is about to explode: " 'Do you think,' he was going to tell her, 'that I alone was made to carry the burden of the whole world on me?' " But, following authorial intention, his mothering wife, noticing his matted hair, begins to wash him. Then figure, purification symbolism, and Joycean epiphany steal Rogin's thunder. The final tableau shows Joan "pouring the water gently over him, . . . the warm fluid of his own secret loving spirit overflowing into the sink" (p. 133). Here is Bellow, after *Augie March*, submitting to the seduction of aesthetic realism. One could say that the story is perfectly coherent, and that the triumph of love over money is perfectly prepared. Love, *schmuv*. We have been given too much grief for a victory of the amniotic sack. The counters of the story and even its rhythm and contour is like *Seize the Day*, but there the circle of moneyed meanness is broken by a knot of grief deep enough only for tears; figurative explanation follows feeling and is not a substitute for it.

"The Gonzaga Manuscripts" is a story taken essentially from discarded drafts of *Augie March*. There as we have seen, Augie is an integral part of the Committee for a Reconstituted Europe, assuming a serious political character. Bellow transforms him to the equally serious Clarence Feiler, an erstwhile, respectable, lackluster (as his surname indicates) scholar in search of the love letters of the famous Spanish poet, Gonzaga. There is no larkiness here, but the story and novel both illustrate the contemporary climate of ideas, where people are taken as ideational objects rather than individual subjects. Persistent in his search and with enough of Augie's susceptibility to be so victimized, Clarence finds himself in the same situation; the slightly deranged Spanish aristocrat, named Alvarez-Polvo here, wishes to capitalize on Clarence's typically "American" quality—his association with the atomic bomb!—to rid himself of some hereditary stock in a pitchblende mine.

The ending is well prepared for in this new version. Clarence, even though a Feiler, embodies the demands of the heart. He is not merely professionally but personally committed to the recovery of Gonzaga's love poems, poems that, as we might anticipate, run counter to the dominant strain of "modern poetry in English [which] doesn't express much will to live" (p. 162f.). Throughout the story no one can seem to understand the simplicity, the purity, of Feiler's motives. In this sense it is a recent version of the old story: American innocence (purity) survives intact the entrapments of European corruption, while it is at the same time transfigured (innocence as ignorance transformed into felt experience) into knowledge. If the moral is Jamesian, the dramatic exposition is straight Bellow, with nuance of consciousness, in this instance, secondary to satiric exposure.

Bellow drops the ideological trappings of the once political episode. In manuscript, del Nido (Alvarez-Polvo) is, as we've seen, a rich Falangist sympathetic to the Committee for a Reconstituted Europe. He has translated Marinetti, D'Annunzio and a number of Third Reich Germans. He speaks of the coming clash between Asia and the west, which the west would lose because it has no ideology; so one does well to go with the collectivist drift of the times. Augie, to the contrary, maintains that if a man does not go against the so-called will of the times, "he wasn't to be trusted, that riding the wave of the future was only a gilded phrase for submission to murderers, crooks and cannibals" (B.2.12). Since Feiler's frame of reference is literary rather than political, this discussion is dropped. Similarly, an attack on Freud and psychology by the English spinster is dropped. With one exception, Feiler is not involved in ideas, does not grind an intellectual axe. The exception is his view of literature, as the switch from Augie to Feiler, from the C.R.E. to Gonzaga, is accompanied by a switch from political to literary ideas that are remarkably Bellovian.

As his humanist bent would indicate, Feiler speaks for the most precarious of causes, individual humanity. His feelings and ideas crystallize as he explains the appeal of Gonzaga to the intelligent art history student, Miss Unger. (In manuscript she is a ceramics student, less intellectual, more flirtatious, who complains about how slow life in Madrid has become without Manolete [B.2.12]; characteristically, it is *de rigeur* for Bellow to expunge any traces of Hemingway in the final version.) Her role, somewhat enlarged, is to serve as a sounding board for Feiler's insights and admirations. Feiler speaks of the strain on modern art to substitute for a once conclusive faith. What is interesting in his account is the rejection of art as a substitute for religion: "The very best have soon gotten tired of art for its own sake," he maintains. He hints that art may be mocked by morality—witness the career of Tolstoy the reformer, and Rimbaud "who went to Abyssinia [to confront the abyss, no doubt], and at the end of his life was begging of a priest, *'Montrez-moi, Montrez.* . . . Show me something.' " What more is there to say of the modernist moral vacuum than these desperate words uttered so movingly by one of its avatars?

Feiler is sympathetic to the enterprise of the modernists, regards it as an impossible heroism. Considering the price in psychic disintegration, he thinks of them as noble martyrs: "Frightening, the lives some of these geniuses led. Maybe they assumed too much responsibility. They knew that if by their poems and novels *they* were fixing values, there must be something wrong with the values. One man can't furnish them. Oh, he may try, if his inspiration is for values, but not if his inspiration is for words." Here we have the typical Bellovian sympathy for the enterprise of the artist-hero together with the ultimate rejection of it for want of moral substance. The aesthetic (Flaubertian) position—"if his inspiration is for words"—is distinguished from the moral one, and dismissed. Feiler's attraction to Gonzaga is a personalist one. The scholar says, "If you throw the full responsibility for meaning and for the establishing of good and evil on poets, they are doomed to go down. However, the poets reflected what was happening to everyone. There are people who feel that they are responsible for *everything*. Gonzaga is free from this, and that's why I love him."

As if elaborating Feiler's sentiments, Bellow says, in a newspaper interview prior to the publication of *Mr. Sammler's Planet*:

In the eighteenth and nineteenth centuries, when religion faltered, poets became an unofficial priesthood. It was the Blakes and the Dostoev skys and the Tolstoys who found themselves upholding values formerly in the hands of the churches, and writers took upon themselves the task of creating a mental coherence for modern man. But that is not the proper sphere of an inspired imagination. If you look at Shakespeare, he took no responsibility on himself of total coherence. He just spoke of people in the most inspired way. Let philosphers and statesmen provide the coherence.[7]

Here Bellow makes an observation that is, to some degree, self-implicating. For, like the writers he takes to task, he stands somewhere between the claims of personality and the claims of ideas. There are works of his that clearly emphasize one more than the other, but it may be argued that a great part of Bellow's special quality as a writer is the way both are integrated with seeming necessity.

In any case, Feiler's view of Gonzaga, like Bellow's of Shakespeare, posits the mystery of mankind as the highest wisdom. Like Bellow's, Gonzaga's outlook is essentialist. Feiler quotes a Gonzaga letter to his father: "Many feel that they must say it all, whereas all has been said, unsaid, resaid so many times that we are bound to feel futile unless we understand that we are merely adding our voices. Adding them when moved by the spirit. Then and then only." There is a residual religious quality to Gonzaga, as to Bellow, a religiousness of sentiment rather than of perfect faith. Feiler sees this when he says, "Lots of people call themselves leaders, healers, priests, and spokesmen for God, prophets or witnesses, but Gonzaga was a human being who spoke only as a human being." Again, Feiler wishes to lay down the burden of the spokesman for a simpler, more direct truth. Gonzaga had the gift of simplicity, yet it was a simplicity that included the religious outlook. It was natural for him to think of a sanctified element in life. Accordingly when Feiler is offended by del Nido as "the sort of man who cut everyone down to size, Gonzaga included," he thinks of this vulgar character as "precisely the sort of man to whom Gonzaga had written: '*Go away! You have no holy ones*' " (pp. 172ff.). Gonzaga, like Herzog, is an archaic type, and seeking holiness in contemporary Spain is like looking for the proverbial needle in the haystack, or like looking for Gonzaga among his acquaintances. In Gonzaga, literature stands as a criticism of the dismal, power-oriented, failed aristocrats he knew.

Del Nido is the most vivid of these. Looking backward to Iggy Moulton of *Augie March* and forward to Sandor Himmelstein of *Herzog*, he is a mass man, a vulgarian; as such, he is a foil for Feiler's mild idealism. Why concern yourself so with a poet, he wonders, "There's plenty of poetry already, for everyone. Homer, Dante, Calderon, Shakespeare. Have you noticed how much difference it makes?" (p. 179). If literature is feeling and Gonzaga is feeling in its purest form, del Nido is the denial of the purity of feeling.

Clarence "sensed that [he] would have liked to give him the dirt on Gonzaga—revelations involving women, drunkenness and dope-taking, bribery,
gonorrhea, or even murder. Gonzaga had escaped into the army; that was
notorious. But Clarence didn't want to hear del Nido's reminiscences" (p.
180). The revelations remain hypothetical, but Feiler would have borne the
ultimate for the sake of Gonzaga. Women, drunkenness, dope, bribery,
gonorrhea, perhaps, but murder does not seem even theoretically consistent
with the noble gentleness of his outlook.

This compulsion to reduce is given in comic dimension in the final scene
where a hapless aristocrat, Alvarez-Polvo, disappointed for want of a financial windfall, incredulously questions Feiler about his search: "Manuel? The
soldier? The little fellow? The one that was her lover in nineteen-twenty-
eight? He was killed in Morocco." The saddest thing about Spain is that it is
out of touch with its own resources of the spirit. Bellow conveys an atmo-
sphere that may be properly called ironic in the Flaubertian sense. The
denouement with Alvarez-Polvo clutching his dubious portfolio, takes place
in a church under the gored figure of Christ, one of those Spanish Christs
that, with ironic irrelevance, convey the flesh-and-blood cost of human suffering. As Gonzaga wrote, they have no holy ones. If one is going to make
Flaubertian assumptions, contemporary Spain is not a bad place in which to
make them. The story is not quite vintage Bellow in this respect, but it
shows that Bellow is still adept at turning a Flaubertian step of his own. We
even have an implied artist-hero, but here the assumptions are, as we have
seen, strictly Bellovian.

In the story Bellow gives us a portrait of a debilitated Spain, which is what
he gave us even more emphatically in the earlier travel piece, "Spanish
Letter," where the Spain of the Guardia Civil, corrupt patronage, rigged
elections, and phoney political trials is made explicit as a backdrop for Spanish envy. As an American, Bellow is seen as "one of the new lords of the
earth, a new Roman, full of the pride of machines and dollars."[8] The ultimate
insult, made in the story, is to symbolize America by the atomic bomb, as if
this chaotic dynamo were our altar. Feiler's various hosts are saying, in
effect, what a traveling salesman tells Bellow: "America is still looking for a
soul; our soul is very old" (p. 229). Yet where is the Spaniard nowadays who
can seriously stand up for the soul of Spain? No, the putative American
emptiness is only the underside of a more elaborate despair. The soul of
Spain is no longer poetry but envy of American power.

A dramatic advance in the possibilities of the short story form, and in
narrative voice generally, "Leaving the Yellow House" holds a distinguished
place in Bellow's literature of survival. It belongs to that strain of lyrical
personalism that marks *Henderson the Rain King* and *Herzog*, being much
closer to the first in that Hattie is a character having no connection to ideas

or ideology. As if to emphasize his obsessive need to explore the meaning of suffering—here is a source of *Bellow's* virtuosity—the author gives us an almost isolated, septuagenarian heroine in an almost isolated, aging world. Having neither the strength nor wherewithal of Henderson, nor anything like the intellectual energy of Herzog, Hattie seems made to absorb hard knocks on her heavy shoulders. Her being a woman, we are given to believe, is consonant with her ability to endure tough luck and primal necessity.

Precarious to begin with, Hattie's purchase on life is loosened when—partly because of drinking, partly because she sneezed—she loses control of her car, which is then stuck in the middle of the railroad tracks, an analogy perhaps to her own spiritual rut. Calling the impatient Darly to her aid, she is victimized by his callous rescue procedures and breaks her arm. She now realizes the full force of her isolation. Like Henderson, Hattie shows that you don't have to be Jewish to be a survivor. Like Henderson, like Herzog, too, Hattie is one of Bellow's smiling sufferers: "Her face was cleft by her nonsensically happy grin. She was not one to be miserable for long; she had the expression of a perennial survivor" (p. 20). This, to be sure, is survival American style, yet survival it is. Though way out West, this is Bellow country.

In the painfulness of slow recuperation, Hattie senses the onset of mortality. She makes her will—but to whom? There is no one alive who deserves the intimacy of bequest. One of Bellow's most painful isolates, Hattie sees that there is no one left with whom she is intimate. Yet the need for giving in old age, the necessity of pride, of final self-assertion, lead her to a brilliantly perverse gesture. She herself is her true intimate, and she will be benefactor and beneficiary, signing her will over to herself. A damsel in distress aiding a damsel in distress, she transforms the victimization of fate by an irreducible, quixotic narcissism. The triumphs of solipsism are illusory, however, succeeding as gesture rather than deed. Pure as it is in its individualist outline, free as it is from the encumbrances of ideology and ideation, Hattie's fate reaches to a truth that is not a solution. In this poignant story, Bellow may have touched the very bone of inward necessity, but the truth proffered remains problematic in its exclusivity.

Perhaps it is her patrician Philadelphia ancestry that supports Hattie in her declaration of independence. The old American rectitude is a curious analogy to the frequent immigrant desire in Bellow to be a somebody. Conversely, the Jewish geneology is far older than patrician Philadelphia, and Hattie is close to being as alienated as any alien. Hattie's social background implies at once a generosity of heart and a particular sensitivity to decline. Unlike the well-heeled Henderson, and her intimidating but beloved friend India, Hattie has nothing to sustain her but the memories of a fallen past. Old age complicates all this. Our precarious heroine is aware that she "rambled, forgot names, and answered when no one spoke" (p. 29). In the Bellovian manner, Hattie is a character and a case. "Is she still all there?" begins an early version (C.1.3). There was a time when it was all too much: "*I used to wish for death more than I do now. Because I didn't have anything at all. I changed when I got a roof of my own over me*" (p. 37). The house is her identity and she cannot will it to anyone else, for it provides the coherence of a fragmented life. She has seen some kindness but, with the exception of the friend who had willed her the house, she has not been given succor, that more-than-helpful helpfulness, the quality Henderson seeks. Jilted by her mainline husband, too proud for her onetime cowboy lover, childless, "cast off and lonely," she makes the gesture of perpetuity. Of course she will think it through tomorrow, of course she is prepared to live with her straight-laced brother; but this is the moment of truest subjective intensity.

One of Bellow's most impressive short-story flights, "Leaving the Yellow House" is one of the two in Bellow for which there is significant manuscript material. The manuscripts are revealing in that this story shows Bellow breaking through into the third-person, first-person narrative voice, recalling the lyrical "I" of *Henderson* and, more exactly, the shifting third-person, first-person voice of *Herzog*. Narrative as intense, lyric flight develops from earlier versions that are straight third-person, with a heavier proportion of dialogue and delineated minor characters (e.g., Marion, Halfpint). Cut from the final version is the interview at the hospital, the visitors there, the renting of her house, the description of Hattie's daily routine—all to make for a more ultimate solitude. The typical early page (in B.6.2; C.1.3; C.1.4) is heavy on dialogue and light on description. The final version gives us much more interiorized description in pages of solid paragraphs. All of which is to say that Bellow finds a style answerable to greater inner illumination, the third person focusing on the objectivity and limitation of the central intelligence, the first person winning us over with the intimacy of confession, which includes self-castigation. Finally, the final version reveals the making of the will in an unexpected, dramatic and explosive climax not, as in some early versions (e.g., C.1.5) as a casual afterthought after Hattie stays with Marion, and in close proximity to the early description of her as a perennial survivor (C.1.5). The final version dramatizes her isolation, one penetrated by the mad logic of despair. This patrician lady has always taken a special pride in her incarnation as a Western Frontierswoman. The frontier builds American character, and death is the last frontier.

There was a ten-year span between "Yellow House" and Bellow's next published story, yet his skill in the short form had lost nothing by disuse. "The Old System" is curiously related to the first story in that it explores purely personal emotion. Neither dramatizing ideas, nor elaborating an outlook, there is nothing systematic about "The Old System." On the contrary, it is a retrospective idyll, a hymn to the sanctity of primitive emotion. The central character is Dr. Braun, a third generation Jew whose calm reflection frames an emotional violence too implicating for anthropological detachment. The tribal accents are Yiddish, the tribal disputes the laws of the heart. Nor is there any sentimentalizing of the milieu. In a sense, Dr. Braun is the clean American, free of the bloody, old, embarrassing openness, the emotional mess. Yet this older quality, with its cultivation of screams and tears, had a depth of human feeling that may make the current clean American Jew merely antiseptic. The framing of inspired chaos by ordered decency is the essential narrative strategy of a story heavily dependent on the intelligence of its narrator. Such chaos needs the tempering view of a "civilized" voice; such secular, objective, modern perception (Braun is a scientist) on the other hand, pales under the impact of deeply felt life. There is for Bellow, as for others, an enchanted immigrant moment, the moment of graspings and embarrassments, foundations and adventure capital, and, in the truest sense, successes and failures, which the accomplished genteel, and perhaps gentile, present is compelled by its humanity to recall and to cherish.

Like most immigrant chronicles, the story involves dirty laundry. Dr. Braun recalls his cousins, Isaac and Tina, whose sibling rivalry issues into a moving, if grotesque, deathbed scene, where Isaac accedes to Tina's demand of twenty thousand dollars as compensation for what she claims was an exclusion from a lucrative real estate deal many years ago. The deal involved a payoff to the Wasp power structure represented by the calm, polite Ilkington, from which all the siblings but Isaac reneged at the last moment. It is clear that the resentful Tina has no moral claim, equally clear that she has no financial claim (her daughter has been well provided for in her grandmother's will).[9] What claim, then, does she have? None but the mystery of relationship and its consequent forgiveness. This is the gist of the answer given Isaac by the rabbi he seeks out for advice, a marvelous anachronism, who "had the old tones, the manner, the burly poise, the universal calm judgment of the Jewish moral genius" (p. 78). Isaac presents the money, which Tina refuses, but the gesture is well received. Tina then bestows her mother's ring on Isaac, a ring that she rapaciously took on her mother's deathbed. Tears of reconciliation, smiles of grief; an oblique triumph of love—that's what love is (says Leopold Bloom), the opposite of hate. A circular definition perhaps, but one that has all the meaning there is to Dr. Braun.

We know little of Dr. Braun's character but the following: "It was said of him, occasionally, that he did not love anyone. This was not true. He did not love anyone steadily. But unsteadily he loved, he guessed, at an average rate" (p. 48). Clearly a good guess, for anyone to so grasp the meaning of his antecedents—as scientist, Braun significantly specializes in "the chemistry of heredity"—is an act of love. Bellow makes Dr. Braun a scientist to establish not merely an emotional objectivity, but to present the possibility of secular naturalism as well. From the literal end of the story there is the contemplation of flux, the precariousness of consciousness, the almost Lucretian stars "cast outward by a great begetting spasm billions of years ago" (p. 83). Observing with his inner eye the motes given off by "something like molecular processes," Dr. Braun considers these "the only true heraldry of being" (p. 83). The fact that such secularism exhibits itself on a Saturday, the Sabbath, adds to the poignancy Braun feels for what was, in essential ways, a religious past. Bellow's own ambivalence toward religion is dramatized in the Apollonian, Santayanian, "modern" Dr. Braun, with his sense of poetized belief. Jewish feeling, religion as moral mythology, come momentously through to our scientist. His earliest scientific musing—"the feeling of necessary existence might be the aggressive, instinctive, vitality we share with a dog or an ape"—is left in the shade. Though his subsequent, more complex, thoughts are not: "The difference being in the power of the mind or spirit to declare *I am*. Plus the inevitable inference *I am not*. Dr. Braun was no more pleased with being than with its opposite." His past draws him deeply, if temporarily, away from what used to be considered the center of indifference, drenching him in a dark memory of irrational meanings and emotional depths. As for the emotions in the calm light of day, "no one wanted them now. Perhaps the cold eye was better. On life, on death." The allusion to Yeats suggests the aesthetic naturalism of modernism, with all its emotional complication still without the moral yearning of Hebraic tradition. Braun appreciates this intensity, but it is not clear that he is in possession of it: "Oh, these Jews—these Jews! Their feelings, their hearts! . . . These tears [were] only an intimation of understanding. A promise that mankind might—*might*, mind you—eventually, through its gift which might—*might* again!—be a divine gift, comprehend why it lived. Why life, why death" (p. 83). The conception of life as moral purpose, as some not-to-be-despised teleology, is what haunts the scientific mind, and, in this day, who is not a scientific mind? Hence the rhetorical tentativeness of his affirmation. The pride, the madness of this old system had an energy that his new system lacks.

Where *Henderson the Rain King* and "Leaving the Yellow House" portrayed the Wasp as triumphant sufferer, as spiritual survivor, "Mosby's Memoirs" gives us the Wasp as mental aristocrat, as cultural superior, a type we have seen adumbrated in Frazer of *Augie March*. In Frazer and Mosby we have instances of mind civilized to the point of barbarism, of a mental consciousness so complete as to exclude the unruly mess of merely personal disaster. That this anaesthesia of heart can also be "Jewish" we see clearly in

Seize the Day, where the anal retentive respectability of the moneyed Dr. Adler is above being soiled by the floundering agony of his son. Grief, sir, is not a species of idleness. In "Mosby" Bellow comes back to what is a central theme, the indifference to human suffering. "Mosby's Memoirs" is a new version of an old story, an updated version of the narrative pattern in Dostoevsky's *The Eternal Husband* and Bellow's *The Victim* and, more broadly considered, *Seize the Day*. If in technique the story is more complicated than *The Victim* and the Dostoevsky work, in theme it is simpler: the victim here (Lustgarden) is simply victimized and is by no means victimizer. Rather than focusing on the intertwining play of guilt and shame, Bellow here concentrates his energy on the revelation of a monstrous gentility. Unbeknownst to the victim, however, the victimizer must pay.

Mosby is the "bull" to Lustgarden's "mouse" and, like Velchaninoff, he "did not feel quite well" (p. 151). Again, there is a crisis in the life of a well-ordered existence, with "order" carrying a special force in this case. Mosby is presented as a secular Calvinist whose designed world pivots on the dual axes of depravity and self-election. Viewing the famous, mammoth Tule tree, he dismisses the accompanying "golden myth of an encompassing paradise," thinking that "earliest man probably ran about on the ground, horribly violent, killing everything," but conceding that "this dream of gentleness, this aspiration for arboreal peace was no small achievement for the descendents of so many killers" (p. 173). He is in Mexico writing his memoirs. The exotic birds there express, to him, "abysmal depths of aggression, which only man—stupid man—heard as innocence. We feel everything is so innocent—because our wickedness is so fearful. Oh, very fearful!" (p. 151). A penetrating insight this to the extent that innocence is so falsified, and these judgments of darkness are not easily dismissible by the author of *Mr. Sammler's Planet*. But, as Bellow knows, man does more than kill, birds express more than aggression. Mosby's reaction to the lush nature around him is pathological: "Mosby felt ill with all this whirling, these colors, fragrances, ready to topple on him. Liveliness, beauty, seemed very dangerous" (p. 151). This threatened avalanche of sensation materializes in the mind of a man who represents a final stage of western mental consciousness, the positivism that depoetizes and in so doing becomes the spirit that denies. Mosby is a twentieth-century success; he has everything because he believes in nothing. Clairvoyance, pleasure, distinction—there is everything in Mosby's life but feeling. Writing his weighty memoirs, he casts about for comic relief and finds it in Lustgarten, a mere random character, totally non-historic. Like Pavel Trusotsky, he is the sort of born failure whose fate is cuckoldry, another eternal husband. The point of the story is that this essential relationship remains an afterthought to Mosby; indeed, he leaves out of his memoirs Lustgarten's life of mere comic victimization.

At a Paris concert with Trudy Lustgarten—she, too, the wife, never more than an afterthought—he notices in the Czech pianist the labor of culture. Music is emotion intensified, but Mosby is detached: "stone-hearted Mosby, making fun of flesh and blood, and these little humanities with their short inventories of bad and good. The poor Czech in his blazer with chased buttons and the muscles of his forehead rising in protest against tabula rasa." Art is one of man's attempts to authenticate the subjective nature of reality, the primacy of feeling. The pianist by definition works against the notion of *tabula rasa*, against its rationalist implication. Mosby, however, is too much the positivist to even hear the music: "Mosby could abstract himself on such occasions. Shut out the piano. Continue thinking about Comte. Begone old priests and feudal soldiers! Go with Theology and Metaphysics . . . [in] the Positive Epoch" (p. 162). Mosby is an updated version of the sort of intellect the Romantics in their vitalistic naturalism railed against. When glancing at a hummingbird, he thinks smirkingly, "To bless small creatures is supposed to be real good" (p. 162).

The wheel has come full circle, and we see another American gentleman refined beyond the point of civilization, in Eliot's borrowed phrase. In a review of Eliot's *The Family Reunion*, a play which gives added meaning to the phrase, Bellow wonders how a mother and a son getting together after so long could reveal so little emotion and have so little to say to each other. On his part, Mosby reflects that "my parents begot me like a committee of two" (p. 172). After such knowledge, what forgiveness? The narrator tells us that Mosby becomes what the French call *un type sec*, a Senecan who admires Lorca's *clavel varonil*, "the manly red carnation, the clear classic hardness of honorable control" (p. 166). He knows noble excess only in his mental life, developing a mode of discourse so lacerating that Princeton offered Mosby a lump sum $140,000 to retire seven years early.

Mosby's rage derives from sources both personal and historic. On the one hand, there is his life of loveless self-sufficiency; on the other, there is his penetrating intellect stemming from a conservative, patrician sense of order debased, as in Henry Adams. Mosby's insights may appear askew in his reaction to what he takes to be democratic blunderings, as in his view of concentration camps, which "showed at least the rationality of German political ideas. The Americans had no such ideas. They didn't know what they were doing. No design existed" (p. 154). (Very much the sentiment uttered by the rich Falangist in a "political" draft of *Augie March*.) But his excoriation of radical self-righteousness, of sentimental ideology, is much to the point. He scorns the European discovery of Marx and Lenin after the revolution was betrayed, thinking, "should America lose, French internationals were preparing to collaborate with Russia. And should America win, they could still be free, defiant radicals under American protection" (p. 163).

From his conservative vantage he is perceptive on examples of political bad faith: Sartre's calling for Russia to drop atomic bombs on American bases in the Pacific because America was now presumably monstrous, and his exhorting blacks to butcher whites; or Russell's "urging the West to annihilate Russia after World War II" (p. 169), and his weeping at the Londoners cheering the fall of Germans from a Zeppelin, without mentioning that these same Germans had come to bomb the city. From this nightmare of history, comic relief is needed.

Enter Lustgarten, whose name is itself funny, a mocking counterpoint to a life of *unlust*. He has been banished from any Eden of pleasure. Harmless, vulnerable, inept, with a laughable, adulterated idealism, Lustgarten is a secularized *schlemiel*. A former Marxist from New Jersey, he thinks that reading *Das Kapital* and Lenin's *State and Revolution* will give him an edge in business dealings. When his European-black-market dental supply business begins to show a profit, Lustgarten is done in by his German dentist partner. When, at great cost to his family, he imports a Cadillac to turn a double profit, new regulations cancel the scheme. "Mosby realized that compassion should be felt" (p. 163), but the obligation doesn't quite materialize. Hearing of a possibility to sell the car in Barcelona, Lustgarten then hears of a better offer in New Utrecht; driving back exhausted, he crashes in the Pyrenees, lucky to be alive. He is, literally, broken and broken up about his brother's loss.

But Mosby "did not care to sit through these moments of suffering. Such unmastered emotion was abhorrent. Though perhaps the violence of this abomination might have told Mosby something about his own moral constitution" (p. 165). What it should have told him is perhaps too obvious, and is made explicit by the end. For in his qualities of aspiration and suffering, this struggling, messy soul, this Jew, is emblematic of humanity, "mere" humanity. In terms of historical meaning, Mosby later thinks, "Lustgarten . . . didn't have to happen" (p. 176). In his secular Calvinism, Mosby is one of those myopic minds who does not see the trees for the forest. Lustgarten is emphatically non-elect, graceless, emblematic of no meaningful flash of design. But ordinary humanity is what history is mainly about, or ought to be, and ordinary humanity is what Mosby betrays.

One may object that Bellow here falls almost mechanically into the pity-the-victim pattern. Mosby, to be sure, cannot be defended, but one all but feels that Lustgarten doesn't need Mosby to be a near disaster. They do have a "five years later" chance encounter, like Leventhal and Allbee, Velchaninov and Trusotsky, where the buoyancy of life asserts itself like a cork. When last seen Lustgarten had been victimized by his flirtation with Tito's Communism and had lost fifty pounds. Expecting ideological elevation, he had gotten hard labor, and, he finds out, a divorce from Trudy. Now, in the coda—"The thing had quite good form" muses Mosby—Lustgarten is "filled out," successful, married, a father. Back on the capitalist side, he operates a laundromat in Algiers. But later the Algerians threw out the French and expelled the Jews. Lustgarten's life is a Jewish joke, one of those painful comedies, but it is clearly Bellow's intention not to make us laugh. We know little about him personally other than his representative fate, hence the comic element is diminished. Above all, the joke is on Mosby for denying the reality of this fate; he commits adultery with his wife by presenting Lustgarten as merely funny, and "she could not be the wife of such a funny man" (p. 175)—a simple line, almost monosyllabic, that expresses great accusatory power. And more, "Trudy too was funny . . . to him she was a clown. This need not mean contempt. No, he liked her" (p. 175). Beyond this liking stands contempt, distantly related to the classical, aristocratic distinction between serious and ordinary life, between noble figures of public dimension who are better than "we" and merely common, private ones who are lesser, between the tragic and the comic; in Mosby's distorted Calvinism this comes out as a version of the elect and the non-elect.

But Bellow exacts a sort of Chaplinesque revenge on the nearly classical sense of comedy. In the end, Mosby suffocates of his own self-importance. In a patrician version of the Protestant work ethic, Mosby thinks that one cannot "will" oneself into being "a desirable person . . . without regard to the things to be done. Imperative tasks." And recognizing too quickly the discontent that civilization exacts, he thinks of the "monstrous compulsions of duty which deform. Men will grow ugly under such necessities. This one a director of espionage. That one a killer" (p. 176). In seeing that civilization itself can take such a dimension, Mosby is all but cognizant of his own murderousness. Yet in the ostensible world Mosby is "a finished product . . . complete," a triumph of function, in contrast to Lustgarten, the comic relief who didn't have to happen. And in a brilliant, metaphorical *coup de canon*, Mosby is described as art rather than life, form rather than content: "He had completed himself in this cogitating, unlaughing, stone, iron, nonsensical form" (p. 176). The first four qualities assure the fifth or meaningless quintessence, as Bellow expresses an essentially Romantic contempt for an essentially classical notion.

There is a further analogy, in point of civilization, between Mosby and the Mexican tomb, "the mathematical calculations" of which are "perfect," "the precision of [whose] cut stone . . . absolute" (p. 175). The tomb itself reveals a scene of human sacrifice. In his mental set, Mosby, too, has extinguished life, though his sacrifice had no ritual sanction; rather it expressed a contempt for ordinary life in others and, *pari passu*, in himself. In one form of priestly election, one related to the religion of art, such purgation may amount to salvation. The narrator, therefore, says: "Having disposed of all things human, he should have encountered God. Would this occur?" In the Romantic-humanist view of Bellow, of course, no: "But having so disposed, what God was there to encounter?" (p. 176) Here as elsewhere, the perception of the common life is the beginning of wisdom, as the law of the heart is the beginning of perception.

Lacking this, Mosby finds death where life should be; the tombs become symbolic in his own mind of anal retentiveness made racial memory. Everything is measured, ordered, prescribed, claustral. There is room for much here, but not for life; to breathe, Mosby must get out. Salvation for him is no longer spiritual, but biological: "The light was there. The grace of life still there. Or, if not grace, air" (p. 176). His fear of death is related to his recurrent death fantasy, in which he "had died. He continued, however, to live. His doom was to live life to the end as Mosby. In the fantasy, he considered this his purgatory. And when had death occurred? In a collision years ago. . . . The actual Mosby was killed. But another Mosby was pulled from the car. . . . Walked away from the wreck" (p. 174). In a sense, yes. It appears that, like Leventhal, he was lucky, he got away with it. But has he walked away from the shipwreck of his life? His fate, with all its function, is to live the unlived life, a sort of latter day John Marcher whose latent bestiality resides in his having had nothing personal happen to him.

Taken together, the stories are a very illustration of development from the aesthetic realism of the first monologues to the remarkable independence of the original middle stories to the masterly narrative control of the last three pieces. Taken together, they present the growth of an inward moral necessity of man alone, but still definitely there and responsible for his being.

Epilogue

The Dean's December

For some time Bellow had been working on a long non-fiction book about Chicago, which, he came to realize, could only be given its due in fictional treatment. Chicago, he told an interviewer, was "a subject for some kind of poetry, not a factual account," for "the very language you have to use as a journalist works against the true material."[1] Another case of public life drowning out private life. Bellow's protagonist, Albert Corde, a former journalist and professor of journalism turned dean of students at a Chicago university, also knows that "nothing true—really true—could be said in the papers."[2] Inspiration came when Bellow fused the Chicago book with one about Bucharest—a tale of two cities, as was *Humboldt's Gift*. It is as if Bellow of late needs to rub two stones together to make the sparks fly. While this strategy was successful enough in the earlier novel, there is some question as to whether it is in *The Dean's December*. Bellow told the interviewer that the novel materialized as a pleasant surprise: "I wrote it in a year and a half and had no idea it was coming."[3] But he told another interviewer that he had written the novel "under great pressure—a book club deadline"[4] and that he was sick when he finished.

The book does show some signs of strain. Without the usual galvanizing act (e.g., the pickpocket's exposure or the Columbia scene of *Mr. Sammler's Planet*) or galvanizing character (e.g., Henderson), the new novel is one in which Bellow's discursiveness overwhelms his sense of fable. In its casual reflectiveness, it can sometimes read like notes: "That would be a good question. What *did* Corde represent?" (*DD*, p. 131). Occasionally the pain it describes seems gratuitous, as in the kidney dialysis description, where the author seems to be rubbing our noses in metaphysical waste. More importantly, the juxtaposition of east and west remains linear, undramatized, with the result that Bellow's vivid portrait gallery remains too often just that. Bellow's transitions are mechanical: "Now to move to Valeria and the life-support machines" (*DD*, p. 105): "Abruptly, Bucharest again" (*DD*, p. 156);

"To resume" (*DD*, p. 158); "And now, with stormier objectivity, himself" (*DD*, p. 122). In *Mr. Sammler's Planet* the death-bed scene was brief and affecting. Here, within a bureaucratic nightmare, we are given a death-bed scene longer than that in any opera. Valeria's hand stirs by page 127. When, toward the middle of the novel, Corde picks up a manila envelope of mail, the present action intensifies. Event is disproportionately retrospective. Citrine did a stretch of recollection lying down, but Corde spends much of his time in cold, hostile Bucharest under the covers as he ruminates about the "rum" in Rumania.

The *Dean's December* is a tale of two dismal cities. Bucharest is a disaster, an instance of "the penitentiary state." The people who once embraced the Russians and built post-war Rumania are now grovelling under the iron, bureaucratic boot. Yet the "hard nihilism" of the Soviet bloc makes civilized gesture that much more touching. The small female band of intimates in Bucharest are like delicate flowers growing out of stone, the most minimal strumming yet of the axial lines. But from a dramatic point of view they are not worth all the description Bellow lavishes on them. Gigi, for example, is too dull for so much attention. She is not as interesting as the sad communist city itself. In the rendering of urban place, Bellow is as superb as ever.

Where Bucharest is full of debilitation and death, Chicago is full of depravity and decadence, the "soft nihilism" of the west. Bucharest is cold, Chicago is hot, and it seems that Bellow is posing his version of Frost's question—will the world end in fire or ice? A certain darkness has fallen on Bellow's Chicago that makes necessary human connection nearly impossible. The qualified buoyancy of *Augie March* is long gone. Chicago is now "the contempt center of the USA," and there is nothing quite like "the crying ugliness of the Chicago night" (*DD*, p. 44). In fact, "Chicago wasn't Chicago any more" (*DD*, p. 237), according to Alexander Corde. Shades of Heraclitus. We know how bad things are when he judges today's Chicago to be worse than New York. Like other Bellow protagonists, Dean Corde is a reader of Blake, but Blake here means "Cain's city built with murder" (*DD*, p. 285). Representative in many ways of the ultimate nihilism, Chicago is "a mass of data, terrible, murderous" (*DD*, p. 266), like "advanced modern consciousness" itself, which, "because its equipment was humanly so meager, so abstract, was basically murderous" (*DD*, p. 193). Another value seems headed for oblivion, the value of ordinary possibility, of spirit rising out of the democratic mass.

The new novel makes it clearer than ever that "Looking for Mr. Green" is one of the central pieces of the Bellow canon, for the radical split between appearance and reality dramatized in the early work—which, as we have seen, gains currency in such later works as *Mr. Sammler's Planet* and *Humboldt's Gift*—is now dominant in *The Dean's December*. Some lines in the book might have come from the short story. Corde "would have liked to tell his nephew that men and women were shadows, and shadows within shadows, to one another" (*DD*, p. 32). When Corde climbs the stairs to the detoxification center—again the upward quest in a slum setting—he thinks, "If there was another world, this was the time to show itself. The visible one didn't bear looking at." (*DD*, p. 189). The contemplative Dean attends to his surroundings "As if he had been sent down to *mind* the outer world, on a mission of observation and notation" (*DD*, p. 210). His task is "to recover the world that is buried under the debris of false description or nonexperience" (*DD*, p. 243). The Bellow protagonist (merely adumbrated in the early story) is still looking for Mr. Green, though in the novel the obscurity has cultural roots. Still, *doxa* all but buries *episteme*. There is no Platonic harmony. The French Huguenot-Irish Corde might better have been named Discorde.

This critic noted with mistrust Charlie Citrine's lucubrations about the fallen world of appearances. Corde all but lapses into cynicism. "Nobody had a good connection or knew what racket he was in—his real racket," he thinks. Is everything, then, a racket? Not quite. "There was just a chance," thinks Corde, "that he might, at last, be headed in the right direction" (*DD*, p. 32). He notes of Valeria that "for her this world of death was ending. World of death? He surprised himself when he put it that way" (*DD*, p. 133). Again Corde eludes the grasp of nihilism, but in a troubling, passive way considering the energy with which the Bellow protagonist—Herzog, for example—usually assaults it. The line of Shelley about George III that he associates with the unsavory Detillion[5]—"the old mad blind despised and dying king"—is a psychic refrain indicating a lack of paternal principle, secure morality. When, at the end of the novel, Corde stares into the cold of interstellar space, does he derive any more comfort from the sight than does Stephen Dedalus? Herzog ridiculed Heidegger for falling into the quotidian, but what is Corde's emphasis on the falseness of newsprint, the inauthenticity of the everyday, if not Heidegger's *Verfallenheit?* "Social communication is the doom of every truly felt thought"[6] writes the novelist, but the novelist is Mailer, not Bellow. From this premise, Mailer goes subjective and experimental, writing a more verbal fiction (when he isn't doing the usual journalism!). Bellow deeply opposes this direction. Loosening one's moral stance, dismissing tradition as only a joke, going further into subjectivity, into the erotics of art—these merely add to the already existing problem. Tied into monologue though he often is, the Bellow protagonist leaves the way to the objective world open. In *The Dean's December* he does so almost in spite of himself.

For the citizen hero in Bellow, marginal at best, has come on particularly hard times. With his nostalgia for use, his nose for public issues, his distinction as a political journalist, his perception of communist rot, Corde is this hero more clearly than any other Bellow surrogate. He is, in fact, doing his *Harper's* articles on Chicago prisons and hospitals with "the *high* intention— to prevent the American idea from being pounded into dust altogether." But the rhetoric here is excessively defensive. Rufus Ridpath and Toby Winthrop are two black men who prove that the virtue of the citizen is still possible, even if their lives finally leave Corde with anger or depression.

As he leaves the detoxification center Corde's talk about high intentions is immediately qualified by the realization that "the facts were covered from our perception," that "the first act of morality" was to find the real in the garbage of unreality and, odd perhaps for a journalist but not a novelist, "represent it anew as art would represent it." Dewey Spangler, the political journalist and Corde's adversary, is right in scoring "poetry" insofar as it is poetic gesture, "but not insofar as Corde was genuinely inspired. Insofar as he was inspired he had genuine political significance" (*DD*, p. 123). His political significance is the exposure of a spiritual failure. Corde, then, sees significance in the occasional inspired or courageous citizen but not in the conventional "rational citizen's courage," since one cannot be "managerial and noble at the same time" (*DD*, p. 276f.). His Chicago articles are a testimony to this perception. Even academe, in his grim view, is "dominated by the same consensus and ruled by public opinion" (*DD*, p. 301). So much for the politics of civility. Yet the transformation Corde desires may admit only of pragmatic solution.

Is Corde inspired? Can he be, in his own terms, considering that he is a journalist? Only as a maverick superjournalist, perhaps. It is, of course, the novelist who may create inspired art. But there is some question as well as to whether Bellow himself is here inspired. Indeed, the author is so dismissive of everyday life that one may wonder whether realism can do justice to his contempt. Bucharest and Chicago are all but fantastic in their repressiveness, and Bellow is now playing a humanist's version of endgame. It is now the Bellow protagonist who abyssifies.

Yet for all his talk about apocalypse, one ought not to suppose that Corde is enamoured of it. He has "no sermons to preach about the death of cities or the collapse of civilization" being "too much of a Chicagoan to feel up to that," that is, in the last analysis, retaining somehow enough of the ordinary human stuff. Like Herzog, he rejects playing at apocalypse, considering "this poor man's make believe . . . a dangerous distraction." Corde sees clearly that "this *is* a time of the breaking of nations" and, of course, cities. The "real temptation," however, is not that he will advocate the apocalyptic but that he will "hope that the approach of 'last days' might be liberating, might compel us to reconsider deeply, earnestly." More precariously than ever, the Bellow protagonist is on the side of civilization. Mistrusting the prophetic, he tries to hang on against all odds to the ethical. "I personally think about virtue and vice," says Corde, courageously square (*DD*, p. 277). Has he done no more than think about them? Yes: he has reported on two blacks who are virtuous, he has helped bring to justice two blacks who are vicious—and both against considerable pressure of corruption and self-interest. The Bellow protagonist still looks for individual responsibility, but his task has become rather like that of Diogenes because of recalcitrant social conditions. Corde embodies this responsibility. Though he has paid a price, he still says what he wants. His nervous decency is contemporary.

Bellow's greatness as a writer, his powerful counter-energy, comes in reaction to wasteland platitudes, but in *The Dean's December* two unreal cities nearly bury the protagonist's not-so-rugged individualism. At its best, the author's desperate (and often comic) affirmation comes from the central character (e.g., Herzog's murder scene, Henderson's lion's den), from a human, funny voice. Much of his best writing expresses a comic equilibrium between gain and loss. In the new novel the affirmation is itself at a remove, an essentially symbolic enactment of what Corde values but barely expresses in reflection, let alone action. And the humor is nearly non-existent. Bellow is not close enough to blacks to get the necessary personalist charge from them. What he finally derives from Ridpath and Winthrop is a confirmation of his own disenchantment. And his Bucharest ladies, though touching, are too frail an embodiment of tradition to count for very much. Corde's affection for them and for his wife seems small in the destructive flow of events. So the gloom of the book is irremediable, the action flat. The constant crisis has backed Bellow further into the corner. Perhaps Corde's most winning trait, a painfully minimal one, is his availability to disillusion. At least he had better hopes, which is more than can be said of a number of characters in recent fiction. In his mid-sixties, in a difficult time, Bellow is writing a literature of weariness, but he is not writing the literature of exhaustion. Knowing Bellow's feel for the beat of life, knowing the never-to-be dissipated sense of character of the creator of Einhorn, Herzog, Humboldt, one is confident that *The Dean's December* is not the last word.

Notes

Chapter 1. Saul Bellow and the modern tradition

1. Gustave Flaubert, "Style as Absolute," in *The Modern Tradition*, ed. Richard Ellmann and Charles Feidelson (New York: Oxford University Press, 1965), p. 126.

2. Gustave Flaubert, *The Sentimental Education*, trans. Anthony Goldsmith (London: Dent, 1956), p. 62.

3. Paraphrase of "Notebooks," *Herzog*, B.18.12. Used by permission of Saul Bellow.

4. Arthur Rimbaud, "The Poet as Revolutionary Seer," in *The Modern Tradition*, p. 203.

5. D. H. Lawrence, "German Books: Thomas Mann," *Phoenix* (London: Heinemann, 1961), p. 312.

6. Thomas Mann, *Doctor Faustus*, trans. H. T. Lowe-Porter (New York: Knopf, 1948), pp. 248f.

7. Mann, p. 436.

8. Mann, p. 230.

9. Mann, pp. 242f.

10. Mann, p. 375.

11. Mann, p. 236.

12. André Gide, *Lafcadio's Adventures*, trans. Dorothy Bussy (Garden City: Anchor, 1953), p. 254.

13. *The Evergreen Reader*, ed. Barney Rosset (New York: Grove press, 1968), p. 473.

14. Albert Camus, *The Outsider* (*The Stranger*), trans. Stuart Gilbert (London: Hamish Hamilton, 1958), p. 67.

15. Camus, p. 118.

16. Bellow is not alone in his position. The general description of it applies to some considerable degree to Malamud, Ellison, Cheever, Morris, H. Gold, Stern, and others. The C. P. Snow group has certain clear affinities as well.

17. Gustave Flaubert, "An Aesthetic Mysticism," in *The Modern Tradition*, p. 198.

18. Stephen Spender, *The Struggle of the Modern* (Berkeley: University of California Press, 1965), p. 121.

19. "Notebooks," 1967 Gift, 5.17; draft of "Skepticism and the Depth of Life."

20. Saul Bellow, "Where Do We Go from Here: The Future of Fiction," *Michigan Quarterly Review* 1, 1 (Winter 1962) 27.

21. A paraphrase from an interview, *Paris Review* 36 (Winter, 1966): 54.

22. D. H. Lawrence, *The Plumed Serpent* (New York: Vintage, 1960), pp. 272, 275.

23. Saul Bellow, "The Creative Artist and His Audience," *Perspectives* (1954): 101.

24. Saul Bellow, *Dangling Man* (New York: Meridian, 1960), p. 9; further parenthetical page references will be preceded by *DM*. References from other Bellow works, and their respective abbreviations, will be from the Viking Press editions: *AM—The Adventures of Augie March* (1953); *SD—Seize the Day* (1956); *HRK—Henderson the Rain King* (1959); *H—Herzog* (1964); *MSP—Mr. Sammler's Planet* (1970); *HG—Humboldt's Gift* (1975).

25. One may recall Hemingway's praise of Flaubert, in *The Green Hills of Africa* (New York: Scribners, 1935), p. 70: "He was the one we believed in, loved without criticism."

26. Nina Steers, Interview with Saul Bellow, "Successor to Faulkner?" *Show* 4 (September 1964): 38.

27. Saul Bellow, "Literature," *The Great Ideas Today* (Chicago: Encyclopedia Britannica, Inc., 1963), pp. 173ff.

28. Similarly, Bellow, in his own person, attacks Arendt's view of the *nouveau roman* and Nathalie Sarraute's defense of it. Arendt concurs with the bald, dehumanized notion of narrative: "Man as such is or has become unknown so that it matters little to the novelists whom he chooses as his hero and less into what kind of surroundings he puts it" (*New York Review of Books*, 5 March 1964). "It" is right! Bellow answers that this state of affairs "may indicate also a terribly dangerous political condition, for of what has Dr. Arendt written so movingly if not the consequences of such interchangeability of persons? It is in Auschwitz that we see what an outlook can lead to." "Notebooks," C.3.29, "Bellow on Rosenberg on Bellow." Cf. Bellow, "A Comment on 'Form and Despair,' " *Location* I (Summer 1964): 10–12.

29. Saul Bellow, "A World Too Much With Us," *Critical Inquiry* 2, (Autumn 1975): 4.

30. Norman Mailer, *Advertisements for Myself*. (New York: Berkley Medallion, 1966), p. 238; further parenthetical reference will be preceded by *AdM*. References to other Mailer works and their respective abbreviations are from the following editions: *ND—The Naked and the Dead* (Signet, 1948); *AD—An American Dream* (Dell, 1970); *WV—Why Are We in Vietnam?* (Berkley Medallion, 1968); *AN—Armies of the Night* (Signet, 1968).

31. George Alfred Schrader, "Norman Mailer and the Despair of Defiance," *Yale Review* 51 (December 1961): 267.

32. Norman Mailer, *The Executioner's Song*, (Boston: Little Brown, 1979), p. 53.

33. Mailer writes, "The result for all too many patients is a diminution, a 'tranquilizing' of their most interesting qualities and vices" (*AdM*, p. 319, "White Negro"). Why "qualities and vices"? Why not "virtues and vices"? Are "virtues" unreal, obsolete?

34. Approaching the Pentagon the well-dressed Mailer deliberately transgresses by stepping over the low rope and running into the clear, "like a banker, gone ape" (*AN*, p. 151). Hey lookit Nawmin! He lets us know that he was being photographed for a British TV documentary. More fulsome is his concern, at the Patterson-Liston fight, with finding twelve movie stars (as in New York fight crowds). And Rojack's reverence for Shago—a Copa star! Indeed, the celebrated meeting between Mailer and Lowell is mostly glamour, for "he did not speak of his poetry (with which he was not conspicuously familiar)" (*AN*, p. 56).

35. Apropos of his forthcoming novel Mailer says, "Countries as gargantuan and godawful as Egypt did not deserve to dictate terms to one beleaguered Hebrew idea in the desert" (*The New York Times Book Review*, 27 July 1975, p. 2). Mailer's politics, writes the journalist, "appear to be those of Moses, or indeed of God." Without speculating as to God's politics, one can say that Mailer's are not the politics of Moses. Moses broke tablets but not to antinomian effect. (Moses did murder, but only in the most unbearably brutalized of circumstances.) D.J.'s comment on the Egyptian / Jewish axis is perhaps more characteristic of Mailer's interests: "like the asshole belonged to Egypt, man, and the penis was the slave of the Hebes and the Brews, for they got it girdled with a ring of blood fire" (*WV*, p. 7). Sublimation has its pyrotechnics, but, for D. J., when you come right down to it, there is nothing like a fleshpot.

Chapter 2. Saul Bellow and the example of Dostoevsky

1. Irving Howe, "Dostoevsky: *The Politics of Salvation*," in *Politics and the Novel* (New York: Meridian, 1957), p. 51.

2. V. S. Pritchett, review of Alfred Kazin's *Bright Book of Life*, in *New York Times Book Review*, 20 May 1973, p. 3.

3. Philip Rahv, "The Legend of the Grand Inquisitor," in *The Myth and the Powerhouse* (New York: Farrar, Straus and Giroux, 1965), p. 159.

4. Fyodor Dostoevsky, *The Idiot*, trans. Constance Garnett (New York: Modern Library, 1935), p. 208. Quotations from Dostoevsky's novels are from the Garnett translations (Modern Library editions, though the Garnett translations of Dostoevsky's *The Double* [hereafter cited as *D*] and *The Eternal Husband* [hereafter cited as *EH*] are in *The Short Novels of Dostoevsky* [New York: Dial Press, 1951]). For *Notes from Underground*, I have used the Matlaw translation (New York: Dutton, 1960). The Bellow editions from which I have quoted are as follows: *Dangling Man* (New York: Meridian, 1960); *The Victim* (New York: Signet NAL, 1965), hereafter cited as *V; The Dean's December* (New York: Harper & Row, 1982), hereafter cited as *DD;* all other quotations from Bellow are from the Viking editions of his works.

5. Saul Bellow, "Cloister Culture," *New York Times Book Review*, 10 July 1966, p. 45.

6. Dostoevsky, *The Brothers Karamazov* (1960), p. 300; hereafter cited as *BK*.

7. Dostoevsky, *The Possessed* (1959), p. 705.

8. *The Possessed*, p. 247.

9. *Notes from Underground*, p. xiii.

10. *Crime and Punishment* (1956), pp. 354f.

11. *Crime and Punishment*, p. 411.

12. *The Possessed*, p. 268.

13. Raymond Aron, *The Opium of the Intellectuals* (New York: Norton, 1962), p. 80.

14. *Aron*, p. 96.

15. *Aron*, p. 100.

16. R. W. B. Lewis, "Lionel Trilling and the New Stoicism," review of Lionel Trilling's *The Liberal Imagination*, in *Hudson Review* 3 (1950): 317.

17. *Herzog* (New York: Viking, 1964), p. 163.

18. Edward Shils, "Daydreams and Nightmares: Reflections on the Criticism of Mass Culture," *Sewanee Review* 65 (1957): 587–608 passim; "The Theory of Mass

314

Society," in *America as a Mass Society*, ed. Philip Olson (Glencoe: Free Press, 1963), pp. 30–47 passim; "Social Sciences and Law," in *Great Ideas Today* (Chicago: Encyclopedia Britannica, 1961), pp. 245–89 passim.

19. Shils, "The Concept and Function of Ideology," *International Encyclopedia of Social Science*, VII (New York: MacMillan and Free Press, 1968), 66–76 passim; "Ideology and Civility: On the Politics of the Intellectual," *Sewanee Review* 66 (1958): 450–80 passim.

20. Dennis Wrong, "Reflections on the End of Ideology," in *The End of Ideology Debate*, ed. Chaim L. Waxman (New York: Funk & Wagnalls, 1968), p. 123.

21. Bellow, unpublished Notebooks, C.2.7., p. 6, untitled draft for a lecture on the novel.

22. Dostoevsky, *The Diary of a Writer*, trans. Boris Brasol (New York: Scribner's, 1949), p. 787.

23. Philip Rahv, "Dostoevsky in *The Possessed*," in *Image and Idea* (Norfolk: New Directions, 1949), p. 90.

24. Nicholas Berdyaev, *Dostoevsky* (Cleveland/New York: Meridian, 1964), p. 25.

25. Berdyaev, p. 40.

26. Arnold Hauser, *The Social History of Art* (New York: Vintage, 1958), 4: 152.

27. George Steiner, *Tolstoy or Dostoevsky* (New York: Vintage, 1961), p. 154.

28. Rahv, "Dostoevsky in *The Possessed*," p. 101.

29. Herbert Gold, review of *Henderson the Rain King*, in *The Nation* 188 (21 February 1959): 172.

30. Berdyaev, p. 21.

31. Edward Wasiolek, *Dostoevsky: The Major Fiction* (Cambridge, Mass.: MIT Press, 1964), p. 54.

32. Berdyaev, p. 113.

33. The one mitigating factor in Pytor Verkovensky's dossier is his father's relationship to him as a child. Stepan Verkovensky, a caricature of the airy, literary, liberal, may think fondly of Pytor, "the fruit of our first still unclouded happiness," but on the death of his wife, as the MacAndrew translation has it, "the fruit of their happiness was immediately packed off to Russia and his education entrusted to some distant relative residing in a remote backwater" (*The Possessed* [New York: Signet NAL, 1962], p. 13). Similarly Fydor Karamazov disposes of his own, with results even more patricidal in intention. Though there seems to be no evidence of it, Dostoevsky may have wryly contemplated, in a book he knew well, the spectacle of western egotism in Rousseau's *Confessions*, a book whose self-analytical hero abandons his five children and goes on to write a book, a great book, about child rearing.

34. Konstantin Mochulsky, *Dostoevsky: His Life and Work*, trans. Michael A. Minihan (Princeton: Princeton University Press, 1973), pp. 623–4.

Introduction to Part II

1. John J. Enck, Interview with Saul Bellow, *Wisconsin Studies in Contemporary Literature* 6 (Summer 1965): 157.

2. Keith Botsford, Interview with Saul Bellow, "What's Wrong With Modern Fiction." *London Sunday Times*, 12 January 1975, p. 31.

3. Robert Robinson, Interview, "Saul Bellow at Sixty," *The Listener* 98 (13 February 1975):218.

4. Robinson, 219.

5. Letter to Mrs. Dew-Smith, *The Letters of Henry James*, ed. Percy Lubbock (New York: Charles Scribners, 1920), II:55.

6. Francis Steegmuller, *Flaubert and Madame Bovary*, (New York: Farrar Strauss, 1950), p. 284.

7. A. Walton Litz, *The Art of James Joyce*, (New York: Oxford, 1964), p. 8.

8. Litz, p. 31.

9. Litz, p. 36.

10. Litz, p. 9.

11. Robinson, p. 219.

12. Nina Steers, Interview with Saul Bellow, "Successor to Faulkner?" *Show* 4 (September 1964): 37.

13. Letter to the author, 15 January 1982.

14. Keith Cushman, "Mr. Bellow's *Sammler:* The Evolution of a Contemporary Text," in Stanley Trachtenberg, ed., *Critical Essays on Saul Bellow*, (Boston: G. K. Hall, 1979), p. 141.

15. Steers, p. 37.

16. Cushman, p. 141.

17. Cushman, p. 156.

Chapter 3. *The Adventures of Augie March*

1. Robert Penn Warren, "The Man With No Commitments," in Trachtenberg, p. 13.

2. "If we have to resort to German at all, I would suggest the more correct label of *Entwicklungsroman* because the emphasis in *Augie March* is decidedly not on Augie's encounter with objects of culture as it is in Goethe's *Wilhelm Meister*, the prototype of the *Bildungsroman*. No course in Western civilization or lifetime reading plan could satiate Augie's desire for experience . . . the measure of his growth remain[s] questionable as well. Augie is, more than an advocate of 'Bildung' and self-development, a champion of reality." Brigitte Scheer-Schäzler, *Saul Bellow* (New York: Ungar, 1972), p. 57. I agree with Scheer-Schäzler's terminological point and wish that both of these terms were common in the American critical vocabulary. Since they are not, I will defer to the common usage, keeping this distinction in mind.

3. The picaresque often projects harsh satire at the expense of society, so what the picaro resists is something more like destruction. The self-reliance of the picaro is typically a matter of necessity. The traditional picaresque hero might well jump at the chance offered by, say, the Renlings. Augie illustrates what might be called romantic picaresque, resisting the mainstream because he wants to, not because he has to. Many want to adapt Augie, not so the picaro; he is typically excluded, where Augie is often enough courted by conformity.

4. Richard Chase, *Walt Whitman Reconsidered* (London: Gollancz, 1955), p. 36.

5. There is a stray note indicating other ambitious plans for Augie. "Augie when he is a federalist missionary, runs into Mormon boys who are missionaries. Also J [sic] witnesses; anti-vivisectionists." There is no other mention of this anywhere in the extant manuscripts. Bellow adds, "Doesn't want to be what others want to make of him. Stendhal exceptional champion of this" (D.2.3).

6. In an unpublished letter to Lionel Trilling, 11 October 1953.

7. Lionel Trilling, introduction, *The Adventures of Augie March* (New York: Modern Library), p. 196.

8. In a fragment of what may be a scenario for an unpublished short story or, possibly, for a chapter in *Herzog*, Bellow puts Rousseau in an even more critical light: "He is a man that I could never stand if for no more than for the scene he leaves for himself, stubblefaced, milky, in a wig like hemp, weeping at his own opera performed before the monarch, encouraged by the weeping of the women and fancying he'd like to gobble their tears with his lips. Original sin is not always the same; but one lasts a few centuries. His has been ours." "A Visitor Decides to Steal a Photo of the Professor in a Jinnicksha" (B.1.20). Clearly, Rousseau's *Confessions* had a lasting impact on Bellow. The references in *Herzog* are, finally, more charitable.

9. Richard G. Stern, review of *Henderson the Rain King, Kenyon Review* 21, 3 (1959): 658.

10. Occasionally they seem piled-on rather than written, as in the excessive bulge of Trafton's Gym: "the liniment-groggy, flicketyrope-time, tin-locker-chasing, Loop-darkened rooms and the Polish, Italian, Negro, thump-muscled, sweat-glittering training-labor" (*AM*, p. 86). One cannot raise the hyphen to a metaphysical principle. Actually the manuscripts show a cutting down in the hyphenated catalogue and, even more, a cutting down of historical (and mythological) allusions. One may wonder how even in the final version an *ingenu* can have such ease of reference and often penetrating moral perception. The answer is that the narrative is retrospective, sometimes explicitly so.

11. Augie is the only character in Bellow innocent enough to be so compared, and, as my qualifications indicate, here is the exception in Bellow which proves the rule.

12. There are even linguistic echoes of Huck in Augie—"by and by" (p. 273), "I lit out" (p. 274), "ornery" (p. 372), "I reckon" (p. 457)—occasionally full-blown, as is Augie's awed description of Frazer (at his wedding): "He was a *mighty* attractive and ideal man . . . You couldn't *find a subject that stumped him* . . . You *got shivers* on the back and thrills *clear into* the teeth. I was *real proud* to have such a friend come" (*AM*, p. 490; italics mine). It's a long way from Pike County to Humboldt Park. In this instance the prose is merely derivative. The echoes become too strong, literary precedent a crutch, the Huck accent automatic. Some of the echoes are more spontaneous. Augie views the captured Gorman as Huck views the hounded Buck Grangerford or even the captured King and Duke: "I felt powerfully heartsick to see him" (*AM*, p. 165). And Augie, identifying a worker at the morgue, sees with the painful clarity of Huck looking at Boggs: "I recognized him, his black body rigid, as if he died in a fit of royal temper, making fists, feet out of shape, and crying something from the roof of his mouth, which I saw" (*AM*, p. 249). Augie is told that his girlfriend shot him and asks, "Have they caught her?" "Naw, they won't even look for her. They never do"—which is an updated version of "No'm, killed a nigger." In some of this one hears Sherwood Anderson as well.

13. Though there are a few chapters of *Augie March* in magazines, all are close to the novel and show no changes of any consequence. In her bibliography, Marianne Nault (who is generally accurate) describes the chapter called "The Eagle" (*Harper's Bazaar* 87, February 1953) as an early draft. It is, however, late or close to the novel, simply a fusing of two of its chapters.

Chapter 4. *Seize the Day*

1. Ihab Hassan, *Radical Innocence* (Princeton: Princeton University Press, 1961), pp. 315f.

2. Keith Opdahl, *The Novels of Saul Bellow* (University Park: Pennsylvania State University Press, 1967), p. 98.

3. The *Seize the Day* manuscripts are in the Humanities Research Center of the University of Texas library, randomly catalogued and not numbered. I have numbered them according to the order in which they appeared in the microfilm sent to me. Since this is not an even approximate chronological order, I have given a general description of them, including chronological notes. In addition, each manuscript will be identified as "early," "middle" or "late." In the cases of 3 and 5, the manuscript is not single, but fragmented, and duly noted as such.

1   Middle. Typescript. Bears title *Here and Now—Here and Now*, forty-five pages.

2   Early. Holograph. Earliest version, bears title *One of Those Days*, twenty-seven pages.

3   Early. Holograph. Later than 2, but much like it. Bears title *One of Those Days*, thirty-seven pages.

3a   Middle. Holograph. Bears title *Seize the Day (One of Those Days)* Part of Venice episode, not continuous with 3, twenty-four pages. Later than 1.

4   Middle. Typescript. Essentially like 1, but later. Bears title *Here and now—here and now*, thirty-eight pages.

5   Late. Typescript. Bears title *Seize the Day*. Very close to book. (pp. 1–9, 19–30, 70–115.)

5a   Early, Earlier than 1, later than 3. (pp. 50–75.)

5b   Middle. (pp. 45–46.)

5c   Late. Later than 5. Closer to final version. (pp. 94–126,) (134–143.) The *Partisan Review* version comes just after this—they are nearly identical—and is even closer.

5d   Middle. Later than 1. pp. 129–133.

5e   Late. Before 5c. pp. 50–56, 10, 51, 90, 91, 94.

6   Late. Typescript. Bears title *Seize the Day*. Earlier than 5, later than 1 and 9, seventy-one pages.

7   V. S. Pritchett review of *Herzog*.

8   Early. Typescript. Much like 2, just later. Bears title *Here and Now—Here and Now*, sixty-one pages.

9   Middle. Typescript. Much like 1 but later. Bears title *Here & Now—Here & Now!*, eighty-five pages.

Note: the *SD* manuscripts have been recatalogued since I wrote the above. Anyone wishing to check references may consult the microfilm originally sent to me, which is in possession of the University of Texas library.

4. Daniel Weiss, "Caliban on Prospero: A Psychoanalytic Study of the Novel *Seize the Day*, by Saul Bellow," in Irving Malin, ed., *Psychoanalysis and American Fiction* (New York: Dutton, 1965), pp. 279–307.

5. An occasional harsh edge in Wilhelm is expunged in revision, making his unattractive qualities essentially a matter of victimization, not pride, and leaving the way open for something like generosity of response on his part. So, for example, when he tells Perls that he could have handled all of the Rojax territory once assigned

to him, Bellow writes in an early version (2), "He sounded cold and arrogant and vain looks filled his heavy, unhealthy face." This is deleted.

6. Weiss, p. 297. What follows in this paragraph is a summary of Weiss's argument.

7. John J. Clayton, *Saul Bellow: In Defense of Man* (Bloomington: Indiana University Press, 1968), p. 70.

8. This Shelleyan trope is treated more gingerly by the self-analytic Herzog. Cf. *Herzog*, pp. 206f.

9. There is a similar scene in *Herzog* where the central character notices that the subway turnstile is polished by hips. "From this arose a feeling of communion— brotherhood in one of its cheapest forms. . . . The more individuals are destroyed (by processes such as I know) the worse their yearning for collectivity." This remark has a Nietzschean thrust. Not so in *Seize the Day*, where skepticism is parried by wish. Is the intellectual above such longings for *Bruderschaft?* Herzog sees it as a form of false consciousness. Those who have the lust for such communion "return to the mass agitated, made fervent by their failure. Not as brethren, but as degenerates. Experiencing a raging consumption of potato love. Thus occurs a second distortion of the divine image" (*H*, p. 176). He is not being metaphorical, but takes this phrase relating to divinity as seriously as Blake, from whose poem of that title it is taken. Brotherhood remains for him "the most real question." The sentiment Herzog expresses is a typically hard-headed, liberal revisionist (now often called neo-conservative) one. He is an altogether more tough-minded character than Wilhelm. He, too, one may recall, is refused money by his father in a very tense scene, but later thinks that "the old man in his near-demented way was trying to act out the manhood you should have had" (*H*, p. 250). Manhood Herzog has. And Wilhelm? In another interesting parallel, Herzog notes that at his mother's funeral, "How Willie cried in the chapel! It was his brother Willie, after all, who had the tender heart" (*H*, p. 235). Tenderness Wilhelm has in abundance.

10. Erich Fromm, *The Art of Loving* (New York: Harper, 1956), p. 47.

11. Fromm, pp. 42f.

12. Fromm, p. 48.

13. Fromm, p. 26.

14. Weiss, p. 280.

15. Weiss, p. 304.

16. Keith Opdahl, *The Novels of Saul Bellow* (University Park: Pennsylvania State University Press, 1967), p. 108.

17. "Here and Now" was an early title of the book.

18. In the earliest version, the dialogue took an explicitly Reichian turn. Tamkin notes that "people all believe bad things about their own selves when they feel the bad effects of muscular, nervous waste products—bodies with neurotic muscles, character-armoring. They can't hear, feel, taste, smell or see." In addition to not being dramatically right, this apparently seemed too obviously Reichian and was cut, though his description of businessmen spreading "the plague" is a Reichian metaphor that was not cut. Tamkin's wonderful poem, which expresses the submerged "moral" of the story, while it is at the same time a parody of feeling, is a "found" poem in a literal sense. The poem appears verbatim (and in the handwriting described in *Seize the Day*) in the miscellaneous notes of C.3.33.

19. Since beginnings are always important, it is worth noting the transformations of the opening sentence itself. From the early "To look at Tommy Wilhelm, you

would never guess what a bad time he was having but when a man is smoking a cigar it is hard to know what he feels" (2) to the middle "Tommy Wilhelm believed that he was not less capable than the next man when it came to concealing his troubles" (1, 1) we see a heightening of irony and a more dramatic focus on Wilhelm's point of view. The final version, "When it came to concealing his troubles, Tommy Wilhelm was not less capable than the next fellow" (*SD*, p. 1), underscores the irony by reversal and by getting the timing just right.

20. M. Gilbert Porter, "The Scene as Image: A Reading of *Seize the Day*," in *Saul Bellow*, ed. Earl Rovit (Englewood Cliffs: Prentice-Hall, 1975), p. 54.

21. Porter, p. 70.

22. Porter, p. 62.

23. Porter, pp. 59, 57, 63, 56.

Chapter 5. *Henderson the Rain King*

1. Tony Tanner, *Saul Bellow*, (London: Oliver & Boyd, 1965), p. 85.

2. Robert Alter, "The Stature of Saul Bellow," *Midstream* 1, 4 (December 1964): 10.

3. Norman Mailer, *Cannibals and Christians* (New York: Dell, 1966), p. 127.

4. Richard Chase, "The Adventures of Saul Bellow," *Commentary* 27 (April 1959): 329.

5. Alter, p. 10.

6. Nina Steers, Interview with Saul Bellow, "Successor to Faulkner?" *Show* 4 (September 1964): 38.

7. There is one early fragment that shows "Eugene Nail Hendrickson" looking neither remarkable nor gargantuan. He is "not a very attractive man . . . stringy dark-faced and plain." So there is no triangle. Here Henderson is a cameraman and goes to Africa (C.3.22).

8. Letter to Richard G. Stern, 3 November 1959. Bellow explicitly acknowledges some Blakean influence in *Henderson* (as he does in the novel itself by quoting him). He writes, "Last night, reading Blake, the lost children and especially The Little Girl Lost, I began to suspect he must have sunk deeply into my unconscious. Add innocence (the second innocence) per experience, passing by way of lions." In the poem mentioned, the earth rises from sleep and seeks its "maker meek." It is not, however, Blake's peaceable kingdom which Bellow employs in the climactic lion's den scenes. ("The Little Girl Lost" first appears as a poem in "Innocence" but is later transferred to "Experience" for reasons too complicated to go into here.) Another use of Blake (in B.5.6) occurs in Henderson's lament on the state of painting: "No self-respecting artist does portraits any more. The human form divine has gone out, hasn't it! . . . Such war on all that defined a human being in past ages has not yet been seen." Blake again represents the possibility of traditional nobility. Since the picture-motif is, in the final version, an occasion for ironic knocks at bourgeois narcissism, the Blakean aspect of portraiture is dropped; also dropped, partly for its tonal solemnity, is a rather severe condemnation of portraiture as illustrative of upper class degeneracy.

Irvin Stock points to possible echoing of Blake. Plate No. 9 of Blake's "The Gates of Paradise" shows a man starting to climb a ladder to the distant moon. The caption is "I want, I want." The poem introducing the drawing begins, "Mutual Forgiveness of each Vice / Such are the Gates of Paradise." In the introduction to "Jerusalem"

Blake writes, "The Spirit of Jesus is continual forgiveness: he who waits to be righteous before he enters into the Saviour's kingdom . . . will never enter there." Irvin Stock, "The Novels of Saul Bellow," *Southern Review* 3 (January 1967): 33n. For the Jew, though not for Henderson, righteousness first is required.

9. The anthropological detail of the Arnewi section is derived in good part from Melville J. Herskovitz's "The Cattle Complex in East Africa" (Ph.D. dissertation, Columbia University). Herskovitz taught Bellow anthropology, and Bellow has spoken of his former professor's bemused reaction to the novel. The love attachment to cows, the tribal names beginning with A and W (or B) and other details derive from this study. Selectively, Bellow omits such practices as Masai cattle raids as contrary to his artistic intention. See Eusebio Rodrigues, "Bellow's Africa," *American Literature* 43, 2 (May 1971): 242–256 for an essay on sources for *Henderson*, including books by Rev. John Roscoe, Sir Richard Burton, Herskovitz, and others.

10. The aim of Shelley's poem is to lift the gloom of faded revolutionary hopes. The relevant stanzas of the dedication, presented to Mary Wollstonecroft Shelley, follow:

> Thoughts of great deeds were mine, dear Friend, when first
> The clouds which wrap this world from youth did pass
> I do remember well the hour which burst
> My spirit's sleep: a fresh May-dawn it was,
> When I walked forth upon the glittering grass,
> And wept, I know not why; until there rose
> From the near school-room, voices, that alas!
> Were but one echo from a world of woes—
> The harsh and grating strife of tyrants and of foes.
>
> And then I clasped my hands and looked around—
> —But none was near to mock my streaming eyes,
> Which poured their warm drops on the sunny ground—
> So without shame, I spake: —"I will be wise,
> And just, and free, and mild, if in me lies
> Such power, for I grow weary to behold
> The selfish and the strong still tyrannize
> Without reproach or check." I then controlled
> My tears, my heart grew calm, and I was meek and bold.

Buxton Forman believes this to be a reference to school life at Sion House, Brentford, where Shelley, teased by other boys, imagines romantic alternatives; "nothing that my tyrants knew or taught / I cared to learn," writes the poet. Though he experiments with and then discards other parts of these lines as well (cf. B.8.6, 94; B.6.18, 159; B.9.2, 20), Bellow's use of the quotation scarcely relates to the Shelleyan context. Shelley did, however, have more than a passing interest for Bellow at the time of the composition of *Henderson;* witness a quotation from Symonds (written as a note in B.6.10) which does have a rarefied connection to his central character: "Loving, innocent, sensitive, strangely moralized after a peculiar and inborn type of excellence, drawing his inspiration from his own soul in solitude, Shelley passed across the stage of this world, attended by a splendid vision which sustained him at a perilous height above the kindly race of men."

11. Much of the lurid, ceremonial detail of early drafts, in both the Wariri and Arnewi sections, is dropped because of its insufficient dramatic relevance. The

former anthropology student comes to check his wandering concern for local color (e.g., B.6.15, fasting, sacrifices, symbolic pouring of oil on one King Ullo).

12. And his vocabulary made more formal or African-formal, as early colloquialism is removed: "sure thing" (B.7.2) becomes "why certainly": "you have to go with them" (B.5.5), "they require your attendence" (*HRK*, p. 197): "becomes the," "occupies, in consequence, a position of" (*HRK*, p. 196). In one early version (B.5.5), after Henderson insists on paying off the bet with a painting, Dahfu says, "Don't lose any sleep over it." Conversely, Henderson's speech is often modified to the more colloquial, e.g., "be taken away from me" (B.7.2) and "go bust" (*HRK*, p. 212).

13. The Gmilo theme presents a dramatic problem. How can such a civilized man go along with all that mumbo-jumbo? Such consciousness is beyond literal fundamentalism. One early version has Dahfu saying, absurdly, to Henderson, "I am aware, Sungo, that these are false superstitions—but they are more than that. They are also enigmatic forms of what I believe" (B.6.10). This weak expression of poetized religion or mythic sense is not, however, present in the novel. Elsewhere in manuscript we see Dahfu's disciple lamenting, "After all, he *is* a savage" (B.5.10), or saying (punningly?) to the relentless Bunam, "So you killed his father. . . . It was a primitive error. He will forgive it. Why can't you change." (B.5.8) The only dramatic advantage to the sequence is that Henderson can see a man face death with equanimity.

14. Letter to Jascha Kessler, 21 February 1961.

15. Paul Schilder, *The Image and Appearance of the Human Body* (New York: International Universities Press, 1950), p. 9. All subsequent citations of Schilder are from this book.

16. Eusebio Rodrigues, "Reichianism in *Henderson the Rain King*," *Criticism* 15, 3 (Summer 1973): 212–233.

17. Letter to Kessler.

18. Apropos of this sentiment, in an early draft (B.5.3), Henderson addresses an imaginary letter in a curious anticipation of the epistolary Herzog:

> Dear Mr. Dulles
> Inasmuch as many Americans are in the same spiritual plight I may in some sense be said to have made this journey in the service of national interests.

19. The two sections of *Henderson the Rain King* published in magazines, though duplicative of manuscript material, are worthy of note. The first (*Hudson Review* 11, Spring 1958) contains much of Henderson's final language and speech rhythm. It covers from pp. 1–24 and 38–40 of the novel, Chapters I–IV; episodes about the violin, Brother Dick, Old Lady Lenox, Lilly courting Henderson, the Sevcik exercises, and Ricey and her child are not included. The second published section (*Botteghe Oscure* 21, 1958) is a draft of chapters XI–XIII. It contains no frog explosion, no broken bridgework, no allusion to Grenfell or the cloud experiments reported in *Scientific American*. There are frequent verbal changes made after this version, often for greater concretion but, above all, in the Africanizing of Dahfu's English from one that is conventional and flat. Though the actual ritual which will bring on Dahfu's demise and successor is not given, it is clear that he is a doomed man. There is a sense of mistrust and intrigue between Dahfu and Henderson here, yet Henderson clearly loves the chieftan. Henderson fears that some harm may be done to himself by Dahfu's wives during the rain ceremony. He is not as buoyantly admiring of Dahfu as he is in the novel, nor is he yet given to the Romantic view of creation (though he does quote Marvel on resemblance). Deleted from the novel is a long speech on the degeneracy of his class and the cynicism of government.

Chapter 6. *Herzog*

1. In the Steers interview, which appeared shortly after *Herzog* came out, Bellow said that he thought it was his best book: "Its scale is larger. The mind of the hero is more complete" (Steers, p. 38). One should add that Bellow tends to judge his books most generously at the time of publication. He has had little reason to back off from his claim here.

2. Tony Tanner, *Saul Bellow* (London: Oliver & Boyd, 1965), p. 89.

3. Alfred Kazin, *Bright Book of Life* (New York: Dell, 1971), p. 134.

4. On the way to this elevation he is, variously, an ethnologist (B.17.4) or the author of a textbook called *Contemporary Humanities* (B.18.17).

5. Concerned with some possible ambiguity in this formulation, I asked Bellow for a clarification to which he responded: "Real ideas transform, electrify. In the intellectual world people trade in ideas for worldly profit. The men advance their careers, the women add them to their attractions, making themselves more exciting. Just more Dior or Helena Rubenstein." (in a letter dated "Jerusalem May 24 77"). I have, therefore, left my original description unchanged.

6. In a draft of the essay, "Skepticism and the Depth of Life," Bellow attacks Valéry for his typically modernist, and in some ways typically French, disregard for the realities of ordinary life, in words that are like those of his later attack on Nathalie Sarraute. "In speaking of a degree of liberation in which we approach weightlessness and final detachment I was thinking of Valéry's dislike of the demonstrative, of his rejection of character traits, of his opposition, shared by many, to the theatre of the soul, the drama of personality, the exaggeration and overvaluation of eccentricities— the being tired, in short, of our human carrying on. . . . The desire to get away from so many human states may arise from desire to purify the conscious intellect, to increase its power. But it may also contain an element of self-dislike. It may be the most contemporary form of misanthropy" (1967 Gift Box 5.17, 23). The relevant quotation on Saurrate: "Miss Saurrate wants the real, the authentically *real*, not Goethe's 'the beautiful, the good, the true,' but just some tiny, undiluted, undistorted factual matter. . . . I strongly suspect that the hunger for essences—an intellectual hunger—the rejection of 'secondary' attributes, irrelevancies, accidents, distractions, conceal [sic] an intense hostility toward the world." Here, too, is the preference for the older Romantic moral nexus of Goethe, even to the point of moral abstraction. Bellow adds, in what is a critique of Arendt's defense of Sarraute, "It may be that I could not accept Dr. Arendt's portrait of Eichmann, could not believe it, precisely because it was lacking in secondary characteristics" (C.3.29, Bellow on Rosenberg on Bellow).

7. This relaxed description, the inclusion of details for its own sake, must be worked through in the revisions. Excluded from the novel are two local color references to Succoth, the Feast of Tabernacles. In one, we see red-bearded Mr. Gottheil, the tailer, "dressed in a cutaway and opera hat" near his *succah*. From the back porch his wife lowers his dinner in a bucket. "He will eat it in his tabernacle, and perhaps sleep there, to earn a great *mitzva*." Then the narrator adds in an elevated note that in itself would be consonant with the novel, "I cannot help but feel the great power obtained from tradition and from the Bible by these people. One does not have to be an orthodox or even a believing Jew to grasp this power, this essential and deep humanity which sustain [sic] itself in such a setting" (B.17.7). A fine moral. Yet the uncertainty of tone even in the revision is such that the other Succoth allusion takes us in a very different direction. The observant shoemaker Maslansky sleeps in

the *succah* to get a vision of God. A practical joker, young Bogin, calls to him in the middle of the night, "Avrahom." Maslansky wakes up saying, "Hineni! Here is your servant Maslansky." Bogin says, "Well, tuck up your whiskers and kiss my ass" (B.21.2, 156f).

8. Much comes to light in the revisions by way of minor characters. It is worth looking at the metamorphosis of one of these to get a more precise view of the richness of the whole cloth. Valdepenas, the cabbie, will do as an illustration. In his earliest incarnation, he is an anonymous cabbie who advises Herzog not to lose any sleep over the bums who wipe the windshield (B.17.5). Next we see him as Teddy, speaking more vivid Newyorkese: "I'll tell you a coincident" (B.17.9). He is not yet the aggressive, sexual Teodoro Valdepenas of the later versions. The name itself, like so many in the book, gets at the essence of the character, at once an actual Spanish name and a mock-Latin version of "heroic phallus." By B.21.13 we see him combing his thick hair and grooming his little moustache, recognizing Herzog as the older guy who kissed that young-looking chick and interposing some of his own wisdom on the subject. "I broke up with a sixteen year old broad last week. I come in, she's reading a book. I say, 'Baby, listen, with Teddy you don't read books.' I slapped the book out of her hand," a macho gesture that stands in sharp contrast to Herzog's fumbling with his Tikhon-Zadonsky-reading wife. Not that this is the solution. When the girl says, "Okay so let's get it over with" (B.21.13, 280), he assures her that Teddy's gonna take his time. In the novel it is, more realistically, a magazine, and his retort to the girl is spicier: "In my hack, that's where I hurry. You ought to get a punch in the teeth for talkin' like that." He concludes to an astonished Herzog, "A broad eighteen don't even know how to shit" (*H*, p. 223). Valdepenas, a Puerto Rican who knows some Yiddish (the fat guys who pay the window cleaning bums "shiver in their pupick"), some genteel phraseology (it finally comes out just right—"You know, I think I got a coincident to tell you"), and, of course, street talk ("Keep sockin' away, Doc") is an example of that New York candor which Herzog finds so striking. Each of the paren- thetical examples appears in the late B.22.5, 267ff., showing again how Bellow often saves the best, or most memorably formulated, for last.

9. The Sono episode, like the Napoleon Street sequence, appears in a fragment which apparently antedates the manuscripts of the novel. In *Don Juan's Marriage* the names are Kikiku and Bryer. There is a womb-bath, and Bryer considers marrying Kikiku.

10. Fyodor Dostoevsky, *Notes from Underground* (New York: Dutton, 1960), p. 23.

11. Dostoevsky, p. 31.

12. Ihab Hassan, *Radical Innocence* (Princeton: Princeton University Press, 1961).

13. "Nietzsche Contra Wagner," *Viking Portable Nietzsche*, ed. and trans. Walter Kaufman (New York: Viking Press, 1964), p. 663. All subsequent references to Nietzsche will be from this volume and cited in the essay as *VPN*.

14. There is some question as to the accuracy of this label as Herzog applies it to himself. Analysts I have spoken to seem to think that this describes a state more severely alienated than any Herzog inhabits.

15. Blake, "The Four Zoas", *Selected Poetry and Prose of Blake*, ed. Northrop Frye (New York: Modern Library, 1953), p. 236.

16. Elsewhere, Herzog's references to Nietzsche are not so balanced or "cheer- ful." In an early draft of the Strawforth letter, he writes that "Whitehead, Ortega and Nietzsche are the modern writers who deal with risk. This is nothing but the social Darwinism on which many writers, notably Bernard Shaw, blame the disasters of this

century" (B.18.12, 37b). Again, an uncomplimentary reference: "Curious how the Continental disdain of British genius as lacking in original conceptions betrays ideological disorders—Nietzsche's contempt for Darwin's mind is an example" (B.18.12, 141). Finally, and most critical of all: "You never hear me crying out about the decay and degradation of the highest values. Like a Nietzsche or a Burckhardt or a Henry Adams, or any of those Christian Fatalists or two-bit prophets of doom, who call themselves Royalists, Classicists, Aristocrats" (B.21.29). Here he simply links Nietzsche, for whom he has much admiration, to the strain of modernism for which he has no admiration at all.

17. A few of the *Herzog* "stories" deserve notice (others are too close to the novel). The *Saturday Evening Post* story (237, August 1964), a selection that is *ersatz* since it focuses on plot highlights, has the virtue of pivoting around the central scene. Two more authentic sections appeared in *Esquire*. The first (56, July 1961) is an early version of the trip to the Vineyard and includes the Miss Thurnwald incident. It is all told in the third person, with letters. Compared to the final version the style is flat; things are told rather than dramatized. We are told, for example, that he bought clothing to forget his second divorce. There is no tension in the men's shop, no New York enervation as such. We are told that he does not want to see Juliana's mother because "we'd be confronting each other like a pair of losers; I don't want to be in your psychological category" (p. 118). Similarly, he leaves the Vineyard (after an overnight), not because of any dramatic change in consciousness as in the novel, but because "he realized the Vineyard was not a good place for writing letters." The tone is placid. And Herzog is not as hard either. Broken up over his second divorce (he has two sons here) he almost cries. This is one of the drafts in which Herzog finds aphorisms in a woman's hand and joins in the game. The selection shows how conscious Herzog is at an early stage of the limitations of subjectivity in this novel of subjectivity. After noting that his isolation is "very funny" because he argues with himself, he adds, in a letter to Dr. Bhave, that man "is not likely to be free by himself." And he says in reference to a letter to Tolstoy, after a man "has declared himself king of infinite space inside his own nutshell, he becomes insidiously sickened by what he has done. A reality of his own creation makes him ill" (130). The *Esquire* piece called "A Letter to Dr. Edvig" (60, July 1963) is later, though all but the final part of the Edvig letter in the novel (*Herzog*, pp. 53–65) is here in dialogue. The final part, of course, contains that fine crescendo of pain (on which certain verbal refinements are later made). Much of the novel's dialogue and description of Herzog is not yet present, particularly the idea parts (e.g., Herzog on charity). Nor is there mention of Mady's big, dusty books or Gersbach's Hadassah connection. With the insistent *I* coming through the expanded letter of the novel itself, Herzog's desperation is more intensely expressed. The dialogue in the *Esquire* version is given more or less as summary event. The most remarkable structural difference in this version is the placement of the scene in which Mady announces her intention to divorce Herzog as he puts the storm windows in. Coming near the beginning of the novel (*Herzog*, pp. 8–11), it is here placed between the second and third to last paragraphs of the selection. (This would be *Herzog*, p. 64.) Certain advantages are gained in the change. The crescendo of the Edvig letter is uninterrupted, and, more importantly, the painful comedy of the wound itself is given at the beginning, stunningly, where Herzog's wound is still most tender. The entire scene is rewritten, including the following changes: there is a switch from first to third person, more suitable to comic victimization; there is a much greater focus on Mady; there is a much greater focus on sado-masochism; the Edvig comedy is diminished (the idea that divorce may be right

as therapy but wrong as religion); and Valentine-style hypocrisy is deleted (Mady says, "Try to understand Moses . . . what a failure this has represented to me. *Years of my life.*" Herzog answers, "I'm sorry about that." p. 104).

Chapter 7. *Herzog,* the intellectual milieu

1. Robert G. Olson, *An Introduction to Existentialism* (New York: Dover, 1962), p. 32.
2. Lionel Abel, *Metatheatre* (New York: Hill and Wang, Dramabook, 1963), pp. 140f.
3. Naomi Lebowitz, *Humanism and the Absurd in the Modern Novel* (Evanston: Northwestern University Press, 1971), p. 13.
4. Quoted by Olson, p. 29.
5. Jean-Paul Sartre, *Being and Nothingness,* trans. Hazel E. Barnes (New York: Philosophical Library, 1956), p. 615.
6. Jean-Paul Sartre, *Nausea,* trans. Lloyd Alexander (Norwalk: New Directions, n.d.), pp. 154f. Subsequent citations will be designated by the abbreviation *N* in the text.
7. John Bayley, "By Way of Mr. Sammler," *Salmagundi* 30 (1975): 24.
8. T. E. Hulme, *Speculations* (New York: Harcourt, Brace, Harvest Book, n.d.), p. 33. Subsequent citations will be designated by the abbreviation *S* in the text. All quotes are from "Humanism." pp. 3–71 or "Romanticism and Classicism," pp. 113–140.
9. Lionel Trilling, introd. *The Princess Cassimassima* (New York: Macmillan, 1948), pp. IXf.
10. Arthur A. Cohen, *The Myth of the Judeo-Christian Tradition* (New York: Schocken, 1971), p. 77.
11. Cohen, p. 78.
12. Cohen, p. 81.
13. John R. Harrison, *The Reactionaries* (New York: Schocken, 1967), p. 183.
14. T. S. Eliot, *After Strange Gods* (London: Faber and Faber, 1934), p. 29.
15. Eliot, p. 42.
16. Eliot, p. 48.
17. Eliot, p. 62.
18. Hulme, p. 53.
19. Ortega y Gasset, *The Dehumanization of Art and other Essays* (Garden City: Doubleday Anchor Books, 1956), p. 23.
20. Ortega, p. 28.
21. Robert Boyers et al., "Literature and Culture: An Interview with Saul Bellow," *Salmagundi* 30 (1975): 23.
22. Philip Rieff, *Freud: The Mind of the Moralist* (New York: Viking, 1959), p. 319.
23. Rieff, p. 321.
24. Rieff, p. 322.
25. *The Complete Works of Montaigne,* ed. and trans. Donald M. Frame (Stanford: Stanford University Press, 1957), p. 856.
26. Boyers, p. 9.
27. The motto was not kept by Blake because it worked against unification of the two works.

Chapter 8. *The Last Analysis*

1. Robert Brustein, *Seasons of Discontent* (London: Jonathan Cape, 1966), p. 173.

2. Harold Clurman, *The Naked Image* (New York: MacMillan, 1966), p.46.

3. Nina Steers, Interview with Saul Bellow, "Successor to Faulkner?" *Show*, 4 (September 1964): 38.

4. Saul Bellow, *The Last Analysis* (New York: Viking, 1965), p. VII. All other quotations are from this edition and will be parenthetically designated in the text. Manuscript pagination will be given when available.

5. The actual inspiration for show-biz-celebrity-turned-Freudian-apostle, Bellow once told me, was Artie Shaw, the clarinetist. The first draft of the preface comes a bit closer to him: "I have been especially stirred by jazz musicians, prizefighters and television comics who put on the philosopher's mantle. I find them especially touching. In the tumult of Birdland they are thinking of Kierkegaard. They are preoccupied with Freud and Ferenczi, with Rollo May and Erik Erikson" (B.12.10).

6. Bummidge's strategy for lifting the veil has precedents in the history of psychoanalysis. It was known for a long time, Clara Thompson tells us, that hyponosis could "regress" patients to whatever age desired—one, three, seven—to get to emotions unmodified by later developments. In a further development it was Ferenczi rather than Freud who encouraged his patients to dramatize. "This seems to have developed," writes Thompson, "from the idea that the patient was to re-live his childhood with, as it were, a better parent. So he encouraged the patient to act as if, for instance, he were three years old, even to the point of talking 'baby talk' or playing with dolls, etc. In this the analyst would participate by treating the patient like a three-year old." Clara Thompson, *Psychoanalysis: Evolution and Development* (New York: Grove Press, 1950), p. 186. She cites similar work by Moreno and J. Rosen.

7. Some manuscripts contain Bummidge's idea for a TV script that offers a popular version of the announced theme: "A father and his son. The father wants the son to be the receptacle of his love. The son does not want it." It is the son's birthday. He already has everything—cameras, guns, binoculars, sporting goods, geiger counters, electric guitars, an old submarine, a bulldozer. "We sacrifice everything for your sake," says the father. "The lining is falling out of Mother's mouton coat. There are so many holes in my underpants that in the morning I don't know where to put my foot through. . . . We want you to be happy. We were deprived in our childhood. I had to peddle papers and came home with numb fingers. I hunted for toys in ashcans." Father offers son a helicopter, but he can't land it on the roof. "That's where I keep the solar batteries you gave me last Xmas," says sonny. Father offers a cyclotron, and ICBM—offers, finally to have himself crucified. "Love and suffering," he says. "That's the only ending." The television people, with some justification, think that "this is the end of Bummidge on commercial TV" (B.13.1, 28–35).

8. Bummidge does say, "The little infant shows me the way. All impulse. Impulse is the soul of freedom," a Romantic but hardly a Freudian insight (*LA*, p. 70). This is one of a number of vatic utterances Bellow smiles at.

9. *Do It Yourself* is an early title (B.12.7, 19). Other titles are *The Upper Depths* (B.13.3); *Know Thyself* (B.13.4); *Bummidge* (B.14.2); *In a Beautiful World (or off the couch by Christmas)* (B.14.6); *Crash Program* (B.14.17). *The Last Analysis* was one of the early titles (B.13.12). The locale of the play shifts from Central Park

South (too rich) to Central Park West (better) to a loft in a warehouse on the West Side (perfectly seedy).

10. In another version the superego is associated with both parents, who always wanted him "to be thirty years old. I should be a bachelor of steady habits. I should wear long underwear winter and summer. I should sing like Chaliapin. Gargle. Part my hair in the middle. Have clean fingernails. Bring home my whole paycheck. Honor my Father and my Mother. Speak when spoken to and leave no odors. Always lose to Papa at Casino. Sit in the synagogue all day on the holidays. Have no genitals" (B.13.10, 31f.).

11. Philip Rieff, *Freud: The Mind of the Moralist* (New York: Viking, 1959), p. 343.

12. The revisions show Bummidge discussing his troubled dreams with the "analyst" from the beginning. "If you were not sick," says the "analyst" in an early version, "you would be unwell. Everybody is sick. . . . You can be just a little too sick—too oral, too anal, too, too. . . . You must seek adult genitility." Bummidge replies, "That's not what Dr. Brown says" (B.12.5). The utopian neo-Freudians are left out of *The Last Analysis:* orthodoxy is enough of a utopianism there. The "analyst" is trying to interpret a dream which is present in many manuscripts. Bummidge is standing on a stepladder in a swimming pool or body of water, sometimes carrying a blazing torch, when an old man with a beard floats by on his back. "A beard indicates a father, but the water is generally amniotic fluid—the womb," says the tentative "analyst" (B.12.5) in a reading of Freudian symbolism which the final version retains. Usually the "analyst" has more to say. For example, "Maybe, Mr. Bummidge, you want to rise above your fathers. Maybe you have gone as high as you can on the ladder" (B.12.4). In one version the dream is prefaced by Leonardo DaVinci telling him, "Why don't you make a stained-glass suit?" (B.12.2, 6). The "swimming pool is the womb," says the "analyst." "Leonardo is a father figure. The suit is your exhibitionistic tendency. The blow torch is your Prometheus tendency. You want to get higher than your father, that's the stepladder. Ambition. By analyzing yourself you want to bring light to the world" (B.12.2, 6). Another version holds that rising no higher on the ladder "means you recognize a limit to your ambitions" (B.13.4). Clear enough? Other versions show a somewhat different interpretation. Mott tells Bummidge, "Well, obviously, the stepladder is the legs of the mother and the water is the birth fluid" (B.13.12, 14). Or even: "What's the stepladder trying to tell me," wonders Bummidge. "A pair of legs. They fold in and out" (B.13.1 I, 10). Perhaps Mott and Bummidge are not as skillful in symbol interpretation as the "analyst." In any case, Bellow is having a good time with this patently Pop set of symbols. The final version cuts down on the details of the dream while it emphasizes its opaque quality. "I found myself in a swimming pool, not swimming, not wet. An old gentleman with a long beard floats by. Such a long white beard, and rosy cheeks," says Bummidge. To which the "analyst" responds, "The material is quite mixed. Water stands for the amniotic body of waters. A beard refers to the father figure" (*LA*, p. 26). His earlier dream of "a male with breasts" is even more of a caricature of Bummidge's sexual ambivalence (*LA*, p. 12). A fragment of this earlier dream gives a good example of Bellow's verbal glitter. "The pig turned into a huge fellow" becomes "The pig squirmed and writhed like a living knockwurst and turned into a huge fellow" (B.13.2, 13). "Living knockwurst" changes to "phantom knockwurst" (B.12.10), and we have the essential verbal savvy of the final version (*LA*, p. 12).

13. The *Partisan Review* version of the play, an early one, begins in this way. It

contains two acts, two scenes in each. All of the material is in manuscripts, often verbatim (e.g., Act I, scene 1 and B.13.3, I, 1), though not in the order of the play. Bummidge is here more of the wheeler-dealer than he is in the later versions. He bribes anyone to help him act out his life and has bribed someone on the program committee to appear on closed circuit television before a meeting of the psychiatric association. Winkleman's psychiatrist laughed himself sick over his last movie. Most of this is not in the later versions. In Act I, scene 2 Bummidge analyzes the pig dream, along with swimming pool, stepladder and bearded old man symbols. All but the pig symbol is later cut. Mott, much diminished in the later versions, is here an active collaborator. As in all the versions, Bummidge recalls his father's violent dissatisfaction with him, having bodyguard Sheldon twist his ear for better recollection. In thinking of the pig Bummidge thinks of Bella. Drawn here in more extreme strokes, he cannot recall having beaten Bella and swears that his mistress is a virgin. The first act does not end with his mock-crucifixion but with Winkleman and Bummidge wrestling for the bag filled with money. In Act II, scene 3 (as Bellow has it) Bummidge pursues his analysis back to the birth trauma, renting a baby to help. He thinks of Bella's pregnancy and simulates her father's assault on him by having a messenger choke him. Act II, scene 4 gives us Bummidge's address to the psychiatric association. In later versions it has two audiences, the psychiatrists and the showpeople (who offer lucrative contracts that he spurns). Bummidge abandons his script and speaks of humanitis. The climax is his re-enactment of the primal scene. He says, in a sentiment retained in the Viking version, "the first birth is awful. But the second is from your own empty heart" (p. 349). The later versions differ in having most of his past re-enacted in the broadcast (in reverse chronological order—vaudeville, marriage, hostile father, weaning difficulties, toilet training, birth). Also the later versions underscore the Lazarus theme. The final version makes much of prophetic rejection. In the *Partisan Review* version, an exhausted Bummidge is lead to a couch. Although he has cried out for value and confessed his vanity and pride, the ending is somewhat inconclusive.

14. Though he begins formally (*LA*, p. 73), he begins without the abundance of formal clichés of earlier versions. For example: "Good evening ladies and gentlemen. . . . You have been invited to be present on what I hope may be a particularly revealing and profitable occasion. I trust you will not resent the intrusion of an untrained talent in your specialty" (B.13.1, III). In the final version the personal voice soon intrudes and is, with its abrupt, emotional accents, far more conspicuous. The revisions, of course, are Bellow's own doing. In one case, however, he took the suggestion of an anonymous editor or director: "Could you for variety sake have slips of paper passed out and the group describing the night of the conception in literary fashion (or perhaps the birth) while Zero pantomines the action. End with the attack of humanitis at his view of the adult world. He's standing in swaddling clothes in the midst of world chaos" (B.12.26). Zero is Zero Mostel who was interested in taking the role at one time. Too bad this did not work out.

15. It is not in the Belasco Theater version. The manuscript closest to that version is B.15.6 (similar to B.13.16). It is called *Bummidge*, marked "Stevens Productions and David Oppenheim" and includes at the end a cast of characters for *The Last Analysis* and the names of the actors who played them. It contains many holograph corrections, indicating that Bellow was revising copiously until the end. Yet the final or Viking version showed still further substantial revision, most notably the ending, with Bummidge as vatic seer. In the Viking version Bellow tells us that he has "dropped several characters, written one new part, attempted to simplify the clut-

tered and inconsequent plot" (*LA*, p. vii). Sheldon, Kalbfuss (as a character rather than a point of reference), a messenger, two of three technicians are removed. Bertram is added. The Belasco version (B.15.6) begins with the golf pantomine and Bummy's guilt at having lost the ball. He discusses the "latent content" of this caddy episode with Mott, who is still the psychologist here. Imogen, here a student at Columbia, and Sheldon, his bodyguard, duplicate each other as naive Bummy admirers, and Sheldon is dropped. Some of the rhetoric of historical allusion (Luther, Galileo, Bruno) is dropped in the final version. In its place is a greater specificity of psychological reference and an elaboration of intellectual content. In the setting, for example, B.15.6 has no Viennese sofa or bust of Freud. More important, Bummidge explains how pa's punishment has made a comic of him, how fragmentation led to comic method (*LA*, p. 41). *Und so weiter*. Also, he lectures more on the new comedy, his own in particular. There is in B.15.6 no early mention of Fiddleman, no nursing home business—the cupidity motif is somewhat revived in the Viking version—and no ratcatcher to net everybody at the end, including his family (with which there is in the Belasco version a sentimental rapprochement at the end). Bummidge's character is made more Christlike. There is no crucifixion at the end of Act I in B.15.6. The language of the playlet is made more vatic, more mysterious, while it at the same time is made more critical, more Bellovian: e.g., the social order makes the best jokes, comedy must be recovered. (This last appears in some earlier versions.) But this is only a prefiguring of the heightened strangeness of the conclusion of the Viking version. In the Belasco version Bummidge acts strangely enough, spurning money, affirming the austere life, accepting his toga and promising that the Trilby will be run like Plato's Academy. He turns the hose on everyone. The parasites leave, but Bella, Max, Sheldon, and Kalbfuss come back. The Viking version gives us Bummy-Christ-Blake-Lawrence-N. O. Brown, a comic savior. He "denies" his sister and says "*Noli me tangere*" to all. Only Imogen understands his transfiguration. He has enough reason in him to say that the Trilby will be run like Plato's Academy. In contrast to the *Partisan Review* ending, both later versions show Bellow transcending humanitis. Other than the substantial differences noted, the Belasco and Viking versions are very much alike. All of the material in these two late versions, except for most of the last inclusions, is present in somewhat different form in other manuscripts.

16. In one version Kalbfuss makes an appearance and is analyzed. "What made you decide to become a butcher?" Bummidge asks. Kalbfuss fears his mother, and the play ends with his saying, "Oh Moma. . . . Don't bite me." (B.13.9, 63) In an earlier version Kalbfuss agrees to lease the Trilby to Bummidge over the objections of Bummidge's family (B.12.11).

17. In some early versions Bummidge is an international success. The Russians are impressed, and the White House requests that he visit the Soviet Union (B.14.19). The Russian ambassador wants to consult with him on the Chinese question. "The Chinese have ceased to laugh," he says. "Now they have exploded an atomic device" (B.15.3, 33).

Chapter 9. *Mr. Sammler's Planet*

1. Jane Howard, Interview with Saul Bellow, "Mr. Bellow Considers His Planet," *Life* 68 (3 April 1970): 59.
2. These include, from the 1967 Gift, IV, 19 and IV, 20 and, from the 1969 Gift, I, 7 (which is marked I, 7 or I, 7A or B or C because the folder contains various

fragmentary versions). "Early" applies only to these. Given the composition of this work, all other manuscripts are, relatively speaking, late. Except where there is some ambiguity, only 1967 Gift manuscripts will be marked with the dates. All others are from the 1969 Gift.

3. Mark Harris confirms more clearly than word of mouth that the scene at Columbia is a fictionalized account of an episode involving Bellow at San Francisco State University. See *Saul Bellow: Drumlin Woodchuck* (Athens: University of Georgia Press, 1980), p. 124. In the context of Harris' discussion the question again arises, why didn't Bellow link at least some aspect of the late-sixties hysteria to the Vietnamese war?

4. By way of comparison, consider a passage from the manuscripts of *Augie March*: "Good old Paris. . . . [The] city didn't oppose you in any life you wished to lead and call the true life. . . . Nothing stopped you from putting on a toga or a zoot suit or a stovepipe hat or cowboy boots. Each was right because none mattered in the place—one set of words was no worse than another. Back of it all was an irony that concealed a horse-laugh that diverted tears and rages" (B.2.12). Though not so openly critical, Bellow is down on masquerading here, too.

5. Harold Rosenberg, "The Politics of Illusion," *Liberations*, ed. Ihab Hassan (Middletown, Conn.: Wesleyan University Press, 1969), p. 122.

6. Rosenberg, p. 127.

7. Perhaps the unkindest cut of all is Bellow's pointing to the *Ubuist* element of the Nazis, particularly in the Rumkowski episode in the Lodz ghetto. Of course, Jarry's playfulness and the Nazis' literalness are two different things. Besides, the Nazis were "idealists." But Jarry does figure clearly enough as an object of Bellow's contempt. Barbara Wright, in the introduction to the New Directions edition of *Ubu Roi* (New York, 1961), calls Jarry a Frederic Moreau who can fantasize, an artist whose impetus is, in Gide's words, the "disgust, the fierce contempt and the icy gaiety [Moreau?] with which both people and things inspired him" (p. 8). *Ubu Roi* gives us nihilistic comedy, presenting us with a hero who is incapable of guilt and is therefore said to be innocent. A power version of infant narcissism, he is forever wallowing in *"merdre."*

8. Sammler contrasts the garrulous Wells to "a great field marshal of words like James Joyce" and even to the French Symbolists. Perhaps because he gives too much to the aesthetic view, perhaps because Sammler would not especially have this knowledge, or this point of view about it, Bellow deletes these literary references. In addition, much of the literary description of Wells is cut. The section undergoes revision to make it more political and less aesthetic. Added is reference to the rioting in Calcutta and to World War II. References to Marx's *Brumaire* and to Trotsky, "a literary intellectual [who] wrote a gorgeous romance about the Russian Revolution, calling it a history" (IV, 12, 143), are cut for the sake of coherence. Here we have a good example of how Edward Shils had some editorial effect on the novel. There is one manuscript, II, 4, in which he makes a number of suggestions, of which the following is typical: "Saul: I think the ensuing pages are brilliant but they are a little too independent of the book's intention. There are too many ideas—and ideas not consistent with the character of Sammler. They are ideas in their own right and I don't think the task you have taken on in the book can afford random brilliance" (II, 4, 192). Shils calls the lengthy climactic discussion between Sammler and Lal "inappropriate in a novel." At times, however, Shils asks for a point of enlargement and clarification.

9. Walter Allen, *The English Novel* (New York: Dutton, 1957), p. 376.

10. Letter to the author, 10 April 1974: "Sammler isn't even a novel. It's a dramatic essay of some sort, wrung from me by the craxy Sixties. The trouble, in these mad times, is that so many adjustments and examinations have to be made for the sake of sane balance and nothing else, and the expenditure of mental energy for mere equilibrium is too costly." Further, in a profile by Richard G. Stern, Bellow is quoted as saying that the novel "dealt with a new state of mind but wasn't under control. I should have gone all out with it" (*New York Times Magazine*, 21 November 1976, p. 48). What this means is made clear by Bellow in the *Southwest Review* interview with Jo Brans (62 [Winter 1977]: 14): "Sammler would have been a better book if I had dealt openly with some of my feelings, instead of filtering them through him"—a better book and a different book because it specifies an element of character not present in the novel now. It is clear that Bellow can be quite hard on his own work. Though it is not hard to identify its weak spots, as Shils does, there is much in character, event *and* idea which make *Sammler* one of his most engaging works. In the 10 April 1974 letter to Fuchs, Bellow says, "you should know that I have learnt (gathered, inferred) one useful thing from you. This is that I've been arguing too much—debating, infighting, polemicizing. The *real* thing is unfathomable. You *can't* get it down to distinct meaning or clear opinion. Sensing this, I have always had intelligence enough (or the intuition) to put humor between myself and final claims. And that hasn't been enough by any means. Hattie in the yellow house and Henderson and The Old System seem to be my most interesting things because they are not argued. You've made me see this more plainly and I'm much obliged." Very gracious, and very interesting, but one suspects that Bellow is making small of his enormous gift—one of his greatest—for presenting us with vivid, emotion-laden, "personal" ideas, whether to champion or annihilate. Would most readers value *Henderson* above *Herzog*? And doesn't *Henderson* contain the argumentative element? It may be that the real thing is unfathomable, but how many would value the unfathomable *Leaving the Yellow House* over the "fathomable" *Sammler*? In the novel there are characters *and* ideas that deal with the unfathomable. (Stern gives us some interesting facts about the novel's genesis. He tells of "a story begun after hearing that his old pal from Tuley High, Oscar Tarcov, had spotted a pickpocket working the Broadway trolleys and didn't know what to do about it. Something here linked with the lives of some Polish Jews Bellow met in New York and Cracow, and Mr. Sammler, who looks like one of them, came into existence to control and express Bellow's feelings about such things as the violence-hunger and civil rot which were conspicuous facts of the late 60's. Or was it Sammler who needed such feelings, and such events, and was more likely to have them? Perhaps there was a confusion here which led to or resulted from rushing the book." It seems, though, on the evidence of the manuscripts, that Sammler [Pawlyk] existed before the knowledge of the pickpocket incident.)

11. H. G. Wells, *The Time Machine* (New York: Berkley Highland Books, 1963), p. 38.

12. *Time Machine*, p. 40.
13. *Time Machine*, p. 42.
14. *Time Machine*, p. 39.
15. *Time Machine*, p. 43.
16. *Time Machine*, p. 46.
17. *Time Machine*, p. 50.
18. *Time Machine*, p. 64f.
19. *Time Machine*, p. 77.

20. *Time Machine*, p. 88.

21. H. G. Wells, *The War of the Worlds* (New York: Berkley Highland Books, 1963), p. 12.

22. *War of the Worlds*, p. 100.

23. *War of the Worlds*, p. 151.

24. *War of the Worlds*, p. 169.

25. For what Bellow considers a more true, and stirring, interpretation of the holocaust, see Alexander Donat's eyewitness account, *The Holocaust Kingdom*. Bellow was moved by the book.

26. Jo Brans, Interview with Saul Bellow, *Southwest Review*, p. 14.

27. Brans, p. 15.

28. There is mention of a moon journey as early as the *Herzog* manuscripts. Herzog writes to the space agency asking to be put in space (an idea which does not originate with Mady): "Dear Sirs, It strikes me that the technical means to go to the moon would not have been available until the spirit of man was ready to leave the earth. Unable to resolve the paradoxes of the spirit and craving an escape from them, having failed to make order within the limits of the earth" (B.18.10, 57f.). This is pretty much Lal's view.

29. There is an essay which compares various versions of *Sammler*. Keith Cushman's "Mr. Bellow's Sammler: The Evolution of a Contemporary Text" (Trachtenberg ed., *Critical Essays on Saul Bellow* pp. 141–157), attempts textual criticism in the strict sense of the word. (Bellow has granted Cushman permission to quote from the *Sammler* manuscripts.) He says, "The textual critic's ideal is to account for and verify every word" (142), an approach that is more urgent when the status of a text, say an ancient one, is seriously a question. His essay is useful in noting some of the essential mechanics, including slips. It is scholarly, but does not attempt to be critical. And he does not notice many changes that do take place. He does notice that as late as the *Atlantic* version there is, toward the end of the novel, a budding romance between Lal and Margotte. The love theme is dropped, as he says, because it "incongruously asserts the power of love in the face of death" (153). Beyond that he comments on the abundance of revision in the last pages of the novel, which improve on the generally similar *Atlantic* version. The revisions are mostly a question of touching up: Feffer is more vividly pinned to the bus, the crowd's psychology is made more clear. Angela is done in harsher strokes: her provoking Baby Doll costume, her fury at Wharton's blabbing to Widick, her explicitly saying to Sammler of her father, "I should ask him to forgive me? Are you serious?" (*MSP*, p. 306). Sammler's moral stance is clarified—as it is in the discourse with Lal—and his words made more pointed. He tells Angela explicitly that her father will die; he enlarges on Gruner's virtues.

Chapter 10. *Humboldt's Gift*

1. Keith Botsford, Interview with Saul Bellow, "What's Wrong With Modern Fiction," *London Sunday Times*, 12 January 1975, p. 31.

2. Roger Shattuck, "Saul Bellow's Gift," *New York Review of Books*, 22, 14 (18 September 1975): 24.

3. A chapter from the Zetland material, somewhat more finished than anything in manuscript appears in *Modern Occasions* 2, ed. Philip Rahv, (Port Washington: Kennikat Press, 1974), pp. 9–30.

4. Letter to the author, 15 January 1982.

5. Though all are from the revised 1978 Gift, manuscripts described as "early" are pre-*Sammler;* those described as middle or late are post-Sammler. Unlike the manuscripts for some of the earlier novels, the Humboldt manuscripts show not much correspondence between manuscript numbering and chronology. Citrine is called Orlansky (J. J. Orlansky, A. A. Orlansky, Albert Orlansky, Thomas A. Orlansky or Albert Beckler, Alec Beckler) in the pre-Sammler manuscripts. To avoid double-name confusion, I have called him Citrine at all times unless a direct quotation describes him as Orlansky, in which case I have bracketed Citrine in the text. (As we have seen in various fragments of the *Herzog* and *The Last Analysis* manuscripts, Bellow had written about Delmore Schwartz well before his death.)

6. Richard G. Stern, "Bellow's Gift," *The New York Times Magazine*, 21 November 1976 pp. 46, 48.

7. While both theosophy and anthroposophy are spiritualistic, there are sharp differences between them. Theosophy is mediumistic and oriental; anthroposophy does not draw away from sensory phenomena, thinking of itself as scientific, western. That Citrine's respect for the occult is a reversal of former tastes is also clear from the following manuscript recollection: "When I was a young man . . . the Old Auditorium Building was a perfect warren of occultists and I often attended meetings there on Sunday afternoons in a spirit of mockery. I sadly admit" (10.1).

8. Harold Rosenberg, "The Orgamerican Phantasy," *The Tradition of the New* (New York: McGraw Hill, 1965), pp. 269–285.

9. Citrine's physical being undergoes a parallel transformation. The early and some middle manuscripts give us a man who looks like "a lean Einstein or a pipe smoking Montaigne" (9.6, 6f.). Often his storklike build and awkwardness are remarked. In a few early versions, though, he is "wide and muscular. Built like a wrestler" (7.9.18). The later versions give us a Citrine who is neither stork nor bear, but a trim, dapper gent whose appearance does not contradict the idea of worldly success. Moreover, Citrine's health is enhanced. Often sickly in manuscript, he is in the later versions something of a health nut. Among Citrine's ailments in early manuscripts are a small cerebral hemorrhage, kidney sickness (8.7), a coronary (7.6), peritonitis and pneumonia when young (9.1), bruxism (teeth-grinding), and comically, candida manilia, a groin rash for which he must sit in purple water of potassium permanganate. Whether poetic justice is being served in the last instance is never stated. The effect of this list is clear. It is part of Citrine's early, bedraggled self, where physical ailment bespeaks a life of grinding undistinction. The appearance of the later Citrine, for reasons already considered, makes for the opposite effect. Also Bellow, for whom falling apart physically has no honorific value, may have thought that one valetudinarian was enough.

10. Interview on Channel 13, New York, 22 March 1977.

11. Jo Brans, Interview with Saul Bellow, *Southwest Review* 62 (Winter 1977): 12.

12. Unique in my experience with the excellent Special Collections unit at the University of Chicago, some of the very early manuscripts of *Humboldt's Gift* were missed and went uncatalogued in the 1978 Gift. Reference to the missed material is made as 1967 Gift.

13. This scene emphasizes urban decay as such. Aretha had slipped on the ice and sprained an ankle so could not come to Denise. The building she lives in is grim; copper cables are stripped, as are the phones. Citrine thinks that if they were to take her to the hospital, her apartment would be vulnerable to theft. On the way over they had passed an autodealer where three men had recently been shot. A black

man's car was repossessed. He killed the men and was killed by the police. Though this scene is deleted, the theme of urban rot is conspicuous in the novel, more dramatically focused.

14. In Steiner's *An Outline of Occult Science*, Ahriman originally is the spirit of awareness of the material world. An excessive awareness has made him a destructive force. Another Steiner term Citrine uses is the Intellectual Soul, which explains all things in terms of sense experience. That Bellow knew of Steiner even as early as *Augie March* is evident from the list of free things Einhorn sends away for; along with reports from the Smithsonian and the *Congressional Record*, pamphlets on Fletcherism, Yoga and spirit rapping, he receives mail from the "Rudolph Steiner Foundation of London" (*AM*, p. 70). Citrine would pass in Augie's eyes as one of those for whom there is something better than what people call reality.

15. Renata's mother undergoes some interesting changes. Citrine says that on their first meeting she "received me with crazy dignity. Shutting her eyes she spoke fluently for ten minutes in three languages." Citrine bursts out laughing. In view of her role in the novel, what the *Señora* says is surprising: "There is no need to be married, of course. Later on you yourself will want it, but you have too many troubles right now." And not so surprising: "Right now the thing to do is establish credit for Renata at the Merchandise Mart" (15.5, 149f.). Also, "to visit clients in the suburbs she needs a car—another Mercedes" (15.5, 151).

16. The loss of his dream girl can be severely wrenching. While in the novel this does not happen until the end, in manuscript he finds himself locked out returning from a trip to Canada. "It was midnight and there was another man with her. . . . I rang her bell. Renata didn't buzz me in, although—I was expected. It was one of those heartbreak idiocies straight out of a book Renata had made me read, *Venus in Furs*, by Leopold s. Von Sacher Masoch. . . . I was fighting the combined humiliations of elderliness and boyish tears, all over a clumsy whore. I went home and had a cry and a fit of rage, slamming the cigar box against the wall and looking for the Masoch book. I wanted to rip it up" (15.5, 137). He calls Sweibel. "Clumsy whore" are words said in rage. They do not apply to the later Renata (except in Denise's eyes), who is not only graceful, but also supportive, would-be wifely. But even in the novel he does not think highly enough of her to marry her. She is the wanted wife only when it is too late, when the separation anxiety and masochistic indulgence overwhelm all sense of choice. The distinguished Citrine becomes at the novel's end a stock loser. The spiritual perception of death (Citrine) succumbs to the financial perception (Flonzaley).

17. There is one early version in which the last scene is recounted by Humboldt (called Delmore). This is the only version in which the lady is identified. "The young lady was Mavis. A delicious girl! A white beauty. An Irish pearl. A female treasury. But what a strange smile. The smile of a tiger. . . . My two fellow editors thought she was the biggest thing ever to hit the Village. They turned her loose on all her enemies. She slashed them to pieces. . . . She gave feminine elegance to their boorish ill-will. . . . And she was a Goy! Imagine their ecstasy! And they were Jews. Marxists! Imagine hers! Just what everyone had been looking for—the great world. They from Brooklyn, she from St. Paul, Minnesota." The Citrine character, whom Delmore calls "Bellow," says, "I disliked Delmore in this state. The poet of ill-will" (20.1, 58f.). Apparently he grew to dislike himself in this state as well. At least the breath of scandal is considerably diminished in the novel itself—though not much in the portrait of Huggins.

18. Elsewhere in early manuscript an atypical, contradictory view is put forth. Where Oscar Wilde thought of Chicago as all that was not art, "a native like Elias Zetland knew that Chicago had *mana*, a powerful charge" (9.6). Being "not art" can be an advantage. Chicago has this charge in much of Bellow's work, even in *Humboldt's Gift* where it has become an essentially negative charge.

19. From an early manuscript, this moralistic, naturalistic speech is more Herzog than Citrine.

20. The Zetland and Citrine characters also merge in earlier versions of scenes that occur in the novel, their meeting, for example. In August 1940 Zetland, like Citrine, rang Humboldt's brass bell. "Humboldt evidently recognized that this was a great event for Zetland, that he was excited, diffident, eager and he was very kind, he put himself out. They had a long, emotional, almost intimate afternoon." They drink gin and take the Christopher Street ferry to Hoboken for clams and beer. "Then coolness for a decade" (19.8, 101). Zetland had written an article about Humboldt "as early as 1939. . . . He still thought well of his work. It was diffuse, sometimes confusing, but it was intelligent, warmblooded" (19.8, 101). This is an early version of the familiar retrospective sophistication of the narrator of the novel, though without much of the dramatized enthusiasm of the young man. "Why had Zetland left landlocked Chicago, ordinary humanity? To see the Atlantic, and nonordinary humanity" (19.8, 103). In the novel he is drawn directly by the poetry of marvelous Humboldt.

One early version has V. H. Tepper (the only time in manuscript Humboldt is so named) meeting Zetland in Washington Square Park. Zetland is put off by his "emphasis on exploitation and his practicality" (19.15, 106). He remembers this scene when he sees him in Washington Square Park ten years later. The poet is more of a busy man than Zetland would like. With Humboldt's five jobs, house in the country, possible stocks and bonds, Zetland ironically notes that "it was understandable that he should go in for bourgeois politics as well." Humboldt says that "Stevenson is a man of culture, a humanist." A recalcitrant Zetland says, "That's really nonsense. . . . Politicians make a show of culture sometimes, yes. . . . Lenin declaimed Lermontov in the Alps, nevertheless he had poets shot and writers suppressed." Humboldt asks, "Do you think I couldn't be useful to the White House?" Zetland answers, "Do you think a bison could be trained for a cotillion?" Humboldt laughs, "Ha-ha. That's all right," adding, "It isn't Fleisher that matters." Zetland says to himself, "O what a big amusing lie!", saying out loud, "Stalin . . . finds graves for the poets in Kamchatka" (19.8, 115f.). Despite this tension, Zetland and Humboldt remain on friendly terms. Zetland meets his financial obligations by doing hack biographies. Humboldt gets him a one-year appointment at Princeton. All of these instances show that at one point early in the composition Bellow thought of a character who would be a composite of himself and Isaac Rosenfeld.

21. Considering Proust, Yeats and Wilde as forerunners of "Delmore" in the art of conversation, Citrine notes, "But these had never eaten in Bronx cafeterias, or in the Automat as well as at the tables of the mighty. For that you needed the famous nephew of Rameau (in terms of 'general precedent'), an inspired talker, a convivial angel, bitter of soul, a passionate ironist, a man who practised the great art of the *salon* even in stables, cellars, sewers." (20.1, 54) Discounting the hyperbole (angel? stables, cellars, sewers?), the point is clear enough.

22. This fragment of eighty-one typewritten pages, in which Humboldt is called Delmore, is, however, marked "Early draft—D. S. Novel." Other preliminary titles

are "A Hole in the Forum" (17.9), "Acting Up" (17.7), "The Bore Expert" (17.2), and, for various Konig (Zetland) fragments, "Charm and Death."

23. Noteworthy in the memoir, in point of possible influence, is an impromptu lecture Delmore delivers at a Princeton party. Part of his ramble is on parody idealism in Dostoevsky: "Just see how Dostoevsky's characters pounced on Schiller, on high sentiment, solemn vows by moonlight, sacrificial love, doomed virtue, justice at any cost. The old boy knew how ludicrous this had become." He cites Old Karamazov talking like Franz Moor in *The Robbers*, wanting to shoot it out with son Dmitri—"A duel—a duel over a handkerchief" (20.1, 74).

24. At the other extreme, Citrine's encounter with Humboldt is fortuitous. A writer, he lives in a coldwater flat on Hudson Street. Humboldt, "around the corner on Christopher St., had been his neighbor" (7.14, 18).

25. Bellow's interest in Von Trenck goes even further back. In a fragment written well before *Humboldt's Gift* or *Mr. Sammler's Planet*, *A Lover From America*, Bernage, traveling in Austria and Germany on a research grant, is doing a study of "Frederick von der Trenck" (C.2.3). Possibly the punning implications of the name attracted Bellow—from drink, as if to say, from hunger. It is surprising that in all of the references made to Trenck, nothing is mentioned of his life imprisonment being caused by military atrocities for which he was responsible.

26. We see another foreshadowing of *Sammler* when, in one version, Citrine tells a friend that he will produce off Broadway *Rumkowski*, his new play. He will do this with the royalties from the musical version of *Trenck*. "You put so much into it, chasing to Poland and to Israel for information," says friend Rosabelle (17.10, 85).

27. There is a more engaging portrait of Friedman in another draft. "I happen to know the foremost American spokesman of Laissez-Faire, a person of genius. . . . I asked him once, when he was walking his dog, whether in assuming a constant level of rational self-interest pure Laissez-Faire didn't overlook the factor of irrationality or madness. He said on the contrary. He said there were only a few things that human beings would always be reliably rational about. Although he is bald and elderly, I could see that as a boy he must have been praised for knowing the answers to all questions. He's something of a Quiz Kid. 'Areas of universal agreement are very few,' he said. 'And the more disorder increases in society, the more we must value these few areas' " (15.17, 50f.).

28. Other small illustrations of this point abound. In one early version (1967 Gift 5.10), Jonas Hamilcar tries to throttle Hilsteiner (Magnasco) as soon as p. 3. In another, Citrine soon relates to an analyst friend that he saw the bedraggled Humboldt on 42nd Street (1967 Gift 5.12, 9). (Cf. the non-meeting of Herzog and Nachman in *Herzog*.) In some shorter early versions, the Plaza scene, where Citrine is alone (no Renata), and the encounter with Huggins occur much nearer the beginning.

29. The Stronson episode, which brings Citrine unwillingly into the mainstream of Chicago criminality, is much worked over. Some verbal changes are worth noting. "Lean on the elbows—that's it spread your legs apart. That's right boys" (16.7) becomes "Bend over sweetheart—that's the way" (*HG*, p. 278); "Okay, what's the story" (10.3) becomes "And which one is supposed to be the hit man? Errol Flynn in the cape, or the check coat?" (*HG*, p. 278). Showing an equal perfection in detail, Thaxter's drink for the sturgeon sandwiches is first Pepsi-Cola (13.8, 271), then Puilly-Fuissé (21.1, 442), and, finally, the correct Piersporter (*HG*, p. 286). The Schneiderman newspaper report of the errant Citrine also gives us unerring detail. The idiom of vulgarity is heightened by the following changes: "Chevalier" (12.5)

becomes "Chevrolet" (*HG*, p. 258), "best sellers" (10.13) becomes "the flick *Von Trenck*," "paid a card debt" becomes "made a card-debt payoff"; "Better go take a poker seminar at the University Charles" is not in the late 12.5.

30. Humboldt's letter undergoes transformations. In an early version Citrine remembers that "Humboldt had written me a letter not long before he died, and after his own fashion apologized for swindling me. It was a very odd letter indeed. Part of it was in language playfully deformed. There had been an entire paragraph of Finnegan's Wake [sic] sentences. I couldn't recall what I had done with that letter. Where was it? . . . I was really too busy to look. Besides, I wasn't about to spend a sentimental morning among my souvenirs" (14.18, 38). In tone and content this is far from the letter of the gift. This is perhaps the letter from Humboldt in Denise's possession, which she will not give up thinking that it might be worth something. Later in the manuscripts, the letter is first seen fortuitously by Citrine at Waldemar's Coney Island place. This is a rough draft of the letter as it appears up to the Corcoran plot, that is, the gift, which is a late inclusion. The gift, a story about a man who falls between his wife and his lover, bears a teasing relationship to Citrine, just as the Amundsen-Nobile-Caldofreddo story, about a mellow memory of professional comrades who were rivals, and a man striving for spiritual redemption, is a minor parallel to the major action.

Chapter 11. Bellow's short stories

1. "Two Morning Monologues," *Partisan Review* 8 (May–June 1941): 231. All subsequent quotations in the story are referred to by page number only. This is the format of all citations.

2. "The Mexican General," *Partisan Review* 9 (May–June 1942): 188.

3. "A Sermon by Doctor Pep," *Partisan Review* 16 (May 1949): 455.

4. "Address by Gooley MacDowell to the Hasbeens Club of Chicago," *Hudson Review* 4 (Summer 1951): 222.

5. "The Trip to Galena," *Partisan Review* 17 (November–December, 1950): 791.

6. Citations from "Looking for Mr. Green," "A Father-to-Be," "The Gonzaga Manuscripts" are to be found in *Seize the Day with three short stories and a one-act play* (New York: Viking, 1956). These stories are reprinted in *Mosby's Memoirs*. Citations from "Leaving the Yellow House," "The Old System," "Mosby's Memoirs" are from *Mosby's Memoirs and Other Stories* (Greenwich: Fawcett Crest, 1969).

7. Interview by Israel Shenker, *The New York Times*, 1 December 1969, p. 38.

8. "Spanish Letter," *Partisan Review* 15 (February 1948): 230.

9. Though, on the evidence of the manuscripts, "The Old System" seems to have been written in its final form almost from scratch, there are some minor revisions of interest. Tina's bizarre sexual encounter with seven year old Braun is first described as follows: "She was drawing him—taking him somewhere. In the dragon-car leaving humankind, to join the demons, her real kin" (1967 Gift, 4.21). The last sentence is changed to the neutral, "She promised him nothing, told him nothing" (p. 54). That Aunt Rose's ring is the one "Isaac had given her many years ago" and that for the possession of it Tina "outfaced him over the body of Aunt Rose. She knew he would not quarrel at the deathbed" (p. 57) are additions to the original manuscript. These revisions tone down the sexual aspect of Tina's grasping character and firm up the material aspect. Like this story, "Mosby's Memoirs" seems to have been virtually written from scratch, with only very minor verbal revisions.

Epilogue. *The Dean's December*

1. William Kennedy, Interview, "If Saul Bellow Doesn't Have a True Word to Say, He Keeps His Mouth Shut," *Esquire* 97 (February 1982): 50.

2. Saul Bellow, *The Dean's December* (New York: Harper and Row, 1982), p. 54. All subsequent quotations are from this edition.

3. Kennedy, p. 50.

4. Al Ellenberg, Interview, "Saul Bellow Picks Another Fight," *Rolling Stone* 363 (March 1982): 16.

5. Detillion is called "Arse Poetica," as was Szathmar in *Humboldt's Gift*. The joke was funny in the earlier novel but not funny enough to repeat.

6. Norman Mailer, *Advertisements for Myself* (New York: Berkley Medallion, 1966), p. 267.

Index

Abel, Lionel, 155–156
Abbott, Jack (*In the Belly of the Beast*), 25
Absurd, the, 155–56, 159
Adams, Henry, 100, 301
"Address by Gooley MacDowell to the Has-beens Club of Chicago, An," 280, 283, 285
Adorno, T. W., 214
Adventures of Augie March, The, 9, 10, 13–14, 53, 57–77 passim, 79, 103, 112, 138, 180, 246, 272, 277–78, 281, 282–83, 289, 291–92, 294, 306
Aesthete, the, 275; in *Axel's Castle*, 4
Aesthetic ideology, 1–27 passim, 54–55, 215; as religion, 228. *See also* Modernism
Aesthetic realism, 4, 95, 220, 280, 282, 291, 304
Alienation, 6, 10, 14, 15, 20, 22, 35, 41–42, 63, 79, 108, 115, 130, 136, 149, 151, 174, 238, 240, 281, 296
Alter, Robert, 98
American Dream, An (Mailer), 26, 132
American literature, 3, 81; modern, 28
Amor fati, 12, 14, 17, 135, 166
Anderson, Sherwood, 28
Anna Karenina (Tolstoy), 37, 40
Anthroposophy, 238, 251, 275–76, 278, 333 (n. 7)
Antichrist, 40; in Dostoevsky, 38
Antichrist, The (Nietzsche), 239
Antinomian, 10, 174, 240
Anti-Semitism, 213, 273; in *The Victim*, 45–47
Apocalypse, 7, 17, 38, 151, 156, 161, 176–77, 308
Apollonian, 26, 299
"L'Après-midi d'un faune" (Mallarmé), 10
Aquinas, Saint Thomas, 155
Arendt, Hannah, 19, 61, 226, 312 (n. 28)
Arnold, Matthew, 258
Aron, Raymond, 33–34, 36, 216

Art of Loving, The (Fromm), 83
Artist-hero, 6–7, 9, 21, 29, 62, 115, 135, 174, 220, 238, 241, 265, 293, 295. *See also* Bellow protagonist; Flaubert, Gus-tave; Joyce, James; Mann, Thomas
"Ash Wednesday" (Eliot), 5
Avant-garde, 216, 259
Avantgarde, 252
Axel's Castle (Villiers de l'Isle-Adam), 4
Axiological, the, 9, 14, 20, 27, 29, 59, 64–67, 79, 83, 86, 92, 130, 133, 144, 306. *See also Augie March*; Dostoevsky, Fyodor; *Herzog*; Postmodernism; *Seize the Day*

Balzac, Honoré de, 165, 183, 187, 196
Barbary Shore (Mailer), 26
"Le Bateau Ivre" (Rimbaud), 5
Baudelaire, Charles, 219, 265
Bayley, John, 162
Being and Time (Heidegger), 158–59
Bellow protagonist, 3, 9, 22, 47, 53, 117, 166, 201, 220, 285, 306–8; as new type of character, 54; relation to artist-hero, 241
Bennett, Arnold, 10
Berdyaev, Nicholas, 38, 39
Berliner, Bernhard, 82
Bildungsroman, 59, 61, 63, 68, 72
"Black Boy, The" (Blake), 148, 156
Blake, William, 15, 74, 105–6, 115–16, 118, 133, 135, 148, 150, 156, 168, 173, 175, 177–78, 206, 240, 279, 293–94, 306, 319 (n. 8)
Bourgeois, 8, 14, 21, 31, 33, 34, 35, 44, 68, 88, 134, 165, 167, 174, 189, 210, 213, 243, 286, 291
Brecht, Bertolt, 30
Brothers Karamazov, The (Dostoevsky), 60
Brown, Norman O., 17, 142, 146, 214
Brustein, Robert, 179
Buber, Martin, 145
Budgen, Frank, 54–55

Burckhardt, Jacob, 16
Burke, Edmund, 34, 60
Butler, Samuel, 258
Byron, George Gordon, 26

Camus, Albert, 8–9, 156
Chambers, Whittaker, 253
Character: in Bellow, 3–4, 13, 53–54, 58,
    104, 112, 114, 115, 122, 140–43, 180,
    188, 192, 208, 221, 233, 280, 285
Chase, Richard, 99
Chicago: in Bellow, 13, 18, 57–58, 64, 74–
    75, 77, 93, 149, 209, 233–51 passim, 256–
    57, 263, 267–68, 271, 276, 284, 287–89,
    305–6, 308, 335 (n. 18)
Christianity, 40, 157, 166–67; and Dostoev-
    sky, 32; and suffering, 84; and Romanti-
    cism, 144, 151, 152, 172–73; and Heideg-
    ger, 158; and Freudianism, 169; and
    Genet, 219; and Rosenfeld, 257
Citizen hero, 9, 12, 22, 29, 61, 64, 115,
    120, 129, 143, 159, 165, 167, 174, 307
Civility, 22, 23, 26, 35–36, 38, 60, 129, 142,
    159, 162, 174, 219, 224, 231, 240, 308
Civilization, 10, 14, 21, 23, 28, 62, 98, 110,
    142, 151, 155, 164, 205, 218–19, 220,
    222, 224, 226, 266, 284, 301, 303, 308
Clayton, John J., 82
Clurman, Harold, 179
Comedy, 20, 22, 33, 40, 44, 55, 61, 64, 66,
    68–70, 71, 76, 89, 99–100, 101, 107,
    119, 125–26, 131, 140, 143, 145–47, 149–
    50, 152, 170–71, 181, 219, 233–34, 237,
    248, 249–51, 276, 278, 280, 295, 300,
    303, 309; and The Stranger, 8; of self-con-
    cern, 15–16, 17, 101, 103, 133, 182, 195,
    239; and ideology, 30, 182; Henderson the
    Rain King as, 118. See also Dostoevsky,
    Fyodor
Common life, 227, 248, 284, 304. See also
    Ordinary life
Confessions, The (Rousseau), 104, 165, 314
    (n. 33)
Confessions of Zeno (Svevo), 15
Conjugal Love (Moravia), 271
Conrad, Joseph, 14
Crab and the Butterfly, The, 285
Crime, 7, 8, 12, 17, 19, 21, 25, 30, 37, 44,
    132, 149, 170, 172, 218–19, 226, 242–43,
    245. See also Aesthetic ideology; Dostoev-
    sky, Fyodor; Freud, Sigmund; Gratuitous
    act; Herzog; Immoralism
Crime and Punishment (Dostoevsky), 8, 31,
    218, 266
Cummings, E. E., 267

Damned, The (Fanon), 23
Dangling Man, 9, 11–12, 34, 40–43, 135,
    283, 286
Dean's December, The, 37, 40, 305–9
Death, 14, 42, 62, 80, 103, 108, 125, 144,
    150, 159, 168, 217, 232, 240, 258, 276,
    284, 297–99, 307. See also Existentialism;
    The Dean's December; Heidegger, Mar-
    tin; Herzog; Mr. Sammler's Planet
Death in Venice (Mann), 6, 9, 15
Death of Ivan Ilyich, The (Tolstoy), 159
Democracy, 16, 131, 135, 162, 167, 301, 306
Descartes, René, 41
Determinism, 13, 65, 71, 75, 79, 112, 290;
    and Dostoevsky, 31; and Allbee, 46–47;
    unconscious as form of, 169–71
Dewey, John, 262
Dickens, Charles, 103, 165, 169
Diderot, Denis, 242
Dionysian, 6, 40, 142, 153, 203
"Dissertation on a Roast Pig" (Lamb), 218
Doctor Faustus (Mann), 6–7, 11
Doppelgänger, 116, 136. See also Double
Dostoevsky, Fyodor, 3, 8, 12, 21, 23, 28–49
    passim, 88, 97, 132, 158, 162, 219, 231,
    242, 247, 257–58, 274, 282, 289, 291,
    293–94, 300, 336 (n. 23); composition of
    The Possessed, 54; and satiric mode, 87,
    145, 184, 186, 215, 253, 255
Double, 42–44, 46, 47. See also
    Doppelgänger
Double, The (Dostoevsky), 39, 43–44
Dreiser, Theodore, 145
Dubliners (Joyce), 4, 11, 55

Eighteenth Brumaire of Louis Bonaparte,
    The (Marx), 216
Eliot, T. S., 4–5, 7, 16, 21, 23, 103, 164,
    167–68, 172, 260, 301. See also Hulme,
    T. E.; Humanism; Jung, C. G.; Mann,
    Thomas; Ulysses
Ellison, Ralph, 161
Essentialism, 133, 229, 294; and moral
    truth, 29; and utopianism, 34; in Joseph,
    42; and ideology, 74; and Lionel Abel,
    156; and liberalism, 236
Esslin, Martin, 155–56
Eternal Husband, The (Dostoevsky), 39, 43–
    48, 300
Ethical, the, 9, 21, 25, 29, 127, 163, 219,
    227, 228, 264, 330–31. See also Dostoev-
    sky, Fyodor; Humanism
Evil: in Bellow, 17, 26, 41, 108–10, 133,
    149, 151–53, 163–64, 166, 169, 293;
    Shils's view of, 35, 37

Excursion, The (Wordsworth), 254
Existentialism, 16, 145, 157, 159, 161–62, 168, 201, 247, 274; Bellow's view of, 26, 145; parody of, 150; and the absurd, 155–57
"Existentialism Is a Humanism" (Sartre), 159
Experience, 15, 58, 106, 109, 119, 176–78, 240, 292

Family Happiness (Tolstoy), 213
Family Reunion, The (Eliot), 301
Farewell to Arms, A (Hemingway), 228
Fascism: political, 7, 130, 173; protofascism, 11; cultural, 17, 130
"Father to Be, A", 280, 289–92
Faulkner, William, 3, 28
Fear and Trembling (Kierkegaard), 21
Fiedler, Leslie, 174
Fielding, Henry, 23, 169
Fifties, 26, 73, 156, 237, 251, 258
Finnegans Wake, 6, 55
Fitzgerald, F. Scott, 23
Flaubert, Gustave, 11, 28, 47, 72, 92, 281, 293; aesthetic realism in, 4; and nihilism, 9; Hemingway as disciple of, 11, Bellow's opposition to, 53; Bellow's method of composition contrasted with, 54–55; Nietzsche on, 152–53; and Sartre, 155; in Bellow, 289; and irony, 295
Forties, 45, 73, 237
French literature, 3–4, 219. *See also* Aesthetic ideology; Modernism
Freud, Sigmund, 15, 26, 64, 82, 84, 88, 112, 127, 142, 180–207 passim, 192, 201–2, 211, 289, 292; and Jung, 5; and Schilder, 112; and Christianity, 169–70; and nihilism, 172; as ideology, 182; and dream symbol, 194; as modernist, and Pascal, 259; and Reich, 261
Friedman, Milton, 270
Fromm, Erich, 83, 88
Function of the Orgasm, The (Reich), 115
Future of an Illusion, The (Freud), 169–70

Galsworthy, John, 10
"Garden, The" (Marvel), 109
"Garden of Love, The" (Blake), 177
Genet, Jean, 218–19
Gide, André, 3, 8, 67
Ginger Man, The (Donleavy), 16
God, 17, 19, 21, 22, 37, 64, 65, 91, 116, 158, 166–69, 176, 230–32, 164, 240, 250, 252, 253, 294, 304; proof of existence of, 30, 31; in Dostoevsky, 37–38; and Christ,

76; Mady on, 144; existentialists on, 150; Herzog turns to, 154; as supernatural sanction of good, 163; and evolution, 220; and nature, 229
God the Invisible King (Wells), 220
Goethe, Johann Wolfgang von, 11, 16, 41, 277, 322 (n. 6)
Gogol, Nikolai, 39, 44, 258
Gold, Herbert, 39
"Gonzaga Manuscripts, The," 280, 292, 296
Good: in Bellow, 9, 12, 21, 25, 35, 41, 49, 66, 77, 83, 88, 107, 108–10, 120, 133, 142–43, 147, 153, 163–64, 166, 168, 172, 228, 248, 258, 264, 268, 284, 293, 301
Gratuitous act, 8, 17, 24, 30, 32, 243, 286. *See also* Gide, André; Mailer, Norman; Violence
Groves of Academe, The (McCarthy), 45

Harrison, John, 167–68
Hassan, Ihab, 78, 149
Hauser, Arnold, 38
Hegel, G. W. F., 31, 155, 157, 161, 163, 173, 216
Heidegger, Martin, 16, 155–56, 157–58, 307
Hemingway, Ernest, 3, 11, 14, 23, 28, 228, 283, 293
Henderson the Rain King, 14, 15, 18, 20, 39, 98–120 passim, 124, 130, 180, 182, 201, 208, 234, 256, 260, 276–77, 295–97, 299, 305, 331 (n. 10)
Heroism, 36, 59, 71–73, 97; in *A Portrait of the Artist as a Young Man*, 4; in Raskolnikov, 8; in Simon March, 13; Mailer drawn to, 25; Augie March renounces, 66; in Thea, 68; in Wagner, 152; Bellow's skepticism about, 153
Herzog, 14–18, 20, 36, 53–54, 85, 121–78 passim, 179, 182, 187, 208, 226, 240, 246, 248, 274–77, 295–97, 331 (n. 10)
History: in Bellow, 4–6, 9, 13, 31, 71, 73–74, 216, 219, 223, 231, 258–59. *See also* Joyce, James; Modernism; Myth
History of Mr. Polly, The (Wells), 213
Hobhouse, L. T., 167
Howe, Irving, 29
Huckleberry Finn (Twain), 28
Hulme, T. E., 16, 133–34, 144, 163, 164–68, 172–76
Human Comedy, The (Balzac), 186
Humanism, 7, 158, 173, 174, 217, 227, 229, 231, 236, 240, 266, 288, 293, 304; in Bellow, 27; in Goethe, 41; Herzog and, 159; Sartre on, 159–61; of disillusion, 161–63;

Hulme on, 162–63; Bellow's art as, 169;
and belief, 176; in Wells, 220; and judgment, 254; the spiritual and, 276
Humboldt's Gift, 21–23, 53, 116, 136, 199,
202, 233–79 passim, 305, 306

Ideology, 40, 42, 61, 65, 71, 74, 142, 144–
45, 156, 292, 296, 301–2; comedy directed against, 31, 33, 34; Shils' critique
of, 35–36; in Hulme, 163; Freudianism
as, 182; and distortion, 253–54
*Image and Appearance of the Human Body,
The* (Schilder), 112
Imitation, 5, 21, 176, 219–30, 231, 232
Immoralism: and artist, 7; undignified aspects of, 7; in *Crime and Punishment,* 8;
in *The Stranger,* 9; in Bellow, 9; as heroic, 12, 16–17, 19, 21; transvaluation of
values, 25; opposition to, 29; in Stavrogin,
30; Herzog counters, 149, 153
Impersonality: in Joyce, 4; in Jung, 5; in
Rimbaud, 5; in Raskolnikov, 7; and Henderson, 114
"In Dreams Begin Responsibilities"
(Schwartz), 272
Innocence, 15, 28, 29, 57–58, 67, 69, 74–
75, 105–6, 116–17, 119, 173, 177–78,
192, 193, 222, 240, 259, 264, 286, 292,
300
Island of Dr. Moreau, The (Wells), 213

James, Henry, 54, 100, 220, 222
James, William, 258
Jewish-American writing: and postmodernism, 27; and Russian literature, 29; and
humanistic liberalism, 162
Jewishness, 26, 45, 85, 116, 136, 138, 149,
167, 172, 252, 258, 274, 290, 296, 298–
99, 302; and the ethical, 21, 25, 228; and
meaning of suffering, 82, 84; and family,
117, 135, 198; ambivalence about, 157;
and obligation to choose life, 159; and
Original Sin, 166; and liberal-democratic
tradition, 166; and third-generation
American, 226, 298; Bellow protagonist
removed from, 251; and belief, 322 (n. 7)
Joyce, James, 4–6, 10, 47, 264, 291; Bellow's method of composition compared
with, 54–55; in Bellow, 289
Judeo-Christian tradition, 25, 49, 105–6,
109, 116–17, 147, 284
Jung, C. G., 5, 22, 118, 194, 201, 231, 244

Kafka, Franz, 103, 281, 287–88
Kazin, Alfred, 121

Keats, John, 9, 156
Kessler, Jascha, 112, 115
Kierkegaard, Søren, 21, 63, 146, 151–52,
162, 200, 206
King Lear (Shakespeare), 19

Lafcadio's Adventures (Gide), 8
Laon and Cythna (Shelley), 107
Lardner, Ring, 28
Last Analysis, The, 179–207 passim, 261
Lawrence, D. H., 6, 10, 14, 167, 216, 225,
273
"Leaving the Yellow House," 280–81, 295–
97, 331 (n. 10)
Lewis, Wyndham, 165, 167–68, 252
Liberal Imagination, The (Trilling), 34
Liberalism, 36, 61, 73, 227, 239, 254; attack
on, 5; Mailer on, 24; Mailer as, 24; Bel-
low's sympathy with, 33; Nietzsche on,
153; and humanism, 161–3; and Herzog,
167; Eliot's opposition to, 167; as essen-
tialist, 236
Lipset, Seymour Martin, 174
Little Dorrit (Dickens), 162
Litz, Walton, 54–55
Locke, John, 34
Lolita (Nabokov), 15–16
"London" (Blake), 177
"Looking for Mr. Green," 280, 287–89, 306
Lost Girl, The (Lawrence), 11
Love, 57, 59, 64, 70–72, 77, 78–97 passim,
105, 119, 136, 140, 141, 145, 148, 153,
156, 158, 160, 162, 190, 196, 239, 254–
57, 298–99, 284
"Lovesong of J. Alfred Prufrock, The"
(Eliot), 260

Madame Bovary (Flaubert), 4–5
Mailer, Norman, 307, 312 (n. 33); and im-
moralism, 17; and Bellow, 23–27; on *Hen-
derson the Rain King,* 98–99, 119; Ro-
mantic criminality in, 132
Mallarmé, Stéphane, 4, 18, 169
Manichean dualism, 26, 35, 40
Mann, Thomas, 6, 16
Marcus Aurelius, 230
Marcuse, Herbert, 17–19, 142, 146, 214
"Marriage of Heaven and Hell, The"
(Blake), 106, 133, 177–78
Marxism: in Bellow, 19, 33, 35, 36, 73, 134,
145, 156, 161–62, 177, 216, 252–53, 258,
270, 301–2. *See also* Ideology
Meister Eckhart, 20, 177, 230–31, 276
"Mexican General, The," 280, 282–83
Middle of the Journey, The (Trilling), 45, 220

Mill, John Stuart, 34, 60–61, 153, 162, 167, 258
Mills, C. Wright, 36
Milton, John, 34
Misanthrope, The (Molière), 182
Mr. Sammler's Planet, 18–22, 23, 30, 36, 189, 198, 204, 208–32 passim, 243, 254, 266, 269, 272, 290, 293, 300, 305–6
Mochulsky, Konstantin, 4
Modernism, 55, 77, 79, 80, 88, 101, 114, 121–78 passim, 214, 239, 250, 254, 265, 276–77, 292–93, 299; as aesthetic ideology, 3–27 passim; in Mailer, 26–27; revolutionism gains from, 33; release from, 72; influence of, 215; backwash of, 218; resurrection of body in, 251; irony of, 283
Molière, 182
Montaigne, Michel de, 173
"Mosby's Memoirs," 280–81, 299–304
Moses, 67
"Mourning and Melancholia" (Freud), 171
Murder, 7, 8, 12, 14, 17, 30, 40, 48, 66, 70, 85–88, 94, 107, 117, 129, 130, 141, 148–50, 153, 161, 189, 210, 218, 243, 264, 273, 286–87, 292, 295, 303, 306
Myth: Bellow's use of, 5, 6, 9, 11, 14, 215–16
Myth of the Judeo-Christian Tradition, The (Cohen), 166

Napoleon, 7–8, 12, 13, 67, 73, 115, 165, 227, 265
Nausea, 4, 168, 262
Nausea (Sartre), 159–61
Neill, A. S., 262–63
New Criticism, 5
New York: in Bellow, 18, 47, 62, 83, 92–93, 105, 209–10, 227, 233, 237, 251, 252, 255–57, 267, 284, 290, 306
Nietzsche, Friedrich, 8, 10, 16, 25, 50, 109, 115, 150, 152–54, 157, 200, 206–7, 239
"Nietzsche Contra Wagner" (Nietzsche), 152
Nihilism, 18, 85, 144, 152, 218, 262, 307; and Gide, 8; and Camus, 8–9; and Bellow, 9; and heroism, 16; and postmodernism, 27; and Dostoevsky, 30, 38; and existentialism, 157, 159; and death, 168, 172; and revolution, 217; Renata as, 250; east and west, 306
Notes from Underground (Dostoevsky), 31, 39
La Nouvelle Héloise (Rousseau), 165

"Ode: Intimations of Immortality" (Wordsworth), 204
"Of Experience" (Montaigne), 173

"Old System, The," 281, 297–99
Olson, Robert, 158
Opdahl, Keith, 78, 86
Oblomov (Goncharov), 118
Opium of the Intellectuals, The (Aron), 33
Ordinary life, 16, 20, 162, 176, 231, 272, 288, 291, 302–3, 335 (n. 20); in *Crime and Punishment*, 8; in *Madame Bovary*, 4; in *Ulysses*, 5; and humanism, 27; in *Augie March*, 73; in *Herzog*, 130, 134, 135, 140, 145, 151–53; Heidegger's view of, 157–58; as mendacious, 204; Citrine's distance from, 245; in *Dean's December*, 307, 308
Original Sin, 5, 157, 163, 166, 167–68, 206, 231, 316 (n. 8)
Ortega y Gasset, José, 169
Orwell, George, 19
Outline of History, The (Wells), 220

Parsifal (Wagner), 152
Pascal, Blaise, 259, 261
Pericles, 67
Personality (personalism), 3, 36, 68, 71–72, 94, 154, 164, 167–68, 176, 236, 294, 309; and Dostoevsky, 38; tradition of the American, 64; Hulme on, 163; lyrical, 295
Philosophy in the Bedroom (Sade), 217
Picaresque: in Bellow, 13, 59, 61, 66, 69, 71–72, 73, 75, 315 (n. 3)
Plato, 272, 273, 287–88
Plumed Serpent, The (Lawrence), 11
Podhoretz, Norman, 14
Poe, Edgar Allan, 248–64
Poète maudit, 22, 115, 238
Portrait of the Artist as a Young Man, A (Joyce), 4
Possessed, The (Dostoevsky), 32, 38, 54, 215; Lenin's view of, 36
Postmodernism, 10, 110, 126, 229; Bellow and, 4; comedy of, 16; Bellow opposed to, 27
Pound, Ezra, 10, 16, 165, 167–68
Primitivism, 15, 25, 73, 98, 110, 113, 217, 263, 284
Pritchett, V. S., 29
Protestantism, 36, 116, 170
Proudhon, Pierre, 17
Psychoanalysis, 88, 110–11, 127, 171, 182, 196, 207, 252, 255, 259–260; Bellow's view of, 26; as utopian, 33, 181; and Wilhelm, 81; and Schilder, 114–17
Psychoanalysis: Evolution and Development (Thompson), 326 (n. 6)

Quest: in Bellow, 27, 29, 40, 54, 66, 98, 104, 201

"Question Answered, The" (Blake), 178

Rahv, Philip, 37
Rameau's Nephew (Diderot), 31
Rank, Otto, 194
Reason: in Bellow, 15, 18–20, 133, 156, 162, 172
Red and the Black, The (Stendhal), 7, 241
Reich, Wilhelm, 19, 26, 79, 111–12, 115–16, 251, 258–59, 261–63
Riesman, David, 26, 237
Religion: in Bellow, 15, 22, 29, 33, 42, 78, 79, 82, 84, 117, 145, 157, 164–65, 168, 170–71, 176, 228–32, 238, 251, 293–94, 299
Revolution, 18–20, 33, 38, 73, 177, 189, 244; as style, 10; in Mailer, 27; as crime, 30; and Dostoevsky, 33; Joseph rejects, 42; aesthetic imitation of, 215–16; and nihilism, 217, 224; eclipse of, 227; perversion of, 255; Reichianism as, 258; apocalyptic, 273
Richardson, Samuel, 23
Rieff, Philip, 172
Rimbaud, Arthur, 5, 10, 21, 62, 134, 219, 239, 265, 293
Robbe-Grillet, Alain, 3
Roman Catholicism, 37
Romanticism, 9, 11–12, 15, 25–26, 38, 66, 68, 92, 114–16, 117, 140, 154, 157–78 passim, 182, 198, 217, 220, 226, 229, 231, 240–41, 254, 285–86, 301, 303, 322 (n. 6); in *The Red and the Black*, 7; criticism of, 16–17; Bellow and, 26; Mailer and, 26; mock, 88; and Henderson, 105–6; and vitalism, 111, 116; and criminality in Mailer, 132; and recapturing of time, 133–34; Bellow's ambivalence toward, 135, 154; and Christianity, 144; and alienation, 149; Sade and, 217
Rosenberg, Harold, 216, 237
Rosenfeld, Isaac, 115, 134, 234, 256, 259
Rousseau, Jean-Jacques, 11, 17, 60, 66, 86–88, 135, 163–65, 170, 175–76, 182, 220, 316 (n. 8)
Russell, Bertrand, 158
Russian literature, 3, 28–29, 79

Sade, Marquis de, 17, 21, 23, 30, 32, 132, 153, 217
Saint Genet (Sartre), 158
Salinger, J. D., 28
Santayana, George, 299
Sarraute, Nathalie, 168, 312 (n. 28), 322 (n. 6)
Sartre, Jean-Paul, 3, 158, 168, 262, 302; on

violence, 23; Aron on, 33; and nausea, 155; on humanism, 159–61
Schilder, Paul, 111–15
Schiller, Friedrich, 47
Schopenhauer, Arthur, 232
Schrader, George, 24
Schwartz, Delmore, 233, 235, 267, 333 (n. 5)
Science and the Modern World (Whitehead), 175
Science of Life, The (Wells), 220
Season in Hell, A (Rimbaud), 239
Seize the Day, 14, 78–97 passim, 260, 289, 292, 300
Self: in Bellow, 3, 9, 16, 39, 40, 69–70, 132, 140, 158, 233
Seneca, 230
Sentimental Education (Flaubert), 4
"Sermon by Dr. Pep, A," 280–85
Sexuality: in Bellow, 10–11, 18, 35, 44, 72, 102, 126, 142, 144, 169, 171–72, 216, 220, 232, 249–50, 255, 260–62, 264, 271, 273
Shakespeare, William, 25, 207, 294
Shape of Things to Come, The (Wells), 220
Shattuck, Roger, 233
Shelley, Percy Bysshe, 147, 240, 307, 320 (n. 10)
Shils, Edward, 26, 34–37
Sickness Unto Death (Kierkegaard), 168
Sixties, 26, 36, 174–75, 208, 213–14, 216, 221, 225, 231, 249, 273, 331 (n. 10)
Slavery and Freedom (Berdyaev), 247
Songs of Innocence and Experience (Blake), 177
Sorrows of Werther, The (Goethe), 165
Soul: in Bellow, 3, 6, 9, 13, 22, 39–40, 48, 117, 148, 158, 160–62, 177, 241, 250–51, 253, 275–78, 280–81, 295, 302
Spender, Stephen, 10
Steegmuller, Francis, 54
Steiner, George, 38
Steiner, Rudolf, 22, 177, 230, 236, 238–40, 246, 250–51, 278, 334 (n. 14)
Stendhal, 8, 11, 165, 249, 315 (chap. 3, n. 5)
Stern, Richard G., 235, 241, 267, 319 (n. 8), 331 (n. 10)
Stevens, Wallace, 23, 267, 273
Stoicism: in Bellow, 26; in *The Liberal Imagination*, 34; liberal, 45; and Sammler, 228; Roman, 229; and Christianity, 230
Strakhov, N. N., 38–39
Stranger, The (Camus), 8–9, 281
Symbolism, 20, 55, 78, 95, 176, 291

Tanner, Tony, 98, 121
Thesis novel, 3

Thirties, 73, 237
Thoreau, Henry David, 76
Time Machine, The (Wells), 213, 220–22
"Time of Her Time, The" (Mailer), 24
Tocqueville, Alexis de, 131, 162
Tolstoy, Leo, 3, 20, 23, 67, 159, 248, 258, 262–63, 266, 283, 293–94; Dostoevsky on, 37; and Dostoevsky, 39
Totem and Taboo (Freud), 170, 202
Tradition, 9, 14, 18, 79, 99, 117, 142, 149, 157, 167, 228–62, 307; religious, 33; ideological distrust of, 35; and civility, 35; and the novel, 55, 73; and Eliot, 167; and Romanticism, 175–76; precariousness of, 309; power of, 322 (n. 7)
Traherne, Thomas, 240
Trilling, Lionel, 64, 67, 156, 161
"Trip to Galena, The," 280, 285–87
Trotsky, Leon, 34, 67, 70–71, 282
Twain, Mark, 61, 145
Twenties, 73
Twilight of the Idols (Nietzsche), 153
"Two Morning Monologues," 280–82
Typee (Melville), 106

Ulysses, 5–6, 54–55, 206
Unheroic hero, 66, 77, 97, 241, 283; Bellow drawn to, 25; Augie as, 68; Huck and Augie, 75. *See also* Heroism
Utopianism, 14, 17, 20, 33, 118, 120, 133, 177, 189, 215, 284, 289; imaginative, 4; and psychoanalysis, 26; and Dostoevsky, 31–32; and essentialism, 34; Wrong's defense of, 36; and Basteshaw, 65; and science, 88; and Reich, 116; Herzog skeptical of, 167; psychoanalysis as, 181, 201; sexual, 216–17; in Wells, 219; and "Christian Enthusiasm," 255

Valéry, Paul, 258, 279, 322 (n. 6)
Value: in Bellow, 27, 145, 147, 157, 159, 164, 167, 172, 175, 203, 205, 243, 250, 293–94
Victim: in Bellow, 12, 13, 21, 29, 69, 71, 79, 84, 89–90, 108, 140–41, 145, 173, 190–91, 232, 254, 264, 300, 302
Victim, The, 12, 45–48, 162, 286, 300
Violence: in Bellow, 24, 85, 117. *See also* Gratuitous act
Voice: in Bellow, 53, 55, 98, 103, 122, 124, 130, 234–35, 245
Volpone (Jonson), 182

Wagner, Richard, 152–54
Walden (Thoreau), 200
War and Peace (Tolstoy), 20, 266
War of the Worlds, The (Wells), 220, 222
Warren, Robert Penn, 57
Wasiolek, Edward, 39, 44
Wasteland, 4, 14, 15, 16, 17, 92, 130–31, 134, 154, 207, 309
Weber, Max, 35, 217
Weiss, Daniel, 80, 84
Wells, H. G., 10, 19, 210–11, 213, 219–24
"White Negro, The" (Mailer), 30, 132
Whitman, Walt, 59, 114, 145, 175, 201
Why Are We in Vietnam? (Mailer), 25
Woman: in Bellow, 26, 32, 71, 85, 112, 127, 200, 244, 250, 254
Woolf, Virginia, 10
Wordsworth, William, 11, 26, 135, 192, 254, 257
Work, Wealth, and Happiness of Mankind, The (Wells), 220
Wrong, Dennis, 36

Daniel Fuchs is Professor of English, The College of Staten Island, City University of New York. He has also taught at the University of Chicago and the University of Michigan, has been a Fulbright Lecturer in American Literature at the University of Nantes and the University of Vienna, as well as Visiting Professor at the John F. Kennedy Institute of American Studies, Free University of Berlin. He is author of *The Comic Spirit of Wallace Stevens* (Duke University Press) and of numerous essays on contemporary American writing, one of which, "Ernest Hemingway, Literary Critic," won the Norman Foerster Prize as the best essay published in the journal *American Literature*. He has recently been a fellow at Yaddo.

Of related interest

American Literature and the Universe of Force
Ronald E. Martin

The Short Stories of Ernest Hemingway
Critical essays
Jackson J. Benson, *editor*

American Literary Scholarship
An annual
James Woodress *and* J. Albert Robbins, *editors*

The Tragic Vision of Joyce Carol Oates
Mary Kathryn Grant

Robert Frost
Modern poetics and the landscapes of self
Frank Lentricchia

The Circle of Eros
Sexuality in the work of William Dean Howells
Elizabeth Stevens Prioleau